KU-779-216

Contents at a Glance

Table of Contents

Introduction

Welcome to *American Politics for Dummies*.

Growing up in Britain in the 1980s and 1990s, my first memories of America were from popular culture. I remember watching *ET, SpaceCamp* and *The Goonies,* and loving every minute of their optimistic and adventurous views on American life. I wanted to be a part of that world, wanted to go to high school in Middle America, play baseball and drive a car at an early age. Life was so much more exciting over the other side of the pond than here in Britain.

It was this love of American popular culture that started me on the path to discovering American politics and society. I began to think about the backdrop to these and other movies, about how actors could become political figures, and how America was a superpower dictating world affairs. I wrote this book as an introduction to the US – to give you an idea of the rich and complicated world that is American history and politics.

About This Book

To make your reading experience go smoothly, *American Politics For Dummies* follows a few important rules. For example, new terms show up in *italics,* followed by their definitions. A key word or term in a bullet list stands out in **bold.**

Sometimes, I couldn't resist including information that is interesting but not critical to your understanding of American Politics – maybe a story about a major player in government or excerpts from a speech that had an impact. You see these bits in shaded grey boxes. I hope that you find them interesting, too, but feel free to breeze right by them if not.

Throughout the book, I direct you to further information where it might come in handy. So, for example, when I talk about election cycles in Chapter 12, I might direct you to Chapter 10, where I go into detail about elections of all kinds.

Foolish Assumptions

To write this book, I had to make a couple of key assumptions about who you are. I assumed that you have an interest and some knowledge about America, and I assumed that you're interested in learning more about its history and politics. For those of you who feel that your understanding of America is limited, don't worry. We all have to start at the beginning sometime, and I wrote this book keeping you in mind. It's not a difficult read, but it is comprehensive, and with each chapter, I'm sure you'll have a better grasp of what's happening in the American political realm.

How This Book Is Organized

This book is organised in six parts to give you a review of the most important subjects you need to know when learning about America.

Part I: Running Down the Basics of American Politics

What's the very best place to start? The beginning, naturally. The chapters in this part give you an overview of the key elements that explain what America is and how it operates. I show you how the country came to be, including the fears and hopes that led to the construction of the constitution, which is the defining document for American government. I also give you a sense of how the government is structured in a federal sense and within the states.

Part II: Discovering How the American Government Functions

The founders of the United States of America worked hard to ensure that they created something new, something that would correct what they saw as the wrongs of British rule in the early days of the colonies. In doing so they created a complicated system of many layers. I show you how those layers function together (and in opposition) and examine whether the system is overloaded.

Part III: Glimpsing Elections and Political Parties

Giving the people input into who runs their government is an essential part of American government, but it has become an incredibly complicated one as the country expanded and grew more diverse. The chapters in this part of the book give you the details on how elections work, including the ways in which two major political parties have come to dominate the political process. I show you the predictable ways in which people vote according to details like where they live and how old they are. I also discuss some of the politics behind politics, like how interest groups work to curry popular favour.

Part IV: Investigating American Politics and Society

Giving the people the power to vote means that all the basic human talents and shortcomings – all the difficulties of reaching agreement and making things happen – are magnified and scrutinised on the world stage. In this part of the book, I talk about changing views regarding race, and I tell you about issues wherein agreement continues to elude politicians and the people they serve. I also talk about tough economic times and the ways government has worked to coax the country through them.

Part V: Looking Into American Politics on the World Stage

America doesn't operate in a vacuum. In fact, its actions and reach are a major part of the world political scene. In this part, I talk about America's mission abroad, its special relationships with various countries, and the ways that America sees and protects itself have changed since the terrorist attacks of 9/11.

Part VI: The Part of Tens

Every *For Dummies* ends with top ten lists of quick, fun, and weird or surprising information. I used mine to cover major political scandals and interesting candidates who ran for office but didn't quite make the grade.

Icons Used in This Book

Those little pictures in the margins are intended to make this book even easier to navigate by calling your attention to certain types of information. I use the following icons throughout *American Politics For Dummies.*

American politics is full of memorable characters (and many that the citizens would prefer you forget). Whenever I highlight the actions or speech of one of them, I put this icon next to the tale.

The way politics operates in theory and the way it plays out in real life are sometimes two different things. Wherever I talk about the politics behind the politics, you see this icon.

Some concepts come up again and again because they're so important to your understanding of the topic. I want you to be able to find those quickly and so highlight them with the icon you see here.

I didn't resist every authorly urge to go deeply into a topic here or there, but you're welcome to skip those bits. When the information gets particularly detailed, I alert you with this icon.

Where to Go from Here

Forget everything you know about reading a book. Well, maybe not everything. But this book is structured so that you can jump in anywhere you like. If you're the kind of reader who has to start at page one and keep turning pages until you hit the back cover, then by all means do. Because this book is also a reference tool, however, you'll get just as much out of it if you flip around according to whatever seems interesting at any given moment.

I wrote each chapter to stand on its own, and so you don't need other chapters or previous knowledge to understand what you're reading. Want to know more about the challenges universal health care has faced in American politics? Flip right over to Chapter 15. Maybe the courts are your cup of tea. You find my rundown of the American court system in Chapter 7. Curious about cycling? Well, you're on your own there.

Enjoy the journey!

Part I

Running Down the Basics of American Politics

getting started

with

American

Politics

In This Part . . .

✔ Trace a new republic's emergence form 13 British colonies.

✔ Understand the what, how and why of the political system the Americans established in the new world.

✔ Examine the US Constitution as it was being produced and as it's viewed today

✔ Dig into the roles liberalism and political parties play in American government.

Chapter 1

Witnessing the Birth of America

. . . .

In This Chapter

▶ Describing the emergence of the new nation

▶ Considering the meaning of democracy

▶ Considering issues in contemporary America

▶ Explaining the emergence of the US on the world stage

. . . .

The United States isn't your typical nation; it didn't emerge from a long process of interactions between a mix of geography and culture, as was the case in Europe. The nation emerged from a fight for liberty – a fight that was based on a new way of dealing with relations between a government and its people. And today, if you look around the globe, you can see how much influence the American concept of government has had. Around half of the nearly 200 countries in the world are democracies, and many of these have emulated the American political system.

This chapter takes you on a sweeping tour of all things American. I identify how America came to be this revered nation by examining its historical and philosophical roots, describe key domestic debates facing the nation today and discuss the role of US involvement on the international stage.

Recounting the Events That Birthed a Nation

The United States came into being when it publicly declared its independence on 4 July 1776. But that was the culmination of a lot of struggle and growth, and the emergence of the 13 colonies that became the first 13 states of the new nation – and a letter that changed politics for generations to come.

Establishing the 13 colonies

The first English settlements in North America were established by companies under the guidance of King James I in order to make money. Two principal companies were given charters: the London Company and the Plymouth Company. The London Company established the Jamestown colony in 1607 in Chesapeake Bay, in what became Virginia. Ten years later it began to grow tobacco, and by 1619 had employed African slave labour. This land had been appropriated from the Native Americans without much consideration for the fact that the company was effectively stealing it. By the 1630s Virginia had been joined by Maryland, founded by Lord Baltimore.

The Plymouth Company was less successful, and its settlement in what's now Maine was abandoned shortly after its establishment. Not until 1620 were the English successful in establishing a settlement – in Plymouth, Massachusetts. These settlers were the famous Puritan separatists who fled England aboard the *Mayflower*.

By 1630, the Massachusetts Bay Company had been established in the area in and around Boston by more Puritan settlers. These settlers were given a charter to govern themselves. Interestingly, anyone considered a freeman and able to vote or hold office had to be a Puritan Christian. Some colonists left and established new colonies; those that thought Massachusetts was too religiously restrictive did so and created Rhode Island in 1636, and settlers who thought it wasn't strict enough formed Connecticut in the same year and New Haven a year later.

The English passed a series of laws – the Navigation Acts – in the latter half of the seventeenth century. These laws ensured that most goods or raw materials transported from one English colony to another had to be carried by English or English colonial ships, and goods such as tobacco and fur intended for sale to other colonies and European powers had first to pass through England and be taxed. While this arrangement was good for England, which saw an expanding Royal Navy dominate the high seas as a result of this wealth creation, the American colonists were less pleased. They complained because the laws restricted their ability to produce manufactured goods and to trade with other colonies in other nations. Just like today, people who think they're paying too much for something will find cheaper ways of getting it. In this instance, smuggling of goods in and out of the American colonies was the result. Smuggling was a source of tension over the next 100 years and eventually led to the American Revolution.

Dear George: The Declaration of Independence

The Declaration of Independence was probably the greatest child-seeking-divorce-from-parents-letter ever to have been written, and one of only a few to have been written by a colony to its former ruler. To cap it off, the declaration of love lost was made public on an international scale.

Written and passed by the Continental Congress (see Chapter 2) on 2 July and published on 4 July 1776, the Declaration starts by explaining that any group wishing to separate from a former ruler needs to provide reasons for doing so. The Declaration begins with the classic sentence, 'We hold these truths to be self-evident, that all men are created equal, that they are endowed by their Creator with certain unalienable rights, that among these are life, liberty and the pursuit of happiness.' Of course, the founders' definition of 'all men' really meant White men and not women or other races. Broadening the scope came much later in the life of America, and I discuss part of that struggle in Chapter 14.

The Declaration goes into great length outlining the injuries inflicted by George III, including refusal to pass laws for the common good, restricting justice and economic growth, and the destruction of colonial lives and property by mercenary armies and insurrections. The Declaration then suggests that the colonists have repeatedly pleaded with the British to grant them greater respect but have found their response wanting.

Finally, the colonists declare they are free people by granting themselves absolution 'from all allegiance to the British Crown' as a new nation with 'full power to levy war, conclude peace, contract alliances, establish commerce, and to do all other acts and things which independent states may of right do.'

The backstory: Opposing colonial power

The Declaration arose from an environment of increasing discontent. From the mid-1700s, colonists were frustrated with the British controlling their destiny. Combined with steady population growth – 2 million people by the early 1760s – was a growing economy and a desire among colonists for further territorial expansion. However, colonists were constrained by a series of British Acts, taxes and royal proclamations that fuelled increasing resentment of colonial rule.

The year 1763 was important in signalling the beginning of the end for British colonial America. The Seven Year War (1756–1763) pitting European powers against each other was echoed in North America as the French and Indian War. It was a battle between the French and the British for colonial domination of the region, and the British won. With the defeat of the French, the colonists believed they could thus expand the territory under their control. However, fearful of Native American rebellion in response to such expansionism, in 1763 King George III issued a royal proclamation forbidding it. Siding with the Native Americans, George III declared that colonists on these lands would have to be removed and, adding to the perceived insult, they would have to help pay for the building of military outposts to protect the border they didn't want.

In the next two years relations between the British colonial powers and the colonists were further inflamed when a series of Acts sought more revenue from the colonies and greater control over their affairs. In 1765, for example, the Stamp Act – used to finance troops based in the colonies – was the first direct tax applied to the colonists. They responded by submitting petitions and boycotting British goods. They also established groups such as the Sons of Liberty, which rebelled against colonial power. Their argument was that without representation in Parliament taxation should not be applied.

By 1767 further Acts had asserted British control over the colonies, and a growing number of colonists were refusing to pay taxes. At one protest against taxes in 1770, British troops killed five people. Referred to as the Boston Massacre, this event became the beacon of resistance against British control. Simultaneously, London relented and repealed all Acts except taxing tea. In December1773, in an incident known as the Boston Tea Party, a group of men dressed as Native Americans raided the East India Company ships docked in Boston and dumped their cargo of tea into the harbour.

Parliament then introduced the Intolerable Acts, severely restricting the powers of the Massachusetts government by placing it under Crown control. In response, the colonists organised themselves and held the First Continental Congress, in Philadelphia in 1774. Twelve of the thirteen colonies sent delegates (Georgia declined), and although disagreements occurred about whether to seek a resolution with Britain or to request legislative parity or separation, they were united in their opposition to Britain's increasing dominance. The Congress issued a declaration on how it wanted Britain to respond to its grievances, and declared it would meet again the following year if the demands weren't met. Before it met again, however, British troops had attempted to seize patriot weapons and the revolution began.

The Second Continental Congress met in 1775, organised the Continental Army and established George Washington as its commander. A year later, on 4 July, the Congress published the Declaration of Independence, assumed the functions of government and began appointing ambassadors, signing treaties, raising an army, seeking loans from European lenders and issuing money. The battle of Yorktown in October 1782 signalled the end of the war, with General Washington accepting the surrender of the British general, Cornwallis.

In February 1793 the British declared an end to hostilities and in September signed the Treaty of Paris recognising the United States of America as a new nation. The child was officially divorced from its parents.

How to Be a Democracy: The Manual

Creating a new state brought new issues to be addressed, including what the state would look like, how it would respond to the fear of tyrannical rule, and what type of relationship would be formed between government and the people.

Founding forethoughts

In any new game, the rules of play have to be worked out. And new games don't appear in isolation from the experiences of the people developing them; they're driven by those people and experiences. In the case of democracy, the new game developers were also known as the *founding fathers* and were responding to the grievances of the colonists in the 13 colonies. In the wake of their squabbles with King George III, they feared a tyrannical and absolutist leader who dictated terms and did not listen to the needs or wants of the people. Thus, they drew on Enlightenment political philosophy, otherwise known as liberalism, which was being discussed at the time in Europe.

Liberalism proposed a radical reinterpretation of the relationship between the people and those who governed. It suggested that, rather than the ruler having sovereignty and their subjects having to obey them, the people were sovereign and the government was there to work on their behalf. (Chapter 3 tells you more about liberalism.)

Key to ensuring that the government was working in the interests of the people was limiting the powers of the government. The new nation would enshrine individual rights in a Constitution in order to ensure that the government was unable to expand its powers.

Employing a republican state and thwarting tyranny

First and foremost, the founders wanted to establish a state that responded to the needs of the people. They sought to do this by establishing a political system that enabled the people to have their voices represented through elected officials, while also diluting the concentration of power into a federal system that separated powers of government into three branches:

✔ Executive, which enforces the law of the land and is led by the president (see Chapter 4)

✔ Legislature, which makes the law (see Chapter 5)

✔ Judiciary, which enforces the law (see Chapter 7)

Although they liked the idea of democratic government, the founders were also cautious of democracy, associating it with mob rule enabling the majority to dominate all others. In order to avoid this situation, they introduced rights that protected individuals and states.

By dividing the powers of the central government into the legislature, executive and judiciary, the Constitution encouraged struggles between the three branches. In addition to dividing the duties of government into separate branches, the Constitution also details the powers to check and balance the other two branches. Chapter 2 tells you more about these checks and balances.

The Constitution also divided powers between the central (federal) government and the states:

✔ The federal government is responsible for safeguarding civil society from external and internal threats, and for protecting people's individual rights.

✔ Each state government is independent and has its own responsibilities for ensuring that the individuals within its constituency are protected.

Government was divided this way in part as a legacy of the colonial states exercising their own authority in their own areas, and partly because it would ensure that these two levels would compete with each other and ensure that power wasn't concentrated in one area. Thus if one of these two layers of government were to infringe people's rights in some way, those people could then turn to the other layer to address their concerns.

The rights protecting the individual and individual states from the tyranny of the majority were enshrined in the first 10 amendments to the Constitution – collectively termed the Bill of Rights. Chapter 2 covers the Constitution and the Bill of Rights in detail.

Defining 'we' the people

You'd be forgiven for thinking that the phrase 'we the people' used in the Declaration of Independence covered every adult living in the country. But the situation wasn't that simple. Defining who the people are – in other words, who has the rights afforded by the US Constitution – depends on individual and cultural beliefs. The social and political upheavals in US history have had a dramatic impact on who the predominant US culture designates as a member of the 'we' and not the 'others' category.

Race and ethnicity have had a huge impact on the institutional and social development of the American political, economic and cultural system. It's not just a story about how the political system saw the need for change in what constituted 'the people'; it's also about the narratives of the people and how they fought and struggled for equal access and recognition.

Through the 1770s onwards 'the people' were overwhelmingly White men and women and just a few freed slaves and 'civilised' Native Americans. In the immediate aftermath of the Civil War from 1865 onwards and into the Restoration Era, enslaved people were freed, and the definition changed. However, it wasn't until the 1960s that significant advances in terms of political and social equality between races were made. There was a recognition during this period, among increasing numbers of Americans, as well as the government, that the dominance of the White Anglo Saxon Protestant (WASP) culture since the founding of the nation was in need of an overhaul to better reflect the racial and ethnic diversity of the country in the political, cultural and economic realms. This drive for change was particularly focused on the status of African Americans, although the benefits were ultimately felt by all minority groups. The racial and ethnic path of America changed course. Chapter 14 tells you more about race and multiculturalism.

American society has taken 200 years plus to get to where it is today, and by no means has it arrived at destination equality yet. The founders created a political system that can accommodate change and new members, and this unique fight for the rights of the individual to be protected from the tyranny of the majority has stood the country in good stead.

Issues Facing Modern America

The struggles inherent in US domestic policy suggest two things about American society: a narrative of positivity and a belief in change but also a reality that fundamental divisions remain. These struggles, to varying degrees, reflect divisions existing in American society:

- Questions of individual liberty
- Interpretations of the Constitution
- The balance between state rights and federal rights
- The role the federal government should play in regulating the lives of Americans

And while these divisions haven't led to another openly violent and large-scale civil war (see Chapter 14 on that conflict), they do, nonetheless, manifest themselves in a *culture war*. Chapter 15 explores in detail the current issues dividing US society, from gun control to abortion, the power of central government to the death penalty.

Key debates in American society collectively reflect conflicting visions of America's future. Such visions are dependent on differing interpretations of moral authority and gravitate around the concepts of conservatism and progressivism:

- From the conservative view of the world, morality is definable, absolute and unchanging. Irrespective of the era in which a person lives they need to obey the same moral code. While conservatives can be secular, their moral code is typically based on religious texts.

- From the progressive perspective, morality is defined by a person's experiences and not some external and absolute force. It is a product of the changing society in which the person lives.

A lot of debate happens in the United States around issues that illustrate and deepen those conflicting takes on right and wrong. These, too, are covered in Chapter 15.

America on the World Stage

The United States of America was borne from an idea, a revolutionary idea. And it marks the US as an *exceptional* and special state. It has forever proclaimed its unique sense of mission and suggested it is a beacon of freedom and righteousness for the world to admire and follow (see Chapter 17 for more details). As a result, America has felt a duty to promote its political system around the world.

Currently, the US remains the only superpower in the world. It still has the capacity to dominate, shape and determine the future course of world history in a way that no other state can match. However, its period of unipolar dominance is coming to an end. China's rise as an economic and military power, India's growing economic strength and Russia's increasing confidence on the world stage are challenging America's status as the dominant hegemon. Whether a rebalancing of international relations will result remains to be seen, but it is certainly food for thought for policy-makers in Washington, DC. Chapter 18 covers US relations with various other nations.

Chapter 2

Recognising the Constitution as a Living, Breathing Document

In This Chapter

▶ Looking at the lead-up to the creation of the US Constitution

▶ Understanding the three branches of the federal government

▶ Explaining the ideological roots of the Constitution

▶ Explaining how the Constitution has survived for over 225 years

▶ Considering the Constitution's applicability in the contemporary world

*T*he US Constitution is the defining document for the government of the country. It's also a picture of a moment in time when the enlightenment ideals of liberty and freedom manifested themselves in a struggle against tyranny and in defining a new way of running a government. This amazing document set America on a path different from all other nations at the time.

But humans aren't perfect, and the products of our thoughts are equally imperfect. Determining the original intent of the framers of the Constitution and applying its mandates in the modern era continue to be a struggle. This chapter explores the origins of the Constitution, its contents, and how it has managed to survive so long with so few amendments, highlighting key problems with its application.

Setting the Stage for a New Kind of Government

The battle for autonomy was one fought by the colonists over many years – and a steady stream of hostilities major and minor between themselves and their British rulers. Frustration eventually led the colonists to get organised.

Perhaps the most significant result was the First Continental Congress, held in Philadelphia from September to October 1774.

Twelve of the thirteen colonies sent delegates (Georgia declined), and while disagreements existed about how to respond, such as seeking a resolution with Britain or requesting legislative parity or separation, the delegates were united in their opposition to Britain's increasing dominance. They issued a declaration on how they wanted Britain to respond to their grievances, and planned to meet again the following year if they were not met.

The British response was the 'shot heard round the world' – so named because it had an impact on international relations. British troops went to seize patriot weapons in April 1775. Soon after, the Second Continental Congress met and took over the control of the revolution by organising the Continental Army and placing George Washington as its commander. On 4 July, the Congress published the *United States Declaration of Independence*. The Declaration was a line-by-line explanation by Congress of why the 13 former Colonies were rebelling against the British.

The Congress assumed the functions of government and began appointing ambassadors, signing treaties, raising an army, seeking loans from European lenders and issuing money. With one of the chief objections among the colonies being taxation, the Congress did not raise taxes for the war effort but instead requested money from the 13 former colonies.

Over the next eight years the war raged on, until the battle of Yorktown in October 1782 effectively ended it, as General Washington accepted the surrender of the British General Cornwallis. The November 1782 Anglo-American treaty was a preliminary document to establish peace between the two warring parties, and in February 1793 the British declared an end to hostilities. In September that year, the British signed the Treaty of Paris recognising the United States of America as a new nation.

The spluttering first Constitution

The first Constitution was a map to guide how government should operate and how the people should behave. For over a year, delegates from the 13 founding states debated in order to come to a provisional agreement. This working document, otherwise known as the *Articles of Confederation and Perpetual Union*, was submitted in 1777 for ratification.

The 13 founding states were:

- ✔ Connecticut
- ✔ Delaware
- ✔ Georgia
- ✔ Maryland
- ✔ Massachusetts
- ✔ New Hampshire
- ✔ New Jersey
- ✔ New York
- ✔ North Carolina
- ✔ Pennsylvania
- ✔ Rhode Island
- ✔ South Carolina
- ✔ Virginia

The structure of this document addressed the fear of a tyrannical central government by giving power to the collection of individual states – a tactic that meant one single entity could not capture power. Each state retained its independence and sovereignty but collectively came together in the Congress to express their opinions and vote on all foreign- and domestic-related issues. And with one vote for one state, it meant that parity existed among them.

However, not everyone was in agreement over the decentralisation of power: the *Federalists* (those who supported a strong central government; see Chapter 11) disagreed with the intent behind the Articles. They saw Congress's lack of authority to tax and the need to request funds from the states as ineffective. One example of its failure to exert authority was the resistance of some states to honour the part of the Treaty of Paris with the British that forced Americans to repay debts they owed to British subjects. It meant that the US was already reneging on an international agreement, and so the British refused to retire from forts on US territory.

Despite good intentions, the reality was that one vote for each state disproportionately favoured the smaller states. It supported those smaller states that feared the tyranny of the powerful but did not adequately accommodate the states with bigger populations and economies, who thought that their size meant they should have more say. The nascent government needed a new version of itself.

The Constitutional convention

At a new constitutional convention, held in Philadelphia between May and September 1787, the battles reflected the demands of the federalist delegates who wanted the central government to be stronger and the anti-federalists, who preferred that it remained weak.

During the convention, three main proposals arose:

✓ **The Virginia Plan:** Virginia's governor, Edmund Randolph, proposed the James Madison-drafted plan that called for

- A stronger central government

- Separation of powers

- Two chambers of the new Congress to both be apportioned by population

- Power of the federal government to legislate on national issues

- A national *Council of Revision* (comprised of the executive and the judiciary and able to veto legislation by Congress)

The smaller states' delegates opposed the plan because it gave too much power both to the larger states and to a central government.

✓ **The New Jersey Plan:** Presented by New Jersey delegate William Paterson, this plan proposed that federal laws trumped state laws, and that Congress could establish and collect taxes. The executive would be a council of people, not a single person, selected by Congress that would be subject to recall by state governors. Congress would be a single chamber that retained the *Articles'* one-state, one-vote approach so as to minimise the power of the larger states. The federalists rejected this plan.

✓ **The Connecticut Compromise:** Connecticut delegate Oliver Ellsworth suggested that the US was both a nation and a federal collection of states. His proposal blended the other two, with a *bicameral* legislature. To support the balance of power between the states and the central government (*federalism*), the states were to be equally represented in the Senate so that the smaller ones had their voices heard. In the House of Representatives, seats were based on population so as to guarantee that the larger states had a greater voice as a result of having more members.

Bicameralism also served the separation of powers, as any bill that went through one chamber had to go through the other chamber as well. And because the constituencies were different, it meant that the fear of mob rule was assuaged. In order to appease the Southern states, for 20 years slavery could not be restricted, and to boost population, slaves were to be counted as three-fifths of a person when determining the number of members a state attained in the House. (Chapter 14 tells you more about the details and impact of slavery.) It also granted Congress the power to regulate the economy, the defence of the nation, and the currency.

The final text of the Constitution reflected the Connecticut Compromise and was drafted in September. When voted on by the 55 delegates, 39 approved the text and passed it to the states for approval. To become law, 9 of the 13 states had to approve it. The ratification process meant a second and more public round of discussions between the federalists and the anti-federalists.

By mid-December 1787, Delaware, Pennsylvania, New Jersey, Georgia, and Connecticut had approved the new Constitution; however, other states wanted amendments to be added that guaranteed the protection of various rights of the individual (later to be known as the *Bill of Rights*). With guarantees that once the Constitution was passed Congress would make these amendments, three more states ratified in early 1788. Eight states down, and only one more to go.

In June 1788, New Hampshire became the ninth state to ratify, and on 4 March, 1789, the new Constitution went live. At the end of April George Washington became the first US President. In June 1789, Virginia ratified the Constitution and New York did so in July; the last one, Rhode Island, didn't ratify until late May 1790.

True to the word of the Federalists framers who had previously opposed instituting specific protections of individual rights, once the House of Representatives had been established, 19 amendments were introduced to Congress, 12 were passed to be sent to the states for ratification and 10 were approved. Called the Bill of Rights, these 10 amendments became a part of the Constitution in December 1791:

- ✔ **Amendment 1: Freedom of Religion, Press, Expression.** Congress shall make no law respecting an establishment of religion, or prohibiting the free exercise thereof; or abridging the freedom of speech, or of the press; or the right of the people peaceably to assemble, and to petition the Government for a redress of grievances.

- ✔ **Amendment 2: Right to Bear Arms.** A well-regulated Militia, being necessary to the security of a free State, the right of the people to keep and bear Arms, shall not be infringed.

✔ **Amendment 3: Quartering of Soldiers.** No Soldier shall, in time of peace be quartered in any house, without the consent of the Owner, nor in time of war, but in a manner to be prescribed by law.

✔ **Amendment 4: Search and Seizure.** The right of the people to be secure in their persons, houses, papers, and effects, against unreasonable searches and seizures, shall not be violated, and no Warrants shall issue, but upon probable cause, supported by Oath or affirmation, and particularly describing the place to be searched, and the persons or things to be seized.

✔ **Amendment 5: Trial and Punishment, Compensation for Takings.** No person shall be held to answer for a capital, or otherwise infamous crime, unless on a presentment or indictment of a Grand Jury, except in cases arising in the land or naval forces, or in the Militia, when in actual service in time of War or public danger; nor shall any person be subject for the same offense to be twice put in jeopardy of life or limb; nor shall be compelled in any criminal case to be a witness against himself, nor be deprived of life, liberty, or property, without due process of law; nor shall private property be taken for public use, without just compensation.

✔ **Amendment 6: Right to Speedy Trial, Confrontation of Witnesses.** In all criminal prosecutions, the accused shall enjoy the right to a speedy and public trial, by an impartial jury of the State and district wherein the crime shall have been committed, which district shall have been previously ascertained by law, and to be informed of the nature and cause of the accusation; to be confronted with the witnesses against him; to have compulsory process for obtaining witnesses in his favor, and to have the Assistance of Counsel for his defence.

✔ **Amendment 7: Trial by Jury in Civil Cases.** In Suits at common law, where the value in controversy shall exceed twenty dollars, the right of trial by jury shall be preserved, and no fact tried by a jury, shall be otherwise reexamined in any Court of the United States, than according to the rules of the common law.

✔ **Amendment 8: Cruel and Unusual Punishment.** Excessive bail shall not be required, nor excessive fines imposed, nor cruel and unusual punishments inflicted.

✔ **Amendment 9: Construction of Constitution.** The enumeration in the Constitution, of certain rights, shall not be construed to deny or disparage others retained by the people.

✔ **Amendment 10: Powers of the States and People.** The powers not delegated to the United States by the Constitution, nor prohibited by it to the States, are reserved to the States respectively, or to the people.

Understanding the Government the Constitution Built

According to the Constitution, the US federal government has three brains (legislature, executive, and judiciary) and two hearts (state and federal governments). The interplay of these three branches and levels of government is intended to ensure that no one brain or heart can dominate the others. The three branches of the federal government were designed to have separate functions in running the country, but to keep an eye on each other.

Defining the legislature

The principal mission of Congress is to make laws. Article I of the Constitution defines this legislative branch in 10 sections that range from defining the organisation of the Congress to explaining how members are elected to its powers and limitations.

Congress is split into two chambers:

- ✔ Officials in the **House of Representatives** serve for two years and are elected by the people in a *district* (or subdivision) within their state.

  The number of Representatives is awarded based on the number of people who reside in the state, and there may be no more than 30,000 people per district within a state. Although originally the Constitution stipulated that free persons and three-fifths of all other persons (that is, slaves and American Indians) are to be included in the apportioning of seats, the 14th Amendment abolished the three-fifths clause.

- ✔ The **Senate** represents states equally: each gets two Senators who serve staggered six-year terms; one-third of the Senate is chosen every two years. Senators are elected by popular vote in the state they represent. The vice president (VP) of the United States is also the president of the Senate and so gets to cast the deciding vote in the case of a tie.

Both chambers of Congress have the power to determine the rules regarding how they conduct their own legislative duties and how they punish or expel members. And neither chamber can adjourn for more than three days unless the other chamber agrees.

Section 7 of Article I establishes the legislative process. Except for revenue bills, potential legislation can originate in either chamber, and it needs to be passed by both. The methods for getting from a bill's introduction to its debates and amendments through to – finally – law are thorny and politically fraught. I discuss them in detail in Chapter 8.

Section 8 outlines the powers of Congress, which range from domestic to international and include checks and balances on the other branches (which I discuss in detail in the 'Putting auxiliary precautions in place' section later in this chapter). Congress has the power to do the following:

- Borrow money on the credit of the nation
- Regulate commerce with other nations, among states and with Native American nations
- Regulate and fix standards for weights and measures, and coin money
- Punish those who counterfeit US-issued coins and securities (such as government-backed bonds)
- Establish post offices and construct roads for transporting the mail
- Provide copyright protection to inventors and authors
- Create federal courts below the Supreme Court and determine the jurisdiction (geographic location) of the courts in operation
- Define piracy and punish those who commit piracy on the high seas and offences against international law
- Declare war
- Raise and support an army (but finance it for only two years)
- Provide and maintain a navy
- Regulate and govern land used by the military
- Call on militia to fight against attacks from internal and external enemies
- Raise, arm and discipline militia to fight in the service of the US
- Create all 'necessary and proper' laws that enable it to carry out all its other powers

Outlining the executive

Article II discusses the identity, organisation, and powers of the executive branch of government – basically the portion that has the responsibility for the daily administration of the nation, including enforcing laws. The president is the leader of the executive branch.

Article II contains vague language and is not organised as thematically as the other articles. This disorganisation reflects the debates over what the powers of the executive should be during the time that the constitution was drafted. The unintentional result is that presidents have been able to greatly expand their powers by interpreting the looseness of the text to suit their needs.

To be eligible to run for the presidency, a person has to have been born in the United States or a citizen of the US at the time of the adoption of the Constitution in the late eighteenth century. The other requirements for eligibility are that the person has to be over the age of 30 years and must have been a resident of the US for 14 years (the 14-year rule related to the founders wanting those born outside of the US to have had sufficient time to have adopted the American way of life and thus not seek to alter its path by imposing *Old World* political views).

According to Section 1 of Article II, the president and vice president are to be appointed for four-year terms. Appointment is decided by popular vote but directed through a series of electors from the states – the *Electoral College*, which I tell you about in Chapter 10. The number of electors is dependent on the number of Senators and Representatives each state has, and the president is the one with the majority of elector. Originally, the vice president was the person with the next-highest number of votes, but nowadays the VP is chosen by the presidential candidate in the primaries.

Section 2 enumerates the powers of the president. The president can:

✔ Determine how the military and the state militias are deployed in the service of America's interests

✔ Pardon and grant amnesty to individuals either convicted or likely to be prosecuted for federal crimes, unless that person has been impeached

✔ Make treaties with other nations (although they require approval from two-thirds of the Senate)

✔ Appoint 'Ambassadors, other public Ministers and Consuls, Judges of the supreme Court, and all other Officers of the United States' (with the Senate's approval)

✔ Fill federal vacancies without Senate approval if the Senate is in recess, although the Senate must confirm the appointment by the end of the next session otherwise the position is again vacant

Section 3 affords a chaotic jumble of powers to the president. Those are to:

✔ Address Congress outlining the State of the Union

✔ Offer policy directions to Congress on how the Union can be improved

> ✔ Convene a joint session of Congress to address important national or international events, such as a terrorist attack or an economic crisis
>
> ✔ Receive, as the head of the nation, ambassadors and other dignitaries from abroad
>
> ✔ Appoint all federal employees

Section 3 also demands that the president 'take Care that the Laws be faithfully executed'. Section 4 details that any officer from the executive, whether it be the president, vice president or any other civil officer, will be removed from office if impeached and found guilty of 'Treason, Bribery, or other high Crimes and Misdemeanors'.

Article II also details the line of succession of the presidency and what to do in case the president dies, resigns, or is incapable of carrying out his duties, and the 25th Amendment (1967) clarified the line of succession. If the president is removed from office, one way or another, the vice president becomes president.

Defining the judiciary

Article III discusses the judiciary, which is tasked with interpreting the laws of the land. Article III contains only three sections and appoints the powers of the judiciary to a single Supreme Court, along with other lower courts as required according to the wishes of Congress. And in order to offset any possible political influence on judges by politicians, their wages cannot be reduced during their time as a judge.

All federal judges are appointed for life unless they resign as a result of bad behaviour. The reach of judicial power includes jurisdiction over cases brought to the Supreme Court by US states, citizens, the US government or foreign states or citizens. A key element of the American legal system is that all trials, except impeachment, are to be conducted with a jury, and are to be held in the state in which the crime was allegedly committed.

Most cases heard by the federal court system involve the federal government as the defendant or the plaintiff. Typical cases usually cover possible violations of the US Constitution, bankruptcy, patent cases, cases between citizens of different states, and particular types of criminal cases, such as kidnapping or illegal drug importation into the country. The federal court system is divided up into three sections:

> ✔ **Trial Court.** The trial courts are usually the lowest level of courts, where all criminal and civil cases are first heard.

- ✔ **Appeals Court.** A court of appeal is an important layer in the court system because any ruling made by a lower court that is appealed will end up here. These cases can range from civil to criminal cases.

- ✔ **Supreme Court.** The role of the Supreme Court is to be the court of last resort on all issues relating to lower court disagreements over interpretations of the US Constitution or federal laws. A case can come from a state's own court of last resort or from a federal appeals court. Also, according to the Constitution, those cases that refer to 'Ambassadors, other public ministers and Consuls', as well as those involving a state as a party in a trial can be heard in the first instance in the US Supreme Court. This means that the court can have *original jurisdiction* (that is, it can hold a trial which seeks the facts of a case as opposed to being an appeal court that interprets the Constitution).

The 50 states along with the District of Columbia and the Commonwealth of Puerto Rico have their own state court system, and they are basically a duplicate in structure and form of the federal court system. The kinds of cases heard by these courts include most criminal cases, personal injuries, family law (marriage, divorce, and so on), most contract and *probate* (wills and estates of dead people) cases. As a result, it deals with many more cases than the federal system at 30 million to 1 million.

The final section concerns treason. It defines treason as an American citizen fighting a war against the US or supporting an enemy of the US in some way. To convict someone of treason, two witness testimonies must be provided or a confession presented in open court. Someone found guilty of treason may be penalised but that conviction doesn't carry over to her descendants.

Creating a Limited Government, and Other Major Concerns of the Framers

The American political system was a reaction to British governance, tyranny and revolutionary war. It came at a time when human nature wasn't looked upon too favourably and so contained checks and balances that prohibited too much concentration of power in the hands of one entity.

The writers of the Constitution wanted to ensure that individual liberty was preserved and private property protected from the reach of government. While the government should have the authority to rule, and raise taxes to maintain law and order and protect from external threats, it must not go beyond those duties. And this constraint was to be achieved by the government being accountable to the people.

Philosophical roots of the Constitution

Social Contract Theory was the political philosophy that drove the organisation of government. Key exponents of this theory include Thomas Hobbes, John Locke, Jean-Jacques Rousseau and Thomas Paine. This theory acknowledges that, although the individual loses the physical freedom inherent in a state of nature (that is, where no society or government exists and individuals can do whatever they want whenever they want), they do gain *civil freedom,* which is the freedom to do what they want within certain restrictions.

Social Contract theorists suggested that this kind of freedom was better than an absolutist government that controlled people. They suggested that a new world should be established whereby a social contract between individuals and government created a civil society. In exchange for protection, the individual releases his right to participate in government on a day-to-day basis but does so on condition that elected officials are accountable to the people. Civil freedom is constrained by an agreement not to hurt other individuals.

In other words, no one can be completely free and get along in a society. People need some reasonable way to keep order and be protected, and that protection necessitates some sacrifice of freedoms.

James Madison, a politician, political theorist, founding father and the fourth US president, wrote in defence of these checks and balances in the *Federalist Papers* (a series of pamphlets written between 1787 and 1788 deliberating on the future path of the American political system). In Paper 51, he noted that, 'if men were angels, no government would be necessary. If angels were to govern men, neither external nor internal controls on government would be necessary.' He went on to conclude that the problem with a government run by men over men meant that 'you must first enable the government to control the governed; and in the next place oblige it to control itself'. The key influence keeping the government in check is the people; however, Madison warned that, despite this check, 'experience has taught mankind the necessity of auxiliary precautions'.

This commitment to a limited government was a critical force behind the establishment of a balance between state and federal rights, the separation of powers between the three branches of the federal government and the enshrining of the rights of individuals and states in the Bill of Rights.

Putting auxiliary precautions in place

Giving sovereignty to the people isn't without its pitfalls – especially in an environment where trust hasn't exactly been established. Thus two types of auxiliary precautions were introduced that would provide further guarantees of life, liberty and the property of individuals.

Institutional arrangements

Two types of institutional arrangement help ensure the government doesn't expand its scope – the division of powers between the state and the federal government, and the separation of powers between the legislature, executive and judiciary.

- **Federalism:** Article 4 of the Constitution defines the relationship between the states and the federal government. Everyday affairs of government that relate to the individual are determined by state governments and local politicians. The central (federal) government is responsible for safeguarding people in civil society from external and internal threats and protecting their individual rights.

  This system suggests that all states are equal and should respect each other's 'public Acts, Records, and judicial Proceedings'. Each state government is independent and is responsible for ensuring that the individuals within its constituency are protected. Dividing government into state and federal layers ensured that power wasn't concentrated in one area. And if one of these two layers of government were to infringe the rights of people in some way, the people could turn to the other layer to address their concerns. To ensure the federal government was restricted in its scope, the 10th Amendment stated that it only had those powers that were explicitly mentioned (*enumerated powers*) in the document, while all other powers (*unenumerated*) that weren't visible at the time would be automatically transferred to the state and the people.

- **Separation of powers:** By dividing the powers of the central government into the legislature, executive and judiciary, the Constitution encouraged struggles between the three branches. Each branch is given specific duties: Congress legislates, the executive runs the government and implements laws and the judiciary adjudicates on legal and constitutional matters.

  In addition to dividing the duties of government into separate branches, the Constitution details the means by which each branch can apply checks and balances to the other two. Table 2-1 lists the ways in which such checks and balances operate. This system is further reinforced by the legislature being divided into the House of Representatives and the Senate. (See Chapter 5 for further details.) It reduces the ability of Congress to amass power, as its powers are divided. One example is the case of impeachment. The House of Representatives, by a simple majority, determines whether such a case exists in relation to a particular official. If it does, the Senate acts as the jury and hears the case. A guilty verdict requires the support of a two-thirds majority of the Senators.

Table 2-1	Checks and Balances	
Legislature (Congress)	*Executive (President)*	*Judiciary (Supreme Court)*
Checks the executive: Laws made in Congress control the scope and powers of executive departments and agencies Can approve or reject the Executive's federal budget request. Can impeach and try executive officials, including the president. Can override a presidential veto. Senate approves all key departmental appointments and US ambassadors and all treaties negotiated by the executive with other countries.	**Checks the legislature:** Can veto legislation passed by Congress. Can recommend legislation to Congress in order to support his policy agenda. Can pardon convicted individuals and grant amnesty to those likely to be prosecuted for federal crimes. Can call special sessions of Congress to resolve unfinished or new business.	**Checks the legislature:** Through judicial review, the courts can declare laws unconstitutional.
Checks the judiciary: Senate approves all federal judges appointed by the president, including Supreme Court justices. Can impeach and try judges. Can create and abolish court systems, as well as alter the size of the Supreme Court. Can restrict the jurisdiction of courts to hear certain cases.	**Checks the judiciary:** The president appoints all federal judges, including Supreme Court justices.	**Checks the executive:** Chief justice presides over impeachment trial of executive officials, including the president. Supreme Court can declare a presidential action, such as an executive act, unconstitutional and require it to be changed.

Bill of Rights

The Bill of Rights protects the rights of the individual and the states from the federal government. As I show you in 'The Constitutional convention' section, earlier in this chapter, states would ratify the Constitution only if certain amendments were added. The 13 newly established states approved 10 amendments that together are referred to as the Bill of Rights. Flip back to 'The Constitutional convention' section to see the full list of protections afforded by this document.

Amending the Constitution

Article V of the Constitution outlines the amendment process, which is important for keeping the Constitution in sync with a changing society and the needs of its people. The writers weren't so arrogant as to believe they had all the answers to a perfect society, and so they provided a framework that enabled elements of the Constitution no longer relevant to be replaced, and new elements to be added. The intention of the amendment process was that it shouldn't be easy – the framers didn't want change to be constant or to eradicate the initial intent of the document.

An amendment can be passed only if overwhelming national consensus backs the change. Both the states and the central government, through Congress, can instigate an amendment process. Through either of these two vehicles are two ways in which an amendment can be ratified:

- ✔ **Via Congress:** With a two-thirds majority in each chamber, the House of Representatives and the Senate have to agree to make an amendment. The amendment can then be sent either to the state legislatures or to specially convened conventions in the states for approval. Either way, for ratification, three-quarters of the states must agree to pass the amendment. To date, 33 amendments to the Constitution have been approved by Congress to pass to the states for ratification.

- ✔ **Via the states:** If two-thirds of states petition Congress for a national convention, it can be set up to propose an amendment that's then sent to the states for ratification. Similar to the first vehicle, the amendment can be sent either to the state legislatures or to specially convened conventions in the states for approval. Either way, for ratification, three-quarters of the states must agree to pass the amendment.

In the 225 years since the Constitution was introduced over 11,500 amendments have been proposed but only 27 have been ratified. If you discount the first 10, as they were essential ingredients required in order for the Constitution to be approved by the states in the first place, only 17 new amendments have been approved.

Interestingly, all 27 amendments were ratified using the first vehicle, whereby Congress sends an amendment to the states for approval; 26 were ratified by the state legislatures and one by a Constitutional convention (the 21st Amendment, which repealed the prohibition of alcohol in 1933). Although states have attempted to propose a national convention, this vehicle has never actually been employed. The wording of the text in Article V doesn't detail the scope and identity of a national convention, and so the states have been reluctant to agree to one.

Ensuring the Survival of the Constitution

Something must be working: the United States of America is still a nation, its Constitution has changed very little and its political system is based on the same fundamental principles that guided its founding. Despite challenges and crises, the document remains at the foundation of the government, and many elements contributed to that longevity.

A symbol of unification

The United States is a nation of immigrants. Although, initially, immigrants came predominantly from Europe, as the years went by more and more came from other regions of the world. With a range of languages, cultures and customs, all competing for the attention of the identity of each new citizen, one common language helped formulate a common identity between them all and that is the sense of being a patriotic American. Key to that patriotism is the US Constitution. And part of its attraction is the fact that it can be interpreted and reinterpreted, changing society for the better by making it more inclusive. The wording of the Constitution and its reinterpretation has allowed, for example, equal access to education and equal voting rights for all. Whether this is the reality for most immigrants isn't the issue here; what is, is the belief in what the Constitution offers them as new migrants.

'Short, ambiguous and imprecise'

The Constitution is a small document at about 12 pages or 8,000 words long. (By way of comparison, the 1996 South African constitution is about 80 pages or 53,000 words long.) Its brevity can be considered a weakness or a strength. Responding to specific issues outside what the writers considered important can be difficult with a document so brief, for example.

Because the document is ambiguous, conflicting positions can be put forth as equally legitimate interpretations – and this ambiguity is the interface between the wording of the Constitution and the Supreme Court. Judicial interpretation of how the Constitution is applied is how ambiguity is resolved. However, the power of interpretation is also why, in one Supreme Court era, *separate but equal* (see the 'Original intent vs. a living constitution' section below for an explanation) could be justified and why, in another era, it was seen as unconstitutional.

The power to interpret the Constitution leads to Supreme Court justices wielding inordinate power over the future direction of American society. A position of such power isn't determined by an accountable or elected official but by people appointed by the president and confirmed by the Senate. Once appointed, they can sit in the Supreme Court until they die, and are duty bound to nobody or nothing in making their decision in court (see Chapter 7 for more details on the Supreme Court). This realisation raises the following questions: first, should the Supreme Court defer to the will of elected majorities and, second, should the text of the Constitution be interpreted narrowly or broadly, with original intent or as a living document?

Original intent vs. a living document

The Constitution can be interpreted in two main ways today: It can be seen as a fixed document that should be interpreted in the light of its original context or as open to interpretation to provide a better fit with evolving contemporary principles. Those contrary positions have important implications for determining appropriate behaviour on the part of the federal government and American citizens.

From the original intent perspective, the expansion of federal government, as happened during the Great Depression, is likely to be viewed negatively. Original intent also suggests that Supreme Court decisions such as *Brown vs. Board of Education* (1954), whereby the constitutional nature of the *separate but equal* doctrine that justified black and white children being educated separately, was repealed, and *Roe vs. Wade* (1973), whereby the Court decreed that a Texas statute declaring that a foetus could only be aborted to save the life of the mother was unconstitutional under the rights to personal liberty and privacy guaranteed by the Constitution, demonstrate the problems of Court rulings based on contemporary principles. In defence of an original intent interpretation of the Constitution, President Reagan's Attorney General, Ed Meese, commented in 1985 that, 'Those who framed the Constitution chose their words carefully; they debated at great length the most minute points. The language they chose meant something. It is incumbent upon the Court to determine what that meaning was.' However, he suggested that it was not incumbent to go beyond the meaning and seek new interpretations.

From the perspective of ensuring that interpreting the Constitution fitted in with evolving contemporary principles, issues that addressed contemporary inequality would be viewed more favourably. Justice Joseph Brennan (served 1956–1990) commented that the document was so broad and its definitions of its limitations so vague that it was impossible to assume what the writers always intended. Interpretation was thus inevitable and essential. In 1985, Brennan commented that the Constitution ultimately 'embodies the aspiration to social justice, brotherhood, and human dignity that brought this nation into being'. This being the case, it was thus right and proper for the Court to interpret that separate was *not* equal in terms of education and that a woman was constitutionally guaranteed the right to have an abortion.

The Downsides of the Document

While the power of the Constitution to be interpreted as a progressive tool for shaping an American society that's more equal and representative is to be lauded, that doesn't mean that the American political system created out of this document doesn't have problems. Two general complaints are that it's out of date, and that it gets in the way of progress and action.

Out of date and unworkable

Because the US Constitution was written so long ago it means that the people that wrote it were referring to a society that no longer exists; its problems then are not all the same problems that society faces today. As a result, it does not provide solutions to contemporary problems and so causes issues when its out-of-date elements are applied. Those who regard the Constitution as unworkable highlight points like the following:

✔ The fact that only 27 amendments have been made shows that the amendment process is too unworkable and change is therefore unlikely.

✔ The applicability of certain elements of the Constitution no longer holds. For example, the second Amendment refers to 'the right of the people to keep and bear Arms' in order to ensure 'the security of a free State'. During the colonial and independence periods, citizens formed militia to protect themselves from foreign aggression (including on the part of Native Americans); arms were thus necessary to carry out their duties. Now that a standing army exists to protect the nation, is the right to bear arms still applicable?

✔ The Electoral College (EC) causes a number of problems that a directly elected process would not. The EC is considered out of date and unworkable for five key reasons:

- The candidate with the greatest number of votes technically could lose because she didn't actually win the required 270 EC votes to claim victory (see Chapter 9 for further details on the EC).

- Smaller states are overrepresented, and the EC votes aren't evenly distributed by population. The system tends to favour rural rather than urban states.

- The system discourages independent and third-party candidates and thus isn't a fair reflection of the will of the people.

- Candidates spend fewer resources (time and money) in states where they have no chance of winning, and more in states where they have a high chance of winning, which skews the political messages of the candidates to favour those contested groups in the swing states at the expense of the other citizens in those and other states.

- Nothing forbids an elector from disregarding the will of the people to give his vote to a different presidential candidate.

Inefficient and paralysis inducing

The Constitution's development of a split between the federal and the state governments, the separation of federal powers into three branches and the bicameralism of Congress was bound to create an inefficient organisation. This was precisely what the framers wanted to do so that no one group could usurp the power of the others. However, in recent years, the difficulties of delivering gun control, reforming healthcare, resolving federal budget debates and using government shutdowns as political footballs have inspired growing discussion on whether these checks and balances are actually design flaws. Maybe this purposeful inefficiency is too inefficient.

Contemporary American politics induces paralysis in other ways, such as the political redistricting that ensures a political party obtains or maintains dominance in a particular area (see Chapter 10 on redistricting) or political parties' difficulty in creating a national and concentrated political agenda that can be supported by all party actors at the local, state and national levels in order to drive change (see Chapter 11 on political parties for further details).

Another example of this structurally induced paralysis is what happens when a divided government exists. When one party holds the White House and the other controls at least one of the chambers of Congress, political gridlock results. Each party doesn't want the other's policies to succeed because that situation could hamper their own future electoral success. Legislation doesn't progress, and political decision making on the welfare of America is driven by ideological differences.

Chapter 3

Grasping the Structure of Democracy in Action

*P*ut simply, a *democracy* is a political system that governs a group of people based on the idea that power is derived from the people; it enables all people in a society to have a say in how they're governed. But that leaves a lot open to interpretation. Within this chapter I outline the different types of democracy and situate the American system within them. I also identify the key aspects of the American political system to give you an idea of what US democracy looks like in practice.

Situating America within the Modern Democratic Family

Democracy is a mode of governing states, the first example of which was the city-state of Athens in ancient Greece (fifth century BC). In the century following, some 1,500 democratic city-states existed in the Mediterranean area now known as Greece. Seems natural, then, that the term *democracy* derives from the Greek word *demokratia,* which refers to the *demos* (the common people) and *kratos* (the system that rules).

Being a democracy enables a government to claim that its actions are supported by the people, conferring a sense of legitimacy on a government's decision making that other types of political system don't have.

In a modern democracy, according to political scientist Robert Dahl, two underlying dimensions are essential:

✔ Contestation, meaning that individuals are free to express themselves and to arrive at decisions without arbitrary attacks from the state

✔ Inclusiveness, which enables the individual to participate in the political process and be able to vote freely and fairly, and for those votes to be counted equally and without discrimination

Generally speaking, democracy comes in two distinct types, depending on how immediate the link between the people and the government itself:

✔ **Direct democracy** is the ancient Greek system and places decision-making power directly into the hands of the people. When the government has to make a decision, the issue is presented to the people with a number of possible options. Each eligible individual has the right to choose their preferred option.

In practice, this type of democracy works better with smaller groups of people. Decisions are made through referenda, petitioning the government for change and requesting a recall of an elected official.

Fully operational direct democracies are rare. The federal government of Switzerland employs this system most closely, and two *cantons* (regional governments similar to states in the US) in Switzerland employ it fully. One problem with direct democracy is that it can restrict the liberties of certain minority groups because the electorate can introduce legislation that's illiberal in nature. In Switzerland in 2009, for example, a referendum was held on whether to ban the construction of minarets on mosques. Even though the federal government was against the vote, over 57 per cent of the population and 22 out of the 26 cantons voted in favour of the ban.

✔ **Representative democracy** (also called *indirect democracy*) utilises a mediator between the people and the decisions made by the state. Citizens elect officials to represent their interests at the local and national level, transferring responsibility for making decisions regarding law, administration and other governance issues to the elected representatives.

Representatives may meet the needs of their constituents by listening to the demands of the citizens and voting accordingly or by acting as specialists in the field of politics and thus making decisions based on what they think is in the collective best interests of the people. Most officials in a representative democracy tend to employ both these approaches.

A problem with this kind of democracy is that, while elected by the people, these representatives also have competing interests that they consider must also be dealt with. In the US, for example, the interests of the citizens compete for the attention of elected officials with those of special interest groups (see Chapter 13 for more on these). As a result, people's interests aren't always attended to, which raises the question of how representative elected officials really are. However, power still resides with the people, and is exercised through regular elections, as well as referenda, petitions and recalls. So citizens can deselect officials and replace them with new ones if they no longer want them in office.

To further understand how American democracy is situated within the democratic family, you need to know that within these two different types of democracy there are two different ways democracy can operate: parliamentary and presidential.

Parliamentary democracy

Parliamentary democracy is the political system practised in the UK, Canada, Australia, New Zealand and Ireland, whereby whatever party wins the most seats in the legislature (parliament) also earns the highest office. The winning party leader becomes the executive head of government, usually known as a prime minister.

One way in which the head of government is accountable to the legislature is that the legislature can propose a *vote of no confidence* in the government. A vote of no confidence can bring down the prime minister's government and force an election to appoint a new government, and strip the prime minister of her job.

What makes the parliamentary system unique is that the head of government is typically a member of the legislature himself. Thus the separation of power between the executive and the legislature is not as definite as in a presidential system (see below). However, a benefit of this system is the speed at which the executive can propose legislation to the legislature and get party members in the chamber to vote in favour of it. And the more members the sitting government's party has, the more likely it will be able pass legislation to further its policy agenda.

The head of government is responsible for proposing legislation, setting the government's policy agenda and appointing the cabinet ministers who are heads of the executive departments. The other part of the executive is the head of state, who performs ceremonial duties and has no formal powers in the legislative process. This person is regarded as apolitical and represent the interests of the nation, meeting and greeting other dignitaries from around the world. In some countries the monarch is the head of state, as in the UK; in others, it's a president (not to be mistaken with presidential democracy) who's elected by the population, such as the Irish president.

A legislature typically comprises two chambers (*bicameral*) that debate and vote on legislation. All lower chamber members are elected by popular vote, while members of the upper chamber are sometimes elected by that method (as in Australia) or are appointed by the head of state following guidance from the head of government (as in Canada and the UK). Some legislatures, such as that in New Zealand, are *unicameral*, meaning they have only one chamber.

Presidential democracy

In a *presidential democracy*, which operates in countries such as the United States, Mexico and Brazil, the president is both the head of the executive and the head of state. A presidential democracy is often called a republican state.

The president in a presidential democracy is in charge of running the government departments, such as the treasury and defence, including by appointing (and sacking) the cabinet ministers who run them. He also represents the state on official visits to other countries and receives foreign dignitaries.

A key difference from a parliamentary democracy is that, in this system, the executive is completely separate from the legislature. The legislative and executive branches have specific duties, independent of the other, in a way that doesn't occur in a parliamentary system. Supporters of this system suggest that it's much more stable than a parliamentary system because legislation is more thoroughly analysed by competing interests in a system of checks and balances (see Chapter 8 on how an idea becomes law for further details). Also, whichever party wins the majority in the legislature has no bearing on who is appointed president because the presidential election is separate. And because these powers are separate, the president cannot control the legislature in the same way as can a prime minister; equally, however, they can't be forced out of government by a parliamentary vote of no confidence.

The separation of executive and legislative branches does have drawbacks, though. Delays in getting things done can occur, particularly when one party controls the legislature and another the executive. Ideological differences between these two parties can cause atrophy and lead to a breakdown in government efficiency.

Similar to a parliamentary democracy, the legislature in a presidential democracy typically comprises two chambers. In order to ensure that these two branches of government check each other, the president has the power to veto all laws made by the legislature and the legislature has the power to override the veto.

Examining American Politics Today

The structure of the government is but one element contributing to how it actually works within ever-changing (and ever-diverse) American society. The ideal would be clear majorities and black-and-white breakdowns of issues, but of course wherever humans are, there also are a wealth of viewpoints. How those find voice within the American system of democracy has a lot to do with what gets done – and doesn't. Some concepts about how to make democracy work have stood the test of time, as have certain key factions behind them.

Liberalism in general

Liberalism as a concept emerged from the ideas of political theorists from the 1600s onwards who sought to identify a relationship between the citizen and the state that wasn't based on the predominance of the state over the individual. The political systems operating in Europe at the time suggested that the government or monarch awarded people rights. Liberals, in contrast, believed it was the other way round – people were given rights by God and they then awarded government the right to rule.

Liberalism suggests that people are sovereign, not the government. I like to think of liberalism as akin to a computer operating system. The system doesn't tell you what programmes to use or what websites to click on, but it does ensure that you have access and the right to use or see whatever you want. What the system won't allow you to do, though, is to restrict access for others. And in that way, liberalism recognises that the freedom of the individual to do as she wants is paramount within the political, economic and social realms.

A liberal state's role is to be an enabler – to foster the free exchange of goods, services and ideas. In order to guarantee the right to do as you please, the government should operate only to ensure that your rights are protected, and do no more. This situation is what's called *limited government* (see Chapter 2 for further details). The only constraint on an individual should be that he's not allowed to infringe the rights of other individuals. All people are thus viewed as having equal rights to do as they please.

From this perspective, private property and free markets are encouraged. Private property is viewed as the product of the individual's labour and, as such, is a manifestation of an individual's rights. It means that a liberal state must protect the rights of ownership; no one or no thing should be able to take away the property of an individual. A free market is one in which no governmental constraints are placed on the ability of one individual to trade with another. Free markets should thus be encouraged in a liberal state because they're much more successful in promoting wealth than any other economic model; individuals should be entrepreneurial and free to do as they want.

American liberalism

The breed of liberalism that evolved in the US was somewhat different from European liberalism. And with this difference came a different interpretation by government. While limited government is a feature of all types of liberalism, it is absolutely integral to American liberalism.

The US Constitution limited the powers of the government by ensuring that they were diluted between branches of the federal government and the states. And in order to safeguard the rights of the individual, such as freedom of expression, the Constitution included a bill of rights. The government was incapable of going beyond its mandate. Including these systems protected future American society by thwarting tyrannical rule by an overly powerful executive or legislature.

As a result of states having sovereign power and the rights of the individual being protected, over the years a rejection of attempts, or perceived attempts, by the federal government to attain more powers than constitutionally allotted has evolved on the part of the American people. Defence of these rights has become increasingly dogmatic and has bred hostility to any argument that suggests their revision even if it could benefit society as a whole. A classic example is the fight to maintain the right 'to bear arms' contained in the 2nd Amendment (see Chapter 15 for more details on this subject). Although solid data demonstrates that gun-related accidents and fatalities would be reduced by placing controls on gun ownership, many people see doing so as an attack on individual freedom.

Contemporary American political ideologies

Conservatism and liberalism are the prevailing ideologies within American politics, but in this case, liberal is used in a different sense to that describing a theory regarding the role of government. People who describe themselves as liberal refer to a set of ideas that generally promote human rights and the role of government to reduce inequalities among individuals. Those who describe themselves as conservative are more inclined toward tradition and a minimal role of government.

From the perspective of a political scientist, today conservatives and liberals are completely different beasts from those of 100 years ago. The upcoming sections represent my best shot at defining what these terms mean to contemporary Americans.

American conservatives

Conservatism in contemporary America isn't that easily defined. That said, it can be examined in two key ways – individualist and traditional conservatism:

- ✔ **Individualist conservatism** is strongly supportive of the historical tradition of protecting the personal liberties of individuals as enshrined in the Constitution's Bill of Rights against the feared encroaching federal government. It follows that they want to maximise the rights of the individual over the power of the state. They are thus, for example, a supporter of free market capitalism as it minimises state involvement in the affairs of people.

- ✔ **Traditional conservatism** has its roots in European conservatism and focuses more on society as a whole than on the rights of the individual. It suggests that the traditions and norms of the past society deserve to be maintained, and so previous discussions on things such as religion, law, society and politics greatly influence the current direction of society and government. This kind of conservative is far more cautious regarding changes in government and the direction of society than others.

Just to confuse things further, a person who identifies as a conservative could employ both of these approaches in defining their own conservative identity. Using a pick 'n mix approach to choosing a political identity is a perfectly acceptable way to navigate the political, economic and social arenas, but it also means that two conservatives may take contradictory political positions on issues while still both validly calling themselves conservative.

Someone who identifies with individualist conservatism is more likely to support restricting the power of government in all political, social and economic arenas. She'll oppose government regulation of business, restriction of a citizen's access to guns and government determination of how people should live their private lives (for example, same-sex marriage legislation). A more traditional conservative will also be unlikely to support radical changes regarding acceptable behaviour in the private sphere but will base her views on traditional religious values rather than individual liberty.

American liberals

American liberals today have much in common with the social liberals of Europe; they oppose economic and social inequality and believe that the state should be involved in dealing with these problems. They tend to support an economic model that drives the economy through public as well as private involvement. Referred to as a market economy, the state's involvement is based on the recognition that unfettered markets are danger-ous in terms of the good of society. Liberals think government should regu-late industry to ensure businesses follow safety guidelines for workers and goods.

'Liberal' in the US usually refers to a person's standpoint on issues of social and economic justice. Liberals advocate government involvement in address-ing social issues such as unemployment and poverty. Often, they're in favour of government affirmative action programmes that elevate underrepresented minority groups in education and the workforce.

Liberals are also known for social politics such as supporting women's rights, providing access to abortion and legalising same-sex marriage (see Chapter 15 on the fault lines in American society for more details).

Of course, liberals can and do pick and choose which aspects they identify with most – just as conservatives do. They can be simultaneously pro- and anti-government but in relation to different issues. A good example is being pro-government involvement in dealing with the inequality facing African Americans in terms of educational opportunities and anti-government arbi-trarily spying on its citizens, thus infringing their personal liberty.

American libertarians

Libertarians demonstrate an impressively dogmatic consistency. They believe in the maximisation of an individual's freedom and independence to choose how to live their lives. The state should thus play an extremely lim-ited role in the social and economic affairs of individuals.

Different parts of the libertarian platform sit comfortably with both liberals and conservatives of different stripes. They support the free market and non-interference in people's social lives. Take same-sex marriage as an example. According to the Libertarian Party's 2012 election manifesto, 'sexual orienta-tion, preference, gender, or gender identity should have no impact on the government's treatment of individuals, such as in current marriage, child cus-tody, adoption, immigration or military service laws'.

Essentially, libertarians don't believe that the government should play a role in people's private lives. A liberal shares this view but disagrees with a libertarian's call for the closure of government welfare programmes. Unsurprisingly, many people identify as libertarian or agree with aspects of libertarianism as a result of its crossing over with both liberal and conserva-tive attitudes. A 2013 survey revealed that 7 per cent of Americans are consis-tently libertarian while a further 15 per cent lean in that direction.

American political parties: Two behemoths and a spate of also-rans

While political parties have come and gone over the near 240 years since independence, the ideas behind them have remained pretty consistent. One party has tended to support the rights of states and the individual and the other a stronger central government. These two positions have historically been known as the anti-federalists and federalists, respectively.

Two main parties exist in the United States today: the Republicans and the Democrats. It's safe to say that most conservatives identify with the Republicans and most liberals with the Democrats, but some wings of these political parties reflect elements of conservatism and liberalism. Blue Dog Democrats, for example, are predominantly fiscally conservative but tend to be politically and socially liberal (see Chapter 11 for further details on the ideological wings of the two parties). And of those libertarians out there, 45 per cent identify with the Republicans and only 5 with the Democrats. The other half identify either as independents or with another political party.

As a result of the varying stages of political realignment in the course of American political party history, the two parties that have emerged and consolidated have a tremendously rich and ideologically varying past. In one party you can have candidates and the electorate both supporting and opposing healthcare reforms. The next two sub-sections outline a number of key wings that operate within the Democratic and Republican parties while the third examines some of the lesser-known parties.

Republicans

The Republican Party is also known as the *Grand Old Party* (GOP) and was established in 1854. Because the GOP has many different wings, trying to determine the overall theme of the party is very difficult. Some wings are more popular at some times than others, and so the party will morph into that position in order to gain votes. However, Republicans tend to be perceived as supporters of minimal state engagement in social and economic issues, low taxation, and tough penalties for criminals.

Most people tend to associate this party with key figures such as Presidents Ronald Reagan and George W. Bush. However, the party is more than these individuals. The Republican Party has seven key wings:

> ✔ **Fiscal wing:** Affectionately called (by some) the *neo-liberal economic order*, it supports a reduction in government spending, including on welfare programmes, lower taxes, a balanced budget, deficit reduction, free trade and the deregulation of the economy.

- ✔ **Libertarian wing:** This group supports a whole range of issues, including supporting the free market and the rights of states versus the federal government, and is against taxation and large government expenditure. It's predominantly against an interventionist foreign policy and supports the removal of military bases throughout the world.

- ✔ **Neoconservative wing:** Concerned more with foreign than domestic policy, this wing aims to maintain US global supremacy. It supports acting aggressively to protect the US position, using strategies such as the promotion of democracy. President George W. Bush's interventionist foreign policies in Afghanistan and Iraq exemplify the neoliberal approach.

- ✔ **National security wing:** This wing aggressively defends American interests around the world. It supported the Bush administration's (2001–2009) foreign policy but has also criticised its weakness in relation to restricting immigration.

- ✔ **Religious right:** This group includes mostly fundamentalist Christians, evangelicals, traditional and conservative Catholics, Mormons and some orthodox Jews. Their social conservatism supports traditional moral and social values such as marriage being purely between men and women. They're against abortion (pro-lifers) and stem-cell research (because it involves testing on human embryos).

- ✔ **Moderate wing:** Un-affectionately referred to by some as RINOs (Republican In Name Only), this wing is fiscally conservative and so believes in balanced budgets, deregulation of industry and lower taxes (which is good from a more typical Republican perspective) but also socially liberal (which is bad) and so supports issues such as gay rights, gun control, environmental protection and is pro-choice. It includes people such as former California Governor Arnold Schwarzenegger and former New York City Mayor Michael Bloomberg.

- ✔ **Tea Party:** Established in 2008 and more a movement than a wing of the party, it's partly conservative, partly libertarian and partly populist, and so focuses on limited government, fiscal conservatism and a strict adherence to the Constitution. It opposes government-controlled programs such as welfare or healthcare insurance for all Americans.

Democrats

The Democratic Party has been operating in various guises for over 200 years, and since the 1930s has been the party representing liberals seeking change in society via legislation and government programs. Examples of Democrat-driven legislation include the 1964 Civil Rights Act, which outlawed discrimination based on race and gender, and the 2010 Affordable Care Act, which enabled more Americans to access affordable healthcare.

The Democratic Party has five significant wings, which, similar to those of the Republican Party, include liberal, conservative and libertarian positions:

- ✔ **Left wing:** This wing includes progressive and liberal democrats who have a less militaristic approach to foreign policy; some were opposed to the 2003 war in Iraq. They're against social conservatism, support civil liberties and help disadvantaged people through government programs covering, for example, employment and health care.

- ✔ **Centre wing:** Otherwise known as the New Democrats, this group typically supports tax cuts and the use of military force; it supported the war in Iraq and favours reducing government welfare funding.

- ✔ **Conservative wing:** This wing includes the Blue Dog Democrat faction established in the mid-1990s as a voice for conservative or moderate minded members, particularly concerning economic issues.

- ✔ **Libertarian wing:** Not a large part of the party, this group supports issues such as civil rights and separation of church and state, and opposes gun control and large government expenditure. Its foreign policy is non-interventionist, citing the problems that arise from taking an interventionist approach.

And the rest: Smaller political parties

A number of other national and regional political parties exist in the United States, but their impact in shaping the political landscape is limited. The success of any third party is somewhat hampered by the broadness of the two main political parties and their ability to incorporate multiple ideological platforms.

The Libertarian Party is probably the closest thing there is to a third party in the US today. It's the party for those who believe in small government and greater freedom for individuals to do as they please. It has approximately 250,000 registered party members across the country. And as of 2012, nearly 600 elected officials occupy state positions ranging from mayors to members of school boards.

The 2012 presidential election results provide an indicator of the size of the Libertarian Party. The presidential candidate was Gary Johnson, a former New Mexico governor, and his running mate was James P. Gray, a former California state court judge. Nearly 1.3 million out of the 129.2 million people who voted did so for the Libertarian Party; that's about 1 per cent of those who voted.

Other small national and regional parties play some role in the political life of America. One of these, the Green Party, has shown more success than most. Its main platform is protecting the environment but it also supports the practice of non-violence, grassroots democracy, political decentralisation and social justice initiatives, including universal healthcare and a living wage for workers (one that enables people to enjoy life and not just survive it). As of late 2012, the Green Party had just over 130 elected officials. In the 2012 presidential elections, the Green Party presidential candidate was Jill Stein, a medical doctor, and her vice presidential candidate was Cheri Honkala, a human rights advocate. They received about 460,000 votes, which worked out as a 0.36 per cent share of the popular vote.

Other, more single-issue and local-based parties also exist, such as the United States Marijuana Party, which seeks the legalisation of cannabis and an end to the 'War on Drugs' and the New York-based Rent Is Too Damn High Party, which focuses on lowering rent and reducing poverty in the city.

Additionally, independent candidates – those not affiliated with any party – run in local, state and national elections. Perhaps the most famous of all independent candidates is businessman Ross Perot, who ran for president in 1992 alongside his vice presidential candidate, retired vice-admiral James Stockdale. They ran on a libertarian-inspired platform and received nearly 20 million votes and nearly 19 per cent of the popular vote. Perot ran again in the1996 election as the Reform Party candidate, although his popularity had waned and he received only 8 million votes and 8.4 per cent of the popular vote. Still, both runs are evidence of the space for third-party candidates.

The size of the United States, the fact that there are 50 states, and the multiple layers of government mean a lot of elections are based on local issues. Being able to create a party that speaks to all those local spaces is very difficult, and even more difficult when two parties already dominate, and encompass multiple wings that address particular facets of their total ideologies. At present, there is very little chance for a third party to ever develop any significant foothold in the national consciousness of America. Thus, the US is stuck with two parties for now.

Although third parties can't touch the two established political parties in terms of fundraising or reach, they can have a bigger impact than one would think, and at critical junctures. In the 2000 presidential election, when the Green Party candidate Ralph Nader received 2.74 per cent of the popular vote, it was suggested that political plurality led to a fate worse than death – a Republican victory. Gore, it was felt, lost the election because people who voted for Nader would otherwise have voted for him.

Part II

Discovering How the American Government Functions

Running through a Very Broad Overview of How a Bill Becomes Law

1. **A bill is researched, drafted, and introduced by a Senator or Representative.**

2. **The bill is assigned a committee in whichever chamber (House or Senate) it was introduced.**

    The committee discusses the bill in meetings and public hearings. At this stage it is *marked up* (revised) to reflect the discussions and then the committee votes on it. If the vote enables it to continue on its path, it is put onto the calendar for a vote by the entire chamber, accompanied by a report that explains its costs, purpose and amendments so far.

3. **The bill is read, debated, possibly amended, and voted on.**

4. **It goes to the Congressional Budget Office for review.**

5. **The bill is introduced in the second chamber of Congress.**

    It goes straight to the floor for debate or is sent to the appropriate committee, debated, amended, and then reviewed, debated and voted on by the chamber.

6. **It is passed or, if it has been amended, it goes back to its originating chamber for another vote.**

    If legislators agree with the change, the bill goes to the next stage; if they disagree then it can be bounced back to the other chamber or a special joint conference committee attempts to unify the different chambers' versions of the bill.

7. **The bill is sent to the president for approval.**

Find out how the system oversees itself through checks and balances at www. dummies.com/extras/americanpoliticsuk.

In This Part . . .

✔ Dig into the roles liberalism and political parties play in American government.

✔ Investigate the roles and responsibilities of the three federal branches of government: the executive, legislature and judiciary.

✔ Discover how these three branches interact with each other in ways both productive and challenging.

✔ Dive into the depths of federal and state bureaucracy. Are they effective on the large scale that the vast American population requires?

✔ Follow the process of an idea becoming law as it moves through both chambers of Congress — and past (or into) a lot of potential pitfalls.

Chapter 4

Exploring the President's Role as Executive

. . . .

In This Chapter

▶ Identifying the individual elements of the Executive

▶ Understanding the formal and informal powers of the president

▶ Explaining the traits that make for a successful president

▶ Exploring public perceptions of the president

. . . .

*T*he executive branch of the federal government is extremely powerful in both domestic and foreign affairs. At the head of this branch is the nationally elected president of the United States. The president swears an oath to 'faithfully execute' his responsibilities as president and to 'preserve, protect and defend the Constitution of the United States'. It includes ensuring that the nation is protected from foreign aggression and proposing a policy agenda that serves to improve the lot of American citizens.

But life is never that easy, and the president and the executive face many obstacles when carrying out their duties. This chapter analyses the different elements of the executive, examines the powers of the presidency, identifies what makes a successful president and outlines how the average American has perceived the various presidents in office since the Cold War.

Understanding the Executive Branch

The executive isn't all about the president. Three other parts of the Executive also play vitally important roles in this branch of government, without which the president's ability to carry out his duties would be extremely limited. These are the Executive Office, the vice president and the *Cabinet*, or the heads of the federal government departments. This section discusses the powers, roles and responsibilities of these four elements of the executive.

President

According to the Constitution, the president is in charge of the executive branch of the federal government, making him the highest elected office holder in the federal government and responsible for how it operates. Additionally, the President represents America, to Americans and to people around the world.

Presidential election and terms

In order to be eligible to run for the presidency, a person has to have been a citizen of the United States at the time the Constitution was adopted in the late eighteenth century or to have been born in the US. Today, what this effectively means is that only Americans born in America are able to be president, unless, of course, you were born more than 225 years ago – or, if you believe a small faction of dissenters, you're Barack Obama, who was allegedly born in Kenya (actually he was born in the fiftieth US state, Hawaii!).

The other requirements for eligibility are that the person has to be over the age of 30 and must have been residing in the US for 14 years (although the 14-year rule actually no longer applies as it relates to the founders wanting those born outside of the US to have had sufficient time to have adopted the American way of life and to thus not seek to alter its path by adhering to Old World political views).

The president is chosen through the Electoral College (EC). It is a complicated system that was originally designed to accommodate the needs of the less populous southern states during the founding of the nation. The 538 electors of the Electoral College each have one vote and are divided according to the number of Senators and Representatives in each state – plus Washington, DC. You can find out more about the particulars of the Electoral College in Chapter 10.

The US presidential election is often referred to as an *indirect* election because the candidates aren't directly elected by the people but through electors. These *electors* are officials from a particular state who are tasked with voting for the presidential candidate who has the most votes (popular vote) in that state. For example, California has 55 EC votes and so has 55 electors. Whichever presidential candidate wins the popular vote in California wins all 55 of its Electoral College votes. To become president, a candidate must win 270 EC votes (a simple majority – one more than half of the votes).

According to Article II, Section 1 of the Constitution, each presidential term is to last four years. While no such restrictions were placed on the number of terms a president could take up, because the first, George Washington (1789–1797), held only two terms, a precedent was set that was to last until

President Franklin D. Roosevelt (1933–1945) took office. He won an impressive fourth term in office during the Second World War.

In 1951, the Congress and states ratified the Twenty-second Amendment, which stated that a president could run for two terms (eight years) only. An exception would only apply if the vice president assumed the office of the president with less than two years of that previous president's term left to run, won the next election and was then re-elected. Only once since this amendment was ratified could this situation have occurred. After the assassination of President Kennedy in November 1963, vice president Johnson became president and ran in the 1964 presidential election and won. Because he only held office for one year of Kennedy's term (less than the two years prescribed), he could have run for president in the 1968 election as well, although he didn't.

In 1967, the Twenty-fifth Amendment was ratified, clarifying the presidential line of succession. Because in eight instances an elected president had been removed from office – as a result of death, assassination and resignation – and because in eight instances a vice president had either died or resigned, it meant that technical issues not thought out at the time of the writing of the Constitution needed to be dealt with. The order of succession is as follows:

- ✔ If a president is removed from office, one way or another, the vice president becomes president.

- ✔ If a vice presidential space becomes available as a result of removal from office or promotion, the president gets to choose his candidate, although both chambers of Congress also have to approve his choice.

- ✔ If a president is unable to carry out his duties, whether by his own determination or that of the Cabinet or Congress, the vice president becomes acting president. The president can resume his duties if he decides he is able to and the Cabinet or Congress don't oppose that decision. In the case of opposition, a two-thirds majority in both chambers must decide that the president cannot carry out his duties.

Presidential responsibilities

As the head of the executive branch, the president functions in seven key positions. Each one is important in its own right, and all involve the president being the head honcho. No wonder presidents experience delusions of grandeur!

- ✔ **Chief executive:** The power of the chief executive is afforded to the president by the Constitution. The president runs the federal government by appointing members of the Cabinet and other key positions, ensuring that the government fulfils its legal obligations. The president employs *Executive Orders* (EOs) that are designed to help the government carry out its duties.

- ✔ **Head of state:** Similar to other heads of state, the president is responsible for representing the nation on foreign trips and receiving foreign dignitaries. Heads of state are, in effect, the symbol of the nation in the same way that the Queen represents the UK and the Commonwealth. In this role, the president also gives speeches on non-partisan issues, such as on the Fourth of July celebrating Independence Day.

- ✔ **Chief diplomat:** The president is both the chief negotiator for foreign policy and the chief architect of foreign policy. He is responsible for representing the US at treaty negotiations, developing US responses to international issues and explaining to the American public US foreign policy actions. The president also has the power to conduct foreign relations by formally acknowledging a state's existence, allowing the exchange of ambassadors and agreeing to international agreements by employing *Executive Agreements* that do not require Congressional approval. The president also has the power to nominate candidates for ambassadorships to represent the US in other countries and the United Nations.

- ✔ **Commander-in-chief.** The Constitution places the president in charge of the military. He is in ultimate charge of determining its size, focus and where it should be deployed. While the president is supposed to determine how a war is conducted and Congress to determine which countries or peoples America goes to war with, since the Cold War the powers of the president have expanded and he now has the ability to determine foreign interventions (see Chapter 7 for details of the conflicting roles of both branches at times of conflict).

- ✔ **Chief legislator:** The president has a principal role in both the passing of laws and in setting the policy agenda for Congress. The president is responsible for submitting a budget to Congress for the federal government. It is important for the president to have it approved because it ensures that his political agenda is implemented. The budget pays for the agenda but Congress can, and does, reject budgets. This calls into question the power of the president to lead on national issues, and opposition can be evidence of presidential weakness. While Congress has the sole power to legislate and pass Acts, the president has to sign those Acts before they become law. Through the power of the veto, the president can choose not to sign an act into law. Chapter 5 tells you more about the law-making process.

- ✔ **Head of political party:** The president is the nominal head of the party, and supports party candidates in local, state and federal elections via endorsements, fundraising and attendance at rallies. And I say nominal because political parties in American are less coherent beasts than their European, Australian and Canadian counterparts (see Chapter 11 on the two-party system for further details).

Executive Office of the President

The *Executive Office of the President* (EOP) is the group of staff members closest to the president and headed by his chief of staff. It's a way for the president to exert his power and influence over the other elements of the executive branch of the federal government, in particular, those civil servants who have some degree of influence whose support is required for implementation of presidential policy.

The Office of the Vice President of the United States and the Office of the First Lady are two more well-known elements of the EOP. Perhaps the most important office, in terms of directing the mission of the EOP, is the Office of the Chief of Staff – typically a former politician who is a confidante of the president. She runs the EOP, negotiates with various government officials such as Congresspeople in implementing the president's plans, decides who gets to meet the president and is in charge of where the president goes and when.

While some positions require Senate confirmation, such as the Director of the Office of Management and Budget (OMB), the majority of positions are appointed by the president. Being appointed engenders loyalty to the president and encourages the office holder to carry out their duties in accordance with the president's wishes. However, the situation's never that clear cut when it comes to politics. The loyalty of the EOP is complicated in that Congress has the *power of the purse* (see Chapter 5 on the Congress for further details) and so determines whether or not the president's requests for funding are approved.

In 1939 President Roosevelt established the EOP with congressional approval, when it passed the Reorganization Act. It required an organisation to support the president in the development and implementation of his policy plans. The first two elements of the EOP were the establishment of the White House Office (WHO) and the Bureau of the Budget (now known as the OMB), which help the president implement and enforce his policies through the executive departments. As the years went by, more people were employed and more offices created.

According to official figures, about 1,800 people currently work in the EOP, although, in reality, that figure is likely to be significantly higher because it only accounts for those who are paid for by the EOP. Lots of other people are seconded from other federal departments and agencies but are paid for by their home institutions. But the situation wasn't always like this. Before President Roosevelt came along, most presidents had very few resources to rely on. When Thomas Jefferson was president (1801–1809), he had only two members of staff – a messenger and a secretary. And they were paid for out of his own pocket and not government funds. During Herbert Hoover's presidency (1929–1933), over a hundred years later, there were still only 35 people on his staff.

Obviously, the EOP has expanded exponentially. Currently, nearly 50 separate offices, councils and advisors support the president in carrying out his duties. Some of these are much bigger and more important beasts than others, and so have more members of staff. The president also has the power to modify, add or delete these elements of the EOP as he sees fit.

The OMB is the largest part of the EOP and has over 500 employees. These employees involved in developing and implementing how presidential policies are to be implemented by the government bureaucracy. It means that, at any one time, they could be developing health, defence or environmental programmes. Some of these employees are actually seconded from different departments, such as the White House Rural Council and the Office of National AIDS Policy.

Vice president

While this role is technically a part of the Executive Office of the President, I've given the vice president his own section – mainly because I feel rather sorry for the person who assumes this undervalued role.

The Constitution only details how the vice president is elected and that his principal duties are two-fold.

 ✔ He gets to take over as president should the president leave office as a result of death, illness, impeachment or resignation.

 ✔ He gets to be a president of sorts in that he's President of the Senate, and gets to cast the deciding vote in a tie in the Senate.

Despite a general attitude of cynicism towards the office (see the nearby sidebar. 'A bucket of warm spit' and other personal observations on the role of the vice president'), the modern vice president has attained more powers. Sometimes these are determined based on the whims of the president, sometimes on the personal relationship between the two and sometimes because the practical necessities of running the country demand it.

Some presidents consider the vice president a necessary evil and don't engage that person in the day-to-day political operations of government, while others consider the VP an essential part of the deliberating process. A classic example of non-engagement was when Truman became the vice president for President Roosevelt after the 1944 presidential election. In the two months after being appointed vice president in January 1945 until Roosevelt's death and his taking the presidential oath in April 1945, Truman wasn't briefed on the country's war plans and didn't know the US was developing an atomic bomb. President Bush's vice president, Dick Cheney (2001–2008), in contrast, accumulated more responsibilities for the vice president's office than most, as a result of his relationship with the president. More permanent changes do occur, however, which make this office more important; for example, since 1949 the vice president has been a member of the National Security Council established in 1947 to advise the president on national and security issues.

Before the Twelfth Amendment was ratified in 1804, the vice president was neither appointed by the presidential candidate nor chosen directly by the electorate. The role was granted to the presidential candidate who scored the second-highest number of votes in the general election.

In a presidential general election today, the vice presidential candidate is part of the election ticket. He's typically chosen for his ability to bring in votes from other ideological wings of the party, help unify the party and generate more support for the presidential candidate from the party establishment, grassroots members and funders. And, in another act of canny vote grabbing, the vice president is normally from a different geographical part of the United States.

'A bucket of warm spit' and other personal observations on the role of the vice president

Since the founding of the United States, successive vice presidents have been rather cynical about the office they hold. The first vice president, John Adams, who went on to become the second president, once complained to his wife that 'my country has in its wisdom contrived for me the most insignificant office that ever the invention of man contrived or his imagination conceived'.

And this irreverent attitude to the office was supported by President Woodrow Wilson's vice president, Thomas Marshall (1913–1921), who quipped: 'once there were two brothers. One ran away to sea, the other was elected vice president, and nothing was ever heard of either of them again.' And in referring to the health of Wilson after he suffered a stroke in 1919, Marshall stated that 'the only business of the vice president is to ring the White House bell every morning and ask what is the state of health of the president'.

President Roosevelt's vice president, John Nance Garner (1933–1941), was equally sanguine and is reputed to have said, that his office was 'not worth a bucket of warm spit'. Even a noted historian, Arthur Schlesinger Jnr., commented, in 1974, that 'the Vice President has only one serious thing to do: that is, to wait around for the President to die'.

A good example of bridging the ideological divide is Republican presidential candidate Abraham Lincoln opting, in 1864, for a Southern Democrat, Andrew Johnson, to run as his vice president. Lincoln thought that this move would demonstrate to the electorate in the South that he wouldn't ignore their voices in government decision making. And an example of geographic differences is the appointment by the East coast Bostonian presidential candidate John F. Kennedy, in 1960, of the Southern Texan Lyndon Johnson.

When the party isn't clearly divided, the rules of vice president-choosing change. In that case, the presidential candidate can appoint someone who is neither ideologically nor geographically different. Candidate Clinton's nomination of Al Gore as his running mate is a double example: both were from the South and both represented the New Democrat wing of the party (see Chapter 11 on the two-party system for details of the different party wings).

While I present the vice president as a neutered position, maybe all political capital is not lost for them. In modern times, assuming the office of the vice president has also been seen as a stepping stone to the presidency itself. So, while the vice president's powers may be limited, the role does provide a convenient national platform for a run as a future presidential candidate. Since 1956, 15 presidential elections have taken place. Ten of these have featured the incumbent president, four the incumbent vice president and one no presidential or vice presidential incumbents. Only time will tell, but a distinct possibility exists that the 2016 Democratic candidate will be the current vice president, Joe Biden.

Cabinet

Today, the Cabinet comprises the president, vice president and the heads of the 15 executive departments (otherwise known as the federal departments). These heads are called secretaries: the Secretary of Defense for the Department of Defense; Secretary of the Treasury for the Department of the Treasury; and the Attorney General for the Department of Justice (yes, there's always one who wants to be different).

Similar to the EOP members of staff, the Cabinet members are appointed by the president. That said, they must also be approved by the Senate in what's known as confirmation hearings. In spite of this complication, Cabinet members' loyalty is overwhelmingly to the president; their position is dependent on his favour. Because the president can replace a secretary when he wants to (although, politically, it's not always the right thing to do, irrespective of their possible incompetence), it is in the interests of the secretaries to implement the president's plans.

The Cabinet and the heads of executive departments were briefly mentioned in Article II of the Constitution in referring to the president's power of appointment. But there haven't always been 15 departments with a seat at the Cabinet table. The earliest departments, and thus secretaries, were the Departments of State, the Treasury and War (in an Orwellian twist, that department is now known as Defense), which were founded in 1789. And the most recent newcomer is the Secretary of Homeland Security, which joined in November 2002.

After the vice president, the speaker of the House of Representatives, and then the president pro tempore of the Senate (typically the longest serving member of the majority party in the Senate), the heads of these 15 departments are in line for the presidency if something were to happen to the president. The 15 departments are aligned in the succession in order of their establishment. Here are the details of each of these 15 departments:

- ✔ **Department of State:** The Secretary of State is one of the leading advisors to the president on international affairs. This department is responsible for conducting diplomatic relations with other states and international institutions in pursuit of US foreign policy objectives. Currently, these objectives include continuing the fight against terrorism, protecting the current international order and providing foreign assistance via the US Agency for International Development (USAID). The Department of State currently has 58,000 employees and submitted a budget request of $46.2 billion for 2015.

- ✔ **Department of the Treasury:** The Secretary of the Treasury (top bean counter) advises the president on how the government can fund its policy plans. This department is responsible for promoting stable economic growth, increasing employment and encouraging international trade through fiscal policies such as tax collection. It has over 100,000 employees and an operating budget of $15 billion.

- ✔ **Department of Defense:** The Secretary of Defense advises the president on military operations, and is one of the most powerful positions in the Cabinet as a result of the size and spending of their department. With 2.1 million people working full time (1.4 million of those being on active duty) and a further 1.1 million in the National Guard and Reserve Forces, this person manages a lot of people. Combined with a yearly budget of around $500 billion, you can see why the Secretary of Defense has a lot of sway. The Department of Defense comprises the Navy, Army and Air Force and has a host of military command offices such as the National Security Agency. Its mission is to protect the US from attack, and to provide humanitarian assistance and peace-keeping troops if required.

✔ **Department of Justice:** The Attorney General runs this department and is the principal legal adviser to the president. This department enforces the laws of the federal government and protects the public from crime and terrorism through its multiple agencies, such as the Federal Bureau of Investigation (FBI) and the Drug Enforcement Agency (DEA). It employs more than 110,000 people and has an operating budget of about $27 billion.

✔ **Department of the Interior:** The Secretary of the Interior is the head of the department that advises the president on conservation and the use of federal lands. And herein lies the paradox – on one hand, it has bureaus that are responsible for conserving the national parks and, on the other, it charges mining, oil and other natural resource extraction companies to operate on federal lands. It generates yearly revenue of about $14 billion, costs about $18 billion to run and employs 70,000 people.

✔ **Department of Agriculture:** The Secretary of Agriculture oversees the farming industry and regulates the industry to ensure food production is conducted in accordance with legal standards, helps the industry expand into foreign markets and supports rural communities. It has a yearly budget of $150 billion and employs nearly 100,000 people.

✔ **Department of Commerce:** The Secretary of Commerce reports to the president on matters relating to national and international business. The department ensures international partners are abiding with trade agreements, issues patents and trademarks and controls export licences for sensitive materials and technologies. It also helps develop models for predicting the weather and behaviour of the oceans. It operates on a budget of $8.8 billion and employs nearly 47,000 people.

✔ **Department of Labor:** The Secretary of Labor runs this department, which is responsible for ensuring that industries and businesses comply with federal employment laws pertaining to health and safety, the minimum wage and employment discrimination. In doing so, it develops better working conditions for employees and protects retiree pension and healthcare benefits. It has a budget of about $12 billion, with a further $2.35 billion being provided for programmes to create more jobs and training opportunities for US citizens in 2015. It employs 18,000 people.

✔ **Department of Health and Human Services:** The Secretary of Health and Human Services is responsible for ensuring the health and wellbeing of American citizens, including food and drug safety and the prevention of outbreaks of particular diseases; it also funds and runs the Medicare and Medicaid health insurance programmes for the over-65s and those in poverty. It has a budget of $967 billion (85 per cent of which goes to Medicare and Medicaid), the biggest by far of all the departments, and employs about 77,500 people.

✔ **Department of Housing and Urban Development:** The Secretary of Housing and Urban Development is responsible for a department that enforces federal housing laws, increases homeownership, provides access to affordable housing and helps communities by providing grants for economic development. It employs about 10,000 people and has a budget of $47 billion.

✔ **Department of Transportation:** The Secretary of Transportation reports to the president on matters relating to the regulation of planes, trains, automobiles and boats and the development of the transportation infrastructure. Bureaus include the Federal Aviation Authority (FAA), which is responsible for all matters relating to air transportation. It employs about 55,000 people and has a budget of $77 billion.

✔ **Department of Energy:** The Secretary of Energy is in charge of the department responsible for keeping the lights on in America. It regulates the nuclear, fossil fuel and alternative energy industries, and the decommissioning of nuclear weapons. It has a budget of $28 billion and employs over 16,000 federal and 100,000 contracted staff.

✔ **Department of Education:** The Secretary of Education is responsible for this department, which distributes funds for educational programmes, oversees the school system, conducts research, enforces federal laws prohibiting discrimination and resolves problems within the educational system. The Department of Education employs over 4,000 people and has a $67.3 billion budget.

✔ **Department of Veterans Affairs:** The Secretary of Veterans Affairs reports to the president on issues relating to military veterans. The department is responsible for providing mental and physical healthcare facilities, running military cemeteries, organising educational and work-related programmes and providing home loans to veterans. It has a $163.9 billion operating budget and employs about 235,000 people.

✔ **Department of Homeland Security:** The Secretary of Homeland Security is the new kid on the block, and is responsible for thwarting terrorist attacks on American soil. In 2002 it incorporated 22 former executive branch agencies such as the US Customs and the US Secret Service into one department to protect the borders, enforce immigration rules and prevent or respond to human-made or natural disasters. It employs 240,000 people and has a budget of $38 billion.

Discovering the Powers (and Limitations) of the Presidency

The presidency isn't as powerful as one might imagine. Public perception affords the president more power than is actually the case according to the Constitution. And this impression is understandable if you consider the president's role as a figurehead in American politics. When deliberating on the powers of the president, the writers of the Constitution were conscious that they did not want the office to replicate the absolutist British tyranny they had fought during the War of Independence. However, alongside the Constitutionally granted powers, the president has also attained more informal powers that have played an important role in expanding how he can achieve his objectives.

Defining executive powers

In order to thwart the concentration of power within one body, the framers of the Constitution separated power into three branches: the executive, legislature and judiciary (see Chapter 5 for a discussion of the legislature and Chapter 7 for the judiciary). Article II of the Constitution dictates that the president of the United States has the authority to run the executive branch and is responsible for doing so.

The president has a range of formal powers, including keeping the other two branches in check. The president has the power to:

- ✔ Make treaties with other nations, although doing so requires approval from two-thirds of the Senate

- ✔ Veto any laws that have been passed by Congress if he doesn't agree with them

- ✔ Propose laws to Congress

- ✔ Submit the federal budget to the House of Representatives for approval

- ✔ Appoint federal officials to carry out the laws of the land

- ✔ Nominate justices to the Supreme Court and judges to the federal court system, although, again, they have to be confirmed by the Senate

- ✔ Pardon and grant amnesty to individuals either convicted or likely to be prosecuted for federal crimes

Understanding presidential powers

As the years have gone by, as new realities have emerged that were not previously accounted for, as presidents have ruled and as scholars have queried, the Office of the President and the powers afforded it have grown and changed.

Increasing powers of the office

The Second World War was a key era in the presidential assertion of more powers than afforded it by the Constitution. Pre-Second World War, Congress had a legitimate role to play in foreign policy; it had the power to declare war, not the president. After the war, however, the balance of power (that is, the benefit of the doubt) shifted to the president. A key reason for this development was the advent of the atomic bomb and its acquisition by America's Cold War foe – the Soviet Union. Because a quick decision would have to be made in regard to launching a nuclear attack, and the debating chamber that is Congress was seen as an unlikely candidate for doing so, the president was thus given the power to 'press the red button', or meet nukes with nukes and send the country into war.

The number of executive agreements relating to treaties has also greatly increased. These agreements don't require Congressional approval; however, under a 1937 Supreme Court decision, they have the same influence. This decision greatly eroded Congress's ability to engage in foreign policy: before 1939, the president had made about 1,200 executive agreements while Congress had ratified approximately 800 treaties. After 1940, a similar number of treaties were ratified but over 13,000 executive agreements made, demonstrating that no Congressional oversight had been sought (Chapter 6 has more on the complicated relationship between the executive and Congress in terms of foreign and domestic policy).

Utilising the power of persuasion

Presidential powers also derive from more informal sources. According to President Harry Truman (1945–1953), 'all the president is, is a glorified public relations man who spends his time flattering, kissing and kicking people to get them to do what they are supposed to do anyway'. And perhaps the most famous and insightful analysis of presidential leadership is Richard Neustadt's *Presidential Power and the Modern Presidents: The Politics of Leadership* (1960). Not only was this book used to examine the successes and failures of various presidents, it was also used by presidents themselves to work out how to persuade people to support their political agendas. Kennedy famously had a copy of this book in the White House.

Neustadt claimed that the overriding power of the president is the 'power to persuade', meaning that the president derived power not only from the Constitution, as detailed in Article II, but also from his reputation and associated national and international prestige. Limitations on the president's power, according to Neustadt, arise because the American political system is based on shared rather than separated powers. Thus separate institutions share power (the legislature, executive and judiciary); federal and state governments share power; and the power of the government is restricted by terms detailed in the Bill of Rights.

In sum, the US government is large, and powers are dispersed into varying local, state and federal levels. The president cannot just demand that his policies be implemented – the fragmentation of government is too great.

Working across political layers

Each level of the political party, whether local, state or national, is autonomous. These autonomous levels aren't coherent entities pushing in the same direction, which means that multiple constituencies and interests can shape and influence that level of government or political party. Take, for example, a Republican member of Congress and a Republican president serving simultaneously. While they're members of the same party, they depend on different interests on the part of the electorate. Members of Congress represent the local interests of their district or state; unless confronted with a crisis, they won't overly concern themselves with national issues if they don't relate to their constituents.

A member of the House of Representatives from Montana, for example, wouldn't worry about the problem of over-populated cities such as Los Angeles (with a population of nearly 4 million) and the impact of car pollution on residents when the largest city in Montana has a population of a mere 100,000. A president, in contrast, does have to take these local as well as national issues into account when making decisions. What this situation means is that representatives at the different levels aren't dependent on each other; a president, for example, has little influence in determining which members of his party should be nominated to represent it in a state or federal general election.

When the president wants someone to do something for him, he has to acknowledge that, because of these multiple layers of government and party, he's competing with other interests also vying for their attention. And it's here that the president must use his power to persuade. To accomplish this task, the president must instil fear or demonstrate that it's in the official's best interests to do what he wants – and this process is called bargaining.

Another factor in determining whether someone will support the president's position is if sufficient public interest is shown in the measure. If public support is evident, it's in the interests of the official to support the president; if no public support exists, the official can resist. To ensure allegiance, the president does have a number of powers that can help in the bargaining process. He has the power to appoint people to various offices, veto appointments and help fundraise for someone running for office or, if the individual is in government, give their department an increased budget for pet projects.

Thus, the president can use his status and authority to persuade people to follow him. Obviously, however, this use of power isn't a one-way street. Support comes at a price; people will want something in return. They conduct their own cost–benefit analysis regarding whether supporting the president aides their interests. What Neustadt exposes is the complicated world of bargaining that the president must engage in, in order for his policies to be supported and enacted. Not quite the all-powerful figure the Office of the President presents to the outside world.

Judging What Makes a Good President

Many measures can be applied to deciding whether a president can be judged a success. And as many surveys serve up these tools of assessment. They all, however, and to varying degrees, overlap each other in terms of what's being measured.

In determining the individual criteria required for determining whether a president is successful, it's important to include:

- ✔ The ability of the president to attain her legislative priorities
- ✔ Whether he has been re-elected for a second-term
- ✔ Levels of public approval
- ✔ Foreign policy successes
- ✔ Strength of the economy
- ✔ Ability to use the veto to halt legislation that doesn't fit with her political agenda

Fred I. Greenstein, in what's become a regular update on presidential greatness, has published one of the most famous books on this subject: *The Presidential Difference: Leadership Style from FDR to Barack Obama*. Greenstein analyses the last 13 presidents and suggest six criteria for judging their success. He also uses these criteria as a tool to predict future presidential success. The six criteria are:

- ✔ **Public communication:** How well did the president communicate to the public his message regarding the path he wanted to take America down? Key to successful communications are good speech writers and plenty of rehearsals. Greenstein suggests that Roosevelt, Kennedy, Reagan and Clinton were examples of good communicators.

- ✔ **Organisational capacity:** How successfully did the president build a good team that worked well for him in the executive office? Advisers should not always agree with the president but challenge him to solve problems. The ability to create effective institutional structures is also important. Key to success is the ability of the president to encourage aides to debate competing points while in the same room. Two notable proponents of this policy were Franklin D. Roosevelt and Eisenhower.

- ✔ **Political skill:** Could the president get his way? A successful president can assert himself in the overly bureaucratised political system in order to get people to implement his policies; to do so, he must gain a reputation as a determined politician. He must also engage the public in order to obtain support for his policies. President Johnson is lauded as one of the best political operators, using the legacy of Kennedy to persuade the public, members of Congress and the bureaucracy to support his political agenda.

- ✔ **Vision:** Did the president have a clear and viable vision, and could he inspire others to follow it? Pragmatic politicians such as George H.W. Bush were criticised as lacking in vision and holding inconsistent and conflicting positions; the same has been levelled at Obama. In contrast, Eisenhower and Nixon established clear and consistent policies that connected to an overarching narrative.

- ✔ **Cognitive style:** How well did the president get to the heart of a problem and propose solutions? In terms of foreign policy, Nixon is a great positive example. During his time in office he began ending the war in Vietnam, normalised relations with Communist China and negotiated a reduction in nuclear weapons with the Soviet Union. Reagan, on the other hand, is seen as a failure because of his inability to grasp the details of his government's policies.

✔ **Emotional intelligence:** Did the president have a firm understanding of his own personality, limitations and strengths? Johnson, Nixon, Carter and Clinton are all examples of presidents who had personal issues that impaired their ability to act. Johnson was liable to mood swings, Nixon was overly suspicious, Carter was inflexible, which meant that he had a problem engaging with Congress, and Clinton was emotionally challenged and had a series of affairs.

Ranking the presidents

On discussing presidential power in 1960, Richard Neustadt wrote that Americans liked to 'rate' presidents' leadership skills. Judging how good a president is in absolute terms or relative to others is still an enjoyable pastime for many people. A few years ago (2010), I participated in the first poll of US presidents by British-based academics organised by the School of Advanced Study at the University of London. It examined the performance of 40 presidents based on five areas: vision and agenda-setting, domestic leadership, foreign policy leadership, moral authority and positive historical legacy. The results were interesting. The top five included no presidents post-Second World War. Roosevelt, for example, topped the polls because of his impact in dealing with the challenges of the Great Depression and the Second World War; US academics, in contrast, typically place him lower down, perhaps reflecting the different attitudes of Europeans and Americans in regard to the responsibilities of central government. The top five are as follows:

1. Franklin Delano Roosevelt (1933–1945)

2. Abraham Lincoln (1861–1865)

3. George Washington (1789–1797)

4. Thomas Jefferson (1801–1809)

5. Theodore Roosevelt (1901–1909)

Of the most recent presidents, Reagan (1981–1989) took the top spot, in eighth position, Carter (1977–1981) was eighteenth and Clinton (1993–2001) was nineteenth. Surprisingly, Kennedy (1961–1963) only managed fifteenth position and George W. Bush (2001–2009) scraped in at thirty-first. It was too early to judge President Obama (2009–); however, according to other polls, he doesn't appear to be faring so well either.

Chapter 5

Considering the Power of Congress

● ●

In This Chapter

▶ Introducing the powers of Congress

▶ Mapping the organisation of Congress

▶ Understanding the role of committees, Congressional staff and political parties in Congress

▶ Discussing the changing demographic makeup of Congress members

▶ Explaining what the public think about Congress and its members

● ●

*O*ne of the most interesting places in American politics, Congress plays a vital role in the running of the United States in both domestic and foreign policy fields. Legislators from all over the country meet in Congress to represent the interests of their constituents at the national level. It's where these elected members propose bills, debate them, and vote them into law.

In this chapter I explore a whole range of issues that help explain the power and beauty of the Congress, from describing its structure to discussing the role of committees. I also consider the bad reputation that Congress has developed among the American public and how, as time goes by, its public image is getting worse rather than better.

Understanding Congress

Congress is a powerful legislative body with powers assigned to it by the US Constitution. It is split into two different chambers: the House of Representatives and the Senate.

The principal mission of a legislative body is to make laws. Debating the subject of a bill is an essential part of that mission and is instrumental to whether a bill becomes the law of the land (see Chapter 8 on how an idea becomes a law for more details). That journey is typically a very long one, with lots of opportunities for the bill to die.

A principal criticism of Congress is thus that it's too slow to react to the political, social and economic issues facing America. However, Congress is also a body that represents the electorate and thus should consider the multiple competing interests of a very diverse nation (see Chapter 12 on voting behaviour for an overview of the diversity in American society). Therefore, a slow debating chamber provides the opportunity for representatives to compromise and provide solutions that accommodate the various needs of all interested parties.

Powers of Congress to check and balance

The first of the seven articles that make up the Constitution concerns the legislative branch, Congress. I think the very fact that Congress is the first subject discussed in this map of the future political system illustrates the importance the framers attributed to it. The article explains the logistics, roles and responsibilities of Congress (see the following section for the list of Congressional powers).

To balance the power between large and small states, the Constitution establishes two chambers of Congress (this is called a *bicameral* system and refers to the division of the Senate and the House of Representatives). Always vigilant against the possibility of tyrannical rule by one institution, the framers gave separate powers to each chamber, effectively instilling competition between the Senate and the House of Representatives. For example, the House has the sole power to introduce laws designed to raise revenue and decide to impeach the president or a federal judge, while the Senate confirms presidential nominations, approves treaties and tries impeached members of government accused of ill-doing. And because both chambers have to agree to a bill before it's passed to the president for his signature or veto, compromise is as important as competition.

A further source of conflict is the disconnect between local and national interests. Because Senators are elected on a state-wide basis and Representatives are elected on a district-wide basis (*districts* are geographical areas below the state level that are organised for voting purposes), both local and regional interests influence which draft legislation they support – and those don't always align.

Grasping the make-up of Senate and House

Creating a bicameral legislative body was no accident. The framers were extremely concerned with fairness and balance – with creating a way for all people to be represented. Thus they crafted two very different bodies of representatives, apportioned in very different ways:

- ✔ The Senate gives equal weight to the interests of each state. It was established to counter the framers' concern that the larger states would dominate the smaller states and lead to majority rule. Each state elects two Senators who represent the state as a whole. Thus today 50 states are represented by 100 Senators.

- ✔ The make-up of the House reflects each state's population, and representatives are voted to office within districts. Thus a representative serves a portion of the state that they're from. Today there are 435 representatives, and every 10 years a government census (counting how many people live in the US and where) moves the number of seats dependent on shifts in the population.

On one side of Congress – the Senate – each state is represented equally. A state with a small population has the same voting rights as states with much larger populations. The 21 smallest states represent 12 per cent of the nation's population and have 42 per cent of the nation's Senators. The smaller states could therefore work together to block legislation that negatively impacts them. In fact, they are just over the 41-vote threshold required to end a filibuster (see Chapter 8 on how an idea becomes law for details on filibusters).

Each Senator has a six-year term, which is supposed to relieve them of the immediate pressures of public opinion – although this doesn't seem to be the case today what with 24 hour news coverage! To ensure that no one group would dominate the Senate in one election and compromise the stability-inducing aim of the chamber, elections are staggered. Every two years only one-third of the Senate is thus up for election. If you fancy becoming a Senator, you have to be at least 30 years old, a resident of the US for at least nine years and a legal resident of the state you want to represent.

Whereas the Senate represents the states, the framers wanted the House of Representatives to reflect the will of the people. Whilst the framers were concerned about the rights of smaller states being protected, they were also concerned that the more populous states should not be held hostage to minority rule. It meant that the number of Representatives (also known as Congressmen and Congresswomen, or just Congresspeople) would be determined by the population within the state. The more populous a state the more representatives it gets, and thus, greater influence in submitting and getting legislation passed that reflected their interests as a large state. When compared to the overrepresentation of small states in the Senate, these House stats offset this imbalance, as required under the terms of the Constitution.

After the last census in 2010, the top 8 most populous states accounted for 220 of the 435 seats in the House, which would give them a majority of three seats. The intention behind having the people vote for the Representatives is that it better reflects the needs of the people at the time of an election. This situation is further reinforced by all members of the House running for election every two years. It enables significant shifts in the focus of the House within one election. In the 1994 elections, for example, the Republican Party gained 54 seats to reach 230, which put them in the majority for the first time since 1952.

If you want to be an elected member of the House, and my sincere best wishes to you in this busy and thankless job, you need to be at least 25 years old, a US resident for over seven years and a legal resident of the state in which you're running.

Representation in the House in relation to population, as determined by the Constitution

In the 2012 elections, the average population size of a district was just over 700,000 people. This large figure somewhat compromises the aim of the framers, who wanted Representatives to represent a smaller number of people so that they'd have a better idea of their local situation and thus better serve their interests. In fact, the Constitution states that, 'The Number of Representatives shall not exceed one for every thirty Thousand'. However, in 1911 Congress fixed the number of Representatives at 435 – the number it still is today. What that fixed number has meant is that average district size has mushroomed as the US population has increased. A disparity between states also exists regarding the number of people in each district. Montana, for example, has a state-at-large district with one member of the House representing nearly 1 million people, while Rhode Island has two members for a population of just over 1 million, which is about 500,000 per member. This disparity has led for calls for the House to expand its number of Representatives. While sticking to the 30,000 limit set in the Constitution would mean having an impractical 10,000 Representatives, calls have been made to expand the number to 1,000.

Enumerated vs. implied power

Congress's powers can be broken into two categories:

- ✔ **Enumerated powers** are those explicitly given to Congress.

- ✔ **Implied powers** are those that haven't been expressly granted by the Constitution but that Congress must have if it's to exercise its enumerated powers.

Each branch of Congress has a range of powers that it uses to carry out its duties, including keeping the other two branches in check. Their joint or closely related powers include the following:

- ✔ Impeaching (House) and trying (Senate) the president or judges if they're deemed to have done wrong.

- ✔ If no presidential candidate in a general election has an Electoral College majority (270 out of 538), the House will choose the president and the Senate will choose the vice president.

- ✔ Congress can override a presidential veto on a bill that's passed Congress with a two-thirds majority in each chamber.

- ✔ If a new vice presidential candidate is required, the nominated person requires the approval of both the House and the Senate.

- ✔ Congress has the power to declare war but the same text of the declaration must be passed by the House and the Senate.

- ✔ Congress has the power to make a constitutional amendment with a two-thirds majority vote in both the House and the Senate.

- ✔ Congress has the power to create federal courts below the Supreme Court if it so chooses and determine the *jurisdiction* (geographic location) of the courts in operation. (As the size of the country and its population expanded and the number of states grew, a new federal court system was able to be established.)

- ✔ Congress has the power to alter the size of the Supreme Court.

- ✔ The House and the Senate each have the power to pass or stall a bill passed in the other chamber if it doesn't agree with the text.

- ✔ Congress has the (implied) power to create all 'necessary and proper' laws that enable it to carry out all the other (enumerated) powers.

- ✔ The Senate or the House are only able to adjourn for more than three days with the permission of the other chamber.

- ✔ All the records of the House and Senate proceedings have to be published in their respective journals.

Each chamber also has separate responsibilities that the other chamber is not involved in:

- ✔ All key departmental appointments and US ambassadors made by the president, such as the Secretary of Defense or the US ambassador to Australia, require Senate approval.
- ✔ All treaties that the US government has negotiated with have to be approved by the Senate.
- ✔ All federal judges appointed by the president have to be approved by the Senate.
- ✔ Congress has the power to create and collect new taxes. All revenue-collecting bills must originate from the House.

Clinton's 1988 impeachment

In 1998, Bill Clinton became the second US President to be impeached. (The first was Andrew Johnson in 1868, who was impeached on numerous counts of 'high crimes and misdemeanours'. But that's another story.) Clinton's impeachment concerned the controversy around his relationship with White House intern Monica Lewinsky. Having an affair is not an impeachable offense, but lying about it to a court is. Clinton had denied the affair, not only to the media but also before a grand jury who had questioned him about his affair in the context of a wide-ranging investigation of various allegations of corruption by the president and his wife. It was Clinton's lies that got him into legal hot water.

There are two stages to Congress' impeachment process. Firstly, the articles of impeachment (accusations) are put to the House of Representatives, where a simple majority vote is taken to determine whether these articles should be considered formal allegations. At this time, Republicans were the majority party and, since Clinton was a Democrat, it is perhaps not surprising that the vote didn't go his way. Proceedings moved to the Senate, where he was tried very much as if he were in court.

On 9 February 1999, nearly a month after proceedings began in the Senate, votes were cast and Clinton was acquitted on both counts. Despite the efforts of the prosecution and defence, it seemed that most Senators were persuaded by loyalty rather than legal argument. Not one Democrat voted to convict Clinton on either charge, and very few Republicans made the leap the other way.

Sussing Out the Structure of Congress

Congress doesn't begin and end with Senators and Representatives. Those are the people in charge of making things happen, but how they organise among themselves and the people they rely on to do their jobs creates a complicated network of Congressional committees, staff and agencies that work together (and against each other) for the sake of legislation.

Committees

Congressional committees – small groups of legislators who come together to focus on special issues – are vitally important structures in the federal system of governance. If Congress is the legislative chamber, think of its committees and subcommittees as both the debating and investigative engines of law-making.

In total, 45 different committees operate in Congress. Within the 21 committees in the House of Representatives are 96 subcommittees, in the Senate are 20 committees and 68 subcommittees, and four committees are joint affairs between both chambers.

Committees focus on domestic and foreign affairs and have four major roles:

- ✔ They identify and convene hearings to investigate a particular issue that's under the committee's jurisdiction, such as submitted draft legislation, federal government actions or specific individuals. They invite interested parties to present their thoughts and findings on the issue being discussed. These hearings are typically open to the public, and sometimes are shown live on TV and the Internet.

- ✔ They draft new legislation and scrutinise and redraft legislation that the president and other members of Congress have submitted (see Chapter 8 on how an idea becomes law for more information).

- ✔ Publish reports on the findings of their investigations.

- ✔ Examine executive actions and individuals.

- ✔ In the Senate, some committees are responsible for approving presidential appointments in the federal judiciary, ambassadorships and key federal employees such as the various secretaries of government departments (for example, the U.S. Department of the Treasury).

Within each chamber, four types of committees exist:

- ✔ **Standing committees:** These committees are the most important because they report on legislation submitted to them by the House and Senate floors. For example, one Senate committee, the Committee on Appropriations, is concerned with setting the level of resources required to fund the federal government. It has 12 subcommittees working on a whole range of domestic and foreign policy issues.

- ✔ **Select or special committees:** These ad hoc committees are set up in order to examine a particular issue that's not covered by a standing or other committee. They usually expire when their task is done, and are investigative rather than legislative. The investigations into the assassinations of President Kennedy and Martin Luther King are good examples. Other select committees are permanent in nature and have oversight functions, such as the appropriately titled House's Permanent Select Committee on Intelligence.

- ✔ **Joint committees:** These committees are permanent and comprised of members from both chambers of Congress. Some focus on housekeeping issues, such as the Joint Committee on the Library, which concerns the administration of the Library of Congress (the research library of the US Congress and apparently the largest library in the world). Others focus on major issues facing the United States, such as the Joint Economic Committee that examines the economic situation and suggests changes to economic policy.

- ✔ **Conference committees:** An *ad hoc* committee comprised of House and Senate members, this committee arises when different versions of the same bill are passed in both chambers. Its aim is to reconcile the House and Senate versions of the (usually controversial) bill to make it acceptable to both chambers and continue on its path to becoming law.

While a crossover exists between domestic and foreign issues, most committees do focus on the domestic. And some have amazingly conflated agendas, such as the Agriculture, Nutrition and Forestry committee. Most committees have subcommittees that deal with specific areas of the committee's work. The Agriculture, Nutrition and Forestry committee, for example, has five subcommittees:

- ✔ Commodities, Markets, Trade and Risk Management – includes oversight on topics such as the production of agricultural crops, commodities and products; fresh water food production; and futures, options and derivatives.

- ✔ Jobs, Rural Economic Growth and Energy Innovation – includes oversight on topics such as rural economic revitalisation and quality of life; rural job and business growth; and renewable energy production and energy efficiency improvements.

✔ Conservation, Forestry and Natural Resources – includes oversight on topics such as conservation and protection of natural resources and the environment and the use of pesticides.

✔ Nutrition, Specialty Crops, Food and Agricultural Research – includes oversight on topics such as nutrition and food assistance; school and child nutrition programmes; and local and healthy food initiatives.

✔ Livestock, Dairy, Poultry, Marketing and Agriculture Security – includes oversight on topics such as animal welfare, and marketing and promoting US products.

The power of the chair, and committee composition

As committees are the engines of debating and law-making in Congress, committee chairs are very powerful people. The chair, who's appointed by her party caucus at its pre-session convention, has to make a series of decisions that shape the future path of the committee. Perhaps the most important powers are legislative related. The chair has the power to:

✔ Set the agenda of what topics will be discussed and when.

✔ Call hearings and choose who should appear in front of them (and use the legal power to subpoena reluctant witnesses).

✔ Chair the meetings and the rewriting of bills that have been submitted by the floor of the chamber they're in. (This process is called *marking-up* and more details on it and the other committee processes can be found in Chapter 8 on how an idea becomes a bill.)

✔ Choose how the rewriting is to be achieved, and how the report outlining the amended bill is passed back to the chamber floor.

✔ Make administrative and organisational decisions on who gets appointed to the committee staff, how the committee budget is to be spent (although in conversation with the minority party members) and determine what information is to be released to the public.

✔ Make changes to the committee rules, such as the amount of time a committee member can ask questions in an oral hearing, pertaining to the previous Congressional session by informing Congress of such changes within a specified time. This detail is important because it's another example of the chair shaping how topics are to be discussed by controlling what the members can do.

As the power of the political party agenda becomes more concentrated and party polarisation becomes more prominent, the power of the chairs is gradually being eroded as political deals replace the committee's debating and refining role in law-making (see the 'Looking at Political Parties in Congress' section, later in this chapter, for more on this).

Unsurprisingly, because committees are so important Congresspeople set a lot of store on getting a place on one or two. And obviously some committees are more powerful than others. If you're an aspiring committee member, your journey won't be easy. The first hurdle to jump is being nominated by the party *caucus* (the elected officials from your party in the chamber you sit in) at the beginning of the two-year Congressional session. Typically, you'll choose a committee or committees that you're interested in or have experience of (for example, a former lawyer might go for the Senate judiciary committee). An added pressure of being dependent on the party and towing the party line is that, if you decide to leave the party caucus, you have to surrender your seat on whichever committees you work on.

The second hurdle is whether your party is in the majority or minority in the chamber you work in. If you're a Republican and your party is in the majority, there'll be proportionately more Republicans on the committee than Democrats. In fact, in most committees the majority party gets to choose how many committee members the minority party gets, although this tends to be loosely based on the number of seats that party has in the chamber. Currently in the Senate, for example, are 53 Democrats, two independents who vote along Democratic Party lines and 45 Republicans. And in the Senate Committee on the Judiciary are 10 Democratic Party members and eight Republicans. The chair of the committee is a member of the majority party. The leading minority party member is called the *ranking member*.

In order to ensure that you're not spreading yourself too thin, a series of restrictions exist. In the House of Representatives, a member can

✔ Serve on only two committees and up to four subcommittees.

✔ Chair only one committee or subcommittee.

✔ Serve as chair only three times in a row.

In the Senate, although a similar number of committees and over 60 subcommittees exist, only 100 people are available to sit on them rather than the 435 in the House. It means that you're much more likely to get a place on the committee you really want.

Three types of committee exist, ranked in terms of importance and classified by the Senate as A, B and C. A Senator can sit on no more than two A committees, one B committee and as many C committees as he wants.

Congressional staff

Senators and Representatives sit on the shoulders of great men and women (most of the time). That's what should be scratched on the doors of Capitol Hill. If it wasn't for the staff and support agencies organising and providing expert advice on a whole range of issues, it would be safe to say that most elected politicians would be swimming around Washington like goldfish in a bowl.

Each Senator and Representative has staff members to help them conduct their duties in relation to their constituents in their home states and districts, and to help them on legislative issues, particularly on topics based on their committee and subcommittee assignments. These staff will be divided between their constituency and Washington offices. A Senator can have as many members of staff as she likes, but a Representative is restricted to 18. Six positions are usual in a member's office:

- **Chief of Staff:** The chief is the most important person to the Senator and the Representative, and is directly responsible to that Congressperson. As well as managing the office and the staff, the chief is in charge of prioritising which constituency and legislative issues should be dealt with immediately.

- **Legislative director:** This person is in charge of developing the elected official's legislative agenda. He arranges what legislative assistants and correspondents concentrate on, and handle the member's key agendas and class A committee commitments.

- **Legislative assistant:** These are experts in a particular field that's of prime importance to the member because it involves her constituency or relates to committees and subcommittees she's a member of. For example, if a number of military bases are in her state she may well have a legislative assistant working on military-related affairs. Her job involves keeping up-to-date with subject-related issues and drafting relevant legislation. She also manages the correspondent working in the same field.

- **Legislative correspondent:** The correspondent provides support for the assistant on legislative issues, greets visitors to the office and responds to constituent requests for information, tours and so on.

- **Press secretary:** This person is the face of the elected member and it's important that he scrubs up well and can relate and talk to multiple audiences. He's the spokesperson for the member and liaises with the media. He also develops and implements his media strategy in relation to legislative issues and keeps the member up-to-date on key topics he may be questioned on by both constituents and the media.

✔ **Staff assistant:** The principal responsibilities of this role are receiving visitors at the front of office, answering the phone, passing on requests to the relevant person in the office, and generally doing everything in the office that no one else is doing. Typically, this is the first job you get when you've finished your degree in political science and you want to head to the capital and work in politics.

Supporting agencies

Say an elected member is on a committee and is involved in a hearing investigating the ineffectiveness and wasteful practices of a particular department. To prepare for the questioning, she asks the Congressional Research Service (CRS – works exclusively for Congress providing non-partisan legal and policy advice to Senate and House committees and individual members) for details on this department. She also asks the General Accountability Office (GAO – also exclusive to Congress and provides non-partisan information on how efficiently the federal government spends taxpayers' money) for details on how much this misguided programme has cost the American taxpayer. And finally, if she works for the Senate and House budget committees or, for example, the House ways and means committee or the finance committees, she can also ask the Congressional Budget Office (CBO) to report on budgetary operating issues and write a cost estimate for all bills that have passed through the committee and back to the chamber floor for debate and then a vote (see chapter 8 on how an idea becomes a bill for further details).

These meetings, along with reports and targeted answers responding to specific questions, are supplied by the three agencies and help the member form the basis of her questioning. If these two agencies didn't exist it would make interrogating the federal government departments and agencies that much more difficult to do. It would hamper the aims of the framers of the Constitution because members of the legislature would be unable to sufficiently carry out their power as a checker of the Executive and its various offices.

Looking at Political Parties in Congress

The party in the majority, whether in the House or Senate, plays a powerful role in determining a whole range of Congressional activities.

In the House and Senate, determining the future trajectory of each party's plans in each chamber is set in the initial Republican Party conference and the Democratic Party caucus at the beginning of the Congressional session. It's at these events that a whole series of decisions are made.

The leaders of the parties are elected, including (contingent on whether your party is in the majority or minority):

- The Senate majority and minority leaders
- Speaker of the House
- Minority leader of the House
- The whip (who's tasked with ensuring party members vote along party lines on important legislation, liaising between the party leadership and its elected members and co-ordinating strategy within the party caucus)
- The chairs and vice-chairs of the party in the two chambers
- The chair of the campaign committee

At the party conference or caucus the members get to vote on the chairs and members of committees. It's a source of power for the leaders because to gain a place on a committee party members have to toe the party line.

The chair can change the rules governing the operation of the committee, and because the majority party chooses the chair, the party leadership can exert some pressure on that chair's decisions. The majority party in each chamber also has the power to decide if committees should be created, abolished or extended. Another source of power for the majority party is that it can determine the administrative resources for each chamber, which means that it can shape what it wants the chamber to focus on during that Congressional session.

In the Senate, the majority leader isn't as powerful as the House speaker, partly because he doesn't preside over the chamber (the vice president does) and determine what legislation gets discussed or referred, and partly because of the anarchic nature of the Senate where one Senator has the power to dictate policy through a filibuster whereby they stand and speak uninterrupted and do not yield in order to kill the debating time for the bill (see Chapter 8 for the lowdown on filibusters). The consequence of filibustering is that urgent issues facing the US, such as debt, immigration and global warming, aren't addressed as debate and legislation are delayed.

One tool the majority leaders in the Senate have at their disposal is the power to determine what types of amendments can be made and how much time is scheduled for debating them, although it's contingent on persuading Senators to agree with these decisions.

The House speaker is the leader of the majority party and has many more formal powers than her Senate equivalent. She has tremendous influence in determining which bills become law, and thus can shape the future path of the country. Her powers include:

- ✔ Determining which bill will be passed to which committee, meaning that if she wants a bill to pass or die she gives it to the committee she knows will support the party line.

- ✔ Appointing the chair of the Committee of the Whole, which comprises all members of the House and through which most legislation is debated.

- ✔ Scheduling of the Congressional session – which bills get discussed and which bills die.

- ✔ Appointing the members of the majority party to the Rules Committee (which develops special rules determining how legislation gets passed to the floor).

- ✔ Determining who gets to speak in the chamber when discussing amendments (a very powerful tool because the opposition can obviously be silenced).

- ✔ Shaping conference committees (committees made up of Senators and Representatives tasked with consolidating their respective versions of the bill into one coherent bill) via the power to appoint House members. The speaker (along with their party leaders) can set a deadline by which a committee has to report to the chamber and even tell its members the number and type of amendments they can make.

The number of Representatives the majority and minority parties have impacts the influence they have in the House. Simply put, if one party has a majority, then it can forward its legislative agenda in the House with relative ease but there are other factors to consider, like the number of seats they have on the committees. If the party is in a majority in the House then they will automatically get more seats; the larger the majority, the greater the number of seats. If the minority party is barely a minority, then it will have large representation in the committees and a greater influence on whether a bill is reported back to the whole House.

Viewing Public Perceptions of Congress

Rarely does the American public view Congress in a positive light. And that's not necessarily always a bad thing. The Constitution purposefully created a separation of powers by dividing them between Congress, the president and the judiciary, with each checking and balancing the others in various ways. On top of that is the division of federal and state power (see Chapter 2 on the Constitution for further details).

The US political system is *designed* to be slow and cumbersome because the founders didn't want a system that concentrated power in one place; they feared absolutism and tyranny exercised by the few. That said, when polls reveal that vast numbers of people are dissatisfied with the actions of Congress, the individual members in that sitting of Congress, along with the parties they represent (as parties do play a key role in setting the Congressional legislative agenda), have to take some responsibility.

Polling data is the only reliable way that experts can gauge the positive and negative public perceptions of Congress. Historically, Congress tends to have low approval figures because of its structural responsibilities, and when the country is facing a domestic or foreign crisis, Congress is seen as being responsible either for the crisis or for America's poor response to it.

Since 2005, approval ratings for Congress have pretty much tanked, with no more than 25 per cent of Americans approving (although that figure did go up in the first eight months after President Obama was inaugurated in January 2009). Figure 5-1 shows you approval ratings. One example for these low polls occurred in the summer of 2011 when President Obama and the Republican House were arguing over his request to raise the government's *debt ceiling* (a figure that determines whether the federal government can borrow money for its budget). By November 2011, Congress had only a 13 per cent approval and 81 per cent disapproval rate. And this low approval rating was maintained through October, when the federal government had to shut down for just over two weeks and put government employees on unpaid leave. This did not do Congress any favours. Since then, approval figures have stayed rock bottom and do not show signs of improving.

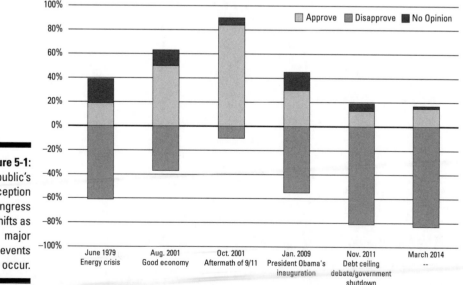

Figure 5-1: The public's perception of Congress shifts as major events occur.

Chapter 6

Sibling Rivalry: Congress and the Executive

. . . .

In This Chapter

▶ Introducing the powers of the Congress and the executive

▶ Understanding the relationship between Congress and the executive in domestic policy

▶ Detailing the eras that define the power balance in congressional and executive relations

▶ Discussing the relationship between Congress and the executive in foreign policy

▶ Explaining how Congress asserted itself in 1970s foreign policy issues

▶ Reviewing the deference of Congress to the executive after 9/11

. . . .

*T*he relationship between the two elected branches of the federal government has been good, bad and ugly – usually all three at the same time! When designing the political system, the founding fathers did not design these siblings to be best friends but to be rivals. Their system of checks and balances injects competition for power into the interactions between the system and the individuals. It's a nifty approach to dealing with the negatives of human nature: make those in charge fight it out among each other but ensure they play within the rules of the game.

The power dynamics between Congress and the executive have shifted over time, due to each wrangling for more power and in response to international and domestic events. I think that it's fair to say that in terms of foreign policy, the executive has taken the dominant position and even usurped the powers of Congress somewhat. In domestic policy, Congress has maintained its position of dominance.

This chapter examines the shifting powers of Congress and the executive, relative to each other, in domestic and foreign policy. (See Chapter 5 for details on the Congress and Chapter 4 to find out more about the executive.)

Congress is also known as the *legislature* and is the body that makes laws. It consists of two chambers: the Senate and the House of Representatives. The executive is the branch that determines how laws made by Congress are to be implemented. It includes the federal departments and agencies such as the Department of the Treasury. The head of the executive is the president.

Outlining Powers of the Congress and the Executive

Whilst Congress has the power to make laws, the executive has the responsibility to carry out government policies as determined by the three branches. Here's how those powers break down.

Congress:

✔ Can apply legislative pressure to shape government policy through its power to write laws.

✔ Provides oversight on the executive branch as a check on its power by

• Interrogating key presidential appointments to determine whether they can take up their positions.

• Using its committees to examine the federal agencies under the president's control in order to root out fraud and waste, stop illegal or unconstitutional activities, evaluate the success of a programme, conduct hearings in order to develop new or amend existing legislation, and ensure the executive is honourably complying with legislation.

✔ Comments on contemporary issues and ensuring further public and government discussion by issuing simple and concurrent resolutions. (These aren't legally binding but serve to get Congress's message out. Chapter 8 tells you more.)

✔ Uses directives within legislation to elicit an official response from the department or agency the bill is directed towards.

✔ Can decide to finance or restrict funding on certain projects by federal departments or agencies. (This is called the *power of the purse*.)

✔ Can shape the policies of the US government by providing informal advice on government policy by attending meetings with the president and various US federal department and agency officials.

The president:

- ✔ Runs the federal government, including the 15 executive departments that help develop and implement the president's policies.

- ✔ Represents the nation on foreign trips and receives foreign dignitaries to America.

- ✔ Serves as chief negotiator of foreign policy and chief architect of foreign policy, represents the US at treaties, explains to the American public US foreign policy actions, and develops US responses to international issues.

- ✔ Nominates candidates for top political positions such as secretaries of departments, ambassadors, and judges.

- ✔ Acts as commander-in-chief of the military, and is in charge of determining its size, focus, and where it should be deployed.

- ✔ Has a principal role in both the passing of laws and in setting the policy agenda for Congress through suggesting legislation for Congress, getting the federal budget passed and having the power to veto legislation.

How Congress and the Executive Address Domestic and Foreign Policy

The principal goal of a government is to run the country. As much as a government is organised to ensure the nation is protected from outside interference, most of its dealings concern domestic-based issues. The *preamble* (introduction section) to the US Constitution pretty much confirms this prioritisation of domestic affairs over foreign ones. And the Constitution places Congress at the heart of US government.

The Constitution was established in order to create a 'more perfect Union, establish Justice, insure domestic Tranquility, provide for the common defence, promote the general Welfare, and secure the Blessings of Liberty to ourselves and our Posterity'. There are six active components to this statement, and four of them directly speak to domestic issues whilst one speaks to foreign issues ('common defence'), another can speak to both domestic and foreign ('secure the Blessings of Liberty').

It has been said that America, effectively, has two presidencies; one concerns domestic and the other foreign affairs. In the domestic context, the presidency has a competitor in an active Congress that has its own view of running the country, and in the foreign context, the presidency is much more powerful in shaping and determining government actions.

There are a couple of important structural factors that help define this relationship between the two branches. The executive is elected on a national basis and the head, the president, is minded to look at the health of the nation in domestic and foreign affairs. The Congress, on the other hand, whilst a national body that determines national issues, is also predisposed to looking at domestic affairs. This is because Congresspeople represent people in their constituency. And it is the issues that affect the constituents in the local area that are of primary importance when they vote. Therefore, any elected politician who ignores the voices of the electorate is likely to be a one-term wonder. It is no surprise then, to hear that domestic policy makes up most of the work of congressional committees.

Domestic policy

The powers of domestic policy afforded to the two branches have not undergone the same angst-ridden changes as responsibilities for foreign affairs have (see the upcoming section, 'Foreign policy'). Whilst attempts are sometimes made by Congress and the president to usurp the powers of the other, neither is willing to back down on their constitutionally granted powers. This being the case, the Congress and the executive fight each other over domestic affairs, which is just what the Constitution intended.

The powers of the executive in the domestic scene are to run the federal departments, interpret legislation and ensure regulations are followed, as well as implement the president's direction policy agenda. Congress has the principal role in making and shaping government domestic policy because it determines what legislation drives that policy, and has the power to defund programmes that it thinks the executive is misapplying. (For an example, turn to the section on the 2013 Republican Congress's effort to defund Obamacare in Chapter 15.)

Since the 1930s, there has been an expansion in the role and responsibilities of the federal government as controlled by the executive to areas it did not previously cover. This expansion was driven by the Great Depression and the decision by President Roosevelt to expand the scope of the federal government to deal with issues such as poverty, healthcare, employment, and regulating the banking industry at the national level (see Chapter 10).

Directed by the president, through a whole series of new departments and refocusing of old departments, the powers of the executive have continued to increase. And this expansion has become a permanent feature of the office.

These changes have not, however, led to depreciation in the role and responsibilities of Congress in developing domestic policy but given the president has a little more say in certain types of policy.

When Congress dominates and when the executive dominates

The dominance of one branch over the other, in terms of governing the nation, depends on the type of policy being employed. Scholars tend to suggest three types of policy-making:

- ✔ **Redistributive policies** are determined through an interpretation of the 'general welfare' principle outlined in the Constitution's preamble. These are the most controversial because they usually involve Congress legislating to take resources (usually through taxation) from one group and spreading them to those less advantaged. The president tends to dominate this process as the benefits of these policies usually are nationwide, which is counter to the congressional members' focus on supporting the demands of their constituents only (it might be counter-intuitive to them to work in the interests of people who aren't their electorate). Redistributive policies include federally funded or sponsored social welfare programmes such as food aid for low-income families, unemployment insurance payments for those who have lost their jobs, and Medicare (health insurance to all those over 65).

- ✔ **Regulatory policy** involves the standardisation of practices to protect the public from harm. There are three main types of regulation: labour, business, and the environment and energy. Labour policies are designed to protect the American workforce – by ensuring equal pay for men and women, and health and safety standards to protect people from accidents, to name a couple of examples. Congressionally dictated business regulation includes ensuring standards for fair competition between companies and restricting the dominance of one company in the market at the expense of others. In regulating the environment and energy sectors, Congress has outlined how federal government agencies such as the Environmental Protection Agency should enforce policies on issues such as pollution and getting rid of waste. Concerning energy regulation, Congress established the Department of Energy in a 1977 act in order to deal with the American energy crisis and dependence on foreign energy supplies. It concentrated research, regulation and energy policy under one roof. In this category, responsibility for action is more equally shared by both the president and Congress.

- ✔ **Distributive policies** involve federal support for programmes designed to benefit a particular constituency. This type of legislation is mostly influenced by Congress, as providing for the needs of one's constituents keeps Congresspeople in or out of office. As a result, these policies tend to be less ideologically driven than the other two types, as an ideological platform is highly contentious when it comes to passing benefits on to constituents. No benefits equal an unhappy electorate, and an unhappy electorate equals fewer votes for the incumbent.

Typically, these policies are paid for by general tax revenues, and exist in the shape of farm subsidies, research grants, infrastructure and *pork-barrel spending* (federal funding of local projects that benefit the Representative's standing in the area and help his re-election campaign). This type of spending is an integral process in the way Congress shapes and makes domestic policy. However, with the economic crisis of 2008 (see Chapter 16) and the rise of the Republican Tea Party, things could be changing. Pork-barrelling, for example, became policy *non-grata* by the public, so much so that any attempt to add a local project to an appropriations bill could derail re-election efforts. With the fear of electoral failure amongst Representatives, there was, according to *Citizens Against Government Waste*, between 2010 and 2012 a 98.3% reduction in proposals, and an 80% reduction in appropriation funds from $16.5 billion to $3.3 billion.

A more assertive Congress

There are three eras of congressional activity since the end of the Second World War within which the power relations shifted between the two branches.

- ✔ During the **bipartisan conservative era** (1947-1964), Congress often looked to the president to take the lead on issues confronting the nation. National parties were unable to impose unity amongst their members and so it was usually the moderates of both parties who would tend to control the outcomes of legislation (see Chapter 5 for further details). In this era, divided government was not problematic. It meant that a president did not have to appeal to a party when pushing legislation but to the middle ground, and that was more workable.

- ✔ In the **liberal activist era** (1965-1978), the success of President Lyndon Johnson meant that a series of liberal policies could be implemented by relying on Democrats in Congress rather than a coalition in the previous era. Johnson broke the hold of the conservative Democrat and Republican coalition. When Nixon took power in 1968, it was a divided government but the president did not confront the liberal Democrat Congress, in part, for fear of causing bad publicity to his presidency. However, after winning a massive victory in 1972, he had the authority to de-fund congressional programmes and veto bills that were too liberal. In response to this attack on the liberal agenda by Nixon, and the fear that conservative Democrats in Congress were hampering its implementation by siding with the Republicans, the leaders of the party consolidated their power over the independent-minded members. And when the unelected Republican President Ford came to power in 1974, these changes and the manner in which he took office were not conducive for productive relations with a Democrat-dominant Congress. This division between the president and Congress was further reinforced when the Democrat Jimmy Carter won the presidency in 1976. With his campaign being driven by Washington, DC, outsider status, relations between him and the Congress were not fruitful; Congress asserted its independence and authority even though it was led by the Democrats as well.

✔ The **post-reform/party unity era** (1979 to today) is a further consolidation of the party reforms of the previous era. It has demonstrated the new reality that presidential legislative strategies cannot rely on cross-party support as they had in previous eras. And so, by the 1980s, party identity between political parties had become much more visible (see Chapter 11 for more about the two-party system), and the need for a Democratic Congress to assert itself, for example, during the Reagan years in the White House (1980-88), had become an ideological as well as an institutional objective. And there's nothing like partisan politics to get the blood rushing! In this era, the president has relied on the power of the veto to stop opposing agendas from becoming law. Whilst a president can stop laws from being implemented in these instances, a veto is essentially a negative tool as it does not enable them to develop alternative legislation. During this period, the Republicans took a leaf out of the Democrats' book and equally consolidated party control over members. The Republicans were dominant in Congress, and under the tutelage of Congressman Newt Gingrich from 1994, they dominated the legislative process with their *Contract with America*. That document promised the people a conservative revolution to change the direction and focus of America, including reducing the size and excess of Congress, implementing tax cuts, and ridding America of crime. In this divided government, the gloves were off, antipathy between the branches was running high and Congress was flexing its muscles. Clinton vetoed regular bills passed by Congress 36 times during his eight years in office and only one of those was overruled by Congress and became law (see Chapter 7 for further details of the law-making process).

As you can tell, divided government is not a good idea for presidential and congressional cohesion. From the 96th Congress (1979-1981) until the 113th Congress (2013-2015), there have been 18 congressional sessions, and 14 of those have been divided government.

Foreign policy

In the making and shaping of foreign policy the Congress and the executive have clearly defined roles and responsibilities. The Constitution gave Congress the sole power to declare war, raise and maintain the military, finance or restrict American foreign interventions through exercising its budgetary power, and give consent to executive-nominated US ambassadors and to international treaties. Presidential powers were to develop foreign policy, receive foreign dignitaries as the head of government, and dictate how that foreign policy is conducted.

Over time, some of these powers have been shaped by the realities of the domestic and international political scene and by the constant battle for control between the executive and legislative branches. One example of the shifts has been the role that executive agreements have played in American relations with other states, replacing the role of treaties. *Executive agreements* typically are employed to make international agreements; they're decisions made by the president that do not require congressional approval but under a 1937 Supreme Court decision have the same influence. To give you an idea of the massive erosive impact this had on Congress's foreign policy engagement: before 1939, the president had made about 1,200 executive agreements whilst Congress had ratified about 800 treaties. After 1940, a similar amount of treaties were made but over 13,000 executive agreements were made.

WWII and the need to reshape who's in power

World War Two (WWII) is seen to be a watershed moment for Congress's loss of power in shaping foreign policy. Prior to WWII, there was a more traditional interpretation of the Constitution by the three branches. Congress had a legitimate role to play if it chose to assert itself in foreign policy, and when Congress and the president were in disagreement regarding foreign policy, the benefit of the doubt went to Congress.

After WWII, the balance of power shifted to the president. A working atomic weapon was the impetus for the shift. In August 1945, the US dropped two atomic bombs on Japan, killing between 150,000 and 240,000 people. The devastation of the weapons caused a major rethink in foreign policy decision-making and elevated the role of the president as the Commander in Chief. This was emphasised by the emerging Cold War between America and the Soviet Union, and their respective allies (another dimension to this war was the ideological battle between democracy and communism). In case of an atomic (and then a nuclear) attack from missiles or bombers that could launch and be hitting the US within 30 minutes, the decision to respond had to be made literally within minutes.

Whilst the power to declare war is with the Congress, the president has the duty to protect America. Making a decision to respond by 'pressing the red button' (releasing nuclear weapons) is both protecting the US and a declaration of war. Congress is a debating chamber and therefore not the best place in the American political system to respond to an immediate threat to the safety of the US. In order to facilitate the presidential power to respond to a nuclear attack (amongst other issues), temporary emergency legislation was enacted. It was initially passed during WWII but lasted for the duration of the Cold War (1945-1991). It embedded both a legal and cultural expansion of presidential powers in foreign policy at the expense of Congress, which has been difficult for Congress to claw back. It led to a new interpretation of the Constitution whereby the executive has prerogative in foreign affairs and defence of the country, even if this overrides constitutional constraints such as the power of Congress to declare war or the increase in executive agreements over treaties (see 'Foreign policy' earlier in this chapter).

Gulf of Tonkin incident in 1964

A classic example of congressional acquiescence in its foreign policy duties is the 1964 Gulf of Tonkin Resolution that precipitated an expanded US military role in Vietnam. Congress's actions were in response to two incidents. A US ship was engaged in combat with three North Vietnamese Torpedo boats and then two days later was supposedly attacked again (although a National Security Agency report confirmed the second attack was non-existent).

Congress passed the Gulf of Tonkin Resolution in August that year, giving the president the power 'to take all necessary measures to repel any armed attack against the forces of the United States and to prevent further aggression'. And it was under this authorisation in successive years that President Johnson increased US troops in Vietnam to over 500,000. Whilst clearly at war with the North Vietnamese government, there was never an official declaration of war by the US through Congress. If Congress was serious in its desire to exert its power in foreign policy, it could have either passed a resolution declaring war on North Vietnam, or, if it did not approve it could have defunded the war effort through drawing down on the purse strings. But it did neither. It carried on with the ambiguous *status quo*.

Congress exerting its powers over foreign policy

By the mid-1970s with the Watergate scandal (when the Republican President Nixon resigned over sanctioned break-ins at the Democratic Party offices) and the disaster of the Vietnam War, Congress attempted to claw back some authority, or at least restrict presidential powers in foreign policy. A series of Congressional interventions, including legislative pressure, achieved these efforts.

The 1973 War Powers Resolution was one such attempt. It was vetoed by President Nixon but passed into law because over two-thirds of Congress supported its introduction into public law. Its purpose was to reassert the power of Congress in 'collective judgment' with the president regarding 'the introduction of United States Armed Forces into hostilities, or into situations where imminent involvement in hostilities is clearly indicated by the circumstances, and to the continued use of such forces in hostilities or in such situations'.

The Resolution means that the president has to notify Congress of deployment of armed forces in actual or imminent hostilities within 48 hours of their start and then obtain congressional authorization within 60 days to continue. If Congress refused to support the conflict then forces would have to be withdrawn within a further 30 days. However, Congress's ability to fully reassert its constitutionally awarded powers had been compromised somewhat by the detail. It effectively gave the president the legal authority to wage war without a congressional declaration for the first time ever, albeit only for 90 days. It can therefore be seen that the resolution did not curb presidential powers to declare war, it legitimised them! Not a smart way of doing legislative business.

Continuing the elevation of executive powers after 9/11

After the September 2001 terrorist attacks, Congress authorized a resolution that was similar in language and reach to the one it approved after the Gulf of Tonkin incident. On 14 September 2001, it gave the president the authority to 'use all necessary and appropriate force against those nations, organizations, or persons he determines planned, authorized, committed, or aided the terrorist attacks [. . .] or harbored such organizations or persons, in order to prevent any future acts of international terrorism against the United States by such nations, organizations, or persons'.

The resolution passed the Senate with no objections and the House with only one. Perhaps understandably, given the heightened emotional situation in the days immediately after the attacks, members of Congress felt that this was the right response. It is perhaps less easy to understand the decision by Congress, in early October 2002, to abrogate its responsibility in checking the executive in a non-heightened emotional environment (there were no horrific terrorist attacks on the US immediately before voting), when it passed the act enabling President Bush to use the US Armed Forces in Iraq in a way that 'he [Bush] determines to be necessary and appropriate to (1) defend the security of the US against the continuing threat posed by Iraq and (2) enforce all relevant UN Security Council Resolutions regarding Iraq'.

These Congressional actions are clear evidence of Congress's deference to the executive in foreign affairs. It is relinquishing its constitutionally determined co-responsibility. There seems to be no political will in Congress to enforce or strengthen the War Powers Resolution and reclaim its position of authority. Maybe it suits members of Congress to defer to the president in foreign policy because they won't be criticised if things go wrong. And because of their fear of upsetting their re-election campaign, they are reluctant to vote against the president. This is particularly so in a time of war, as the electorate tend to get behind the president and to go against the grain may be electorally foolish. The counterargument is that Congress is able to influence foreign policy-making by methods like proposing bills, holding committee hearings on international relations, and engaging in foreign policy agenda setting through raising awareness of issues through public campaigns.

Chapter 7

Understanding the American Court System

*R*unning the United States successfully isn't just about the decisions made by elected politicians or their controlled government departments and agencies. It's also about ensuring the rule of law. For without the legal system and a working independent judiciary democracy would be in chaos.

In this chapter, I explore the American court system, from the state through to the federal system. In particular, I discuss how the unelected US Supreme Court is at the heart of American democracy what with its power to shape and influence the country's politics and society.

Glimpsing the American Court System

America is made up of two important layers of government: state and federal. Think of a state as a mini-me version of the United States of America. It's organised in the same way and does similar things. A state does what it does in one little jurisdiction, and these jurisdictions combine to make one big federal system. They both have god-like statuses in that the legislature at the state and federal levels can and do write laws on how American state and society should operate. This division of government is called *federalism* (see Chapter 2 for further details), and this way of governing is referred to as being run by the *rule of law.*

Although the state court system has to enforce the federal Constitution and statutes (laws made by Congress), most cases that go before it are issues relating to that state's own constitution and statutes made by its own legislative body. (Yes, the United States has more than one constitution – 52 if you include the 50 states plus the Commonwealth of Puerto Rico and the US Constitution. File this little fact; it comes up a lot in pub quizzes!)

Although most states have a Supreme Court, this chapter principally discusses the Supreme Court of the United States of America. But in order to understand its role in American life we need to think about how it fits within America's legal world.

A court is created by a government to settle disputes between two or more groups. It's a place where decisions are made by a jury (made up of a number of citizens) or judges. Each individual case has a *plaintiff* (those who issue a lawsuit against someone or something, such as a company) and a *defendant* (those who are being judged to see if they did something wrong).

Whether a case goes before a jury or not depends on a number of factors, including what happened and what type of punishment is required. Decisions made in courts can have consequences not only for those people personally involved in a case but also for how future similar cases play out.

The state and federal court systems in the United States are powerful for three reasons:

- ✔ They were developed from English *Common Law* meaning that decisions made by judges are based on previously made decisions by judges on cases that have similar facts (called *acting on precedence*).

- ✔ If the case heard involves a *statute* (Congress-made law), the court judicially interprets what that law means and can, through *judicial review*, determine that the law referred to or any actions resulting from that law are unconstitutional.

- ✔ The decision about whether a law is unconstitutional can be passed up to the Supreme Court, but if the Supreme Court agrees that it's unconstitutional, the law will generally be out on its ear. In this case, Congress would either need to write a new law or propose a constitutional amendment. Securing a constitutional amendment is very difficult because so many arms and branches of government need to agree to the change. In the nearly 250 years since the US Constitution came into force, only 27 amendments have been passed.

The state courts

Each of the 50 states along with the District of Columbia (DC) and the Commonwealth of Puerto Rico has its own state court system. Except for DC (a special case), each of these has its own constitution and laws that establish its court system.

The state court system deals with state constitutional issues and statutes, as well as US Constitutional issues and statutes. The kinds of cases heard by these courts include:

✔ Most criminal cases

✔ Personal injuries

✔ Family law (marriage, divorce and so on)

✔ Most contract and *probate* (wills and estates of dead people) cases

That caseload makes for a seriously busy court system, with approximately 30 million cases going in front of these courts every year. In comparison, the federal court system appears less significant, dealing with only about 1 million cases a year. Also, approximately 30,000 state judges exist compared with only around 1,700 federal judges.

In different states, state court judges are appointed in a number of interesting ways that may include elections, appointment for a set number of years, appointment for life or a combination thereof. In Tennessee, for example, the state governor initially appoints the Court of Appeal judges and then, after eight years, an open election is held to determine whether they can continue in post.

Trial courts

Trial courts are the lowest level of courts, where all criminal (when the state is one of the parties involved, usually prosecuting an individual for breaking the state's laws) and civil cases (when cases are between individuals or organisations) are first heard. Typically at the level of trial courts, there will also be some specialist courts that deal with specific legal issues, such as a probate court, a juvenile court or a family court. Some states have an even lower court often referred to as the county court, which deals with cases such as minor criminal issues, traffic offences or small claims.

Court of appeal

Most states have a *court of appeal*, although these courts may have different names. The state of Delaware, for example, calls its court of appeal the *Superior Court* (but it's not that superior because a Supreme Court is actually above it!).

A court of appeal (appellate court) is an important layer in the court system because any ruling made by a lower court that's then *appealed* (has its ruling made is re-examined by a higher court) will end up here.

These cases can range from civil to criminal types of cases, and these courts are sometimes referred to as *intermediate appellate courts*. They're intermediate because in most states the Supreme Court has *discretionary review* enabling the justices to pick and choose what they want to hear. But ten states (including New Hampshire and Delaware) don't have this layer. In these instances, all criminal and civil appeals go to that state's Supreme Court. It means that those justices are extremely busy. In New Hampshire, for example, the Supreme Court deals with approximately 1,000 cases.

Court of last resort

Each state has what's called a *court of last resort*, often known as a *Supreme Court*. This court is the highest court in the land (jurisdiction) and has the power to decide on cases relating to both constitutional law (what the constitution states) and statutory law (laws made by the state's legislature).

The aim of this court is to provide all the courts below it with a clear understanding of how a particular law should be interpreted. (It doesn't always meet that goal, as I show you later in the chapter.) All decisions made are *binding*, meaning they have to be followed by the state and federal courts. However, if the decision concerns a federal issue (such as an interpretation of something outlined in the US Constitution) it can be appealed directly to the US Supreme Court for a ruling as it's the court of last resort for the US Constitution.

Reading about court cases in different states can be confusing because courts in different states can have the same name but different roles. For example, the court of appeal in Delaware is called the Superior Court while, in California, the Superior Court refers to its lowest level of courts, the trial courts where all criminal and civil cases are first heard.

The federal courts

The state court system is basically duplicated in structure and form in the federal court system. However, the federal court system isn't as busy because it doesn't have the same scope of civil or criminal jurisdiction that the state courts have. The federal court is determined by the rules set out in the US Constitution. Most cases heard by the federal court system involve the federal government in some capacity either as the defendant or the plaintiff. Typical cases usually cover one of the following:

- Possible violations of the US Constitution
- Bankruptcy
- Patent cases
- Cases between citizens of different states
- Particular types of criminal cases, such as kidnapping or illegal drug importation into the country

To provide an extra layer of confusion, some cases can be tried in either the federal or state system – it's up to the plaintiff to make this decision. On behalf of a concerned group, the federal court system can also be tasked with reviewing actions made by federal agencies, such as a decision by the Food and Drug Administration (FDA) to allow a new drug to be available on the market.

Article III of the US Constitution lays out the powers of the federal court system (see Chapter 2 for further details). It determines that the court of last resort is the US Supreme Court and that the US Congress has the power to determine the size and scope of those courts below it. At the time the Constitution was written (in the late eighteenth century), only 13 states existed. As the United States expanded, a need developed for a greater number of lower courts, and today the federal court system is huge.

Below the Supreme Court are 13 courts of appeal, which include 12 *regional circuit courts,* which hear cases that come from a particular region of the United States (for example, the 11th Circuit includes cases heard in federal courts from the states of Alabama, Georgia and Florida). The 13th court of appeal is called the *Federal Circuit,* which is thematic not region-based and concentrates on issues such as patents, coming from specialist courts such as the US Court of International Trade).

In all 13 of the courts of appeal a defendant or prosecutor (plaintiff) can appeal a lower court's ruling. They can suggest, for example, that the judge did not properly apply the law. If the court of appeal determines there's no case to be heard, the original ruling of the lower court stands. If the appeal is *upheld* (that is, the court agrees with the appeal), then someone found guilty of a crime, for example, could be found not guilty and released. Alternatively, the court could decide to send the case back to the lower court for a retrial. Below the 12 regional circuit courts of appeal are the 94 district courts, which are the trial courts where all criminal and civil cases are first heard (similar to the trial courts in the state system).

Understanding the Supreme Court

The role of the Supreme Court is to be the court of last resort on all issues relating to lower court disagreements over interpretations of the US Constitution or federal laws. When compared to the powers of the executive and the Congress it doesn't sound like its powers are extraordinary, but they are quite immense. The Supreme Court is the final arbiter in determining whether the democratically elected branches (president and members of Congress) have, by what they've done, acted constitutionally. And what's striking about its powers is that this body is an unelected and undemocratic body. Justices are appointed by the president and confirmed by the Senate but after that's done, no external forces can direct how they make their decisions. And they are justices until they die or quit, so no awkward re-elections required.

Explaining how a case makes its way to the Supreme Court

A case can be passed on to the Supreme Court in one of three ways:

- ✔ **From a state Supreme Court.** A decision made by a state's Supreme Court can only be heard by the US Supreme Court if it relates to federal issues. It can't, for example, consider a criminal case involving bank robbery where the deposits stolen were not insured by a federal agency. If a case does concern a federal issue and one of the parties doesn't like the decision made by the court, the disgruntled party can request that the case be heard by the US Supreme Court. About one-third of all Supreme Court cases are appealed from these courts.

- ✔ **From a federal court of appeal.** Any decision made by one of the 13 federal courts of appeal can be appealed to the US Supreme Court. Similar to the process whereby a case is passed on to the Supreme Court from the state system, one of the parties in the case can appeal for a hearing or the court itself can appeal directly in a case if it determines that a state law is unconstitutional. About two-thirds of cases heard in the US Supreme Court arrive via this route.

✔ **The case involves a specific type of VIP or a nation-state.** According to the US Constitution, those cases that refer to 'Ambassadors, other public ministers and Consuls' as well as those involving a state as a party can be heard in the US Supreme Court. This means that the court can have *original jurisdiction* (in other words, it can hold a trial which seeks the facts of a case as opposed to being an appeal court that interprets the Constitution). This provision is hardly ever used and only about 40 such cases (most relating to disputes between states) have been heard since the Supreme Court has been operating.

Dealing with a case

If you're at school or university, your yearly body clock will prepare you well for being a Supreme Court justice. Term starts at the beginning of October and involves two three-day working weeks in which they hear cases (oral argument); the court is then in recess for two weeks while they write opinions (their decisions). This routine continues throughout the year until April. From April to June the Supreme Court sits only to announce opinions or to provide decisions on whether a case will be heard. During this period the justices hold regular conferences in which they decide which cases should be granted a review.

That routine depends upon the four stages a case goes through on its journey through the Supreme Court.

Petitioning the court

If a party wants a federal or state court decision to be reviewed by the Supreme Court it has to issue a *petition for writ of certiorari* to the court. This petition typically argues that a decision made by a lower court was incorrect on an important question of law and needs the Supreme Court to make a final decision so as to prevent confusion in similar cases. The Court then decides whether to grant a hearing.

For a hearing to be granted, four of the nine justices have to agree (this necessity is unoriginally called the *rule of four*). If a hearing is granted it doesn't mean that the Court disagrees with the prior decision of the lower court, only that a case for review exists.

The Supreme Court has a limited capacity and needs to be very picky about which cases it will give its time to. Not many writs make it through the first hurdle. By the end of the 2010–2011 term over 7,000 writs had been submitted but only 79 (just over 1 per cent) of them were taken up for oral argument.

Hearing a case

Two stages are involved in a case being heard by the Supreme Court:

✔ First, the parties have to prepare *legal briefs*, which are specially pre-pared documents outlining their legal arguments supporting why their position should be chosen by the Court. Experts in the subject matter can also write a report (*amicus curiae*) in support of either the petitioner or respondent. These briefs and *amici* aren't brief at all and are often very long.

✔ Second is the oral argument itself, and each side has 30 minutes to pres-ent their case in front of all the justices and to answer any questions. The attorney presents the key facts of the case and then raises her argu-ment about why the law should be interpreted in a particular way. If the need arises, justices can agree to extend the allotted time for arguments.

Standing in front of the Supreme Court justices can be a daunting task, par-ticularly when your argument is legally weak and your performance is poor. In one case regarding the withholding of evidence from a defendant's attor-ney in a murder trial, an attorney presenting a case in front of the Court was asked whether he had ever considered just abandoning the case due to the weakness of his argument. Ouch.

Debating a case

After the three days of hearing cases the justices hold a conference to discuss their opinions on the cases heard (and vote on new petitions of *certiorari*). No one except the justices can sit in on the meetings, and when discussing a case, the Chief Justice talks first and others follow by seniority. Each justice gets to talk and ask questions without interruption. Whilst I am sure that a justice will at times be frustrated with the perspectives of the other eight jus-tices, by enabling all justices the opportunity to fully develop their thoughts all voices are equally respected.

A vote is held after the debates and a simple majority of five (out of nine) is required for a decision to be made. Interestingly, justices are able to change their minds after the vote when draft opinions are being circulated between the nine. Typically, the senior justice writes the majority opinion unless the Chief Justice voted as part of the majority. If a dissenting opinion exists, the senior justice of those dissenters will write it or appoint someone to write it.

Writing an opinion

After an initial decision has been made at the conference, an opinion is drafted. During this process the justices initially tasked with writing the opinions get help from their law clerks (assistants) to write draft opinions, which are then circulated to the other justices for comment. The aim is to persuade at least four other justices to support your position. Whilst the court is supposedly removed from politics, this process is a prime example of horse-trading as they are trying to win influence for their position. Five types of opinion result from this messy but vitally important process in determining an outcome:

- ✔ **Majority:** When five or more justices agree on the reasons a case should favour either the petitioner's or the respondent's argument.

- ✔ **Plurality:** When four or fewer justices agree on the reasons for support- ing one of the parties and the other five or more do not have agreement on their positions. This situation is basically a non-decision and causes complications in the lower courts because it leaves attorneys without a clear position from which to argue or rule on a case.

- ✔ **Concurring:** When a justice supports the arguments made in the major- ity opinion but thinks that other legal issues explain their support for a party's position.

- ✔ **Dissenting:** An opinion by those justices who do not agree with the major- ity decision. Whilst the dissenters have no legal power to determine future cases, their reasons can set the groundwork for a future majority opinion. The Court at some point in the future may listen to another case focusing on similar issues but have a different perspective on the outcome.

- ✔ ***Per curiam*** ('for the court'): An unsigned opinion that's unanimously made and requires no explanation. These are typically non-controversial opinions, such as when the Court decides that the case shouldn't have gone for a hearing.

Looking into the Politics within the Supreme Court

The Supreme Court has the tricky job of trying to balance the cynical reality of politics with the task of being seen as distant and objective. As the third branch of government, it needs to be seen to be separate from the state and federal systems and as blind to politics, popularity and social norms. In sup- port of that notion, the Court doesn't refer to anything except legal argument when making its decisions, which means it should take a neutral stance as it makes judgements on the future course of American politics, economics and society.

This neutral stance is a vital myth. Many years ago you might have read text books that suggested it was a reality. However, since the early 1980s, this myth has been eroding. Perhaps we've all just become a bit more cynical but nowadays saying that the Supreme Court is a deeply political beast won't shock anyone. Throughout the following section I outline some of the reasons why the Court is political.

Analysing the political world that surrounds the Supreme Court

Politicians, citizens, businesses and other interested groups want their perspectives to be sanctified by law. If they win a case at the Supreme Court, then it enables them to fight off their opponents by saying that their way is the right way and all must conform to the ruling. One ruling can literally change the path of American society. Because the stakes are so high, a lot of effort and resources are put into arguing a case. And the rewards are so great because the Supreme Court is the court of last resort; its decision holds ultimate authority (and it rarely goes back on a previous ruling). These politicians and other interested groups lobby the Court by submitting cases for it to hear and writing the expert *amicus curiae* briefs.

Leveraging the make-up of the court

Because there are multiple ways in which a justice can make an opinion on a case, two justices can develop opinions on the same case that are completely different but equally legitimate. The make-up of the Court is therefore vitally important. The more justices that have a particular political position whether conservative or liberal, then the more likely they will employ the same approaches to making opinions, and the more likely their opinions will be the same. If there are more liberal justices than conservatives then this is great for the liberals of America but not for the conservatives. Thus the nomination process can get quite heated; there is a lot riding on it.

The political identity of the justices also has an impact on the types of cases they are willing to grant *certiorari* to; in the 1970s, for example, the Court was liberal and death penalty cases were routinely heard, whereas today, with a more conservative court, they're not.

Presidential power to appoint

Under the US Constitution the president has the power to appoint a Supreme Court justice, who must then be confirmed by the Senate. In choosing a justice, the president can have an impact on the future direction of America far beyond their presidential term. Justices are appointed for life and can only be removed from office if they retire, die (which is bad news) or are impeached 'for, and Conviction of, Treason, Bribery, or other high Crimes and Misdemeanors' (which is equally bad). Only one Supreme Court justice has been impeached and that was Samuel Chase in 1804, although he was acquitted by the Senate.

Not surprisingly, the president is going to appoint someone who represents his fundamental political ideologies. While no conditions are placed on who should be appointed a justice, judges from the lower courts have normally been appointed (who were also once attorneys). Whether the president is a conservative or a liberal, they're likely to look through the opinions the candidate made as a judge or the cases they fought whilst an attorney to determine whether they hold similar views on key issues like abortion, federalism, gun control and so on. Of course, no guarantee exists that the newly appointed justice will fulfil presidential expectations!

Senate confirmations

Senate confirmations are particularly relevant when a *divided government* exists (when one party sits in the White House whilst the other holds Congress). The Senate Judiciary Committee first holds a hearing then reports back to the Senate floor and a final vote is held for confirmation. A judicial appointment during a divided government is a perfect opportunity for the Senate to assert its power relative to the president. As of 2014, 112 people have been appointed to the Supreme Court whilst 29 have been unsuccessful in their nomination, 12 of those being outright rejections in a Senate vote. Although that's a pretty good success rate, the confirmation hearings in the rest of the cases were far from easy affairs.

Throwing influence within the Court

On top of politics outside the Court, the interactions among the justices are also a case of politics in action. After a conference vote, justices are appointed to write the various opinions that are pertinent to that case.

If there is a majority opinion, for example, and the Chief Justice is not in that group then the senior justice can either write the opinion himself or appoint one of the others who voted for it to write it. If she chooses someone else, it is because she may determine that this person has a better knowledge of the subject or because he is more likely to write an opinion that other justices are more likely to sign up to.

Impeachment of Samuel Chase

The issues surrounding the 1804 impeachment, and subsequent acquittal, of Samuel Chase were an important landmark in securing the independence of the Supreme Court from the other branches of government. Samuel Chase had a prestigious legal career and was actively involved in politics. He was an elected representative for Maryland by the age of 23 and was one of the signatories of the Declaration of Independence in 1776. In 1796, George Washington appointed him a Supreme Court Justice.

Whilst Chase had been a strong anti-federalist in his younger days (campaigning for less power in central government), in his time on the Supreme Court his perspective was strongly federalist, and he spoke out in favour of strong central government. Whilst this would have suited George Washington and his successor John Adams, when anti-federalist Thomas Jefferson became president in 1801, they saw each other as enemies. Their relationship would not have been helped by the fact that Chase had vociferously campaigned for Jefferson's opponent during the election. In 1803, Chase spoke against Jefferson's government before a grand jury, accusing them of pursuing policies that would lead the country into a 'mobocracy, the worst of all possible governments'. Jefferson was outraged and became determined to remove Chase from the bench.

Anti-federalist Congressmen drew up a series of allegations against Chase, known as articles of impeachment. These articles largely concerned his behaviour in the circuit courts (at the time Supreme Court Justices also presided over circuit courts), and suggested that his partisan political views had corrupted his ability to fairly distribute justice. The House of Representatives served Chase with eight articles of impeachment in 1804, at which point proceedings moved across to the Senate to try him on these eight counts. Whilst the prosecution did its best to paint Chase as corrupt and incapable of continuing in his role, Chase's defence argued that the case had been cooked up by the anti-federalists and that Chase had done nothing worse than express a position in opposition to Jefferson. In the end, Chase won the day and was acquitted on all counts.

To this day, Chase remains the only Supreme Court Justice to have been impeached. The failure of Jefferson to remove Chase from the bench serves as a historic symbol of the independence of the judiciary within the American political system.

Remember that a justice can change her vote after a conference, so a majority opinion in a conference may turn into a minority opinion if people aren't comfortable with the argument made. The justice appointed to write the opinion therefore makes compromises and seeks to influence others.

In contentious cases, a lot more political manoeuvring occurs. An opinion writer may modify the opinion in order to bring more justices on board. And it is not until the opinion is made available to the public or read out in court that the opinion becomes a final ruling.

Making a well-timed exit

If Supreme Court justices weren't bothered about the political scene, they'd probably hang up their gowns on their sixty-fifth birthdays and retire to condos in Florida. But that's not usually how it happens because the final act of political influence involves choosing when to retire in order to ensure that their replacement is made under a president with whom they're aligned ideologically.

A good example is the case of Justice Thurgood Marshall. Marshall was appointed to the Court by a Democrat President, Lyndon B. Johnson, in 1967. He was a civil rights lawyer for the National Association for the Advancement of Colored People (NAACP) and was the attorney who won the *Brown vs. Board of Education* case (1954) at the Supreme Court on desegregation in schools. During his time as a justice, Marshall supported prominent liberal causes, including abortion rights and opposing the death penalty. And, although in the late 1970s and throughout the 1980s he suffered ill health, he refused to resign during a Republican presidency. He kept going until the age of 82, when illness made it impossible to continue. Unfortunately for him, a Republican was still in the top job and his replacement was a certain Clarence Thomas, whose road to appointment got a little slippery, to say the least. (Find out more in the sidebar 'The close-call appointment of Clarence Thomas'.)

Recognising that a justice may be active or passive

You can look at the political nature of the Court from one more angle: whether justices or a court can be considered liberal or conservative. As a short-cut to understanding whether they're liberal or conservative, we need to examine their jurisprudence record regarding when they were active or passive.

How the Supreme Court decides: One theory with six parts

How do the nine justices make a decision on a case? Since the Supreme Court first met in 1790, thousands of cases have gone before it and thousands of opinions made. As the law evolved and new precedents were set and reset, methods of decision making expanded. Philip C. Bobbitt, an American Constitutional expert (and, interestingly, the nephew of the thirty-sixth President of the United States, Lyndon B. Johnson), suggested that six types, or *modalities*, of Constitutional decision making exist. Unfortunately, each of these modalities has an inherent problem:

✔ **Historical.** The justice relies on the *original intent* of the framers and ratifiers of the Constitution in the latter part of the eighteenth century to determine outcomes to cases. Basically, the justice is asking what those 50 men (and yes, no women were involved) would have said about the issue at hand. Of course, ever being certain of the answer to this question is impossible. And obviously in cases where the issue (for example, stem cell research) would've been impossible to imagine in the 1700s, it might not be a very helpful approach to take.

✔ **Textual.** A justice will interpret the text of the Constitution literally through the eyes of an 'average person on the street'; that is, what they would mean by those words. This approach overcomes the problem of being stuck in the past, but is tricky in other ways. For example, the Eighth Amendment states that a person has the right not to suffer cruel or unusual punishment. The justice has to decide what's considered cruel and unusual, but in different periods in American history different answers will result.

✔ **Structural.** A decision is made based on understanding the Constitution as a whole. It considers the particular provision within the context of the separation of powers between the three branches of government as well as the relationship between the states and the federal government (for more on this, see Chapter 2). However, this approach can only be employed when cases consider the separation and division of powers.

✔ **Doctrinal.** A justice uses the decisions made in previous cases, and the series of principles that are established, to guide her decision. Of course, this approach is only possible when a previous case exists that's sufficiently similar to draw upon.

✔ **Ethical.** A justice looks to the values contained within the constitutional and democratic traditions of America when making a decision.

✔ **Prudential.** Should the Court consider the consequences of its judgement? From a legal argument it shouldn't, because a decision should be made on principle not on foresight. But from a political standpoint, consequences are very important. In being prudential justices are acknowledging that decisions do not operate in a vacuum. They're impacted by and have an impact on society at large. To varying degrees justices are aware that, in order for the Court to maintain legitimacy and authority, it has to speak to the American people. Its opinions have to be both popular and grounded in the Constitution. This is why, in vitally important cases, the Court seeks a unanimous decision. It reinforces the legitimacy of the decision and thus the institution itself.

Justices are referred to as:

- *Activist* when they judge that laws made by the legislature are unconstitutional and therefore that the elected body has not fulfilled its obligation to protect, for example, certain groups from the majoritarian view.

- *Passive* (or restrained) when they go along with what the legislature has suggested.

Whether liberal or conservative (court or justice), activism and passivism have been used by both groups. Not only is this situation political because a justice's decisions are examined through a bi-polar liberal or conservative framework but also because a justice will respond differently to a statute dependent on whether being active or not supports how she identifies her political philosophy.

- A **liberal judge** will be concerned about protecting the minority from the tyranny of the majority and is probably more at home as an activist. When a minority is at risk of being treated unsympathetically by an 'intolerant majority', for example in the *Brown vs. Board of Education* case, a justice can intervene and apply a new interpretation of a constitutional right in order to determine what's just and fair.

  Sometimes, however, a justice will use judicial restraint and act passively. For example, when a statute declares an act is illegal, such as burning the *Stars and Stripes* (the American flag) as a form of protest, but a justice objects, he is exercising judicial restraint. The justice declares that the dissenter's First Amendment rights (freedom of speech) are being infringed by not being allowed to burn the flag. In this case, the justice is not making a new policy or establishing new legal rights but interpreting the law as written in the US Constitution (*Texas vs. Johnson* 1989).

- A **conservative judge** will be more comfortable being passive. In fact, some conservatives propose that a justice should always be passive. If the law isn't illegal, beyond reasonable doubt, the Court should defer its position – but most people don't take this argument totally seriously.

  However, since the Court has become more conservative in its make-up, judicial activism has become an acceptable framework for decision making. Conservative judges are typically active in terms of upholding unconstitutional laws that restrict commercial advertising and what corporations and wealthy people can spend on their favourite political candidates (for example, *Citizens United vs. Federal Election Commission* 2000).

Revisiting Supreme Courts in the Modern Era

A Supreme Court gets its title from the name of the Chief Justice who's holding office. Obviously, some Courts have had more influence than others in shaping American society. And whether you think the Court was good, bad or indifferent will depend on whether you're liberal or conservative. This section reviews the last four Courts by looking at some of their key themes and influential cases. I also pass judgement on the political identity of each court.

The Warren Court (1953–1969)

During the 16 years of Earl Warren's role as Chief Justice, the Court dealt with a number of politically explosive issues. It engaged with desegregation, the rights of people accused of criminal acts, reapportionment (population size of electoral voting districts), the role of religion within public life and birth control. President Eisenhower appointed Warren as Chief Justice in 1953 and as the cases went by and the tallies were added he was upset that a former three-term Republican Governor of California was more liberal than expected. It goes to show that a president never knows how a nominee will vote until he actually does so. Warren's approach considered the social issues of the day and was an activism that sought to redress the failures of political institutions to protect the rights of minorities. In the case of *Brown vs. Board of Education* (1954), for example, Warren addressed the constitutional nature of the *separate but equal* doctrine outlined in *Plessy vs. Ferguson* (1896), which had meant that black and white children were educated separately. For over 50 years the Court had refused to engage in reviewing the constitutional nature of this doctrine. The Warren Court voted unanimously, although with some persuasion, to declare that in the case of school education 'separate educational facilities are inherently unequal'. The social implications were immense, leading to a series of stand-offs between the state and federal governments. It included Arkansas Governor Orval Faubus calling the State National Guard to block African-American students from entering a high school. President Eisenhower responded by calling out the 101st Airborne and federalising the National Guard.

Verdict: Liberal activist Court (conservative voting only 34 per cent of the time)

The close-call appointment of Clarence Thomas

In 1991 Republican President George H. W. Bush nominated Federal Court of Appeals Judge Clarence Thomas as a justice in the Supreme Court. With over ten years in the White House, the Republican Party was on its sixth nomination to the Supreme Court, which meant that the Court was expected to have a Conservative majority. The implications for its impact on American society were great. Could the Court overturn, for example, the right for women to have an abortion (as in *Roe vs. Wade 1973*)?

Battle lines were drawn by liberal and conservative politicians and interest groups over the nomination. Feminist and civil rights organisations attacked Thomas because they thought he would rescind *Roe vs. Wade* and continue to oppose *affirmative action* (support for under-represented minorities in employment, business and education). The Democrats could refuse to accept the president's nomination should they desire. His responses to questions on his judicial philosophy were dampened down so as not to cause any major objections from the members of the judiciary committee and his nomination just about squeezed through. However, by the end of the committee hearings an FBI interview with a former employee, Anita Hill, had been leaked. The interview had included details of alleged sexual harassment of Hill by Thomas. Hill was asked to appear before the Judiciary Committee to discuss her accusations. Committee hearings were recorded and appeared live on C-SPAN (public service TV) and on all the other TV stations. Hill gave testimony (and Thomas was questioned) about, for example, the size of his penis, and that he had watched a film called *Long Dong Silver*. Other people who worked with him testified against and others testified in favour. The political theatre on display during his confirmation had a detrimental effect on public perception of the Supreme Court and all other parties involved. He was just confirmed by a 52–48 vote; 41 Republican and 11 Democrats. After he joined the Court media interest in his private life died down. Whilst the outcome was that Thomas was still made a Supreme Court justice, the level of vitriol in his nomination process provides an important insight into the willingness of people to go to many lengths in order to influence the political identity of the Supreme Court.

The Burger Court (1969–1986)

During the Republican presidency of Richard Nixon, four justices were appointed, including Warren E. Burger as the Chief Justice. To some, the Burger Court heralded a new era in Supreme Court decision making. It suggested an ambition for the Court to be more conservative in its outcomes and reverse some of the previous Court's liberal decisions. Although moving to a conservative agenda was not as clear cut as expected (particularly around abortion), this Court did do some pretty conservative things. For example, in 1986, in an act of conservative restraint, the Court refused to strike down a Georgia statute stating that sodomy was illegal (*Bowers vs. Hardwick*). Other important issues the Court addressed include a mixed record regarding the right to religious practice in a public setting, of free speech (such as the right of the press when the Court refused the US federal government's request to stop the *New York Times* publishing a government report critical of its engagement in the Vietnam War), gender equality and affirmative action.

Roe vs. Wade (1973) is perhaps the most famous liberal activist decision of the Burger Court. In a 7–2 decision, the Court decreed that a Texas statute declaring that no foetus could be aborted unless to save the life of the mother was unconstitutional under the rights to personal liberty and privacy guaranteed by the Constitution. The Court's decision balanced the right to privacy with an interest to protect the health of women from the dangers of abortion and the protection of the life of the foetus. It detailed that in the early stages of the pregnancy (first trimester), the right to privacy was paramount but was increasingly replaced by these other interests in the second and third trimesters. On reflection, the Burger Court is often seen as a transitional one between the liberalism of the Warren Court and the conservatism of the Rehnquist Court.

Verdict: Combination of liberal and conservative positions (conservative voting 55 per cent of the time)

The Rehnquist Court (1986–2005)

Even before Republican President Nixon appointed him to the Supreme Court in 1972, William Rehnquist was renowned for his conservative criticism of judicial liberalism. In 1957, as a law clerk for one of the justices of the Warren Court, Rehnquist published an article criticising the influence of liberal law clerks, suggesting that they provide support 'for the claims of Communists and other criminal defendants, expansion of federal power at the expense of State power, [and] great sympathy toward any government regulation of business'. When Rehnquist became a justice he continued in this vein by dissenting in the *Roe vs. Wade* abortion case and making a number of judgements favouring the rights of states over the federal government (federalism). When President Reagan promoted him to Chief Justice, he was expected to continue the conservative revolution. Unfortunately for the conservatives, these expectations were not met. For example, the court did not reverse the right for a women to have an abortion (although they did add some further restrictions to abortion). Another famous case which angered conservatives was the decision to accept flag burning as a constitutionally protected act under the First Amendment, in *Texas vs. Johnson* (1989).

The Rehnquist Court did make significant conservative advancements in other areas of the Court decision making, particularly in terms of the relationship between the federal and the state governments. Prior to the mid-1990s, congressional power to regulate all types of activities was achieved through the Court's interpretation of the Commerce Clause detailed in the US Constitution. The clause refers to the prohibition of state legislatures from passing statutes that are against or excessively burden inter-state commerce and it served as a kind of short-cut to making lots of things illegal. This legislation, for example, could regulate a restaurant that did not allow African-Americans to eat-in because the food served had previously crossed state lines (*Katzenbach vs. McClung* 1964). However, by 1995 the Court had begun to restrict the definition of what could be regulated by the Commerce Clause. In *United States vs. Lopez*, for example, the defendant was charged because he had brought a gun to school, which violated the 1990 Federal Gun-Free School Zones Act. The law was passed under the Commerce Clause, which stated that possession in a school could lead to a violent crime and thus impact the general economic conditions. The Court rejected this argument on the grounds that it did not deal directly with issues concerning commerce.

The Rehnquist Court was also famously and contentiously involved in settling disputes of a very political nature. In a 5–4 decision (*Bush vs. Gore* 2000; see Chapter 20 for further details of this case), it was the first time that the Supreme Court had played *the* decisive role in determining the outcome of a presidential election. It ultimately awarded the Office of the President of the United States to George W. Bush on the basis that the manual recount of voter cards as determined by the Florida Supreme Court violated the *Equal Protection Clause* (suggesting that all people in a state must be treated equally under the law) of the Fourteenth Amendment. It ruled that the recount violated this clause because different standards of counting were applied in different counties. It also suggested that time pressures meant that applying a uniform standard were unrealistic. This was a great case for exposing the political ideologies of the justices. Conservatives Scalia and Thomas argued that the recount violated the Equal Protection Clause; however, in 46 previous cases where it was argued (during the time of these two justices), Scalia and Thomas held only two times that it was unconstitutional.

Verdict: Conservative but not to the degree hoped (conservative voting 55 per cent of the time)

The Roberts Court (2005–)

John Roberts was recruited to the Supreme Court after Rehnquist's death and at the same time a new conservative justice, Samuel Alito, also joined. These new appointments instilled hope amongst the conservatives, which was realised when the Roberts Court made key decisions on abortion, campaign finance reform, gun control, criminal sentencing, affirmative action and capital punishment. Was the Court finally turning to the conservative side of the force? Sitting on the conservative side of the ring are Roberts, Scalia, Thomas and Alito while on the liberal side are Ginsburg, Breyer, Sotomayor and Kagan. Sitting pretty in the middle is Reagan-appointed Anthony Kennedy, who is the swing voter. However, in 5–4 rulings in which Kennedy was the deciding voter he's tended to vote with the conservatives. In the 2010–11 term, for example, 20 per cent of all cases were split 5–4 rulings, with a near complete division based on ideological divides. Of those decisions, Kennedy voted with the conservatives 70 per cent of the time. One such case was *Citizens United vs. Federal Election Commission* (2010), which concluded that the government couldn't stop corporations or labour unions from unlimited spending on political activities, including during elections, as long as such funds weren't directed to a candidate's election campaign. This conclusion led to the rise of the Super PACs (Political Action Committees) designed to raise unlimited finances for advocating for or against a political candidate. The impact this decision had on electoral politics is revealed in the 2012 presidential election: Republican-focused Super PACS received $225 million and the Democrat Super PACS received $92 million to fund pro-Romney and anti-Obama and pro-Obama and anti-Romney campaigns, respectively.

Verdict: Conservatively orientated (conservative voting 58 per cent of the time)

Chapter 8

How Does an Idea Become a Law?

The point of making laws is to make government more efficient, run more smoothly and respond to the needs of the people. At least that is what they're supposed to do. Of course, this isn't always the effect of every bill submitted or passed into law.

Any newly elected member of Congress is bound to arrive with lots of ideas on how to make the country a better place. In order for their ideas to have any impact they need to get involved in the process of law making.

In this chapter you find out how difficult it is for an initial idea to move through the bureaucratic system of government and become an enacted law. I take you through this journey from where the initial idea comes from, through to its early stage of development in committees and sub-committees, to discussion on the floors to both chambers, and finally (if it makes it that far) to the president's desk.

Taking a Bill from Idea to Introduction

Proposing, making, and implementing a bill is a tricky business with many factors supporting or hampering a successful journey. Following the rules and regulations of the Congress keeps it complicated: in the House alone, the rule book is about a thousand pages long with over 25 volumes of previous precedence that defines House procedures. And this journey begins when a member of Congress introduces a potential law – a *bill* – by one of several methods.

Bringing ideas to the table

Elected members get ideas about new laws from various places, including, on occasion, their very own minds. In general, ideas for legislation arise from one of the following five sources:

- ✔ **Constituents.** If a significant number of a member's constituents feel strongly about an issue, he or she may be inclined to support the issue by introducing or co-sponsoring a bill into Congress. This is especially likely if it is politically expedient for the member – if, for example, the bill touches on a topical issue and an election is just around the corner.

- ✔ **Interest groups.** For every issue under the sun, multiple *interest groups* (affiliations of people intent on affecting laws about a given topic) exist. These groups work to change the world according to their goals, usually at cross-purposes with another interest group with goals of its own. Interest groups can support lawmakers by giving them money to run an election campaign or support them by helping to write (or even writing outright) a draft bill on an issue to submit to Congress. Chapter 13 gives further details on interest groups and their influence on the political system.

- ✔ **Congressional committees.** For various duties within Congress, committees and subcommittees that address those duties exist. (See Chapter 5.) One of the many congressional committees, such as the House Armed Forces committee or sub-committees such as the Senate's Foreign Relations committee's European Affairs, can also suggest legislation to address issues raised in committee discussions.

- ✔ **Members of Congress.** Individual members of Congress who are experts (or like to think they are) on a particular issue can draft and submit a bill.

- ✔ **The president's office.** In supporting an issue close to him, the president can develop draft legislation and ask members of Congress to submit a bill for consideration. (Chapter 4 gives further details on the role of the president.)

Of course, these categories are not independent of one another and often an elected member will feel pressure from several places to introduce a bill.

Submitting the idea: Bills and resolutions

With an idea in place, a legislator's next move is to get it down in writing and pass it along to the rest of the gang (or some subsection of it).

In consultation with their chamber's legislative counsel, a Senator or Representative develops the policy idea into the appropriate legislative language required for submission as a *draft bill*. Think of the *legislative counsel* as the translators that help legislators turn their ideas on how to improve government into a draft bill. This working bill employs the technical language required for its successful implementation into the government bureaucracy.

In the Senate, a bill may have many *sponsors,* or legislators responsible for drafting the bill in the first place. In the House of Representatives, a bill can have only one sponsor (also known as the *primary sponsor*). And once the bill is ready to be submitted onto the floor, the sponsors ask other legislators to join as *co-sponsors* of the bill in order to gain more support and increase the chances that the bill will get over all the hurdles it needs to in order to become a law. An *original* or an *initial* co-sponsor is someone who puts her name to the bill before it's introduced to the Congress for discussion but did not write the bill. And those who were unsure of sponsoring the bill at the outset can add their names to the list supporting the bill as *additional co-sponsors* after it has been submitted.

A submitted bill that is intended to become law may come in any of three flavours, depending on its purpose and scope (although public bills are the most common):

- ✔ A **public bill** impacts the general population rather than a specific group. For example, a bill to increase the minimum wage would be a public bill.

- ✔ A **private bill** impacts a specific person or group rather than the public-at-large. In many cases, private bills are immigration requests for people who seek permanent resident status.

- ✔ **Joint resolutions** work just like bills do with one exception: They can be used to craft an amendment to the US Constitution. (Chapter 2 tells you more about the constitution.) Typically, legislators use a joint resolution for issues such as requesting a declaration of war or establishing temporary investigative commissions (for example, the 9/11 Commission).

Another kind of resolution, called a *non-binding resolution,* enables the chambers to organise their day-to-day operations or express an opinion on an issue. These resolutions do not become laws and so do not require a presidential signature. Two kinds of non-binding resolutions exist: A *simple resolution*

concerns matters in the chamber that it comes from and does not require a vote from the second chamber, whilst a *concurrent resolution* must be passed to the other chamber for voting.

Introducing the bill

Introducing a bill is a momentous occasion for a sponsor, as it is the culmination of a many hours work. A bill is introduced when the sponsor, with the aid of the legislative counsel, has ironed out all the creases in the draft bill and decided that it's ready to begin its journey. Only an elected member of one of Congress's two chambers (House of Representatives and Senate) can submit a bill.

In the House, a bill is introduced when the Congressperson who is the primary sponsor drops it in the clerk's box, otherwise known as the *hopper* during any time that the House is in session. The hopper is a wooden box at the front of the floor attached to the rostrum near where the *Bill Clerk* official sits.

The process is a bit less theatrical in the Senate, where a bill is normally submitted to the clerks on the floor at any time of the day, as long as the Senate is in session. A Senator typically just hands a copy of the bill over without making any formal comments on its submission, although sometimes it can be more formally introduced on the Senate floor by the Senator reading out the bill along with a statement of support.

When a bill is submitted, the clerk of the chamber in which it was submitted gives it an official designation that shows where it originated and includes a unique number. In the House of Representatives, that designation starts with H.R. or H.J.Res. (which stand for House of Representatives and the House Joint Resolution). Senate bills are named either S. or S.J.Res (which stand for Senate and Senate Joint Resolution). Numbers are issued sequentially, and the whole shebang (for example, H.R. 2642) identifies that bill throughout its legislative life.

Referring the Bill to Committee

Before a bill becomes law it must be scrutinised by members of Congress, first within a committee. There are 45 different committees in Congress (21 in the House, 20 in the Senate and 4 joint committees). The process by which a bill gets referred to a particular committee differs ever-so-slightly in the two chambers:

✔ **House of Representatives:** In the House of Representatives, once a bill is submitted in the hopper it is then referred by the presiding officer (the Speaker of the House or someone delegated from the majority party) to the specific Congressional committees that have responsibility for the focus of the bill. A bill typically falls under the jurisdiction of one committee, although some do fall under more than one committee. In this instance, one committee will be designated the primary one and is in charge of leading the drive of the bill through the legislative process.

✔ **Senate:** In the Senate, a bill is passed to the presiding officer who, with advice from the clerks, determines which committee to send it to for discussion. The vice president of the US is the Senate's presiding officer, although that person rarely sits in the chamber; the position then is sub-contracted typically to the leader of the majority party, who then sub-contracts out to junior Senators of the majority party to give them on-the-job training. Although, if there is more than one committee that could comment on the bill it will only be referred to the committee that has jurisdiction for the principal focus of the bill. Rarely, a bill in some of these multi-jurisdiction cases is referred to more than one committee.

Sorta like trying out for the Olympics: A bill's chance of becoming law

If you are an elected member of Congress and you submit a bill or joint resolution, you probably won't see it become law in the two years that session of Congress sits.

To give you an understanding of just how much congressional business is done, here are some figures for the 112th Congress (January 3, 2011 to January 3 2013):

✔ In the House, 6,722 bills, 122 joint resolutions, 845 simple resolutions and 147 concurrent resolutions were introduced.

✔ In the Senate, 3,715 bills, 51 joint resolutions, 630 simple resolutions and 65 concurrent resolutions were submitted.

That's more than 10,600 bills and joint resolutions combined.

Exactly how unlikely your bill is to become law depends partly on the Congress you're a member of. In the 102nd Congress (January 3, 1991 to January 3, 1993), only 610 laws were made – out of 10,507 bills and joint resolutions proposed. That's about a 1 in 17 chance that your bill becomes a law. Sounds like bad odds, but you'd have been even worse off if you were a hopeful legislator in more recent sessions. In the 112th Congress, 10,610 bills and joint resolutions were submitted but only 283 public and 1 private bill were passed into law. That's about a 1 in 37 chance of a bill or joint resolution becoming law. (Flip over to Chapter 11 for details on why the 112th Congress had a record low number of laws passed.)

After a bill has been designated a number and given a committee, it appears in the next copy of the *Congressional Record* – the daily record of everything that is said on the floors of the two chambers and of all proposed bills.

The bill is then sent to the *Government Printing Office* (which does what its title suggests: prints government material), where it is printed and distributed to both chambers and to the presiding committee chairs. It is then also made available to the public.

There just isn't enough time to consider every bill that makes it into committee, so a bill can die at the behest of the committee chair as soon as it arrives. The committee chair is a member of the party that is that chamber's majority party and a powerful person who decides which of the thousands of submitted bills gets airtime in the committee. If it is on a subject that they and their party are not interested in exploring then the bill gets ditched.

Investigations and sub-committees

After a committee has been allocated a bill to discuss, the committee chair (who is a member of the majority party in the chamber), is responsible for appointing the sub-committee that will investigate the subject of the bill. Sometimes a chair decides not to appoint a sub-committee, and it goes to the committee-at-large. This happens either because the chair wants the bill to be rushed through the committee in order for it to become law quickly or to kill the bill. An investigation involves a *hearing*, or formal discussion of a bill by the committee or sub-committee. The hearing is set up to question the details of the proposed bill. The centre point of the hearing is to invite a series of interested parties to present their thoughts on the issues the bill discusses. Although not necessary for a bill to be approved, public hearings are typical of important bills.

If a bill proposes federal investment in new railway infrastructure, for example, then interested parties would include experts from government departments and agencies such as the Department of Transport, trade unions such as the Amalgamated Transit Union and interested business parties such as the industry trade group the Association of American Railroads.

Each expert presents an oral testimony and answers questions from the committee or sub-committee and submits a longer written testimony that details his or her perspective. Witnesses are generally invited to testify, but those who are unwilling to attend can be subpoenaed and thereby legally required by the committee or sub-committee to testify.

By definition, an elected member likes to talk, a lot. To ensure that no one member hogs the stage during a hearing, each member has five minutes to interrogate the witness. If a member or a staffer wants to ask more detailed questions, then they can have up to one hour with the committee's or sub-committee's permission.

To attract more attention to the issues raised in the bill, holding a public hearing is a good tactical move for a committee or sub-committee. Because it's open to the public, it encourages engagement and interest in the bill. If it is interesting to the public or a particular constituency that has friendly relations with media groups, then the media will also be interested. And if the committee or sub-committee favour the bill and there is enough interest generated by these two then it is likely to generate interest amongst congressional colleagues – essential if the bill is to become a law.

In addition to the formal hearing, a committee or sub-committee will also have staff members examine the bill in more detail and will also engage in private discussions with witnesses, particularly when the bill concerns matters that could hamper national security or compromise the operations of law enforcement.

The minutes of a hearing are made public after it's over. Anyone can access those minutes by going to the relevant committee's website.

Marking up or killing the bill

The committee or sub-committee *marks up* a bill. This meeting is typically open to the public and is the final meeting by a committee or sub-committee to decide whether the bill should be reported to the floor of one of the chambers of Congress. The decision is based on the information gleaned from its investigation, after the multiple perspectives on the bill's content are discussed and voted on.

The members debate the bill, suggest amendments (or even propose completely new text), or suggest the full committee effectively kill the bill through what's called *tabling it* – postponing further action until some other time. For a bill to be a success and make its way to the chamber floor it needs to pass a simple majority vote of the committee members. If the investigation was done first by a sub-committee then it would be the same process, and if it passed the sub-committee it would then be voted on by the committee at large.

For any bill that it accepts, the committee submits what is called a *report* to its parent chamber (the Senate or House of Representatives). The report outlines the background, content, aims, and impact of the bill. It includes a financial costing of the bill to the federal budget by the Congressional Budget Office. A report can also include the meanderings of committee members that support or oppose the bill.

If the bill is reported favourably to the chamber (in other words, the committee fully support the bill) then none or only minor amendments to the wording of the bill are made and it is submitted to the chamber floor for discussion. Based on the committee or sub-committee investigation, however, a committee may decide that a bill is important and should go to the chamber floor for discussion but requires significant amendments. In the latter instance, there are two options. Either the bill is reported back to the chamber whereby the complete text of the bill is replaced with new text, or, the committee may report a new *clean* bill with the recommended amendments. In the latter, the chair is usually the one to propose this new bill (starting again at the hopper). This new bill will be forwarded to the relevant committee just like any other bill but will usually have a smooth journey through the committee, and will be reported back favourably without amendments to the chamber floor for discussion.

Bills *tabled* (put aside) by the committee at this stage are effectively toast. What adds salt to the wounds is the fact that once snubbed by the committee the original bill will never be seen again for the remainder of the two year duration of the congressional session. This is because once a session ends all bills that are stuck in a committee or sub-committee and have not been referred back to the chamber floor have to go through the entire process all over again. The death of a bill at this stage (although statistically likely) is a sad event for all those who've put in hours of hard labour to get it so far.

Taking a Bill onto the Floor of the First Chamber

Being approved by committee is a big hurdle for any bill to clear. After a bill has been reported to the chamber it came from, it is entered in that chamber's calendar and is eligible for discussion on the floor. The majority party leadership has great power in determining whether a bill or joint resolution at this stage is given an expedited date, a later date – or no date for a scheduled debate, which effectively kills its chance of becoming a law. As a result, making it onto the floor for debate is another layer of political machinations by parties to pass before a bill can move on to the next stage. The way the House and Senate handle this part of the process varies.

Debating a bill in the House of Representatives

In the House of Representatives, bills and joint resolutions that are reported from committees are placed on a House calendar that determines how and when bill will be debated. There are four calendars that a bill is streamlined into:

- ✔ **Union Calendar:** Most public bills and resolutions come under this calendar and concern finances such as government taxation, revenue or appropriations. Its official title is the Calendar for the Committee of the Whole House on the State of the Union.

- ✔ **House Calendar:** Public bills or resolutions that do not cost the government anything go onto this calendar.

- ✔ **Private Calendar:** The place for those bills and resolutions that impact only specific people or groups and not the public at large.

- ✔ **Calendar of Motions to Discharge Committees:** Bills and resolutions are typically arranged for discussion by the floor in order of their submission, but because there are thousands of bills to be discussed in a Congressional session, not all of those bills have a chance to be discussed. This special calendar enables the more important bills and resolutions on the Union and House calendars or even those in committees to be fast-tracked.

Whenever the House votes and there is a requirement on the number of members attending, it automatically assumes there is a legitimate quorum of at least 218 members. Only when a member raises an objection is a count required.

Using the special rule

The special rule process on how a bill can be fast-tracked provides a really interesting window into the formal procedures of the House of Representatives and is the process most employed for passing legislation.

The chair of the committee that has reported the bill can ask the *Rules Committee* (the committee in charge of determining the terms of debate for a bill to be discussed) to speed up the delivery of a bill for discussion. Whether that happens has a lot to do with who's in charge and where that party stands on the legislation: the Rules Committee's membership disproportionately favours the majority party, which has nine members to the minority party's four. The majority party therefore has the power to fast-track bills (known as a *special rule*) that suit its ideological agenda. When a special rule is used, the Rules Committee (and therefore the majority party) can really shape how things go for the bill. In discussion with the majority party leadership, this committee, along with the committee chair that the bill was reported from, determine the specific nature of the bill's special rules for being introduced to the floor. They can include the following points:

- ✔ The original text of the bill or resolution that was reported from the committee can be automatically replaced by text from the Rules Committee (called a *compromise substitute*).

- ✔ The amount of time members can debate the bill or resolution can be restricted in order to speed up its passage to a vote on whether to become a law.

- ✔ Certain restrictions that are normal House requirements such as germaneness of an amendment (*open rules*) may be relevant.

- ✔ The amount or types of amendments the House can consider when discussing a bill or resolution can be determined in order to reduce the possibility of slowing the process by dissenters submitting non-relevant amendments (called *closed* or *structured rules*).

- ✔ A series of pre-determined individual amendments agreed upon prior to submission by the majority and minority members tasked with managing debates for their party (called *manager's amendments*).

If the Committee on Rules decides that the special rule should be applied to a bill or resolution, then it typically is placed on the House calendar for at least a day and is then raised by the member who submitted the rule request. They can do this at any time of the session but if they don't request a debate on whether the rule should be implemented within seven days, any member of the Rules Committee can request, at any time of the session, it be debated on the House floor. As soon as the special rule for a bill is raised, a *Committee of the Whole* is requested and the terms of the special rule are voted on. (The rules could be rejected, but the vote is seen as an act of party loyalty by the majority party and so is usually passed.)

The Committee of the Whole has the same role as any other committee in the chamber, except that it is made up of *all* the members of the House. This committee fast-tracks discussion and vote on a bill or resolution because it requires only 100 members out of the 435 to be present to make a *quorum* in order for a majority vote to be legitimate. (In a typical vote on the floor, at least 218 of the 435 members of the House have to be present in order for a bill or resolution to have a legitimate vote.) Therefore, discussion of the bill and possible amendments under the special rule criteria can be done quicker than those that require a full House quorum. This type of committee exists to get bills moving as quickly as possible.

There are two stages to debate on the floor in a Committee of the Whole:

- ✔ **General debate:** Typically an hour wherein a bill gets discussed and possible amendments are raised with 30 minutes given to the majority and 30 minutes given to the minority party. Whilst amendments can be discussed and debated, they cannot be proposed in this debate.

- ✔ **Amendment debate:** Proposed amendments can be made at this stage and follow a line-by-line process or are made on any part of the bill. Amendments must be *germane* – in other words, they have to be relevant to the content. This rule stops a member from strategically placing an irrelevant amendment designed to hijack the bill and kill it on the floor debate. Like any other committee, the Committee of the Whole debates amendments and then votes on whether they should be accepted. Once this has been done, the finalised bill is read out and the committee can decide whether or not to pass the bill to the House for a vote or *recommit* the bill. (Recommitting effectively kills the bill.) And if a bill is approved – with or without amendments – the Committee of the Whole reports to the House floor just as any other committee would.

Suspension of the Rules Procedure

Uncontroversial bills that have overwhelming support and need to be passed quickly are introduced under the *Suspension of the Rules Procedure,* which limits discussion to 40 minutes – 20 for the committee chair who the bill came from and 20 for the ranking minority party member of the committee. No amendments can be made by any member unless proposed under a manager's amendment (when pre-determined amendments by the majority and minority party establishment are introduced – see the earlier section 'Using the special rule'). Bills are made under this process only with the blessing of both party leaderships. A member proposing a suspension can do so only on a Monday, Tuesday or Wednesday whilst Congress is sitting, or on the final days of the session. The Speaker must first recognise the motion to suspend the rules and consider the bill.

In order for a motion to pass under this procedure, the House requires the votes of two-thirds of those present in the House as long as a quorum of at least 218 members is present. If it fails, it is normally because members requested amendments and so the bill can be debated again under a different set of rules that allows for further discussion.

Moving a bill onto the Senate floor

Within the Senate, potential legislation goes onto one of two calendars:

- ✔ The **Calendar of Business** deals with bills and resolutions reported from committees. Senators can also place simple or concurrent resolutions onto this calendar without having gone to a committee.

- ✔ International treaties or nominations for federal appointees go on the **Executive Calendar.**

After bills go onto either of the calendars, the majority party leader has control over the order in which they are discussed on the floor – a big power that can support his political agenda. However, if the majority party doesn't have a super-majority (60-plus Senators), then the importance of compromise with the minority party is essential.

Motion to proceed

A *motion to proceed* is the decision, usually taken by the majority party leader (or a Senator who has been approved by the majority leader) to consider a bill for debate and voting. And it is conducted under the normal rules of the House (see the upcoming 'Unanimous consent agreement' section for details of another way to pass a bill).

Throughout the life of a bill in the Senate, there are no restrictions on debate time (although as I show you later in the chapter, there's always an exception to a rule). Hence, things can get rather undisciplined and messy. The lack of restriction provides a powerful opportunity for a single Senator to derail the bill if she doesn't support its introduction. Unlike in the House, there is no simple majority procedure that can halt a Senator extending a debate or thwarting a vote by just rambling on. This delaying strategy is referred to as a *filibuster* and can be employed at the amendment and final vote stages (see the sidebar 'Strom Thurmond and the longest filibuster' for further details on a famous case of filibustering). Also unlike the House, the Senate has no restrictions on the types or amounts of amendments made to a bill. A bill regarding social security could include amendments on non-germane issues such as stem cell research or national health policy.

The amendment process in the Senate includes the following stages:

- ✔ **Opening statements:** An opportunity for the chair and ranking minority member on the committee that reported the bill back to the Senate floor to outline their reasons for supporting or opposing the bill as it stands.

- ✔ **Amendments, part one:** The first amendments to be discussed, if there are any, are those proposed by the committee that reported the bill to the Senate floor. After they've been read out, a Senator can propose amending the submitted committee amendments, and those new amendments are voted on before the original amendments.

- ✔ **Amendments, part two:** After the committee amendments have been processed, Senators can raise further amendments, debate and vote on them. Naturally, a few rules apply. First, an amendment that has not been successful in a vote cannot be reintroduced as a new amendment unless it includes substantive changes. Second, an amendment cannot propose a change in more than one place in the proposed bill and it cannot alter an already agreed-upon amendment.

- ✔ **Voting:** After the amendment process has been completed the Senate orders the bill to be read a third time (called *engrossing*), at which point no further amendments can be added and the bill goes to a vote on the Senate floor.

If a Senator supporting a bill is wary of an opponent to the bill derailing the voting process then she can request a *cloture bill*, which limits debate and amendments. For a cloture bill to pass, three fifths of senators (a super majority of 60) have to vote in favour of it. Getting cloture on a bill is usually difficult because it's not normal for one party to have 60 seats or more, which means that success requires some degree of bipartisan support. And if it's election time, then the chances of bipartisan support on a defining issue is difficult, as the Senators do not want to be seen to be going against their political constituency.

In a cloture situation, the presiding officer of the Senate is given extra powers including the power to determine whether motions, amendments or other actions are relevant to the content of the bill.

GREAT FIGURES

Strom Thurmond and the longest filibuster

Filibustering is arguably more of a sport than an art, requiring feats of spectacular endurance by Senators determined to put a spanner in the works. The record for the longest filibuster goes to Senator James Strom Thurmond of South Carolina, who spoke for 24 hours and 18 minutes against the Civil Rights Act of 1957. Apparently, Thurmond prepared himself for the epic ramble by having a steam bath to drain himself of excess fluids so that he would not need to use the bathroom. Thurmond began speaking at 8:54 p.m. on 28 August and continued until 9:12 p.m. the following evening. He passed the time by reciting various historical documents including the Declaration of Independence and George Washington's farewell address and even his grandmother's biscuit recipe. Camp beds were brought in for the Senators to sleep on while Thurmond waxed lyrical.

Whenever the majority party does not have a super-majority, the minority party has ample opportunity to threaten to filibuster and force amendments to a bill. In these cases, the minority party is holding the majority party hostage and thwarting its attempts to drive its political agenda as mandated by its victory in the Senate elections.

If successful, then no debate is required for the motion to proceed to a final vote, although there is a delay of two days before the final vote on the bill can happen because cloture still allows for 30 hours to further consider the bill. In the final vote on the floor, a bill requires a simple majority of 51 votes to pass – not the 60 for a cloture.

Unanimous consent agreement

Because Senators have the right to talk for as long as they want on a bill and to propose both germane and non-germane amendments, they technically could debate a bill forever. It's because of these fears of inertia that there's an alternative – a *unanimous consent agreement*. Usually directed by the majority party leader of the Senate, it can fast-track a bill for discussion and provide limitations on discussion time and amendments specific to that bill.

A unanimous consent agreement can be proposed before the bill is first discussed but most likely it will be proposed during discussion of a bill. It is an important interjection because if discussion of an amendment is too lengthy and is threatening to derail the speedy passage of a bill, then the party leaders can arrange for restrictions on discussion of future amendments. If party leaders suspect a particular amendment will be controversial, they can propose a unanimous agreement so that the passage of the bill is not impaired.

However, the phrase *unanimous* is an indication of the difficulties inherent in these agreements. All Senators have to agree with the proposed restrictions, or the bill can't be debated under the specified conditions. Agreeing to particular conditions for a bill under this process can be convoluted; it isn't practical to consult with every Senator on the terms. Objection from a Senator or Senators is referred to as putting a 'hold' on the bill. Once an agreement on a unanimous consent has been made then those rules agreed are golden; nothing changes unless all the Senators agree on that change in a new unanimous agreement, which is unlikely.

Taking the Bill to the Second Chamber

Getting through one chamber is quite a feat for a bill, but it's not the end of its journey to becoming law. In order for the bill to get passed to the president for signing – more of this in the upcoming section 'And the Small Matter of the President's Signature (or Not)' – it needs to be passed by the other chamber of Congress.

Passing the bill to the other chamber

When a bill has been passed by one chamber, it is referred to as being *engrossed*. An engrossed bill is the final version of the bill, including amendments approved voted on by the floor.

It is the responsibility of the *enrolling clerk* to ensure that all amendments approved are inserted into the text of the bill alongside the report by the relevant standing committee of the originating chamber for transfer to the second chamber.

The second chamber typically approves the engrossed version of the bill without suggesting any amendments. In this scenario the bill becomes an *enrolled measure* and is recognised as being passed in identical form by both chambers, is printed out and ready for the president's signature in order to become law.

In other scenarios, members in the second chamber are uncomfortable with the bill or aspects of the bill from the originating chamber and propose their own amendments. If an alternative version of the bill has been approved by the floor, the bill goes back to the originating chamber for consideration. In kind, the originating chamber can amend the amended bill and send it back to the second chamber, and so on – a process referred to as *amendment exchange*. A bill can die in this exchange if one of the chambers refuses to accept the bill proposed by the other chamber. For a bill to become law its text must be accepted in its entirety by the other chamber.

Meeting of the minds: The conference committee

An alternative to the amendment exchange is the *conference committee*. This infrequently-used committee is an *ad hoc* committee comprised of House and Senate members and set up just to reconcile the House and Senate versions of the bill to make it acceptable to both chambers – and thus continue on its path to becoming law.

The bills that usually go to a conference are controversial or major proposals. (Sometimes they're both.) Committee members (usually Congresspeople from the committees that have jurisdiction over the bill) negotiate a compromise bill by combining elements of both chambers' bills.

After a bill is produced, the committee votes. In order for the bill to be reported to the two chambers for a final vote, it must be passed by a majority of Senators and a majority of Representatives. If it doesn't make it, then the two sets of conferees report back to their chamber that no agreement was made; a new conference committee is convened and the process of compromise begins again.

If it passes by a majority of the conferees for each chamber, they write a *conference report* that includes the agreed-upon amendments to the bill. The report is submitted first to one of the chambers for approval.

If approved, the bill will, as is usual of other less contentious bills, make its way to the second chamber for approval. If the first chamber does not approve the amended bill then it can go back to the conference committee for further amendments and resubmitted to the chamber for a new vote. When the bill has been approved by one chamber, the committee's work is done. It is automatically disbanded and can make no further amendments.

An example of a Conference Committee occurred after the Senate and the House passed different versions of the 2009 *American Recovery and Reinvestment Act* (otherwise known as the Stimulus or the Recovery Act – see Chapter 16). The initial Senate and House versions of the bill were sufficiently different to warrant a conference of the two chambers where a synthesised bill was reported back to the House first on February 13 and was passed by 246-183. It moved to the Senate, and later that same day was passed 60-38.

And the Small Matter of the President's Signature (or Not)

After a grueling journey filled with potential pitfalls, a bill or resolution that makes it through the Congressional approval process is lucky indeed – and often bears little resemblance to the one that started the journey. But it's still not at the end of its road. And peril still is possible.

Enrollment and presidential action

A bill that has been passed by both chambers of Congress is referred to as *enrolled* and is passed to the president for approval. The president has 10 days (excluding Sundays) to either sign the bill or veto it.

Earning a presidential signature is, finally and really, the last step in the process. However, it's not a given. The president may decide that the bill is not acceptable and *veto,* or refuse, it.

A veto by a president on an enrolled bill usually occurs when that bill involves a partisan issue that goes against the president's legislative agenda. Also, because the duty of the president, under the Constitution, is to 'preserve, protect and defend' the Constitution, a veto can be an opportunity for a president to formally mark his objection. It is then up to the Supreme Court, if it chooses to take the case, to rule on constitutionality.

There are two types of veto:

- ✔ In a **regular veto,** the president returns a bill to its originating chamber with suggested amendments. In recent years, presidents have been less likely to employ regular vetoes. President Obama has employed only two regular vetoes, President Bush had 12, and President Clinton had 36. President Roosevelt (1933–1945) had the most vetoes with 372.

- ✔ A **pocket veto** occurs when the president doesn't sign or regular veto the bill and Congress is adjourned (for more than three days) during the 10-day window for signing. President Bush never employed a pocket veto, and President Obama has not used it so far. President Clinton used it once. President Roosevelt (1933–1945) had the most vetoes in this category as well with 263.

Interestingly, if the president decides to neither veto nor sign the bill within the 10 days allotted, and there are more than 10 days on the calendar before an adjournment, then the bill is passed into law without the president's signature.

Overriding a presidential veto

A president may approve some aspects of an enrolled bill but not others. In this instance the president may not want to strike the bill down completely but return the bill with suggested amendments to the originating chamber.

The chamber can override the president's regular veto by ensuring that two-thirds of those voting vote against the veto. If successful, the other chamber then has its own vote, which also requires a two-thirds majority on overriding the president's veto. If both chambers are successful then the bill becomes law without the signature of the president. What is perhaps most surprising is that this doesn't happen often.

Presidents totally win the veto game. During Obama's presidency, neither of his two vetoes was overridden by Congress, four out of 12 of President Bush's vetoes were overridden, and only two out of 36 during Clinton's presidency were overridden. Even during President Roosevelt's time in office, which included the most regular and pocket vetoes of any president, still only nine vetoes were overridden by Congress.

When Do the People See a Bill in Action?

Even after a bill becomes law, a number of formalities stand between its being a reality on paper and being enforced out in the world.

1. The bill is sent to the Office of the Federal Register at the National Archives.

2. The bill receives a public or private law number. These numbers begin at 1 for each new session of Congress. Therefore, the fifth public law of the 113th Congress (2013-2015) would be designated Public Law 113-5, and the fifth private law of the same Congress would be Private Law 113-5.

3. The law is entered into the next edition of the *United States Statutes at Large* (the official source for laws and resolutions passed by Congress).

4. The government ensures that the law is properly implemented.

Depending on its type, a new law can be implemented straight away or it can have an implementation date at some point in the future. For the most complicated of laws, there is usually a future start date, as it has to permeate through all the relevant government departments and agencies. The government employees have to be made aware of how the changes a new law has on their operations and the relevant interest groups, businesses and citizens also need to be made aware of how it impacts them.

All in all a law can take a long time before it is in full operation. And if the law hasn't worked as it was intended then modifications need to be made – this means that the poor blighter is back in Congress again.

Chapter 9

Is It Too Much? Deconstructing the Layers and Levels of Government

. . . .

In This Chapter

▶ Analysing the importance of federalism in the American political system

▶ Taking a look at the different levels of government

▶ Identifying why government bureaucracy is often criticised

▶ Recognising why large government is fiercely opposed

. . . .

*T*he sign of a good philosophy for government is not how it would operate in an ideal world, as every system is perfect there, but how it works in the real world, where humans are not always rational and don't always make the decisions you think they should make.

America is a big country, not just in terms of geography but also in terms of government; there are multiple layers of bureaucracy at the local, state and federal levels, and they all need to talk to each other in some way. This chapter examines these layers of government bureaucracy, raises questions over that government's ability to function, and discusses the history behind American culture's fears of large government.

Introducing Federalism: The Basis for American Government

To understand how the government operates, it's important to understand *federalism*, which is a system that administers a single geographic location through two separate levels of government. In the United States, that means

✔ A national government makes laws affecting the entire country and applicable in every state.

✔ Each state that exists within the United States has the power to make laws that affect and apply in only that state.

Federalism helps explain the individual power bases of the state and national governments, and their interactions with each other. Fearful of tyranny, the founders of the American government created a balance between giving the federal government sufficient powers and authority to govern while ensuring that its powers were sufficiently countered by decentralising other powers to the states. And it was this balance between federal and state governments that was ratified in the US Constitution in 1791. Chapter 2 gives you more details about the Constitution and the government it establishes.

The federal government consists of the executive and the government departments under it, Congress and the judiciary, and the individual states. Under Article I, Section 8 the federal government has the power to

✔ Raise taxes

✔ Print money

✔ Declare war

✔ Establish post offices

✔ Raise armies

✔ Make any laws it needs to carry out those duties

Article I, Section 10 of the Constitution determines what powers the states do not have, including being unable to enter into a 'Treaty, Alliance, or Confederation' with another nation, print money, give credit, or charge import or export duties without Congressional approval.

While restrictions are placed on what the states can do, the Tenth Amendment balances the power of the federal government by declaring that 'the powers not delegated to the United States by the Constitution, nor prohibited by it to the States, are reserved to the States respectively, or to the people'. This amendment means that the federal government has only the powers that are written in the Constitution (called *enumerated powers*) while all other powers not mentioned in the Constitution (*unenumerated powers*) are automatically transferred to the state and the people. The power to make laws to carry out these duties has increased the scope and focus of the federal government beyond what the framers anticipated.

Because the power to interpret the Constitution by the various branches and levels of government is a central component of the American political system, federalism has been defined in different ways at different periods in history (see Chapter 2 for further details on the Constitution). People have also suggested new interpretations to determine the relationship between states and the federal government:

- ✔ **Dual federalism:** Also known as *layer cake federalism*, dual federalism refers to a system in which the two levels of government operate separately, and is pretty much the bog-standard definition of how the framers intended it to be interpreted. The powers of government are split between the federal and state levels in order to preserve a balance between the two. This approach operated between the 1790s and around 1930.

- ✔ **Co-operative federalism:** This system, also called *marble cake federalism*, implies that the federal and state governments share power equally in order to resolve common problems collectively and was popular all the way through the Great Depression, the Second World War, the Cold War and up until the 1960s. During these testing times, the country needed the two levels of government to work together. Previous state-dominated projects were transferred to the national stage so that a single unified plan could be implemented. Lines between the two governments' powers are blurred within this approach, which operated from around 1930 to 1960.

- ✔ **Creative federalism:** Also known as *picket fence federalism*, creative federalism allows the federal government to decide what the states need, and then provide them with the resources. It shifted power to the federal government, and is evidenced in the Johnson administration's social and welfare reforms in the 1960s, whereby federal funding to states was contingent on adopting a series of federally determined objectives. This approach operated from around 1960 to 1980.

- ✔ **New federalism:** In response to the states' loss of power during creative federalism, new federalism included a reassertion of powers going back to the state and local governments in order to create a new balance between the two. One principal vehicle for this shift was to remove the conditionality on federally provided block grants to enable states to choose how to prioritise what they should be spent on. This approach operated from around 1980 until 2001.

- ✔ **Bush federalism:** Although not technically a form of federalism, Bush federalism demonstrated an increasing level of federal interference in state issues. The drive for greater national security legitimised increasing federal powers over American citizens and states, such as the passing of the Patriot Act in late 2001 (which strengthened federal powers to ensure US national security but also included giving the FBI the power to search the library records of American citizens). This approach operated during the Bush administration between 2001 and 2009.

✔ **Progressive federalism:** Claimed as a system by the Obama administration, progressive federalism provides states with greater control over issues previously reserved for the federal government, such as environmental and consumer protection. It supports state tailoring of federal regulations in these areas, such as the stricter regulations on vehicle emissions introduced by California. In effect, the federal government sets a benchmark with which the state has to comply and the state can then choose if it wants to go further. This system can be interpreted as a continuation of domination by the federal government dressed to look as if it's respecting the powers of the states. The state has to jump, so says the federal government, but it can choose how high it jumps so long as it conforms to a minimal height set by the federal government. Now that's certainly freedom of choice!

The types of federalism ascribed to the various periods above aren't written in stone and are open to interpretation. What does appear to be evident, however, is that, as the years go by, I see a continuing and increasing expansion of federal powers at the expense of state powers.

Reviewing the Levels of Government

If someone were to ask me to name ten things about American politics that I think are important, then the mechanics of government is probably number seven or eight. And yet, this one area of government is what most people have an intimate and daily connection with. It's the bureaucracy that protects Americans from foreign enemies, grants driving licences, arranges children's education, repairs potholes in the road, offers protection from crime and fire, and picks up the rubbish from outside people's homes. You get the idea. Seen from the other side of the coin, however, that bureaucracy can also restrict the entrepreneurship of large and small-scale businesses and stop kids from setting up a lemonade stand because they don't have a permit. Whether bureaucracy is seen as good or bad, it's definitely everywhere, and at the local, state and federal levels.

Local

The state governments confer authority on the local governments to deal with specific issues through state-made legislation. Americans have more contact with the local government than with the state or federal governments. Local government is organised in four main layers and, according to the US Census Bureau, 90,056 different local governments existed in the United States in 2012. That's a lot of paperwork. These four levels are:

- ✔ **County:** A county's function is to administer state laws within a particular geographic location. It has a number of responsibilities including managing most public services such as parks, hospitals, fire services, libraries, schools, courts, roads and law enforcement. Births, deaths and marriages are also recorded at the county level. A number of key state officials operate within the county jurisdiction, including district attorneys, auditors, county sheriffs and coroners. Some of these are even elected positions. County-made ordinances (legislation) can dictate what types of businesses can operate in a particular zone, for example, but most legislation applied is actually state law. In 2012, 3,031 counties existed.

- ✔ **Townships:** These are traditionally rural geographic locations that are a subdivision of the county; sometimes they're just a different name for a town or city. Most townships have an elected board that includes supervisors who run local services such as rubbish collection and road maintenance; some even include the fire and police services. In 2012, 16,360 townships existed.

- ✔ **Municipalities:** Similar in most states to townships, municipalities are usually a fancy name for an administrative area that's a city or a town. Municipal governments often have elected mayors serving as the executive and elected councillors serving as legislators. They're in charge of running most public services that an average person will come into contact with during their daily lives. In 2012, 19,519 municipalities existed.

- ✔ **Special districts:** These subdivisions of government provide a specialist function within a particular geographic location. Functions include education, waste management and transportation. They're unique entities and even have tax-raising powers to provide the services they cover. School districts, for example, are run by school boards, which can be elected or appointed and are responsible for determining policy issues such as what textbooks the schools can purchase and the ratio of students per teacher. In 2012, 12,880 independent school districts and 38,266 other special districts existed.

State

The US Constitution designates all powers not given to the federal government to the states and the people, including those not even thought of yet. The United States is comprised of 50 states, so 50 state governments exist; however, there are also two state-level governments operating in the Commonwealth of Puerto Rico and Washington, DC.

States are seen as the laboratories of government whereby they test out new ideas on governance without negatively impacting the rest of the country. The term comes from Supreme Court Justice Louis D. Brandeis, who declared in a 1932 court opinion 'that a single courageous state may, if its citizens choose, serve as a laboratory; and try novel social and economic experiments without risk to the rest of the country'. This attitude is particularly evident in controversial examples whereby some states (whether by proposed legislation in the state legislature or by popular vote in a referendum) are willing to make changes that other states do not want to make. Recent examples include the legalisation of marijuana in the states of Colorado and Washington in 2014, and the decision by some states to legalise same-sex marriage. Interestingly, a consequence of the legalisation of marijuana is a battle between the powers of the federal and state governments because it's still illegal to supply and purchase marijuana under federal law even though doing so is legal by state law.

State governments are modelled similarly to the federal government system. Thus there's an executive, legislature and judiciary (although Washington, DC, is an exception as it only has an elected mayor and a council with 13 elected members). Similar to the federal system, these three branches provide checks and balances for each other to ensure that no one branch dominates the political system. Each state also has its own constitution (except Washington, DC, as it's a special case), which determines how its government should run, including how the three branches should interact with each other. These three branches are:

- ✓ **Executive branch:** The top executive official is the governor, who shares executive power with a number of other officials, including the lieutenant governor (second-in-command), secretary of state (business and election official), attorney general (chief legal officer who prosecutes those who violate commercial law), treasurer (runs the state's finances) and commissioner of agriculture (promotes state produce and ensures safety in the industry). All governors are elected through popular vote (typically every four years); the other positions are elected in some states and appointed in others. These officials have similar roles and responsibilities to those in the federal government, such as the Secretary of the Treasury. They run all state programmes, such as those pertaining to medical care and education (which is then devolved to the local level, as described above), as well as regulate industry. In most states, the governor has the executive power to veto legislation proposed by the state legislature, issue executive orders, develop a state budget, make executive appointments and issue pardons to people in prison, including commuting death sentences.

✔ **Legislative branch:** Each state has its own legislature wherein the elected members can propose bills to become law, raise taxes and receive proposals for legislation from the governor. It plays the same role as does the legislature in the federal system, and all bar Nebraska (which just has one) has two chambers: an upper chamber called the Senate and a lower chamber called the House of Representatives, the Assembly or the House of Delegates. State senators usually serve four-year terms in office and state representatives usually two-year terms. The legislatures also approve the budget for the state and have the power to impeach officials.

✔ **Judiciary:** This system deals with state constitutional issues and statutes (laws made by the legislative assembly), as well as US constitutional issues and statutes. The kinds of cases heard by these courts include most criminal cases, personal injuries, family law (marriage, divorce and so on), and most contract and probate (wills and estates of dead people) cases. The state court system is similarly designed to that of the federal system in that it comprises a court of last appeal (usually called a supreme court), a court of appeal (which reviews all decisions made by the lower court) and a trial court (which first hears all criminal and civil cases). This system deals with most cases that come to court in the United States and is very busy. About 30 million cases are heard each year by 30,000 state judges (see Chapter 6 on the American court system for further details).

Federal

Unlike the multiple numbers of local and state governments, only one federal government exists. And its role is to run not just one small geographic location but the entire country. It's a big task.

Fighting taxation without representation in DC

Residents of the District of Columbia (also known as Washington, DC, or just DC) hold a unique position in the US in terms of political representation. DC is the capital of the US, but under the Constitution it was named a federal district and as such is neither a state in its own right nor a part of any other state.

This position has led to some legal anomalies, the most controversial of which is that DC has no representation in the US Senate, and has one delegate in the House of Representatives. Not surprisingly, a great many of its nearly 650,000 inhabitants are pretty unhappy about this situation. Given that these residents pay one of the highest federal tax rates in the country, the fact that they do not get to have a say on how this money is spent must be especially galling.

Whilst nobody claims that the current situation is ideal, the sticking point has been that no administration can agree on how it should be changed. Various options, including granting DC the status of a state, making it part of Maryland, or amending the Constitution have been debated without successful conclusion. The discussion has been rumbling on since the late 1700s, with the most recent failed attempt to change it with legislation under the Obama administration in 2009. Then, as many times before, a bill ground to a halt amidst multiple amendments and legal arguments.

Meanwhile, the people of DC are becoming ever more frustrated. They've adopted the slogan "No taxation without representation" (originally used by the patriots in the American Revolution) to promote their cause. This slogan is seen on the licence plates of cars across the district, including President Obama's limousine. Campaigners have demanded that residents are exempt from paying federal taxes until the situation is resolved.

The population of DC is growing faster than that of any state in the US, bar North Dakota. Having recently passed Vermont in terms of population size, DC is now larger than six states. Some have argued that the rapid population expansion will soon put pay to any arguments that DC is too small to be granted statehood, or that the lack of representation can continue indefinitely. Watch this space.

In short, the federal political system operates like a bigger version of each state system, with an executive, legislative and judicial branch, plus a constitution to dictate how the whole thing functions. (Chapter 2 gives further details on how the American federal system should operate.) The three branches carry out important functions to support the operation of running the country, including keeping an eye on each other to ensure they act in accordance with the Constitution. The federal government is responsible for:

✔ **Executing laws:** The federal bureaucracy 'faithfully executes' the laws given to the Executive Office under Article II, Section 3 of the Constitution, laws which are made by Congress. The Internal Revenue

Service, for example, is told by Congress what federal taxes can be collected and carries out duties to fulfil this obligation.

- **Creating rules:** Congress writes the laws but because the departments and other federal agencies are seen as the experts, they're responsible for writing the rules that guide how the laws are executed. The United States Agency for International Development (USAID), for example, is told by Congress it must implement development and democratisation programmes around the world, but the department determines what they look like and who they employ to carry out these tasks.

- **Adjudication:** Different groups can be in dispute regarding their interpretation of the same bureaucratic regulations. In these instances, they can petition the federal agency involved, which then itself becomes an adjudicator and determines the outcome. The National Labor Relations Board, for example, can adjudicate a dispute between the workforce and management.

To carry out those functions, the federal government is organised into five elements:

- **Executive Office of the President:** Overseen by the president's Chief of Staff, this office provides the president with the support he needs to make executive decisions. Its remit ranges from promoting US trade interests throughout the world to providing advice on national security. Currently 11 principal offices exist, including the White House Office. This last office is the most comprehensive and includes a whole other sub-series of offices such as the Office of Legislative Affairs and the Domestic Policy Council, which are responsible for giving advice on areas such as: issues of immigration policy, health policy, or rural or urban affairs.

- **Executive departments:** These are cabinet-level offices and are headed up by a secretary who is appointed by the president and confirmed by the Senate. Each of the departments concentrates on particular policy areas and has its own budget and staff. Fifteen cabinet-level departments exist (and their titles are pretty self-explanatory):

  - Agriculture

  - Commerce

  - Defense

  - Education

- Energy

- Health and Human Services

- Homeland Security

- Housing and Urban Development

- Interior (responsible for looking after the land, wildlife, water, and energy resources and for managing relations with tribal nations within the US)

- Justice

- Labor

- State

- Transportation

- Treasury

- Veterans Affairs

✔ **Independent executive agencies:** These agencies usually perform specialised functions, and are independent from executive control. They include the Central Intelligence Agency (CIA), which operates to protect the US from international threats.

✔ **Independent regulatory agencies:** These agencies also perform specialised duties by administering laws and regulating important industries and businesses that affect the public. They're typically run by a board or commission of people, and are independent from presidential influence. They include the Environmental Protection Agency (EPA), which protects human health and the natural environment by making and enforcing environmental laws, and the Federal Trade Commission (FTC), which regulates business practices and monopolies. It also includes the National Labor Relations Board detailed above.

✔ **Government corporations:** These are legal entities established by the federal government to provide public services. They're commercial, for-profit enterprises completely independent from government, although they may receive federal funding as well as charge for services in order to operate. They include the National Railroad Passenger Corporation, otherwise known as Amtrak, which is the railroad service, and the US Postal Service.

Considering Criticisms of Government Bureaucracy

As we expect the tide to come in and go out, we can equally guarantee that with government comes significant problems in administering its decisions. *Bureaucracy* is the part of government that is responsible for ensuring that the system operates; it runs the services that clean our streets and our schools, and ensures we pay our taxes. It is effectively everything in government that is not an elected official. Over the course of human history, people have complained about bureaucratic organisations, and the US government is no exception. Experts have ruminated over the problems of the American system, and it is possible to reduce them to seven key criticisms, which hold true at the local, state and federal levels.

- **Expanding nature of bureaucracy:** This refers to the tendency of departments and agencies to want to expand their powers and responsibilities to ensure their continued existence. The knock-on effect is that they'll expand unnecessarily if not kept in-check and the costs of administering them will mushroom.

- **Excessive regulation:** This means that too much red tape (bureaucratic regulations) hinders people's and businesses' ability to go about their daily activities. This situation has a negative impact on entrepreneurialism and can lead to unnecessary rules, regulations and paperwork.

- **Too narrow focus:** Departments fail to see the bigger picture and concentrate on fulfilling their own objectives at the expense of good governance.

- **Confused loyalties:** Departments can sometime end up protecting the interests of those they're supposed to regulate and oversee rather than the interests of the public.

- **Slow-moving beasts:** Typical of all types of government operation, whether legislative or bureaucratic, departments move and respond to changes slowly, which may cause the public to feel frustrated because solutions to problems and new initiatives aren't implemented quickly enough.

- **Responding to averages:** Perhaps understandably due to the size of operations, departments implement rules and regulate industries based on abstracts and generalisations. This approach can sometimes, however, fail to account for individual cases.

✔ **Waste:** Perhaps one of the biggest negative perceptions of government bureaucracy is the inefficiency caused by its large size. The problem is unnecessary spending on goods or services, which is partly a product of the other factors mentioned in this list and partly the result of incompetence. Departments also often work at cross-purposes and duplicate activities, which causes further inefficiencies.

To varying degrees, all of these problems with bureaucracy exist in all the layers of US government, and the degree of intensity is dependent on a whole range of variables including the attitude of the elected officials to reduce these problems, and the capacity and desire by the organisations to resolve them.

Some critics of American bureaucracy are motivated to escalate how problematic a government department or agency is in order to promote their own political agenda. So a problem to one group may not be a problem to another group.

Understanding Opposition to Large Government

Government at the local, state and federal levels is big business. In March 2012, taken together the three levels of government employed approximately 22 million people. When you consider that about 243.7 million Americans were eligible to work in 2012 (all statistics in this section are taken from the US Bureau of Labor Statistics), that's nearly 10 per cent of the eligible working population. For the sake of comparison, 10.8 per cent of those eligible to work in the UK do so in the public sector.

When you consider that figure, 243.7 million people, you can understand why the size of government is criticised. When you consider the range of tasks that all three levels of government carry out, however, it's more understandable. And perhaps even that number of people isn't enough, when you consider that they're responsible for road maintenance to making laws, to educating children and to maintaining the nation's gas supply.

Another question can obviously be raised here, and that's whether or not governments should be responsible for all these tasks. Those opposed to large government think that it's grown too much over the course of US history (for details on what conservatives think, on a range of issues, see Chapter 10 on the two-party system and Chapter 14 on divisions in American society). A Pew Research Center poll conducted in September 2012 revealed that 56 per cent of those questioned would rather have a smaller government providing fewer services and 35 per cent would prefer the reverse. According to Gallup in 2013, Americans explain their support for smaller government by saying they see big government as the greatest threat to the future of the United States when compared with the power of big business and large trade unions. Of those polled, 72 per cent felt this way; in 1965, only 35 per cent did so.

According to Pew, in early 2013, 63 per cent of those polled said they had a 'favourable' opinion of their local government; this view has been fairly consistent for the last 16 years. In relation to state government, 57 per cent expressed a 'favourable' opinion, which was a 5 per cent increase from the year before. But only 28 per cent took a 'favourable' view of federal government. Broken down into party allegiance, attitudes to the federal government are drastically different. Figure 9-1 shows you how those attitudes break down.

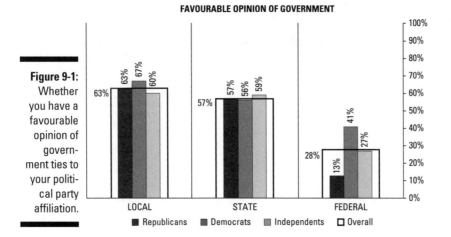

Figure 9-1: Whether you have a favourable opinion of government ties to your political party affiliation.

These views may be seen as surprising, particularly when you consider the fact that nearly 88 per cent of the government workforce is employed at the state and local levels. I'd expect attitudes toward local and state government to be just as negative, if not worse, than those directed at the federal level because that's where people interact most with the system. Opposition to large federal government may thus be seen as cultural, tracing its roots back to the founding of the nation.

Anti-federal-government sentiment is the legacy of a number of factors:

- ✔ The founding fathers opposed absolutist rule of a single all-powerful state, which helped foster an obsession with supporting state rights and individualism.

- ✔ This obsession was reinforced with the ratification of the Bill of Rights (1791), which was introduced to counter government excesses.

- ✔ Over time, cultural mistrust of the bureaucratic arms of the federal government, such as the FBI, developed.

- ✔ The expansion of large government, which started with President Roosevelt's New Deal and the introduction of federal programmes to respond to the Great Depression in the 1930s and continued during President Johnson's Great Society initiative in the 1960s (see Chapter 11 for more details), has helped feed the mythology that small government is better than large and that government should retreat from interfering in the rights of the individual.

- ✔ Coupled with a system of economic liberalism that favours private enterprise over public bodies (as a result of the latter's perceived over-burdening oversight and regulation of business), these points create a potent mix of anti-federal-government feeling as a legitimate counter to large government.

Part III
Glimpsing Elections and Political Parties

Looking Into Voting Behaviour

- In the past four presidential elections going back to 2000, the number of those eligible to vote who did vote has fluctuated from a low of 50 per cent in 2000 to a high of 57 per cent in 2008. In 2012, it had gone down to near 53 per cent.

- In Congressional mid-term elections (those years when no presidential election occurs), the numbers of those eligible who actually vote is significantly smaller at around 38 per cent.

- For comparison's sake, the UK has had somewhat of a decline since the 1992 general election. In 1992, nearly 78 per cent of those eligible to vote did, and by 2001 it had gone down to nearly 60 per cent; it was up again to 65 per cent in 2010. However, if you look at the European Parliament elections held in the UK, the voter turnout was significantly lower at just over 34 per cent.

- The 2011 national election in Canada drew 61 per cent of voters.

- And in Australia, the figures are completely different because voting in the national elections has been compulsory for over 70 years. Whilst about 10 per cent of Australians who are eligible do not register to vote, turnout among those who do is consistently in the early 80s. It certainly ensures that the outcome of the elections is based on the will of nearly all those eligible to vote as opposed to those who can choose whether to vote.

Get the details about which political party dominated which election at www. dummies.com/extras/americanpoliticsuk.

In This Part . . .

✔ Find out about the electoral process in America. Representative democracy can get a lot more complicated than 'who gets the most votes'.

✔ Grasp the role of political parties in American politics, and trace the emergence of the two main political parties.

✔ Look into voting, including who's more likely to vote according to factors like age, education, gender and race.

✔ Investigate the role of interest groups and the media on politics.

Chapter 10

Working through the Electoral Process

. . . .

In This Chapter

▶ Discussing the prolific number of elections for people to vote in

▶ Breaking the elections down to the local, state and federal levels

▶ Working out what the Electoral College system is all about

▶ Understanding how presidents are chosen by their parties and how they're elected

▶ Exploring Congressional elections and how candidates are chosen and elected

▶ Working out how districts are redrawn and the possibility for gerrymandering

. . . .

*T*he United States of America is a *republic*, which means that the power of the state is held by the people, and that they elect other people to represent them in government. Free and fair elections provide the cornerstone of America's identity. What is good about the electorate choosing government officials is that if an official is no good at his job then he can be booted out in the next election, and if he is good at his job then he gets re-elected.

This chapter first discusses the various local, state and federal elections and how many elections are held, and then goes into much more detail on the make-up of contemporary federal Congressional and presidential elections.

Sorry, How Many Elections Did You Say?

According to the US Census Bureau, 90,056 different local governments existed in the United States in 2012; add to that the 50 state governments, the Commonwealth of Puerto Rico and Washington, DC and the federal government, and you have 90,108 different governments in the US. That's a lot of governments. At each level are various government positions that are elected by the popular vote within that constituency. Whatever one says about the United States, you can't say people don't get the opportunity to choose who they want to run government for them.

Nearly all US elections, whether at the local, state or federal level, are governed by the principle of first past the post: the candidate with the most votes wins the election. Thus they have to literally get just one more vote than the runner up to get the job. The American presidential election, however, is organised slightly differently. It's first past the post but divided into states and mediated through an Electoral College (see 'The Electoral College system' section later in this chapter for details).

Local

Local governments are split into four different levels, each of which has a series of elected positions (Chapter 9 gives further details on the breakdown of local government):

- ✔ At the county level, you find a number of elected officials ranging from commissioners who are legislative members for the county government (similar to local councillors in the UK) to district attorneys to county sheriffs. Typically, these officials serve for four-year terms before the position is up for re-election.

- ✔ The township level is a subdivision of the county, and includes elected officials, named *supervisors*, who run the area. They typically serve six-year terms and are responsible for implementing county-made *ordinances* (legislation) for the township, including those relating to:

    - Public works (rubbish collection, road maintenance and so on)

    - Economic development

    - Police and fire services

    - Parks and recreation facilities

    Although not directly elected by the entire electorate in a township but rather through political party primaries, township committeemen and -women play an important role. They're part of the local community and so can best represent the needs of the local people. They usually serve four-year terms.

- ✔ At the municipal level, the chief official is usually an elected mayor; a board of councillors serves as legislators and is in charge of running all public services in the area. Other elected officials can include the chief of police (who runs the police service) or the city clerk (who's in charge of record-keeping and organising council meetings). These positions are usually four-year terms.

Three types of electoral system exist for the council and mayoral positions:

- The *at-large* election is held in one ballot representing the entire area.
- A *district* election is held in a series of sub-divisions of the municipality.
- The *mixed-system* election is a combination of the first two.

✔ At the special district level, elected officials work on running particular areas of government such as schools, weed control (a very important position in the community!) and hospitals. These positions are usually four-year terms and elected by a popular vote.

State

State governments are mini-versions of the federal government in terms of responsibilities to the people who live within them and in terms of administrative organisation. For each of the 50 states, a separate government exists, as is true for the six other state-like administrative areas such as the territories of Puerto Rico and Guam.

Of the state legislatures, 49 are *bicameral* (they have an upper and a lower house), as is the Commonwealth of Puerto Rico, Northern Mariana Islands and American Samoa, while one state is *unicameral* (Nebraska has only one legislative chamber), as are the territories of the Virgin Islands and Guam. Washington, DC, is more like a municipal assembly than a state legislature in that it has a 13-strong council and an elected mayor; however, because of its position of prominence in the American political system, I've afforded it state-like status.

All 50 states are run by a chief executive called a *governor*. In most states a governor is elected to run for four-year terms and can only serve two terms.

In most states, the Senators are elected every four years, with half being elected at each election, and the Representatives elected every two years with all seats being up for election. Most states are also divided up into districts for the elected officials to represent, although in Nebraska, for example, with only one chamber, the Senators are voted in on four-year terms but one district covers the whole state.

Federal

The government of all governments has the big cheese president and the big guns in Congress. A presidential election is held every four years and, correspondingly, all seats in the House of Representatives and one-third of Senate seats are up for election. In the mid-terms (the two years in front and behind an election when the presidency is up), all the House seats are up for election along with another third of the Senate seats.

Presidential Elections

Running for the presidency is a big job in itself, let alone winning and then running the country. A presidential campaign is big business, employing thousands of people involving jobs ranging from social media expert to pollster to campaign speechwriter. Everything a candidate does, says or writes is meticulously debated and analysed – from the candidate's political platform to which haircut presents an image that appeals most to the electorate. And despite all that attention to detail, epic failures still occur (to the delight of opponents and the media).

Electoral College system

The *Electoral College* (EC) is a college unlike any other in the United States – it's not a place but a process by which 538 *electors* representing the states and allotted by population cast votes (based on the popular vote) to determine who serves as president. The people do not directly choose the president; their choice is mediated though the electors. And that doesn't always work so smoothly. Each elector gets one vote; each state is guaranteed at least three electors – one for each Senate seat (all states have two Senators) and one for each Representative. But that brings the total to only 535. The three extra electors are from Washington, DC.

Figure 10-1 gives you further details on the breakdown of the electors per state.

The electors are chosen by the political parties to represent their presidential candidate running in the general election. Electors are typically chosen in recognition of their dedication to the party and are identified either at a state party convention or by the state party's central committee. The voters in each state will then choose the electors who are supporting a particular candidate.

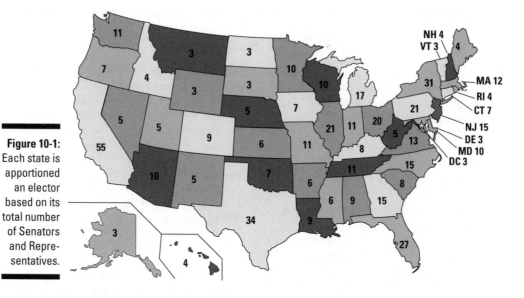

Figure 10-1:
Each state is apportioned an elector based on its total number of Senators and Representatives.

In the 2012 presidential election, if a voter from Texas wanted to vote for the Republican Mitt Romney she'd tick the box for Romney. That vote would then be awarded to Romney. If Romney won the majority of votes in Texas, which he did, the 38 electors nominated by the Republicans and not the 38 nominated by the Democrats would be appointed as official state electors and Romney would get the 38 EC votes.

Typically, if the candidate wins a state by popular vote, he gets all the votes from that state. The exceptions to this rule are Nebraska and Maine. In these two states, a variant of proportional representation is employed whereby more than one candidate can be given electoral votes from one state. A candidate can win the popular vote of the whole state and get EC votes but another candidate can win one of the three Congressional districts in Nebraska, for example, and get one of the five EC votes.

Effectively, the American citizens vote and whoever wins the popular vote in that state wins the EC votes of the electors. Because the candidates aren't directly elected by the people, the presidential election is often referred to as an *indirect* election.

Crazy as it sounds, no federal laws and nothing in in the Constitution forbids an elector from disregarding the will of the people and giving their vote to a different presidential candidate of their own choice. (These dissenters are called *faithless electors* – see 'The faithless elector' sidebar for more on these.) However, just over half of all states do require electors to faithfully represent the popular vote. If they're unfaithful they can be fined and replaced by an elector who will.

The faithless elector

Since the US Constitution was ratified in 1791, 157 *faithless electors* have voted in contradiction to the popular vote. Of these, 71 were a consequence of the candidate having died after the election but before the electors cast their votes and refused to vote for a dead person, three electors abstained altogether from voting and 82 electors changed their votes based on their personal views.

In some cases a contradictory vote is a matter of error and not an act of rebellion. In 2004, an anonymous Democrat from Minnesota was supposed to vote for the Democratic Party candidate, John Kerry, in the general election but ended up voting for John Edwards – the Democratic Party candidate for vice president, as well as voting for Edwards for vice president.

More often, a faithless elector is making a statement. In the 2000 presidential election between Bush and Gore, another Democrat (Barbara Lett-Simmons), this time from Washington, DC, abstained from voting in order to highlight the lack of Congressional representation that district. And in the 1988 presidential election between the Republican Bush Senior and the Democrat Michael Dukakis, Democrat elector Margaret Leach from West Virginia, apparently to expose the problems of the Electoral College, transposed her nominees for the president and vice president and thus voted Lloyd Bentsen for president and Dukakis for vice president. In the 1976 presidential election between Republican Gerald Ford and Democrat Jimmy Carter, Mike Padden from Washington was supposed to vote for Ford, as he'd won the popular vote in the state; however, he voted Ronald Reagan for president just because he wanted to and could, even though Reagan wasn't in the general election. Reagan had lost in the Republican primaries (see below for an explanation of a primary election) to Ford. Fortunately, he did manage to get the vice president right (Robert Dole). These electors weren't punished.

Political parties can also request that electors pledge to follow the popular vote, although this happens in only a handful of states. Fines and pledges are pretty powerful tools of persuasion because the elector is typically a well-respected political party member, state-elected official or someone who has a connection with one of the presidential candidates. No faithless elector has ever been prosecuted. In fact, only a few faithless votes have occurred in American electoral history. The possibility of swinging an election still remains, however, but is improbable.

Because the EC vote is mainly a *winner-takes-all* proposition, those votes tend to over-inflate the size of the victory for the winning candidate in that state. Technically speaking, a candidate who wins 50.1 per cent of the vote in enough states to win 270 EC votes and thus secure the White House but loses by 99.9 per cent in the other states would still win, even though she may have only a small percentage of the overall popular vote. At various times in US history, the winner of the presidential election has actually received fewer popular votes than the loser. The most recent example was Democrat presidential candidate Al Gore, who won 48.4 per cent of the popular vote while the Republican winner, George Bush, received 47.9 per cent.

A step-by-step guide to presidential elections

The political party plays an important role in every stage of a presidential campaign, from organising the primary elections to raising money for the successful presidential candidate, to supporting him in the general election. Because two political parties dominate the American political landscape, voters are in large part electing a party as much as they're electing an individual to serve.

I discuss the process as it's carried out by the two main political parties (Republicans and Democrats), but it's also applicable to others. Ralph Nader, the Green Party candidate in the 2000 election, was nominated at a national convention just as George Bush and Al Gore were.

You do run into some wild cards in American presidential elections. Independent candidates – those who don't represent a party – can skip the primaries and party conventions because they fund their own candidacies, as Ross Perot did in 1992 and 1996. Hey, it's a free country!

Candidate decides to run

A candidate might announce her intention to run up to two years before the election, but usually it's much closer to election time, as she doesn't want the fizz in her decision to fizzle before the race has even started. Candidates often play coy up until the last moment, neither confirming nor denying that they're going to run. Doing so brings up a lot of spin and interest in the candidate; as I write this, tremendous media attention is focused on whether Hilary Clinton is going to run in the 2016 primaries for the Democratic candidate.

Pre-primary phase

The principal aim in the pre-primary phase is to develop name recognition for the candidate so that he's not lost in the sea of contending candidates. Most candidates file papers stating that they wish to create an *exploratory committee panel*, which is a way of setting the tone for their election platform and seeing whether sufficient interest can be gathered by organisations such as trade unions and businesses, donors and the public. The more support they receive, the more money they get; the more media discussion they generate, the more money they get. Of course, a candidate who garners no money or support initially often has a change of heart about running. This phase usually gets going a year or so before the party primaries.

Primaries and caucuses

In each state, party members (or sometimes just interested outsiders) get a chance to have a say about who they'd like to run for their party in the presidential election. Different parties (and different states) have various ways of organising the processes by which this happens. In general, a *primary* is a statewide election open to all voters or voters registered to the party, and a *caucus* is a meeting of party members in which that state's pick for presidential candidate is chosen.

A delegate is a member of a political party and represents a particular presidential candidate in the state where the primary or caucus is being held. The delegates then go to the national conventions to officially nominate the presidential candidate who won that election.

Primaries

Because primaries are official party elections, they have to run according to the rules and regulations of the local and state governments, not the party. The Democratic Party uses *proportional representation* in all its primaries. If Candidate A in a state that has 10 delegates gets 70 per cent of the primary votes, she gets seven delegates; if Candidate B gets 20 per cent, he gets two delegates. The Republican Party follows proportional representation in some states but in others uses a *winner-takes-all* system whereby, if the state has 10 delegates to the convention and Candidate A gets 55 per cent of the vote and Candidate B gets 40 per cent, Candidate A gets all 10 delegates.

Primaries can be *open* or *closed*:

- ✔ An open primary is when registered voters are able to vote in any party primary in the state they live in irrespective of what political party they belong to (but they cannot vote in any other primary for that election).

- ✔ A closed primary is one in which only members of that political party can vote in that party's primaries.

Caucuses

Because caucuses are run by the state political party, election laws don't apply, and so the rules on voting don't have to be so stringent. Caucuses are open to registered members of the political party and involve meetings in the various subdivisions of a state (that is at the local, county and the state levels – see Chapter 9 for further details on these subdivisions).

A series of local caucuses is held on a particular day within a state. In Iowa, for example, about 800 were held for the Republican Party 2012 presidential caucus. In some meetings, members of the party debate why their preferred candidate should be supported by the attendees; these conversations can get pretty lively. In other meetings, members simply write the name of their preferred presidential nominee on a piece of paper.

At this local level, the delegates who represent those presidential candidates who have support above a 15 per cent threshold then go to the next level of the party's presidential caucus, the county level. If, however, supporters of a candidate don't have a viable number (above 15 per cent), they have the opportunity to join another group and boost the number of delegates that preferred candidate gets to carry over to the county caucus.

In Iowa, in 2012, the Republicans had 99 county conventions. At the county convention these delegates then choose their preferred presidential candidates who go to the next stage, the state convention. At the state convention the preferred presidential candidate for the state's political party is known when its delegates are chosen to represent the state at the national convention.

Most states legally bind their delegates to vote for the candidate who wins that state primary at the national convention. However, just to confuse matters further, some delegates at the national convention are *unpledged,* meaning that they do not have a pledge to a particular presidential candidate (called *unpledged*) in the same way that the other, *pledged* delegates, do. A particular kind of unpledged delegate is called a *superdelegate*. These delegates tend to be the big players in the political parties and are a way for the party to exert influence over decisions. In the 2012 presidential national conventions, for example, the Democrats had 794 superdelegates out of 4,090 and the Republicans had 463 unpledged delegates with 123 of them being members of the Republican National Committee.

To win the party's nomination, a candidate needs to gain over half of all the delegates sent to the national convention; in 2012, the Republican Party candidate needed 1,144 of the 2,286 delegates and the Democratic Party candidate needed 2,778 of 4,047.

If one of the candidates drops out of the race, the delegates they've already secured can go to another candidate, either by the determination of the delegates themselves or by the departing candidate. The primary and caucus season usually runs from January to June of the election year.

National party conventions

A *national party convention* is where all the delegates from the state party conventions get to meet and decide who will be their presidential candidate in the upcoming general election. Historically, the national party conventions played dominant roles in deciding who got selected as the party's candidate in the general election.

The convention is now the place for the candidate to formally accept the nomination, to introduce her vice president running mate and to let the electorate and the party faithful know her political agenda for the upcoming general election.

Conventions are broadcast live on TV. They've become carefully managed packages that include keynote speakers to inspire Americans to support the party's political platform and speeches delivered by the presidential and vice presidential nominees.

The federal government gives funding to the parties to both host and provide security for their conventions. In 2012, for example, the federal government provided nearly $18 million each for the Democrat and Republican conventions, and in the 2004 and 2008 conventions $50 million was appropriated by Congress to pay for the security at each party's convention alone. However, parties cannot raise or spend additional money on the convention, and they have to account for all that they spend.

Conventions are big business, and they usually run in either August or September right before the start of the general election.

General election

After the party candidates have been chosen, the internal battles among different members of the same party are over, and it's time for the parties to battle against each other. They do some major battling. Campaigning is an intense and costly business: the 2012 presidential election was the most expensive campaign in US history.

The Obama team, the national Democratic Party and the aligned but independent PACS and super PACS (*political action committees* – see Chapter 12 for further details) raised a little over $1 billion and spent most of that on the general election because as an incumbent Obama faced no primary challengers.

The Romney team, the national Republican Party and the aligned but independent PACS and super PACS raised just under $1 billion but spent more on the primaries than Obama as a result of a competitive primary season.

The spending of nearly $2 billion in the space of a few months is difficult to comprehend, and it certainly isn't distributed evenly around the country. As a result of the Electoral College system and the need for the candidate to receive 270 EC votes to obtain victory, the campaign teams focus predominantly on those states that could swing either way. Voting history and demographics show that the Republicans will almost certainly win Texas, for example, and so there's no point in putting the same amount of resources into that state as they would in Ohio or Florida, where the gap between the two parties is marginal.

Furthermore, Ohio is worth 18 EC votes and Florida 29 – a grand total of 47 votes out of the 270 needed. Because they carry a lot of weight and could go either way in any given election cycle, Ohio and Florida draw considerable interest and funding for good reason.

The big-money campaigns and the intricacies of the Electoral College necessitate a very sophisticated campaign election strategy. A campaign team will have focus groups to test out different candidate positions on key issues, cadres of volunteers knocking on doors and calling people on the phone persuading them to vote for their candidate (or at least not vote for the other candidate!) and databases providing various types of information on people so that they can be targeted with direct mail on issues they think are of importance to that possible voter.

Each party's electoral strategy involves the presidential and vice presidential candidates touring the country attending money-raising events, talking to people and giving speeches on key issues. Three live (TV, radio and internet) debates are held between the presidential candidates and one between the vice presidential candidates. One presidential debate tends to focus on domestic policy, one on foreign policy and one covers both issues; the vice presidential debate focuses on a combination of domestic and foreign issues. About 60 million people watch each of the presidential debates and about 50 million the vice presidential debate. And if you consider that the US population is about 318 million, those are significant numbers.

Congressional Elections

Congressional elections for the House of Representatives and the Senate are much more similar to UK, Canadian and Australian parliamentary elections than they are to the American presidential election.

For a start, Congressional elections give the electorate the opportunity to directly vote for the candidates they want. There is no mediating EC that gets in the way of their decision. They also are similar in that they're national elections voted on at a local level; those eligible to vote must reside in a sub-national geographic location. For the Senate, the sub-national is the state level and has 100 voting members, two members per state. The House of Representatives has 435 voting members from the 50 states and six non-voting members from Washington, DC, and the territories of American Samoa, Guam, Northern Mariana, Puerto Rico and the US Virgin Islands.

A step-by-step guide to Congressional elections

Similar to presidential elections, Congressional elections can be broken into a number of different phases. Unlike a presidential election, they happen *without* dizzying amounts of capital – or interest beyond the state or district.

Candidate decides to run

Before a person becomes a candidate, she generally comes to be well-regarded in the local community. A number of Congressional candidates have been members of the state Senate or House of Representatives. It provides them with the experience and name recognition to run for a higher office. It was, for example, President Obama's position as an Illinois state Senator from 1997–2004 that got him into a position to challenge for an Illinois House of Representative's seat in 2000 (which he lost) and a Senator's seat in 2004 (which he won).

Candidate seeks endorsements

A new candidate generally takes some time to continue building his reputation and meeting people in his community, seeking further endorsements and campaign funding from important local people and businesses.

Party nominates candidate

Most states choose their candidate through a primary, which is similar to the presidential primaries in that they're run by the government (in this case the State Board of Elections) and involve a vote to determine who wins the nomination. Depending on the state, the specifics of these votes take different shapes.

In the Virginia, for example, the Republican Party can choose its candidates in four main ways:

- The primary process as outlined above

- A convention that enables the selection of delegates who then choose which candidates to put forward to the Congressional general election

- Holding a mass meeting, which involves attendees voting at the end of the meeting for their preferred candidate

- Running a party canvass (otherwise known as a *firehouse primary*), which allows attendees to arrive during a particular opening time and then cast their vote for their preferred candidate

In addition to state-by-state differences, the major parties add further wrinkles to nominating strategies. In 2014, the Democratic Party in Virginia's 10th District had a two-week caucus period wherein 300 delegates were chosen by attendees, and these delegates then got to nominate the party's House of Representative nominee for the general election at the nominating convention. This nomination period starts around March in the general election year and can go all the way through to just before the start of the general election in September.

General election

After they're nominated, candidates have all the support from their state and national party, and they have their own election team. That team includes people working similarly to the presidential campaign teams, performing such tasks as

- Developing targeted election material for constituents

- Making radio and TV campaign spots

- Writing campaign speeches for the candidates

The key differences between Congressional and presidential campaign teams are the size of the team required and the amount of resources required to fund the campaign, and these differences arise from the fact that a Senate race is statewide and a House of Representatives race takes place within a district. The average funding for a House race in 2012 was about $1.7 million and for a Senate race around $10.5 million. In the same year, the most a successful House candidate raised was nearly $26 million (Republican Michelle Bachmann) and the most a successful Senate candidate raised was $42.5 million (Democrat Elizabeth Warren). While access to large amounts of money doesn't guarantee victory, it does ensure the candidate has the best chance possible.

Incumbents, challengers and open elections

After you find yourself in Congress, you have a pretty good chance of sticking around – that is, unless you're really incompetent, unlucky or both. Since 1964, the rate of incumbent members of the House gaining re-election has never gone below 85 per cent. It was

- 90 per cent in 2012
- 85 per cent in 2010
- 94 per cent in 2008

In the Senate, re-election of incumbents isn't so high but is still pretty comprehensive. In the same time period it dipped to 55 per cent in 1980 but ever since then the lowest re-election rate was 75 per cent in 1988. In the past three elections, it was

- 91 per cent in 2012
- 84 per cent in 2010
- 83 per cent in 2008

When no incumbent exists (a situation called an *open election*), the race between the candidates is much closer. Those who challenge incumbents clearly have an uphill battle because after someone has been elected, they have a lot of advantages that contribute to remaining in office. Five key interlocking factors help explain incumbency advantage:

- **Developing a strong network:** The daily life of an incumbent (see Chapter 5 on Congress for more details) involves meeting local people and business owners, representing local interests and appearing on the radio and being interviewed. Running an election campaign also involves these duties and so an incumbent will find them much easier than will an opponent.

- **Benefits of being in Congress:** As a member of Congress the candidate has an office team in both Washington, DC, and her home state, which means she can represent her constituents on two levels. By doing a good job and connecting to constituents, the incumbent increases her chances of people wanting to vote for her again. Travel allowances help the member to regularly reach out to all the people and businesses in her constituency. Congresspeople also get free postage on constituent-based leaflets illustrating how great they are and what they've done for people in the district or state, which go a long way in persuading people to vote for them again.

✔ **Previous campaign experience:** Having already won one election, candidates have a pretty good idea about what works and what doesn't. Just as important, they already have a campaign team they can build on.

✔ **Local exposure:** An incumbent in the House has been in office for at least two years (unless a special election was held as a result of the death or resignation of the previous office holder) and a member of the Senate six years. It means that they've pressed plenty of palms, made connections with lots of important people, been on the airwaves a few times, written newspaper articles and hopefully helped out local constituents and businesses. Thus, unless they've done something to upset the locals, they should have positive name recognition, which means that the constituents already have an idea of where they stand on important issues – they're a known entity.

✔ **Capacity to raise money:** Money is an important tool for winning an election. Unlike presidential elections, no federal funding is available for members of Congress; it must be drawn through raising funding from donors, individual contributions from the electorate, self-financing for those who can afford it, support from PACs and super PACs and from the national and state political party committees. And sitting members of Congress have an advantage over any other candidate whether in the primaries or in the general election because they're more likely to receive funds as a result of their status as an incumbent – donors recognise that they're more likely to win the election.

Re-districting and gerrymandering

A *district* is a geographical space in a state that determines which administrative region a citizen's vote is counted in the local, state and federal elections. Re-districting is an important process in ensuring that the state legislative districts and the Congressional districts provide an even distribution of people so that one district doesn't hold a disproportionate degree of power regarding the number of people it represents. However, it also can be manipulated so that elections favour the party in charge.

The decision on whether to redraw a district is based on the US national census held every 10 years. In the 2010 census, for example, four more House of Representative seats were given to Texas for the 2012 elections because the percentage of people living in that state compared to elsewhere in the country had increased. (Chapter 5 gives you a complete rundown of seat changes). Because there's more than just one House seat in most states, and those seats are divided into districts that a member represents, it means when new seats are added those districts have to be redrawn to take the new ones into account. If a seat is added somewhere then a seat must be taken from elsewhere, and thus redrawing has to take place there, too.

Re-districting gives rise to the problem of gerrymandering. To *gerrymander* is to redraw the boundaries between the districts for state and national Congressional elections to benefit one political party over another and ensure that the district maintains a healthy majority of electorate that supports them in that district. It helps ensure that the seat will rarely, if ever, go to the other party. It also means that fewer seats exist which are truly competitive between the parties, and as a consequence it ensures that re-election rates for incumbents are greater, as hardly any incumbents face difficult primary contests.

The people in charge of redrawing or confirming proposed changes are predominantly the representatives themselves in the state legislatures that will benefit from the redrawing; they also have control over the Congressional districts. Of the state legislatures, 37 have the power to control their own legislative district lines and 42 to determine Congressional district lines. The regular legislative process of proposing a bill and passing it also applies to a law redrawing the lines of a district; the governor likewise has the power to veto. Five of these states determine district lines through a joint resolution bill (see Chapter 7 for more on these) that doesn't enable a governor the power to veto. And two of these states require a two-thirds majority in each chamber for a proposed redistricting bill to pass.

In short, in a state where lines are drawn by the legislature, the party that dominates the state legislature gets to determine the redrawing of the lines, and they rarely if ever do that to their own disadvantage.

In six states, federal and state legislative district lines are redrawn by independent commissions whose members are neither elected legislators nor public officials in an attempt to ensure that redrawing isn't party-biased. In two states, no Congressional redistricting can occur as the district is the whole state (called *at-large congressional states*).

Not surprisingly, gerrymandering is seen as a problem by a lot of Americans. When polled, most say they'd prefer that Congressional districts be redrawn by an independent non-partisan commission. And various organisations exist to address this partisan issue across the different states. The difficulty is persuading those parties that are in the majority in state legislatures to relinquish their ability to ensure their political survival by playing partisan politics with the redrawing.

Chapter 11

Understanding the Two-Party System

. . . .

In This Chapter

▶ Introducing the importance of political parties in a democracy

▶ Charting the history of political parties in America

▶ Understanding the continuity between eras of issues facing American politicians

▶ Examining the decline of political parties since the 1960s

▶ Exploring the role of a modern political party in the United States

▶ Describing the different wings of the Democratic and Republican parties

. . . .

The Democrats and the Republicans are the two major political parties in the United States today, and have been for many years. The Democratic Party is caricatured as the home of the liberal do-gooders, who hug trees, smoke dope and protest against government excesses while the Republican Party is the home of uptight conservatives who are predominantly White and against *affirmative action* (equal opportunities for all regardless of colour, ethnicity, religion or gender). This chapter breaks down these stereotypes by revealing that they're more recent than one would at first imagine. It was the Republican Party, for example, that went to (civil) war under President Abraham Lincoln to abolish slavery, while the Democrats were the party supporting it.

In this chapter, I describe the two-party system that emerged in the United States when the nation was founded and explain that, while parties may have died and new ones surfaced to replace them, the issues up for discussion remained the same. I also discuss the emergence of the Democrats and Republicans, detail the role of these two modern political parties in American politics and outline the different wings of the parties.

Outlining the Role of Political Parties in the Modern Era

Most of us scoff and harrumph when asked what political parties are good for; we all get fed up when politicians wriggle out of answering questions (or, and to me more annoyingly, they say something along the lines of 'That's an interesting question but the one I think you should be asking is this and so I'll answer that one instead'). Despite these irritations, politicians do play a vital role – and so do the political parties they belong to. To set us on our way to examining both the evolution and role of political parties in America, I want to first address why political parties are important.

The following points are key to understanding the functions and make-up of a political party in a democracy:

- ✔ It provides a connection between the political system of governance and the people. It enables society to be represented.

- ✔ A successful party identifies what people want and reflects these needs within its policies and programmes.

- ✔ Parties are based on a particular ideology that shapes the policies and programmes they want to implement if elected into government. These policies and programmes are commonly known as the *party manifesto*.

- ✔ A party mobilises voters in an election campaign.

- ✔ Parties are in ideological conflict with one another. Through this conflict different voices (whether in a majority or minority) can be heard.

- ✔ A party is the principal way in which people are selected for appointment to government office or for the legislature.

- ✔ A party is a conduit through which people's interests are represented.

- ✔ The party in the majority will control that particular chamber and the party in the minority is called the *opposition*. The role of the opposition is to monitor the actions of the governing party.

- ✔ A party is a good vehicle for making connections between politicians at the different levels of government (especially in large countries like the United States, which has over 89,000 levels of government, ranging from the federal through to the school district).

- ✔ A party can create connections between people from different political, social or economic backgrounds.

Tracing the American Party System from Its Beginnings

A two-party system has dominated the political landscape since the birth of American political parties in the late eighteenth century. Many parties have existed, with many names, and some parties have even changed their political spots. While some parties have burnt brightly for short periods of time, others have sustained a longer existence; one thing hasn't changed, though, and that's the familiar themes in the political battles America has faced. These battles have been between those who believe in either a weak or strong central government, and between people from the South and North, rural and urban, and agricultural and industrial areas.

And if I can butcher Bob Marley's *Buffalo Soldier*, 'if you know your political parties' history, then you'd know where they're coming from'. Scholars tend to divide the American political system into five distinct periods. Once again, the imagination of scholars has run riot and these periods are referred to as follows: first party system, second party system, third party system, fourth party system and, yes, fifth party system.

The First Party System (1790s–1810s)

Although political parties seem to us now an inevitable part of a working democracy, the framers and ratifiers of the US Constitution were wary of them. By late 1787 a new constitution had been approved by the Confederation Congress and went out to the 13 states for ratification.

In order to persuade the New York voters to support the new Constitution, Alexander Hamilton, James Madison and John Jay wrote a series of essays (*Federalist Papers*) between 1787 and 1788. These essays are an excellent collection of arguments deliberating on the future path of the American political system. The tenth of these papers (imaginatively named Federalist Paper Ten) was written by James Madison and discussed the dangers of political factions (parties). He basically said that political factions are damning indictments on human nature. This is a pretty persuasive argument, although his alternative suggestion of instituting a large republican political system is limited at best and naïve at worst. He suggested that individual representatives should channel the multiple voices of the citizens 'whose patriotism and love of justice will be least likely to sacrifice it to temporary or partial considerations'. He wanted these representatives to give voice to diverse opinions without forming divisive groups around these opinions. However, it seems that not even Madison was convinced by his argument; by the early 1790s he'd co-founded a political party (confusingly titled the Democratic-Republican Party).

Because distrust of political parties was rampant at the founding of the United States, it was largely the unifying character of the first American President, George Washington, during his eight years in office (1789–1797), which held any factionalism at bay. However, as soon as he left office his contemporaries began associating more formally with two opposing camps, the Federalists and the Democratic-Republicans/Republicans/Jeffersonians.

The Federalists were established by Washington's Treasury Secretary Alexander Hamilton and John Adams, his vice-president. The party believed in a strong central government that encouraged state-led economic growth through manufacturing. Such growth was to be made possible by establishing a national bank to help encourage infrastructural development projects such as road-building and through protectionist tariffs to enable industry to become internationally competitive. The Federalists fought for development of industry over agriculture and as such were strongly aligned with business elites from the northeast of the country and more with cities than with rural areas. They also supported the mercantile Britain rather than the revolutionary France.

The Democratic-Republicans were led by Washington's Secretary of State (Foreign Secretary in UK speak), Thomas Jefferson, and James Madison, the leader of the House of Representatives. Until 1791 Madison was a Federalist; however, he was unhappy with the party and broke away to co-found the Democratic-Republican Party. The Democratic-Republicans supported a weaker central government and stronger state governments, distrusted the northeastern industrial elites, opposed Hamilton's national bank and lending plans, had more support in the rural areas and thus backed agriculture as the basis of the American economy and, finally, were more supportive of France than Britain. They feared that a strong central government was likely to be tyrannous and monarchical and strongly supported a republican government that held state power above federal power.

During the 1790s, the Federalists were dominant in Congress. In 1798, they held a majority in both chambers alongside a Federalist President, John Adams. But while this majority enabled them to pass legislation supporting their party platform, it also spelt the party's downfall. The legislation they passed ultimately alienated them from the public and the Democratic-Republicans.

During a time of unofficial war between France and America, Hamilton created a standing army. This army was opposed because it could threaten to dominate the political scene. The Alien and Sedition Acts were also passed by Congress and signed into law by President Adams (1798). The Acts were aimed at weakening the Democratic-Republican Party's position by limiting critical or malicious commentary on the president or Congress. By 1800 the Alien and Sedition Acts had made the Federalists so unpopular that they became a determinant of the Congressional and presidential election campaigns.

Running against Adams in the presidential election, Jefferson gained 61.4 per cent of the popular vote. And in the Senate, by the end of the Congressional session, out of a total of 34 seats (it's less than today's 100 because there were fewer states in the union) the Democratic-Republicans gained seven seats and became the majority party with 18–14 seats (two new seats were added during that session when Ohio was recognised as a state). And, finally, a clean sweep was achieved when the Republicans gained over 20 seats and a clear majority in the House of Representatives.

While the Federalists maintained some political power in the following decade, their unpopular support for the British and ardent opposition to the subsequent war with them (1812–1815) culminated in their disappearance from the national political scene. The Federalists' cause can't have been helped by the fact that the British occupied Washington, DC, in 1814 and set fire to government buildings including the White House (the president's home) and Capitol Hill (Congress's home).

Set in a period of relative international and national stability, the second decade of the nineteenth century is referred to as the *Era of Good Feelings*, with less war and factionalism. On the domestic front, this era was dominated by the Democratic-Republican perspective and it became the only party in town. Next time you have a chat with someone about American democracy and you want to have a little fun, remember to mention that for a decade America was a one-party state.

The power of the Sedition Act

In February 1800 the Democratic-Republican-supporting Philadelphia newspaper, *The Aurora*, published a Federalist-sponsored Senate bill that proposed establishing a special committee to review Electoral College votes in cases of disputes in the upcoming presidential election. Three Republican senators leaked details of the bill to the newspaper's editor, William Duane, who himself decried it as unconstitutional and a blatant attempt to enable Adams to win the next presidential election.

Because Duane had mistakenly suggested that the bill had passed the Senate, when in fact it had just been passed on to a committee for further discussion, the Federalist-controlled Congress declared a special session to charge Duane under the Sedition Act for maliciously talking about the government.

On 27 March 1800, without trial, he was found guilty by the Senate and required to present himself to it. He duly presented himself but, after a delay in proceedings, was asked to come back. He then refused to attend, was charged with contempt and arrested. However, he was never penalised under the Sedition Act as the charges against him were lost. It was a confusing time because Congress was no longer sitting and it was moving from its home in Philadelphia to Washington, DC; oh, and I nearly forgot, the Democratic-Republicans won the presidency and control of Congress in the November 1800 elections.

The Second Party System (1820s–1850s)

Political dissent tends to find its way to the surface even in a one-party state. The good times stopped and unity came to an end with the split of the Democratic-Republicans into two separate parties. Here's how it happened: In 1824 Monroe had been in office for the maximum two terms and it was time to elect a new president. The Federalists having taken their final bow, all four candidates were Democratic-Republicans. And that was a recipe for trouble. On top of the fact that they all represented the same party, none of the four candidates won enough Electoral College votes to gain a majority. The House of Representatives thus had to pick a winner.

In the 1824 election, 131 of a total 261 Electoral College votes were needed to secure presidential victory. (See Chapter 10 on the electoral process for further details.)

Although Andrew Jackson won more states (12) and garnered more Electoral College votes than anyone else (99), because no one achieved a majority of 131 it meant that the House of Representatives had to decide on the winner; it chose John Quincy Adams, who'd received 84 votes (and, yes, this was the first father–son presidential family in American history, his father having been the second US President, beating George H. W. Bush and George W. Bush by over 160 years). This choice caused a lot of infighting, with Jackson supporters accusing Adams supporters of corruption.

Four years later, during the 1828 presidential election, Adams and Jackson were once more pitted against each other. This time, however, Jackson won with an overwhelming majority. It was in the run-up to this election that the supporters of the two candidates began referring to themselves as Democrats (pro-Jackson) and National Republicans (pro-Adams).

The party platform of the newly-established Democrats maintained its opposition to a strong central government by letting the states have more power. It considered itself a party of tradition that looked to the past to find answers to the current day's problems, and opposed banks and corporations (referring to them as state-legislated economic privilege). The Democrats were predominantly supported in rural areas and supported the right of slave ownership.

Run by former Secretary of State Henry Clay after Adams' defeat in 1828, and similar to the Federalists, the National Republicans emerged from Adams' supporters. The 'national' in the title spoke to the need for a strong central government to improve the lives of Americans. Contrary to Tip O'Neill's (former Speaker of the House 1977–1987) famous comment on American politics, that it's all local, they argued that 'all politics *is* national'. They wanted to build a strong economy by establishing a protectionist tariff, creating a national bank and implementing large-scale infrastructure projects such as road construction and a national university.

In the 1832 election, National Republican Clay was overwhelmingly defeated by President Jackson. A year later, the moralising wing of the National Republicans morphed into what became known as the Whig Party. The Whigs, similar to the National Republicans, believed that they could improve the social life of Americans by instituting grand projects such as building schools and hospitals. The Democrats roundly rejected this argument. Over the next 28 years the Democrats and the Whigs fought it out and had a similar number of presidents (although the untimely death of two Whig presidents while in office meant that that party actually spent only eight years in government). During this time the Democrats largely addressed their political agenda by increasing the geographical size of the United States by forcibly removing Native Americans from large areas of land and giving it to small farmers, maintaining slavery and defunding the US central bank set up by the Whigs.

By the early 1800s the geographic border of the United States had increased from the original 13 states. In this expansionist drive (referred to as *Manifest Destiny*; see Chapter 1 for further details), the fragile balance between the pro-slavery states of the South and the anti-slavery states of the North that existed in Congress was in danger of shattering. In the 1840s, Western expansion to places such as Oregon was driven mainly by Northern small farmer families on the promise of fertile land, together with other workers who would be in direct competition with the free labour provided by slaves. These farmers and workers, who were joined by some members of the Whig Party and other parties such as Northern members of the Democrats, were opposed to the expansion of slavery. By 1848 these people called themselves the Free Soil Party and rallied under the slogan 'Free Soil, Free Speech, Free Labor and Free Men'. They elected several men to Congress during this period.

The Third Party System (1850s–1890s)

Arguments about slavery played an important role in the identity of political parties during this era. By the end of the 1860s, old parties had split or died, a new party had consolidated its position (and still exists today), and a civil war had engulfed the nation as a result of difference of opinion on the right of states to maintain the practice of slavery. This was a busy and painful period in American history. The Kansas–Nebraska Act (1854) signalled the end of the Whigs as a political party. The Act enabled a popular vote (of white males) on slavery and people both pro- and anti-slavery rushed into the area in order to register for the vote. In direct response to the Act, members of the Whig Party from the North joined with the Free Soilers to establish the Republican Party (which is the same Republican Party that still exists today, although some changes to objectives have occurred in the intervening years).

As well as opposing slavery, the Republican Party also supported infrastructural development projects, expansion of cities and, in support of the rural, homesteads for farmers. The mainstay of the Southern Whigs joined the Democratic Party. Incorporating the national focus of the Whigs, the Democrats developed a platform that included support for infrastructural projects such as railways. But the Democrats were undecided on the question of slavery and couldn't agree on who should represent them in the 1860 presidential election. Ultimately, the party split into two and the pro-slavery Southern Democrats nominated the current US vice-president, John C. Breckinridge, as their candidate, and the Northern anti-slavery Democrats supported Senator Stephen A. Douglas.

If the Democrats dominated the second party system, it was the Republicans in the third. Starting with the Republican candidate, Abraham Lincoln, winning the 1860 presidential election by a large margin, 24 of the next 36 years were under Republican presidents; in only four years did the Republicans not dominate the Senate; and for 20 years they dominated the House of Representatives. The Republicans fulfilled their manifesto by building a transcontinental railroad connecting western farmers with eastern markets in the expanding urban areas, providing federal lands to homesteaders and, in response to the Civil War, ending slavery throughout the United States.

The Fourth Party System (1890s–1930s)

The two-party system that we know today – the Democrats and the Republicans – emerged during this period of party political history. It was bookended by two extreme events: the *Panic of 1893*, a financial and economic depression that began with the collapse of the railroad industry and included a run on the currency, the collapse of hundreds of national, state and private banks and the failure of commercial, industrial and manufacturing industries, with a resulting increase in unemployment; and the *Great Depression* (see Chapter 16 for full details) caused by the 1929 New York stock market crash, which destroyed American businesses and ruined people's lives for close to a decade.

Leading up to the Panic of 1893, the depression had already hit tenant farmers in the western and southern agricultural areas of the United States by decreasing wheat and cotton production (as a result of drought) and subsequently crop prices, and increasing their debt. By 1892, opposition to those doing business with, and exploiting, farmers, such as money lenders and railroad companies charging high prices to get goods to market, led to the establishment of the Populist Party (or People's Party).

While also attending to the needs of industry workers, the Populist Party ran on a platform of economic and political reforms aimed mainly at improving the lot of agrarian workers. It included reforms that elevated the economic role of agriculture to put it on a par with business and industry, a graduated income tax, public ownership of railroads and an increase in the circulation of currency. It also proposed addressing party corruption by making senators directly elected by the public and not the House of Representatives (see Chapter 5 on Congress for more details).

The party was relatively successful in regional areas but did not quite hit the national stage. By 1896, one faction of the party cozied up to the Democrats, arguing that its agenda would best be achieved by joining them. The other side was suspicious of the Democrats and wanted to remain separate. Ultimately, you've guessed it, the Populist Party split into two factions. With the addition of a chunk of the Populist Party, the Democrats then succeeded in re-establishing themselves in the national political arena with a more populist appeal. However, Democratic President Cleveland was blamed by the Republican Party for the economic depression and William McKinley (Republican candidate) won a convincing majority in the 1896 election. This result spelt the effective death of the Democrats as a successful national party, for six out of the next seven presidents were Republican (28 out of 36 years). The only reason the Democratic candidate won in 1912 was because Former Republican President Theodore Roosevelt ran as a third candidate against the Republican William Taft, thus splitting the progressive vote.

At this time, the progressive identity reflected a movement rather than a party, and several people crossed party lines in order to uphold progressive politics. Based predominantly in the urban areas, these middle-class activists focused on expanding the role of government not for the benefit of business or industry but in the interest of workers. They supported higher wages, improved working conditions, government regulation of food and drugs, and the right for women to vote. The era of government enforcing the liberty of the American people through regulation had begun.

The Fifth Party System (1930s–present)

The final era of the American party political system was established during the Franklin Delano Roosevelt administration. This administration's 'big government' approach and the conservative responses to it have defined the modern party political landscape evident in the United States today.

We shouldn't underestimate the impact of the 1929 New York stock market crash and the subsequent Great Depression on the success of the progressive platform for a new political answer to America's economic and social problems. In 1929 the unemployment rate was 3.2 per cent; by 1932 it had reached

24.1 per cent. Manufacturing output in 1932 was approximately 54 per cent of what it had been in 1929. By 1933 nearly half of all banks had failed. No aspect of American society – people, industry, business and government – was unaffected, and it's not surprising that a backlash against the Republican administration that had presided over this desperate period occurred. In the 1932 presidential and Congressional elections, the Democrats trounced the Republicans. In the presidential election, Roosevelt carried 42 of the 48 states that made up America at the time and the party won huge majorities in both the Senate and the House of Representatives.

Under the Roosevelt administration this era of progressive politics was labelled the *New Deal*. Following on from the ideas of the Federalists, Whigs and Republicans (after the Civil War), the Democrats supported a much more activist central government aimed at creating jobs and providing social security for the unemployed. A whole series of Acts was passed by Congress and signed into law by the president (to see how a bill becomes law, check out Chapter 8) and the federal government was expanded through the development of a series of new agencies. These are referred to as the *Alphabet Agencies* because their titles were all acronyms, such as the Works Progress Administration (WPA) and the Tennessee Valley Authority (TVA). The WPA, for example, was in charge of all public work schemes from construction to employment. Between 1935 and 1943 it had employed 8.5 million Americans, tarmacked 651,000 miles of road, built 800 airports and 78,000 bridges and funded other projects such as a national health survey and a federal arts project.

The aim of these projects was to stimulate economic growth; those hired received $15–$90 per month, which enabled them to feed their families and in turn also injected capital into the economy and created demand for consumer goods (these families had some cash left over to make purchases other than food). The other knock-on effect of these projects was that they provided an infrastructure that modernised America, enabled its businesses to transport goods faster and provided electricity in new places, thus generating new opportunities.

Since the New Deal the Democrats have dominated American politics. They've controlled the Senate for nearly 60 of the last 82 years, the House of Representatives for over 60 years and the presidency for 48 years. This dominance has indicated public recognition of the need for an expanded role of government. In the 1960s, Democrat presidents such as John F. Kennedy and Lyndon B. Johnson continued expanding the role of the federal government into the everyday lives of Americans. They supported legislation that increased the minimum wage and social security benefits, allocated funds for developing poor rural areas, and provided equality for all under the Civil Rights Act (1964). The tide turned somewhat in the 1970s, after underfunding, focus on the Vietnam war and competing interests among government agencies meant the promise of an end to poverty remained unrealised. Americans began to wonder again whether big government was bad.

While the federal government had clamped down on the rights of states and enforced civil rights on resistant populations, its use of heavy regulation had also created enemies in business. Capitalising on this unpopularity, the Republican Party and its supporters saw excessive government as bloated, wasting money and ripe for thinning. The one-term Democratic presidential administration on the cusp of the 1980s was a great example to the Republican Party of what was wrong with America.

In a speech addressed to the public in 1979, President Carter (1977–1981) claimed that a 'crisis of confidence' was occurring in America 'that strikes at the very heart and soul and spirit of our national will'. He described long-term failures of America on both foreign and domestic fronts, inferred that the war in Vietnam was unjust, a growing dependence on foreign oil was problematic and that the government had isolated itself from the American public. This may not have been the greatest campaign for the 1980 presidential election. I can just imagine Carter saying to his team, 'Now guys, don't shoot me down straight away but I've got this great idea . . . .'Seriously, though, what was he thinking? We could pick a couple of lessons out of this approach and write a book called *How to Lose Friends and Influence People to Vote against You*. First, the truth hurts, and when you're blaming an entire nation for its social decay, you're blaming individual people and they're not going to like it, especially if it's true. Second, the messenger will always be shot, especially by the opposition and even more so when election time is looming. Third, when blaming the government for the problems of America, remember that doing so may backfire (for example, it was a Democrat president, Johnson, and not a Republican who presided over the escalation of the Vietnam War). Fourth, listen to that little voice inside your head that's saying, 'maybe this isn't a good idea'.

In his final words in this speech, Carter effectively laid out the Republican Party's 1980 election campaign: 'let us commit ourselves together to a rebirth of the American spirit'. The American public did, Jimmy – just not with you. A key part of Republican presidential candidate Ronald Reagan's election campaign was focused on what Carter had delivered to America during his term in office.

In the Reagan–Carter debate a week before the election, Reagan closed with the following: 'Are you better off than you were four years ago? Is it easier for you to go and buy things in the stores than it was four years ago? Is there more or less unemployment in the country than there was four years ago? Is America as respected throughout the world as it was?' For most people, the answer was a resounding *no* on all fronts. It was a simple but very effective approach. In the election, Reagan won 51 per cent of the popular vote to Carter's 41 per cent and a massive 489 to Carter's 49 Electoral College votes.

Reagan fulfilled his commitment to cut taxes, shrink federal government, deregulate the economy, support states' rights, balance the federal budget and, ironically, boost America's power on the international stage through an expansion of the military – yes, a federal government department.

Carter's Crisis of Confidence speech

President Carter delivered this televised address on 15 July 1979.

[. . .]after listening to the American people I have been reminded again that all the legislation in the world can't fix what's wrong with America. So, I want to speak to you first tonight about a subject even more serious than energy or inflation. I want to talk to you right now about a fundamental threat to American democracy. I do not mean our political and civil liberties. They will endure. And I do not refer to the outward strength of America, a nation that is at peace tonight everywhere in the world, with unmatched economic power and military might. The threat is nearly invisible in ordinary ways. It is a crisis of confidence. It is a crisis that strikes at the very heart and soul and spirit of our national will. We can see this crisis in the growing doubt about the meaning of our own lives and in the loss of a unity of purpose for our nation. The erosion of our confidence in the future is threatening to destroy the social and the political fabric of America.

[. . .] Our people are losing that faith, not only in government itself but in the ability as citizens to serve as the ultimate rulers and shapers of our democracy.

[. . .] In a nation that was proud of hard work, strong families, close-knit communities, and our faith in God, too many of us now tend to worship self-indulgence and consumption. Human identity is no longer defined by what one does, but by what one owns. But we've discovered that owning things and consuming things does not satisfy our longing for meaning. We've learned that piling up material goods cannot fill the emptiness of lives which have no confidence or purpose.

The symptoms of this crisis of the American spirit are all around us. For the first time in the history of our country a majority of our people believe that the next five years will be worse than the past five years. Two-thirds of our people do not even vote. The productivity of American workers is actually dropping, and the willingness of Americans to save for the future has fallen below that of all other people in the Western world.

[. . .] In little more than two decades we've gone from a position of energy independence to one in which almost half the oil we use comes from foreign countries, at prices that are going through the roof. Our excessive dependence on OPEC has already taken a tremendous toll on our economy and our people. This is the direct cause of the long lines which have made millions of you spend aggravating hours waiting for gasoline. It's a cause of the increased inflation and unemployment that we now face. This intolerable dependence on foreign oil threatens our economic independence and the very security of our nation. The energy crisis is real. It is worldwide. It is a clear and present danger to our nation. These are facts and we simply must face them.

In response to the success of the Republican Party, its own failures and the shifting of public support away from the *largesse* of federal government and traditional Democrat economic policy, elements within the Democratic Party responded by creating a new wing and, rather imaginatively, called themselves the *New Democrats*. Key Democrat politicians of the last 20 years such as

Bill Clinton (former president), Jo Biden (current vice-president) and Al Gore (former vice-president) were all members of this new wing. The New Democrats intended to find a *third way*, which would appeal to the middle-classes as well as the Democratic Party's traditional voters (in the UK, Tony Blair's changes to the Labour Party in the mid-1990s, also termed the third way, are a carbon copy). This alternative platform blended cutting taxes for low-income families, the middle-classes and small businesses, welfare reform, and pro-business policies such as deregulation of industries including banking, agriculture and telecommunications. A fiscally responsible Democratic Party was a winner in the elections, and it regained the presidency in 1992 under Bill Clinton.

After 1995 the New Democrats' platform didn't achieve a great deal of success. Yes, the Democrats did win the next presidential election, but it would be 12 years until it became the majority party in the House of Representatives or the Senate. During this time another revolution was occurring – the conservative revolution. During the 1994 mid-term elections (when only Congressional seats are up for election – see Chapter 10 on the electoral process for further details), the Republicans in the House of Representatives creatively made a *contract* with the American people. Under the tutelage of Congressman Newt Gingrich, this contract promised a whole list of conservative changes to the direction and focus of America. With a commitment to reduce the size and excess of Congress itself, the contract also involved a ten-point legislative plan to rid America of crime by making changes to the death penalty (and thus killing more criminals) and building more prisons, deregulation of financial and business industries, tax cuts, increased funding of the defence industry, tax reforms and a balanced federal budget. The Republicans became the majority in both chambers by winning an extra 54 seats in the House of Representatives (230 in majority) and eight seats in the Senate (52).

Considering a Decline of the American Party System Since the 1960s

Up until the 1960s, the parties were viewed as being very important because they, not the individual candidates, were predominately responsible for fundraising, and the caucuses (party committees) chose presidential candidates. In those earlier years, party identification amongst the electorate was high. Because it wasn't yet the television era, the party was responsible for organising a politician's campaigns and making the candidate known to the public.

After the 1960s, the situation changed. Party identification was in decline, and from 1988 through to January 2014 those identifying with Democrats went down from 36 per cent to 31 per cent and Republicans from 31 per cent to 25 per cent whilst those seeing themselves as independents shot up from about 33 per cent to 42 per cent.

Campaigns have become more candidate-centred and issue-centred, the result of which is voters choosing candidates from different parties because they're voting for the candidate and not party ideology. Federal funding for presidential elections is awarded to candidates not parties (although neither Obama nor Romney accepted fund matching in the 2012 elections – see chapter 10 on the electoral process for further details), and since the rise of primaries after the McGovern-Fraser Commission (1968) parties no longer have control over presidential candidate selection as the electorate choose in primaries. (A few states do still use caucuses).

Television enabled candidates to directly appeal to voters, and since the age of the social media this trend has continued. On the Facebook pages of the 2012 presidential election Obama had over 28 million likes and Romney had 5.5 million. In regards to Twitter, at the national political level, around 90 per cent of Senators and House members, and about 42 governors, have an account.

This confluence of factors had led many to believe that the parties are in decline.

'This seat's taken': A failed strike against one party by another

Actor Clint Eastwood has played a few small parts in electoral politics, including being elected mayor of Carmel-by-the-Sea, California, in 1986. But it wasn't until he walked the boards at the 2012 Republican National Convention in Tampa Bay, Florida, that he hit the big time of national politics. In an unfortunately unscripted appearance in support of Mitt Romney's candidacy for president, Eastwood spent his entire time on stage talking to an empty chair, pretending President Obama was sitting in it. He asked him a series of questions on the state of America, and stated that he'd cried when Obama was elected (in a good way) and again when he discovered that 23 million Americans were out of work (in a bad way). In the following excerpt I'm not quite sure what Clint Eastwood was talking about, but it's certainly the best political surrealist speech I've ever heard.

'I would just like to say something, ladies and gentlemen. Something that I think is very important. It is that, you, we – we own this country.

(APPLAUSE)

We – we own it. It is not you owning it, and not politicians owning it. Politicians are employees of ours.

(APPLAUSE)

And – so – they are just going to come around and beg for votes every few years. It is the same old deal.'

What was significant about this speech is that it was delivered live on TV and almost immediately gained notoriety on social media. A Twitter account called *InvisibleObama* had received 36,000 followers within 24 hours. The next day on Obama's official Twitter account was a photograph of him sitting in the president's chair together with the comment 'this seat's taken'. Obama 1–Romney 0.

Examining Modern Democrats and Republicans

Modern Democratic and Republican ideologies represent a great deal of change since the decades when the parties formed. This section explores the breadth of their philosophies, the influence they hold and the ways in which they accommodate the most extreme differences in the political spectrum.

The role of the modern political party

Modern political parties in America play an important role in society through three main avenues: their organisation within the levels of government, the interpretation of ideology from the elected officials' stance, and voting behaviour and the actions of the electorate.

I consider the Democrats and Republicans only in this book because of their national, regional and local dominance in politics. We could explore a number of other national and regional political parties such as the United States Marijuana Party (a libertarian-based party that seeks the legalisation of cannabis and an end to the War on Drugs) or the New York-based Rent Is Too Damn High Party (which focuses on lowering rent and reducing poverty). While such parties are influential as a result of media and public interest, their impact in shaping the political landscape is limited. In this section I outline the party as an organisation of ideologically similar people fighting for similar goals, a party of elected officials that follow broadly similar views on politics and, finally, an entity that citizens identify with and vote for during an election.

Party organisation

When considering the organisation of a political party, it's important to remember the sheer size of the United States, both geographically and in terms of population. The United States is approximately 3.7 million square miles – to put it in perspective, you could fit the UK into it nearly 40 times. The United States has about 314 million people, the UK has 63 million (2012 figure, which includes Scotland; by the time you read this, however, Scotland may be independent), Canada has about 35 million (2012) and Australia has about 23 million (2012).

I mention these statistics because they're important when thinking about the emergence of a political party in the United States. Before the advent of mass communication technology such as the phone, computer and internet or high speed transportation such as the aeroplane, controlling the many chapters of the political parties in rural Alabama all the way through to downtown Chicago would be impossible. As importantly, their interests on particular issues are contingent on completely different local priorities for the electorate. This landscape has thus created very loosely organised and autonomous Democratic and Republican political parties.

If you were to cut a political party in the middle and open it up, you'd see three layers of organisation. These layers muddle along largely autonomously but cohere to work together at election time:

- ✔ **National party:** Forming the top layer, the national party committee and its chair represents the interests of all arms of the party throughout the states, plans the presidential nominating convention (which runs every four years), promotes the general ideological platform of the party, co-ordinates support for candidates throughout the different levels of the party (particularly during election time), raises money for elections and hires professional staff.

- ✔ **State party:** The state party, along with its own state chair, committee and conventions, forms the middle layer, providing support for state candidates, whether that's at national (US Congresspeople), state (state legislators, governors and the second-in-command, the lieutenant governor) or county and lower (city mayors, sheriffs, and members of a school board) level. A state Republican or Democratic party is an organiser; it doesn't tend to play in the policy formation game. While it supports the party's elected officials at the state level, it's a separate entity to the legislative party comprised of elected officials. This relationship is similar to that between the national party and the Congressional members of the party.

- ✔ **Local party:** At the bottom are county, city, ward and precinct organisations and their officers and committees. Also at this level are volunteers, those grassroots supporters knocking on doors and encouraging the electorate to vote. The city mayors and sheriffs also feature at this level of the party.

Elected officials

A second way of considering the two parties is to view them through the eyes of elected officials in the national and state legislatures, as well as during national, state and local elections. Think of the elected officials represented in the legislature, for example the Republicans in Congress, as a separate party that just happens to have the same name as the National Republican Party, Arizona Republican Party and Arizona Coconino County Republican Party. It is a different autonomous arm of the all-encompassing Republican Party, which, while influenced indirectly by these various arms, is nonetheless independent of them.

If the party is in the majority in a particular chamber it has the power to appoint chairs of the legislative assembly and dictate the legislative agenda (that is, what bills get submitted to Congressional committees – for more details on this process, see Chapter 5). The legislative arm of the party will attempt to promote a coherent agenda; however, the strength of this coherence is countered by other responsibilities. A candidate may, for example, want to downplay her party affiliation so as to attract interest from members of the electorate who are either independent or would typically associate with the other party.

The power of the local constituent voter can also have a big impact. If a group of constituents in, say, the 6th Congressional District in Arizona are agitating for national government action because they're concerned about their children inhaling fungal spores from soil disturbed by the construction of a large building upwind from them, they'll pressure their Congressperson to do something about it. Even though supporting the local cause may upset the national, state or Congressional legislative party, if it's election time (and it always is for a Congressperson because they're up every two years) the Congressperson will feel pressured to respond or he may not get re-elected. This is why Congresspeople frequently vote against the party line; this was especially the case in the 1960s and 1970s when Congresspeople voted with their parties only about 50 per cent of the time. Recently, they've been a lot more loyal: since the mid-1990s both parties in both chambers have been regularly hitting 90 per cent and over (although Republicans dropped-off in the mid-2000s but started climbing again thereafter). In the 112th Congress (2010–2012), for example, 48 of the 52 Democrats in the Senate voted along Democratic lines in over 90 per cent of votes cast. In the House of Representatives, 206 of the 245 Republicans voted along party lines over 90 per cent of the time. Christopher Lee from New York wins the record for voting along party lines 100 per cent of the time.

An important reason behind this increase in voting along party lines is the expanded role that the national parties have played in organising elections for party members. The Republican National Committee (RNC) and the Democratic National Committee (DNC) have both developed campaign committees for Congressional candidates that provide funding, advice and support for those willing to conform to their requirements. For the 2012 electoral cycle, for example, which included the presidential election and the Congressional elections (so bound to involve more money), the RNC raised for and spent over $400 million on candidates, and the DNC raised and spent over $315 million. A (new) saying comes to mind: 'Where there's money, there's friendship and conformity.'

Another reason for party loyalty is the replacement of conservative (read Southern) Democrats in the South with Republicans. Often at odds with their own party, these Democrats had frequently built voting alliances with the Republicans in key legislative decisions. One may wonder if they were actually in the wrong party, and indeed these Democrats, over time, either moved to the Republican Party or the voters changed their support to the Republican Party.

This replacement of conservative Democrats with Republicans was kickstarted in 1964 when Congress passed and Democratic President Johnson signed the Civil Rights Act. Conservative Democrats increasingly saw no need to remain in the party as their strategy to hold out against a federally-imposed decision on determining how states governed was rendered obsolete. And in terms of party identification, when he signed the Act Johnson supposedly commented: 'I think we have just delivered the South to the Republican Party for a long time to come.' While no Senate elections were held in the South in 1964, in the House of Representative elections the Republican Party picked up a number of seats in places such as Alabama and Georgia, some of which hadn't voted Republican since the 1870s. By the late 1990s a conservative coalition was dead and the South belonged to the Republican Party.

Party identification among the electorate

The final way of examining the role of political parties is party identification among the electorate and the impact such identification has on voting behaviour. Party identification is important because it provides an opportunity for a citizen to associate herself with an ideological platform. The individual can be an armchair supporter who votes for a party but doesn't engage with it, or an active identifier who joins up and works for it on a voluntary basis. If, as a citizen, I think the federal government is too large, taxes are too high and state governments should exercise more control in my affairs than the federal government, chances are I'll choose a Republican candidate and not a Democrat in an election. While not all Republicans support these positions and not all Democrats oppose them, public perception nonetheless links these platforms to particular parties.

An individual's identification with a particular party is also important from the perspective of that party because such an individual is likely to vote for it. Since 1992, on average, 48 and 42.5 per cent of the electorate has identified with and leaned towards the Democrats and Republicans, respectively. Thus, the more I lean towards the Democrats in terms of ideology, the greater the chance that I'll always vote Democrat in every local, state and national election. This behaviour is called *straight ticket voting*. Rather like a dyed in the wool supporter of a football team, I'll stick with them come what may. The weaker my identification with a party, the more likely I am to engage in *ticket-splitting*, which is choosing to vote either Democrat or Republican depending on the candidate and the office coming up for election.

Symbols of the two parties

The Deomcrats' donkey was first used in American politics during the 1828 presidential election. Opponents to the Democratic incumbent Andrew Jackson called him a 'jackass' as a result of his populist views. In a classic case of reclaiming a negative term, Jackson liked the symbolism of the animal so much that he used it on election posters. However, not until the political satirist Thomas Nast used the donkey in an 1870 *Harper's Weekly* cartoon titled 'Copperhead Press' did it become more indelibly associated with the Democrats. The cartoon referred to Nast's distaste for the Copperhead Democrats, who were anti-Union slavery supporters. The picture showed the pro-Copperhead Press donkey kicking a lion that symbolised Edwin Stanton (recently deceased), who was President Lincoln's Secretary of War. Nowadays the donkey is portrayed as hardworking, diligent and humble by the Democratic Party and as stubborn by its critics.

The Republicans' elephant was first used by Republican presidential candidate Abraham Lincoln in the 1860 election. Not until the 1870s, however, was it popularised as the symbol of the party. Once again, Thomas Nast was behind it – in an 1874 *Harper's Weekly* cartoon called 'The Third-Term Panic', he referred to the Republican vote as the elephant. By 1877 the Republican Party itself was portrayed as the elephant in a cartoon entitled 'Another Such Victory And I Am Undone'. This picture showed a battered Republican elephant at the grave of a Democratic tiger. It referred to the controversial decision made by the Electoral College Commission to award the presidency to Republican Rutherford B. Hayes after a series of electoral irregularities, such as ballot box stuffing and intimidation of black voters (who would have voted Republican), led to the questioning of Democrat candidate Samuel Tilden's electoral victory. To Republicans, the elephant is a symbol of strength, intelligence and dignity; to opponents it's seen as a circus animal.

Two broad churches: Divisions of the major parties

As a result of the varying stages of political realignment that have occurred in the course of American political party history, the two parties that have ultimately emerged and consolidated their positions have a tremendously rich and ideologically varied past. It is for this reason that, within one party, candidates and the electorate could both support and oppose the invasion of Iraq in 2003. The next two sub-sections illuminate this rich and complicated history by examining a number of key wings operating within the Democratic and Republican parties, which are pointers to their diversity. These wings temper the idea that the parties are monolithic entities, which are ideologically straight-jacketed into one view on how the party should respond to a particular issue. That said, over time some wings have developed more power than others, and some wings do hold similar positions on various issues. This diversity within one party can get pretty confusing, so bear with me!

Modern Democrats

Today's Democratic Party has four significant wings:

- **Left-wing:** This wing includes progressive and liberal Democrats who have a less militaristic approach to foreign policy, some of whom were opposed to the war in Iraq. They're against social conservatism, support civil liberties and help disadvantaged people through government programmes, including those to address employment and healthcare. As of 2014, for example, the approximately 80 members of the Congressional Progressive Caucus (a *caucus* is a group of elected officials that sit in Congress) are predominantly made up of Representatives. Just to confuse matters, the only senator in this caucus is Bernie Sanders, who is an independent not a Democrat and is a self-declared *democratic socialist* (not many of them in American politics). Other notable progressives include President Roosevelt, President Kennedy and the former senator to Maine, Paul Wellstone (who tragically died in a plane crash while canvassing for the 2002 Senate elections). Notable liberals include the late Senator Ted Kennedy (Massachusetts) and the Minority Leader in the House, Nancy Pelosi (California).

- **Centre-wing:** Otherwise known as the New Democrats ('The Fifth Party System (1930s–present day)'section earlier in this chapter explains why), these people typically support tax cuts and the use of military force, including supporting the war in Iraq, as well as reducing government welfare funding. This wing includes former President Clinton, former Senator Jo Lieberman and former Secretary of State Hilary Clinton. While he did oppose the war in Iraq, on a number of other issues President Obama can be seen as centre-wing.

✔ **Conservative wing:** This wing includes the *Blue Dog Democrat* faction, which was set up in the mid-1990s as a voice for conservative-minded, or moderate, members. The Blue Dogs are losing importance in the party and only 15 are currently sitting in the House of Representatives. The conservatives are typically fiscally and/or socially conservative and include members such as Senator Bob Casey Jnr. (Pennsylvania), who's pro-life (that is, anti-abortion; see Chapter 15 on the fault lines in American society for further details). It also includes Senators Ben Nelson (Nebraska) and Zell Miller (Georgia). Incidentally, Miller supported Republican President Bush in the 2004 election over the Democratic candidate, John Kerry.

✔ **Libertarian wing:** Not a large part of the party, the free-to-do-anything wing supports issues such as civil rights and separation of church and state, and opposes gun control and large government expenditure. They support non-interventionist foreign policy, citing the problems that arise from taking an interventionist approach, and include people such as the former Democratic Senator Mike Gravel (Alaska).

Modern Republicans

Seven wings are evident in today's Republican Party:

✔ **Fiscal wing:** Affectionately (by some) called the *neo-liberal economic order*, these people support a reduction in government spending, including on welfare programmes, lower taxes, a balanced budget, deficit reduction, free trade and deregulation of the economy. This wing includes notables such as Senator Tom Coburn (Oklahoma).

✔ **Libertarian wing:** Similar to the Democrat variant, this group supports a whole range of issues including supporting the free market and the rights of states versus the federal government, and is against taxation and large government expenditure. These people are predominantly against an interventionist foreign policy, including the removal of military bases in the world, although exceptions to this rule do exist. In a case of family affairs, former Texas Congressman (and former presidential nominee) Ron Paul is against intervention while his son, Senator Randal Paul (Kentucky), is more amenable to maintaining military bases in foreign lands and taking military action. This wing has over 20 self-identified members of the Republican Party members in Congress.

✔ **Neoconservative wing:** Also focused on foreign policy, this wing of the party is concerned with ensuring that American supremacy is unrivalled throughout the world. It promotes acting aggressively to protect the American position via actions such as the promotion of democracy; George W. Bush's interventionist foreign policy in Afghanistan and Iraq is an infamous example of this approach. It included an expanded legal interpretation of pre-emptive attacks to include non-imminent threats (see Chapter 19 on the consequences of 9/11). Other notable neoconservatives include former Secretary of Defense Donald Rumsfeld and former Deputy Secretary of Defense Paul Wolfowitz.

✔ **National security wing:** This wing is firmly focused on the aggressive defence of the United States. It supported the foreign policy of the George W. Bush administration (2001–2009) but criticised its weakness in relation to restricting immigration. This wing includes people such as Arizona senator (and former 2008 presidential candidate), John McCain.

✔ **Religious right:** This wing includes mostly fundamentalist Christians, evangelical Christians, traditional and conservative Catholics, Mormons and some orthodox Jews. These people are socially conservative thus support traditional moral and social values such as marriage being a union between men and women not people of the same gender. They're against abortion and stem-cell research (because it involves the testing of human embryos). Notable members include the founder of the Christian Coalition, Pat Robertson, former governor of Alaska (and 2008 vice-presidential candidate) Sarah Palin, former Attorney General John Ashcroft and, with strong evangelical credentials, President George W. Bush.

✔ **Moderate wing:** Un-affectionately referred to by some as RINOs (Republican In Name Only), these people are fiscally conservative and so believe in balanced budgets, deregulation of industry and lower taxes (which is good from a more typical Republican perspective). They're also socially liberal (which is bad) and thus support issues such as gay rights, gun control and environmental protection. The moderate wing is also pro-choice (it accepts abortion as an option). It includes people such as former governor of California Arnold Schwarzenegger and former New York City Mayor Michael Bloomberg.

✔ **Tea Party:** Established in 2004 and more a movement than a wing of the party, the Tea Party gets special mention because of its influence in nominating Republican candidates for office and its vocal grass roots and Congressional opposition to the Obama administration. It is partly conservative, partly libertarian and partly populist. In late 2013 the Congressional Tea Party Caucus had 46 members in the House of Representatives and five in the Senate. Its focus is on limited government, fiscal conservatism and, in classic politics-speak, a *strict* adherence to the Constitution. Its opposition to President Obama has concentrated on his establishment of healthcare insurance for all Americans (the Affordable Care Act 2009, known by opponents as *Obamacare*) and his supply-side economic stimulus package in response to the 2008 financial and economic crisis. The Tea Party movement was also instrumental in the two-week forced federal government shutdown in October 2013. This situation developed because the Congressional Republican Party would not authorise the appropriations bill (which pays for federal employees) unless the Democrats accepted a defunding of Obamacare. As a result, 800,000 federal employees were placed on unpaid holiday while 1.3 million others worked without knowing when they were going to get paid.

Chapter 12

Taking a Look at Voting Behaviour

. . . .

In This Chapter

▶ Analysing the effects of ethnicity, gender, age and education on voting behaviour

▶ Understanding the changing demographic profile of the United States since the 1996 elections

▶ Considering Republican strategy in light of the shrinking White vote

. . . .

*W*ithout knowing very much at all about an American you meet on the street, you can make a pretty good guess about his voting behaviour. The chances are that if he's a white male, or over the age of 65, or earning over $100,000 then he's significantly more likely to vote for the Republicans than the Democrats. If he has all those characteristics combined, the chance of voting anything other than the Republican is frankly unlikely.

While not an exact science, the relationship between demographic characteristics and how a person votes can be very informative. Research into this relationship is also usefully employed by political parties and their hired consultants because the better they know how the population will vote, the better they can tailor their messages to hit the right note. And if the national party recognises it doesn't have a sufficient number of likely voters in a district, county or state, it may save its money there and spend it where it has a better chance of electoral success. It's politics – what do you expect!

This chapter starts by looking at the effects of ethnicity, gender, age and education on voter turnout. It goes on to explore who votes, looking at all those factors and adding in location and religion for good measure. I use lots of statistics to help you better understand the likelihood of a particular type of individual voting for a specific party and, yes, I predominantly discuss the Republicans and Democrats at the expense of parties on the fringes of the political system (for a full explanation of why this is so, go to Chapter 11 on the two-party system). To make this chapter more digestible I spend most time using data from the 1992 presidential election between George H. W. Bush and Bill Clinton and as the benchmark from which to work when examining the trends. And I focus on a presidential election as it shows a general trend that can equally apply to congressional elections. Finally, I discuss the importance of the White vote for the Republican Party and how its shrinking share means that the party faces a question over whether it adapts its policies to accommodate other groups or aims for an even bigger share of that White vote.

Discovering the Impact of Demographics on Voter Turnout

Voter turnout means simply those people who turn up to the polling station, go inside a booth and register their vote. It shouldn't be confused with eligibility to vote, which in the United States, for federal elections, applies to everyone over the age of 18. Some cities and states allow people as young as 16 and 17 to vote in local and state elections and referenda.

To set the scene on voter turnout, you need to get an idea of recent voting levels. So in this chapter I look at the presidential election year voter turnout since 1996. (Remember that for federal elections in years without a presidential election – called *mid-terms* – the turnout is much lower than during a presidential election; for example, the 2010 mid-term election had a 41 per cent turnout while the 2012 presidential election year had 61.8 per cent.)

Since 1996, voting levels have mainly been rising. In the second Clinton election year (1996), of the 180 million people eligible to vote, 58.4 per cent did so; by the time of the Obama vs. McCain presidential election year of 2008, this percentage had risen to 63.6. In the last presidential election year (2012), voting dropped by nearly 2 percentage points, to 61.8 per cent of the 215 million people eligible to vote.

Ethnicity, gender, age and education are key clues as to whether someone is likely to vote in an election.

Ethnicity

A number of historical events and issues that sit alongside ethnicity and race help determine whether you are likely to vote. In particular, the 1965 Voting Rights Act had a big impact on increasing the Black and minority levels of voter turnout. Figure 12-1, shows that Blacks and non-Hispanic Whites have both the highest population levels and highest voter turnout, making it essential for political parties to listen to their needs in order to court their votes. This figure includes the four largest ethnic groups, starting with the group with highest voter turnout per head (of course, all of these groups are pretty diverse themselves, but that's a whole other book!).

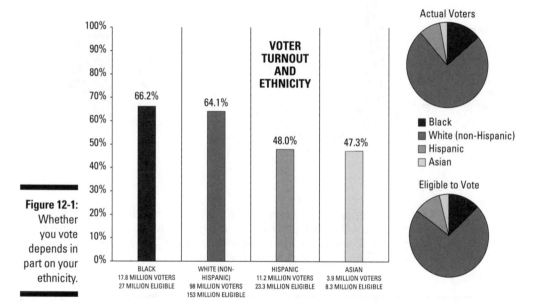

Figure 12-1: Whether you vote depends in part on your ethnicity.

Gender

Gender plays an important role in determining whether a person is likely to vote. Figure 12-2 shows you how many men and women are eligible to vote and how many actually bothered to show up.

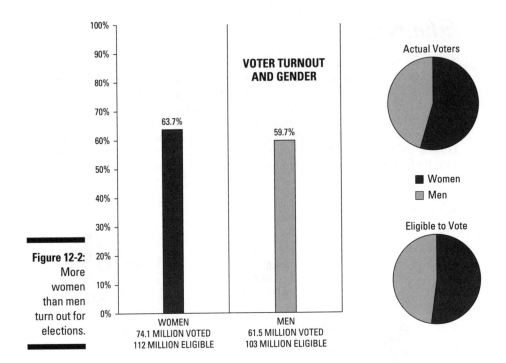

Age

Although younger people have more of a future to worry about than older people, they're much less likely to vote. Table 12-1 shows you how voter turnout steadily rises across the age categories to reach 73.5 per cent of 65–74 year olds, and Figure 12-3 shows you the total number of voters by age group.

Combining ethnicity and gender

Things get especially interesting (and complicated) when we start to combine categories. For example, if you look at ethnicity and gender together, you learn that 70.1 per cent of Black women turned out to vote in the 2012 election, which is a higher rate than any other race and gender combined. And, although women in general are more likely to vote than men, when you consider age and gender together, the group with the highest turnout is men aged 65–74 (74.4 per cent of whom turned out to vote).

In spite of the higher percentage recorded of those who voted in the two elder categories, because their population levels were lower than the middle two categories it meant that the absolute number of votes was significantly smaller.

Table 12-1	Voter turnout by age	
Age Range	*Voter Turnout (Millions)*	*Percentage of Voters Who Voted*
18 to 24	11.3	41.2
25 to 44	39.9	57.3
45 to 64	52	67.9
65 to 74	17.2	73.5
75 and older	12.5	70

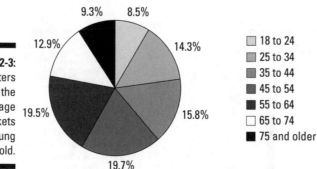

Figure 12-3: More voters fall into the middle age brackets than young or old.

If we take the percentage of those eligible to vote as the indicator of an interest in the political life of the country, then women in all but the 65–74 category out-voted men. Based on this indicator, what comes as a surprise is that the younger, and supposedly more-engaged, generation of 18–24 year olds has the lowest turnout rate of all the categories. Thus, the older you are (whether male or female), the more likely you are to vote. Suggested explanations for why older people are more likely to vote are numerous and include:

✔ They want to protect their federally-funded social security and health-care (*Medicare* – free health insurance for the over 65s).

✔ Older people are less transitory than younger people; they move homes less and don't need to reregister to vote.

✔ Retirees have the time to go to the polling station to vote.

✔ With the high rates of voting amongst retirees, a bit more peer pressure to vote is exercised.

If I were a political candidate, I'd address issues for youngsters in order to encourage more of them to vote *and* tailor policies for those in the middle of their working lives and in retirement so that they vote for me.

Education

Regarding the relationship between education and voting, the statistics are shocking. The suggestion is that people who spend less time in formal education are less engaged with the world around them and so less likely to vote. The US Census Bureau divides education into six categories, which I show you in Figure 12-4.

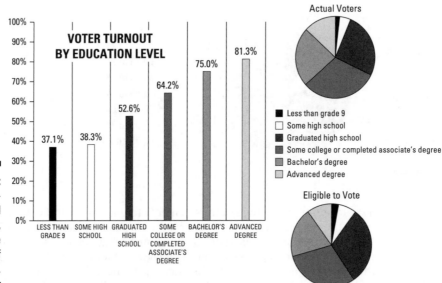

Figure 12-4: As education level increases, so does the likelihood of voting.

Basically, the more years you spend in education, the more likely you are to vote. Clearly, in the light of that knowledge, if I were a moral political party honcho who believed in the role of high voter turnout in a democracy, I'd ensure that people complete as much education as they possibly can.

Of course, these factors don't live in isolation from each other. If I'm Black, what's the probability that I'll complete my education in comparison to a White non-Hispanic student? The answer to that question will ultimately impact the probability of my voting.

Using the Past to Understand the Present and Predict the Future

Relating the impact of the different markers on voter turnout in the 2012 elections is a start, but it provides only an incomplete picture. To elaborate we need to know how these demographic markers relate to which party people vote for. And we need to think about how this voting behaviour has changed over time.

Considering voting behaviour today is like looking at a one-generation picture of a family. It gives you a complete picture of that generation, but that's it. If you want to investigate further, you need to look at the family tree. If 2012 is the most recent generation, then 2008 is the next, 2004 is the one before and so on. By looking at the presidential elections from 1996 we get to observe five generations and see which traits have stayed the same and which have changed. It helps us put into context the final section of this chapter, which looks at how important the 2008 elections were in defining the future relationships of the two parties with the people, and whether there's such a thing as a blue (Democratic) future.

Ethnicity

The White non-Hispanic ethnic group has traditionally been fairly evenly divided in terms of which of the big parties gets their votes. Given that this group makes up most of the electorate, such voting behaviour has tended to keep elections fairly evenly balanced. However, the White majority in the electorate is decreasing very rapidly – from 83 per cent in 1996 to 72 per cent in 2012. The 'As Demographics Shift, Democrats Get the Edge (and Republicans Strategise)' section later in this chapter considers how the decline of the White vote may be fundamentally shifting the balance of electoral politics.

The majority of the Black and Hispanic electorate has given its vote to the Democrat candidate. Not surprisingly, this was especially the case with Black voters in the 2008 election when the electorate had their first opportunity to vote for a Black presidential candidate. But voting Democrat has been a pretty robust pattern from long before the rise of Obama, as Figure 12-5 shows.

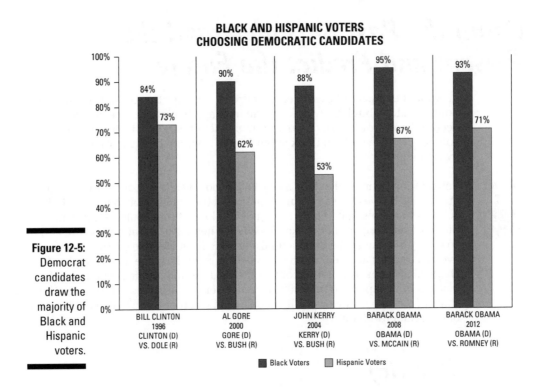

Figure 12-5: Democrat candidates draw the majority of Black and Hispanic voters.

The fact that Black and Hispanic voters consistently favour the Democrats may be gradually becoming more important as the percentage of these minorities in the electorate slowly rises. The Black share of the electorate went up from 10 per cent in 1996 to 13 per cent in 2012, and the Hispanic share went from 5 to 10 per cent over the same time period. During this time, the proportion of Asian voters also rose – from 1 to 3 per cent. While the Asian vote was previously fairly evenly split between the two large parties, this section of the electorate appears to be increasingly leaning toward the Democrats, adding further volume to the growing voice of Democrat-supporting ethnic minorities.

Location

Electoral pollsters break down the United States by region – East, Midwest, South and West (Figure 12-6 shows you these regional divisions) – and by location, meaning whether the voter lives in an urban, suburban or rural area.

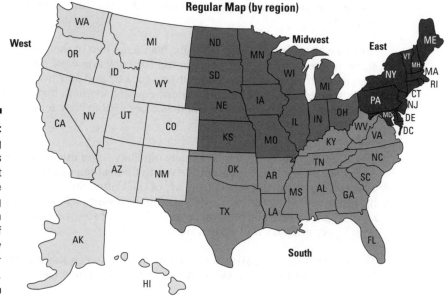

Figure 12-6: Voting behaviour is somewhat predictable according to which region of the country a voter lives in.

Regions

It's true to say that most states in the United States have a track record of voting in favour of a particular party in national elections, and presidential elections provide no better example. It means that candidates will expect certain states to go their way without having to spend too much time and effort on them. The result is that a few states are so close that the candidates' election machines will concentrate on them more than others – why waste precious money on a campaign in a particular state you know you'll win? This category of usually around 12 states is called the battleground, and they're dispersed around the country.

East

The Eastern states of the United States (on a map, this is basically the northeast corner and includes New York, Massachusetts, Vermont and New Hampshire) are known for their wealth, high levels of education and liberal attitudes. These states are also less religious, and more urban than most of the rest of the country. And all of these factors are a good recipe for a Democratic win. The Democrats have soundly brought home the Eastern region, winning between 55 and 60 per cent of the vote there in the last five elections.

However, New Hampshire and Pennsylvania are two of the battleground states where victories for Obama in the 2012 election were significantly lower than in other parts of the region. Obama took 52 and 52.1 per cent, respectively, whereas in other Eastern states he pulled in much higher figures, such as 62.7 per cent in Rhode Island and 58.3 per cent in New Jersey.

Midwest

The Midwest region (which is actually officially – and much more sensibly – named by the Census Bureau as the North Central region) is made up of 12 states in the north and central part of the United States. It contains some big cities, including Chicago, which is the third-biggest in the whole country, as well as vast swathes of farming land. Economically, the Midwest relies on both heavy industry and agriculture.

The Midwest sits precariously in the balance between Republican and Democratic and is thus a key battleground region come election time:

- ✔ In the 1996 election, the Democrats won the Midwest by 1 per cent.
- ✔ In 2000, the balance had tipped towards the Republicans, who also won it by just 1 per cent.
- ✔ In 2004, the Republicans appeared to be consolidating their lead in the region, winning the Midwest by 3 per cent.
- ✔ Their fortunes turned in 2008 when Obama won by a whopping (for the region) 10 per cent.
- ✔ In 2012, the Midwest again sat on a knife edge, with the Democrats getting near 51 per cent and the Republicans receiving near 48 per cent.

Michigan, Wisconsin, Ohio and Iowa are three of the battleground states. And in the 2012 presidential election, Obama won these states by 54.2, 52.9, 50.7 and 52 per cent, respectively.

South

This region is made up of states in the central south and south east of the country. Historically, the South is a rural region, although industry has been growing fast here in the last 50 years or so and urban centres are expanding. The South is poorer, more religious and more conservative than any of the other regions of the United States. This area has traditionally been a homeland for the Republicans (for an explanation of why this is the case, see Chapter 11 on the two-party system), and nothing suggests that this situation is changing.

✔ 1996 was a draw between Democrats and Republicans at 46 per cent apiece, but later elections demonstrate the ascendancy of the Republicans.

✔ In the 2000 presidential election, the Republicans won convincingly with 56 per cent to 43 per cent for the Democrats (in spite of Gore being a Southerner).

✔ In 2004, the Republicans increased their share of the vote to 58 per cent whilst the Democrats went down to 42 per cent.

✔ In 2008, the Republicans dropped to 54 per cent whilst the Democrats increased to 45 per cent.

✔ In 2012, the Republicans won nearly 53 per cent and the Democrats reached almost 46 per cent.

Virginia, North Carolina and Florida are the battleground states in this region, and in the 2012 presidential election Obama won Virginia with 51.2 per cent of the votes, lost North Carolina to Romney, who recorded 50.4 per cent of the votes cast, and squeezed Florida with 50 per cent to Romney's 49.1 per cent. Romney lost Florida by about 80,000 votes; if there were only this many more old White retirees, he could have won!

West

The most sensibly named region! The West is literally made up of the states in the west of the country (including Hawaii and Alaska). The West is the largest of the regions and the most ethnically diverse. It contains ancient cultures, alongside super-modern Silicon Valley. Not surprisingly, the West isn't easy to categorise politically. While the region has usually been won by the Democrats, it is particularly internally divided. The states on the West Coast are strongly Democrat, while many of the interior states (for example, Utah, Arizona and Wyoming) are diehard Republican.

✔ In 1996, the Democrats won this region with 50 per cent to the Republicans' 41 per cent.

✔ In the 2000 presidential election, it was much closer, with the Democrats winning 49 per cent and the Republicans being close with 47 per cent.

✔ In 2004, the Republicans closed the gap, reaching 49 per cent of the vote to the Democrats' 50 per cent.

✔ In 2008, the Democrats stormed into the lead with a 17-point gap, recording 57 per cent to the Republicans' 40 per cent.

✔ In 2012, the Democrats pulled in 54 per cent of the popular vote in the region with the Republicans gaining 43 per cent.

The three battleground states in the region are Colorado, New Mexico and Nevada. In 2012, Obama just about won these three states by 51.5, 53 and 52.4 per cent, respectively. Romney missed out on the combined 20 Electoral College votes by just under 300,000 votes. Whilst this is a high figure, relative to the 129 million people who voted, it's not that many.

Localities

Since this chapter is all about generalisations, I can say that the majority of urbanites tend to vote for the Democrats and the majority of rural types tend to vote for the Republicans. In some elections, this state of affairs has been soundly proven.

In 2012, Obama won convincingly with 69 per cent of the vote in large urban areas of above 500,000 people and 50 per cent in those areas of 50,000–500,000. In the suburbs, the Republicans beat the Democrats but only by a 2 point lead to record 50 per cent of the voters. In the smaller locales, Romney ruled supreme, with 56 per cent of the vote in areas with 10,000–50,000 people. In rural areas, he got 61 percent.

On occasion, though, the rule of thumb has been undermined – for example in 1996, when the Democrats beat the Republicans in rural areas by 1 per cent.

I give you no prizes for guessing that the suburban localities tend to hang in the balance. Sometimes they're blue (Democrat) and sometimes they're red (Republican) but rarely is there more than a few percentage points in it.

Age

Many theories are put forward to explain why people in some categories vote more than others and why people in particular age categories are more likely to vote for the Democrats or the Republicans. According to an old

British adage, 'If you're not a liberal at twenty you have no heart; if you're not a conservative at forty you have no brain'. Whether you agree with the logic behind that statement, the statistics do lend it some truth; that is, if you equate liberal with the Democrats and conservative with the Republicans. I say some truth because the edges of categories are always going to be blurry. And to make life more complicated, comparing different elections with each other is tricky as the age groups in some elections have different cut-offs.

As the earlier 'Discovering the Impact of Demographics on Voter Turnout' section points out, people in the 18–29 age group are the least likely to vote. Those who do make it out on polling day are somewhat more likely to vote Democrat. The Democrats have consistently won this category, with significant leads for over 40 years (only in the 1972, 1984 and 1988 elections did the Republicans win):

Over the last 40 years, in the 30–44 category, the British adage rings *slightly* true and people are becoming more conservative. I say slightly true because, since 1972, the Republicans have not lost 7 out of the 11 elections. Therefore, it must also be slightly false, and, worryingly for the Republicans, the last two presidential elections have demonstrated a change in that trend. Table 12-2 breaks down who's voting for whom by age and party.

Table 12-2	Voting behaviour by age		
Voters aged 18–29			
	Democrat %	*Republican %*	*Independent %*
1992	40	37	23 (Ross Perot)
1996	54	30	16 (Ross Perot)
2000	47	47	6 (Ralph Nader)
2004	60	40	
2008	61	39	
2012	60	37	3 (multiple candidates)
Voters aged 30–49			
	Democrat %	*Republican %*	*Independent %*
1992	42	37	21 (Ross Perot)
1996	49	41	10 (Ross Perot)
2000	45	53	2 (Ralph Nader)
2004	43	57	
2008	53	47	
2012	51.5	46	

(continued)

Table 12-2 *(continued)*

Voters aged 50–64

	Democrat %	Republican %	Independent %
1992	43	39	
1996	47	45	8 (Ross Perot)
2000	50	48	2 (Ralph Nader)
2004	48	52	
2008	54	46	
2012	47	52	

Voters aged 65+

	Democrat %	Republican %	Independent %
1992	50	39	11 (Ross Perot)
1996	51	42	7 (Ross Perot)
2000	56	42	2 (Ralph Nader)
2004	52	48	
2008	46	54	
2012	44	56	

Gender

The first important thing to consider regarding gender and voting is that more women are casting their votes than men (53 per cent versus 47 per cent in the last two elections). Women are significantly more likely to vote Democrat and men are slightly more likely to vote Republican. How this difference has come about has been the subject of much research (and speculation). Surprisingly, 'women's issues' such as abortion rights and equal pay don't appear to have been a major driver of the gender gap.

Opinion polls actually show that the views of men and women closely track one another in relation to issues such as abortion, for instance. Here are some of the other reasons people have come up with to explain this voting behaviour:

✔ Research suggests that women advocate 'big government' more so than do men. This might be because in American society women are more likely to take on family responsibility for healthcare and education, so they'll favour a party that gets involved in these issues, too. (See Chapter 10 on the two-party system to find out more about the Democrats and big government.)

✔ Research shows that women are turned off by big spending on the military, which is an especially Republican habit.

✔ Women are more likely to be the recipients of government aid; that is, they're more likely to be poor, old or single parents. And the Democrats advocate more welfare spending than the Republicans.

✔ Men (white men especially) tend to be more conservative. They're more likely to favour military intervention and to disagree with gun control. I'm sorry this image is such a stereotype, but it's what the research says!

Income

Income is a big determinant in relation to voting Democrat or Republican. The more you earn, the more likely you are to vote Republican. In the 2012 election, 54 per cent of those earning over $100,000 voted Republican in comparison to just 35 per cent of those earning under $29,999. Prior to 2012, pollsters also collected data for the category of voters earning under $15,000; in 2008, only 25 per cent of people in this group voted Republican.

The reasons behind the income differences in relation to voting seem especially straightforward. People who earn more prefer to pay the lower taxes advocated by the Republicans. And people who earn less prefer wealth to be more evenly distributed in terms of the welfare provision advocated by the Democrats. Of course, it's important to remember that big overlaps exist between all the categories I discuss here. For example, if you're poor you're more likely to be female and Black.

As Demographics Shift, Democrats Get the Edge (and Republicans Strategise)

The current demographic changes in America suggest that the future is looking decidedly blue. This section outlines the key demographics that suggest a Democratic future while also identifying the Republican response to this changing situation.

Some have disagreed with the idea that a substantial swing to the Democrats is occurring. Leading conservative commentator Charles Krauthammer, in a 2009 *Washington Post* article on the 2008 presidential election, suggested that Democrat success was the result of 'a historical anomaly' rather than a demographic shift: a combination of 'a uniquely charismatic candidate . . . running at a time of deep war weariness, with an intensely unpopular Republican president, against a politically incompetent opponent, amid the greatest financial collapse since the Great Depression'. To Krauthammer, the shock was that Obama won by only a 7 per cent margin. Political rhetoric aside, Obama successfully won the 2012 election with a 4 per cent margin, suggesting that the only historical anomaly was, in fact, Krauthammer's commentary. And as the sociologist August Comte famously said, 'demography is destiny', meaning that you can't escape from the figures no matter how hard you yell.

A friend once quipped that if the Republicans want to achieve electoral success but remain unwilling to dramatically shift their political ideological base on issues such as immigration, they need to start producing more White voters.

So why does the Democratic majority appear difficult to beat? The answer to this question centres on a combination of two key issues inherent within the relationship between ethnicity and voting:

- ✔ Each ethnic group's impact on the share of the vote
- ✔ The Democrat and Republican shares of each ethnic group

In the 1976 presidential election between President Gerald Ford and Jimmy Carter, 89 per cent of those who voted were White non-Hispanics, 9 per cent were Black and 1 per cent were Hispanic. Twenty years later, in the 1996 election between President Clinton and Bob Dole, the picture was changing so that 83 per cent of those who voted were White, 10 per cent were Black and 5 per cent were Hispanic. In the intervening 16 years the ethnic demographic changes have been even more significant. In the 2012 election between President Obama and Mitt Romney, the proportion of White non-Hispanic voters had shrunk to 72 per cent; Black voters had increased to 13 per cent, Hispanic to 10 per cent and the Asian to 3 per cent.

It remains true that no Democratic candidate has won the White vote since Johnson in 1964. But because of the changing demographic make-up of the electorate, the importance of this fact is diminishing. With the Democrats maintaining healthy advantages in the other ethnic groups of around 70 per cent for Hispanics and Asians and about 90 per cent for Blacks, all Obama needed was to secure 39 per cent of the White vote to secure a 51 per cent victory in the popular vote and 332 EC votes.

In response to this apparent ongoing shift to the Democrats, as evidenced by the outcome of the 2008 and 2012 presidential elections, how does the Republican Party interpret the Democrats' lack of appeal to the White vote and turn it into an electoral campaign strategy? Republican nerds are currently examining two main approaches.

Expanding share of votes and turnout

Assuming that the Democrats will lose even more of the White vote, one strategy is for the Republicans to both expand White voter turnout and increase their share of the White vote. In suggesting this approach, conservative strategists are arguing that they should maintain their appeal to their key group (Whites) and trying to attract the other ethnic groups isn't necessary.

This approach is reflected in the fact that, of the 129 million people who voted in 2012, 92.88 million were White. Of those people, 54.8 million voted for Romney. In total, 60.9 million voted for him, which means that nearly 90 per cent of his votes were from White people.

Suddenly changing its spots overnight is pretty hard for a political party. And actually the Republicans don't have to amend their ideological platform on issues such as immigration. If they were seeking to appeal to immigrant (mainly Hispanic) communities, they wouldn't reject immigration reform, which is what the Republican members of the House of Representatives actually did when they vetoed reforms in February 2014. Their argument is partly supported by the suggestion that a lower White turnout was expected, by about 5–6.5 million, and this group was seen as 'largely downscale, Northern, rural whites', which meant these people were disproportionately likely to vote Republican. If they could get these people to vote in the next election, the number of Whites as a share of the ethnic make-up of the United States would increase and, because Whites are much more likely to vote Republican, a significant boost in votes should result.

This logic is evident in the stats breakdown. As noted, in recent congressional and presidential elections the Republican share of the White vote has been high. This becomes more important when considering the fact that the White group have a larger share of the vote in congressional than in presidential elections thus enabling them to maintain their ideological positioning. In the 2010 mid-term elections, the Republicans had a 62 percent share of the White vote. And since 1992, the share of the White vote for Republicans hovered around the mid- to high-50s with 60 per cent in 2002 and 59 per cent in 2012.

Romney's 59 per cent share of the White vote was quite high compared to other elections such as Reagan's 1980 victory 56 per cent of the White vote, so to expect even high levels may be unrealistic, although Reagan did receive 64 per cent of the White vote in his 1984 re-election. So the suggestion that there is not just a stabilisation of the Republican share but that it is inevitable it will grow is unproven.

Earning votes from other factions

Other conservative strategists suggest that the Democrats' share of the White vote could increase and, if it does, the Republicans will have no chance of success in the 2016 presidential election without significant increases in their share of the other ethnic groups. To attract these voters, the Republicans will have to change their ideological stance on issues such as immigration. On the flip-side, however, if they go too far in trying to address issues of relevance to these new groups, the Republicans may alienate their core voters and ultimately distance themselves even further from the White House in 2016.

These strategists saw 2012 as a loud wake-up call to the fact that the Republican Party was no longer relevant to a large share of voters. Acknowledging this voter deficit among minority groups, in 2012 the Republican National Committee (RNC) commissioned a review of its recent federal election failures and concluded that, 'The Republican Party must focus its efforts to earn new supporters and voters in the following demographic communities: Hispanics, Asians and Pacific Islanders, African Americans, Indian Americans, Native Americans, women, and youth . . . Unless the RNC gets serious about tackling this problem, we will lose future elections; the data demonstrates this.'

Glimpsing possible outcomes

If the Republicans were to pursue a Whites-only strategy (yes, the possible racism that could result from this approach won't be lost on you), a few barriers to success exist. First, in terms of voter turnout in presidential elections, for example, the White vote has been steadily declining, hitting a low of 72 per cent in 2012. The size of this drop cannot be ignored by strategists from all parties when determining their policies; to do so would be folly. For the White-first strategy to be successful, the Republicans would need not only to arrest this decline (which may be possible if the figures stabilise) but also to reverse it (that is, produce White voters at a rate greater than the other ethnicities combined). The long-term voting pattern suggests that minorities aged 18 and under will be the majority within the current decade, meaning that the White share of eligible voters will continue to decline. By the 2016 presidential election, minority ethnic groups are predicted by some to comprise around 30 per cent of those who vote. Based on these predicted figures, the White-only strategy seems troubled.

Second, acknowledging the difficulty of increasing White voter turnout means that an even greater and maybe unrealistic share of the White vote is required for the Republicans to win future elections. Coupled with a continuing loss of votes from the other ethnic groups – approximately 20–80 per cent – relying on this strategy seems even more foolish in the face of the Democrats' continuing appeal to the Black, Hispanic and Asian voter.

According to the statistics, if minority groups do comprise 30 per cent of voter turnout in the 2016 presidential election and the Democrats attain a similar level of support from them (approximately 80 per cent), they'd require only 37 per cent of White votes to win a majority of the *popular vote* (all the votes in the states combined; but having the popular vote doesn't always guarantee possession of the Oval Office, as presidential elections are determined by the Electoral College – see Chapter 10). In this situation, the Republican candidate would need 20 per cent of the other ethnic votes together with approximately 63 per cent of the White vote, which is 4 per cent more than in 2012. Only Reagan achieved that level of success, as an incumbent in 1984.

Third, changes among the White electorate are possibly making the Democrats more competitive. Republican dominance has chiefly been among White voters with no college education. Of all White votes recorded in 1984, 62 per cent matched this demographic; by 2012, it comprised only 36 per cent. The Democrats demonstrate greater success with White voters with at least four years of college education. In 1984, for example, this group made up 27 per cent of the White vote, while in 2012 it had risen to 36 per cent. Other changes include the growing secularisation of White people, a decrease in the number of married White people who vote (who have traditionally supported the Republicans) and an increase in the likelihood of these young people now voting for the Democrats. All of these factors reduce the Republicans' chance of achieving their 63 per cent plus share of the White vote.

Fourth, the impact of the high percentage of White voters who supported the Republican candidates in the last two presidential elections has limited impact, as the majority of them are contained in the southern states. It's no good for the Republican Party to just increase the number of White voters in states where they already have a likely chance of winning the election. For an expansion in the White vote to have any real impact on the Republicans' electoral chances they need to gain a greater number of White votes than first thought, particularly in battleground states such as Ohio, in order for an expansion of the White vote to result in winning more states.

But what if the Republicans do win the next election by employing a White-only strategy? This approach may still not be fruitful in the long term as a means of maintaining Republican competitiveness in the face of a changing demographic climate. Surely at some point the Republicans will need to change tack and the longer they leave doing so, the more difficult it will be.

Chapter 13

Considering the Influence of Interest Groups and the Media

The founding forefathers realised that for republicanism to succeed it had to balance the needs of society with the needs of individual groups within that society. Opening up the political process to all special interest groups would thus establish a balance of power and combat the dominance of a few groups over the many. But some suggest that balance hasn't been achieved and the more financially successful groups have been much more influential in shaping government policy – that money wins, basically.

This chapter examines interest groups in US politics and how they operate around elected politicians trying to influence their behaviour and decision making. It also brings the role of the media into the mix in light of how it, too, influences politics. It then discusses how interest groups and the media aren't islands of influence but also shape and impact each other using public opinion as a driver.

Understanding the Collective Power of an Interest Group

An *interest group* is nothing more than a group of citizens working to promote an idea. Simply put, if someone has an interest in a particular issue, say the right to vote of homeless people, connects with other people who have a similar interest and begins to raise awareness of this subject, they've effectively created a single-issue interest group. Interest groups can have a wide focus or home in on the interests of a particular industry, promoting a political position across a range of issues.

The aim of all interest groups is to influence political decision making related to their area of interest in order to shape policy. This focus on issues around a core subject is what distinguishes an interest group from a political party; a political party will have an opinion on everything because that's what it needs to do. And it's because of this focus that interest groups tend to be policy specialists. While a National Coalition for the Homeless (NCH) policy expert may have an opinion on the level of funding provided for dairy farming, I'd be more likely to go to the Dairy Producers of New Mexico for advice. And while an interest group may support a candidate for political office if they advance its interests, it doesn't put up its own candidates.

Under the Constitution, interest groups are supported by the First Amendment. Congress can make no law that stops people from exercising their right 'peaceably to assemble, and to petition'. This right is as fundamental to American democracy as freedom of speech and freedom of the press.

As the federal government expanded its reach into the daily lives of Americans, kick-started by the Great Depression of the 1930s (see Chapter 16 for details), organised interest groups have tended to focus on its heart – Washington, DC. In fact, as interest groups bloomed during the 1960s so an equal decline occurred in the number of people joining political parties as members. This downward trend was also visible in the mere 50 per cent of people who voted from the 1960s onwards; not until the 1990s did that figure finally return to the pre-1960s approximately 65 per cent.

In general, interests groups have four main functions (although not all of these will be true of all interest groups):

- ✔ They raise awareness of and stimulate interest in particular issues by educating elected officials and the public.
- ✔ They represent their clients and serve as a link between them and the government.
- ✔ They provide information to government, especially data and testimony to Congressional hearings that help shape policy decisions.
- ✔ They provide a channel through which citizens can work together and engage in the political process in order to achieve a common goal.

Theories explaining interest group politics

Three main, conflicting, theories explain how interest groups operate:

- **Pluralist theory:** Originating in the 1950s when a large expansion in the number of interest groups occurred, it suggests that they provide an important conduit in terms of people connecting to the government beyond elections. It also suggests that no one group can dominate others because they can all engage with government in multiple ways and a balance is thus created. It is an optimistic theory as it suggests that most groups operate within the system and don't break laws.

- **Elitist theory:** This theory contests the previous notion that the plurality of interest groups ensures that no one group or position dominates others. It suggests that some groups will generally lose out in government decision making as a result of their lack of resources, inadequate lobbying power, fewer connections with government than their competitors or because they're less receptive to government elites. The interests of industry and big business, for example, tend to take precedence in government decision making over the interests of consumers.

- **Interest group liberalism:** This theory turns pluralist theory on its head by arguing that the presence of multiple interest groups produces a negative rather than a positive outcome. It contends that an inter-relationship exists between interest groups working on a particular issue, the government department in charge of overseeing that issue and the committees and members of Congress responsible for legislation on that issue. As a result, government policy is dictated by that inter-relationship and key decisions are thus not made with an end-goal in mind but to appease various interested parties – very bureaucratic, very political and not very efficient.

Types of interest groups

Interest groups can be broken down into two general categories, according to the focus of their ideologies.

Economic

Currently, most interest groups focus on economic issues. They operate either from the perspective of business owners or workers. Business interest groups aim to protect and promote the interests of businesses by attaining greater profits through seeking tax breaks, government contracts and subsidies, and ensuring their industry is protected from new threats.

Around 80 per cent of all those interest groups with an office in Washington, DC are business-orientated. This includes the National Association of Manufacturers (NAM) and the Chamber of Commerce of the United States, and even groups that promote the interests of foreign governments and businesses seeking preferential treatment.

On the other side are labour groups that fight to maintain and expand the rights of workers. In 2012, 14.3 million labour groups existed; they have more members than any other interest group except the American Association for Retired Persons (AARP), which has 37 million. Most labour unions fall under one of two umbrella organisations: the American Federation of Labor and Congress of Industrial Organizations (AFL-CIO) or the Change to Win Federation. Membership reached its peak in 1956 when about 33 per cent of the non-agricultural workforce was in a union.

Unions fought hard to establish the right of workers to join them but over time this right has been eroded as business groups have chipped away at the right to organise a union in the first place. In 1947, for example, the Taft–Hartley Act partly enabled states to pass laws banning 'closed shops' whereby union membership is a prerequisite of employment. These *right to work* laws existed in 24 states in 2014.

The interests of professional workers are addressed by associations that regulate practices, promote standards of conduct and lobby the government. Examples include the National Education Association (NEA), which was founded in 1857 and currently has 3.2 million members; it promotes greater access to public education for all students and lobbies on educator- and student-related issues. Another example is the American Medical Association (AMA), founded in 1847 and with over 200,000 members in 2012. It advocates for physician and patient rights to better healthcare services and is a supporter of President Obama's Patient Protection and Affordable Care Act, otherwise known as Obamacare (see Chapter 14 for more on this issue).

Non-economic

Many interest groups don't focus on economic concerns but on general public interest issues, single issues, ideological and government-focused issues. To name a few examples:

- ✔ Public interest groups focus on the collective good. They aim to improve society and include health and religious groups.

- ✔ Environmental groups concentrate on raising public awareness of this issue and pressuring state and federal legislatures to enact bills limiting pollution, supporting animal rights and opposing nuclear power stations, for example.

✔ Consumer groups focus on protecting consumers from unsafe products. They've been responsible for a number of changes to business practices and also were instrumental in persuading Congress to establish the Consumer Product Safety Commission in 1973, which regulates consumer products and has the authority to ban those that are unsafe.

✔ Single-issue groups are self-explanatory in that they focus specifically on one issue. They tend to consist of dedicated members driven by a need to promote their issue. Such groups include the National Rifle Association (NRA), which is against all forms of gun control (see Chapter 14 for more details) and the National Right to Life Committee (NRLC), which opposes abortion.

✔ Ideological groups are those interested in a particular way of life. Their overarching narrative permeates every sphere of life. They include religious-based organisations such as the Family Research Council (FRC) and the American Family Association (AFA), which promote a particularly traditional interpretation of family values and advocate for a closer relationship between church and state. Ideological groups also include equality-based organisations that focus on women's and minority rights, for example the National Organization for Women (NOW) and the National Association for the Advancement of Colored People (NAACP).

✔ Government-based groups concentrate on local, state and foreign governments and lobby on issues such as greater federal government funds and tax breaks. They include the United States Conference of Mayors (USCM), which was established in 1932 and aims to support the interests of urban populations in relation to federal policies. Another example is the National Governors Association (NGA), which was founded in 1908 and represents the 55 states, territories and commonwealths that make up the United States. It provides technical assistance to governors, conducts research into public policy issues and represents their interests in negotiations with the federal government.

Shaping policy and opinions

An interest group can employ four key strategies to influence its target and shape policy to its advantage.

Lobbying

Lobbying is simply the process of one individual or group working to influence the opinions of another individual or group. The aim of lobbying is to directly influence policymakers and decision-makers on topics that impact the interest group's constituents. Two types of lobbyists exist: those who are employees of a particular interest group and only work on that issue; and those who can be hired by an interest group to push forward its proposals, a sort of *rent-a-lobby*, if you will.

Because legislation is discussed, written and submitted to Congress, lobbyists tend to operate from Washington, DC – but not always. Lobbyists can also attempt to influence a president's administration by encouraging them to make an executive order that favours their interests (see Chapter 4 on the presidency). Lobbyists influence government decision making in two ways:

- ✔ Direct lobbying involves using personal connections with law-makers, the president and executive cabinet officials as well as their staff to present the views of particular interest groups to the people in government who make decisions.

- ✔ Indirect lobbying involves persuading members of the interest group and other people with similar views to target the decision-makers with letters, emails and phone calls requesting their support on a particular issue passing through Congress.

In order to fulfil the objectives of both types of lobbying, lobbyists with similar goals can combine their resources to create a bigger impact.

Another tactic that lobbyists employ when engaging with law-makers is to offer their services to those elected officials who support their interest group's position. They can provide the member with someone to help devise solutions to political issues by being a source of information and drafting legislative fixes, and help during election campaigns (see the 'Electioneering' section below for further details). Concerns are expressed regarding the democratic nature of this kind of lobbying as a result of its influence on government policy. If an interest group provides the legislator with help developing prospective legislation, for example, it's possible it will serve that group's interests and not necessarily those of the general population. However, some people argue that interest groups aren't actually as powerful as they at first seem, given the other influences that compete with them, such as the needs of the electorate; opposing interest groups may also cancel out each other's influence. What's clear is that lobbying for an interest group can help rally its members and help raise money for its cause.

Litigation

If an interest group can't persuade the government to change policy or the legislators to propose new laws, it can always sue for change. Groups representing a range of interests, from those supporting the rights of ethnic minorities to those representing the interests of corporations have all used the courts as a way to gain an advantage by changing government policy.

Interest groups can employ *class action lawsuits*, which enable a large number of people in a similar position to have their cases heard together. This tends to happen in cases that concern consumers and environmental issues and involve suing a business or a federal agency regarding their actions or inactions. Because the US has a series of laws that protect the environment, such as the Clean Air Act (1967, with amendments in 1970, 1977 and 1990) and the Clean Water Act (1972), class action litigation has become a useful tool for environmentalists. This is because these laws include provisions that enable citizens to sue businesses if they're not following the legal guidelines.

Another way to influence government policy in the courts is to submit *amicus curiae* briefs (groups filing reports that support either the petitioner or respondent – see Chapter 6 for further details on this process) to the federal or state courts.

Electioneering

Electioneering is when an interest group helps a candidate win elected office because that person supports the group's position on an issue or issues. Interest groups need to keep people in office who are sympathetic to their causes, which is why they help officials running for all levels of US government office to win an election. Because national and state elections are staggered, it means that a citizen has the opportunity to vote in an important election pretty much every year. And that means that the electoral cycle is constantly spinning.

Interest groups can help candidates in multiple ways, including developing campaign strategies, running election campaigns, providing financial contributions, publically endorsing them and encouraging their own affiliated individual members to vote for them. The key tools for promoting a particular candidate or issue that a candidate supports are the Political Action Committee (PAC) and the Super Political Action Committee (Super PAC). They operate in slightly different but important ways:

✔ A PAC is typically used by an interest group to directly provide financial resources to a particular candidate running for office, rather than individual or political party contributions.

A PAC can give up to $10,000 to a candidate's election committee for use in the entire electoral cycle process, $5,000 in the primary and $5,000 in the general election. A PAC may also contribute $15,000 to a national party election committee. As well as giving money, a PAC can also receive money. It can receive up to $5,000 from other PACs, party committees or individuals in any calendar year.

The 2011–12 federal election cycle involved presidential, House of Representatives and Senate elections (as well as a whole series of local and state elections). The International Brotherhood of Electrical Workers' PAC, for example, contributed $2.5 million to a whole series of House and Senate campaign committees for individuals. And as you'd expect, being a union, 98 per cent of it went to Democratic Party candidates.

✔ A Super PAC has slightly different regulations. It is technically known as an *independent expenditure-only committee* because, while any interest group, business or individual can receive or contribute as much money as they like in supporting or opposing a candidate, political party or even an issue that certain candidates support, it prohibits any liaison with a candidate's campaign committee and does not allow for direct financial contributions to their campaign. The unlimited amounts that can be raised and spent far outweigh the negatives.

By July 2013, 1,310 Super PACs were registered. According to OpenSecrets.org (the Center for Responsive Politics), in the 2011–12 federal cycle over $828 million was raised by Super PACs. The top 100 contributors gave 57 per cent of that money, and nearly $610 million was spent. The distance between a Super PAC and a candidate's current campaign team isn't always clear cut and the waters appear a little murky. Take Restore Our Future, for example, the conservative super PAC that supported Romney. It was established in 2010 to support his primary and then general election campaign. A number of Romney's 2008 presidential Republican primary campaign team were on the Super PAC board, such as Charles R. Spies (2008 general counsel) and Carl Forti (2008 campaign political director). Would it be unreasonable to suggest that they had an idea of what kind of support the 2012 Romney campaign team would need in the primary and general election?

Public engagement

In bringing attention to a particular issue, an interest group wants to control public debate by shaping what gets discussed and how. If a lobby group persuades the public to support an issue, chances are that the public will start putting pressure on their elected officials. They may, for example, start calling them up or writing letters asking why they aren't supporting this particular side of the issue.

Recognising what makes an interest group successful

The amount of money being pumped into interest groups every year leads to an expectation of success. Three key factors influence an interest group's chance of success:

✔ **Size matters:** The smaller the interest group, both in terms of focus and members, the more efficient it will be in achieving its goals. This is because small interest groups tend to include those with an economic business-supporting or single-issue focus rather than a consumer or broad ideological interest. Because their goals are more specific than larger organisations or those with a broader range of ideological goals, they're much better organised.

✔ **Focus:** Even interest groups with a broad membership base can be very successful if they're focused on an ideological position that fully engages those members. Generally, these are single-issue interest groups that have a rigid and uncompromising approach to a particular subject such as abortion.

✔ **Resources:** Of course, the more resources an interest group has, the more likely it is to be successful, although leadership and financial mis-management can off-set this logic.

Looking at the Role of the Media in American Politics

Not only do interest groups have an important impact on American politics, so too does the media. To understand the media's influence, this section discusses what the mass media is and how it shapes and is shaped by other influences. The *mass media* – radio stations, print media such as magazines and newspapers, TV stations and the whole range of Internet-based sources, including social media, personal blogs and online journals – is essential to the health of democracy. In fact, it's often described as the Fourth Estate; that is, the fourth branch of the American political system designated to keep in check and balance the other three branches (executive, legislature and the judiciary – see Chapter 3 for further details). Under this shining cloak the media is seen to provide three services:

✔ As a *public representative* the media keeps in check elected politicians and government officials by holding them accountable for their actions.

✔ As a source of *public information* the media keeps the populace up-to-date on important issues that concern them.

✔ As a *public watchdog* the media provides investigative journalism that objectively examines key issues determined important to the populace.

However, this may be a somewhat romantic interpretation of the role of the media. In the rest of this section I describe some of the complications that make the media a little less shining knight and a little more corporate pawn.

Media ownership and its political impact

The more media owners there are, the more voices people can choose from, meaning the system is more representative. That's true of media in much the same way as the plurality argument applies to interest groups. (See the previous section, 'Understanding the Collective Power of an Interest Group'.

However, this argument can only stand if multiple voices actually exist. And since the 1980s a rapid decline has occurred in the number of organisations that control the media.

In the 1980s around 50 large media organisations controlled most of the media; by the early 2000s that number had shrunk to six and controlled about 90 per cent of all mass media. In 2012, those organisations were

- News Corporation (owns 28 TV stations such as Fox News, 20th Century Fox film corporation, print media including the *Wall Street Journal* and *New York Post* and HarperCollins publishing)

- CBS (owns 29 TV stations, over 130 radio stations and Simon & Schuster publishing company; it also sells billboard advertising space around the world)

- Time Warner (owns a range of media companies, including CNN, HBO, Warner Bros. and DC Comics)

- Viacom (owns over 160 cable channel stations, including MTV and the children's channel Nickelodeon, and Paramount Pictures)

- Disney (owns multiple TV stations such as ABC and the sports network ESPN, nearly 300 radio stations, a series of film production and distribution companies and print magazines)

- Comcast (owns over 24 TV stations including NBC, film companies such as Paramount Pictures and the broadband company AT&T Broadband)

Damaging accusations are levelled at the role of the media in American politics as a result of this situation. In particular, it means that distribution of information is controlled by the few, which raises the question of whether the mass media in the US can truly fulfil its supposed duty as the Fourth Estate.

While the Federal Communications Commission (FCC) regulates and provides licences for public service broadcasting, the media companies focus on providing revenues for their shareholders. Advertising is the prime source of such revenues and big advertisers are big corporations. The interests of large corporations are likely to conflict with the mass media's role as a public representative, source of unbiased information and public watchdog. If, for example, a corporation doesn't want its record on a particular issue to be discussed in a particular documentary, it could cancel its advertising contract and thereby reduce the revenue of the media company. A culture is possibly thus created whereby the media company doesn't want to rock the boat.

Deregulation of radio station ownership under the 1996 Telecommunications Act is an example of the concentration of media ownership unduly and powerfully impacting the American political scene. Before this Act, an organisation could own a maximum of 40 stations, thereafter it could own as many as it wanted. Clear Channel Communications Inc. currently owns more than 1,200 radio stations. In 2003 a member of Texan country and western band The Dixie Chicks commented at an event in London that US foreign policy made her 'ashamed that the president of the United States is from Texas'; as a result, Clear Channel Communications (along with a number of other companies) banned their music from some of their stations' playlists. Differences of opinion regarding US actions in the world during the early 2000s were thus being marginalised in the public sphere.

Politicians manipulating the media

While I have portrayed the media conglomerates and their underlings such as news producers as the big bad wolves in all of this, it would be wrong to think that no other wolves are in the forest or that these conglomerates don't have weaknesses that can be exploited. Politicians and government agencies have the capacity to shape media organisations' news content in order to advance their interests. Campaigning for elections, for example, takes place in the media. It means that candidates running for office must have an effective media strategy in order to present their positions on various issues and persuade constituents to vote for them and not for anyone else.

Key to a successful strategy is positive exposure of the candidate on the different media platforms such as social media or television. Positive exposure ranges from serious interviews on the relevant issues to chats with radio talk show hosts to political campaign commercials. A candidate needs to try to appeal to the emotion of the audience as opposed to its logic, which is most successfully done with the sound bite and the photo opportunity. Campaign sound bites get to the heart of messaging and Obama's 2008 campaign tags 'Hope', 'We can change' and 'Yes we can' are very good examples; they set the tone of the campaign from which all else followed. However, the power of political advertising has its limits; it can't fully change a person's opinions on an issue but is more likely to activate a latent position already held by that person.

Politicians are increasingly connecting with the public via the Internet and social media channels. Twitter, YouTube and political blogs have had a huge impact on shaping the way people access information. And more and more people in America are using these sites. According to a 2013 Pew Research Center poll, 73 per cent of Americans over the age of 18 use social media, regardless of, ethnicity, household income, education, age, gender and so on. As a result, its role in the world of politics has expanded exponentially from being a source of fundraising (in the 2012 campaign Obama raised about $650 million from online sources and Romney raised about $500 million) to a means of influencing and shaping the public's response to news (see Chapter 10 on the two-party system and the case of Twitter and President Obama in the 2012 general election).

The Three Amigos: Combining Interest Groups, the Media and Politics

Interest groups, the media and politics aren't islands of influence; at different levels they can influence each other, which is why unpacking exactly what or who is responsible for why something happens is difficult. Media organisations can directly shape political decisions, and politicians can equally shape how media organisations respond and report on issues. Interest groups can influence government policy, as politicians can shape the conclusions some interest groups reach. These are all direct examples of influence; however, they can also all influence each other in some capacity via an indirect route and that's through the mediator of public opinion.

Public opinion can shape political decisions, politicians can shape public opinion, public opinion can be shaped by media organisations, and interest groups can shape and be shaped by public opinion. The reduced ownership of the mass media can have an undue influence on shaping public opinion on issues, which some would argue was the case with whether the US should invade Iraq.

Any decision by a media organisation to exert its influence could be related to a number of factors. As part of the corporate elite, such an organisation could, for example, be supporting a decision made by the ruling government at the time. It may also be in its interests not to upset the government because its broadcasting licence is up for renewal or it requires government support for a new merger or acquisition. The owner of the company may simply want to persuade others of their perspective.

The flip side of these examples is that the ruling government may actively pressure, whether implicitly or explicitly, the media organisation to support its case. An elected member of the government may also want to persuade the public to support her efforts and will utilise the media organisations to present their case in the best possible light. Alternative positions may thus be ridiculed or not discussed as a result of the wishes of the government; likewise the media organisation itself may also decide to treat a particular issue in this way, consciously, unconsciously or independent of government influence.

An interest group, too, may seek to raise the profile of its position and persuade members of the public to support it by utilising the influence of the media. If an interest group has successfully managed to sway public opinion on an issue, then it becomes very difficult for elected officials to support an alternate position, particularly when an election's around the corner.

Part IV
Investigating American Politics and Society

Five Ways Religion and American Politics Mix

- From the first days that Europeans settled the North American continent, there was always a religious dimension to society; the Puritans, for example, settled because they wanted to escape persecution in the Old World.

- Integral to the decisions made by the framers of the US Constitution when writing out the future path of the nation was a clear recognition that people should not be persecuted for their religious beliefs, and that no one religion or denomination should dominate over any others by being the official religion. This recognition led to formal rules within the Constitution that ensured that there was separation between the church and the state.

- Through the years, the US Supreme Court, as interpreters of the Constitution, determined in court opinions that government should play no role in facilitating one religion over another. And in the *Engel vs. Vitale* (1962) case, this led to declaring officially-sanctioned prayers in school unconstitutional.

- Despite these secular formalities, the US is, and always has been, a religious nation, and the separation between religion and state is not at all clear-cut. A massive majority of Americans practice religion and think it is important in their daily lives.

- Religious identity translates into political party identification. Of Evangelical Christians, 40 per cent are Republican whilst 34 per cent are Democrats. For Jews, 23 per cent identify as Republican whilst 65 per cent are Democrats. Of Muslims, only 11 per cent are lean or are Republican and 63 per cent identify with Democrats.

Glimpse the document that started the society by visiting www.dummies.com/extras/americanpoliticsuk.

In This Part . . .

✔ Look into the changing makeup of the American population, and the sometimes painful ways that these differences have played out in politics.

✔ Explore the fissures in American culture. Examine key issues, like abortion and gun control, that continue to raise heated debate.

✔ Identify the causes and consequences of the 2008 financial and economic crises on the American economy, politics and people.

Chapter 14

Investigating Race and Multiculturalism

In This Chapter

▶ Taking a look at the racial and ethnic make-up of America

▶ Consider the results achieved by the Civil Rights Movement

▶ Using race and ethnicity to examine America today

Race is an important issue in American society today, and has been since significant numbers of Europeans landed on the continent's shores in the 1600s. The European White domination of other races and ethnicities has fundamentally shaped the politics, economics and culture of the country, as has the resilience of those people.

In this chapter, I examine the foundation and development of the state using the lenses of race and ethnicity, and their impact on contemporary America. I explore the impact of racial and ethnic identity on the institutional and social development of the American political, economic and cultural system. It's not just a story about how the political system saw the need for a change in what constituted 'the people', it's also about the narratives of the people and how they fought and struggled for equal access and recognition.

One Nation, Many Identities

Understanding the past provides a key to understanding the present. And so here I review the racial and ethnic make-up of the country since its founding. I focus on two major racial and ethnic groups and the role they played in the history of the US – Native Americans and African Americans. While other groups played and do play an important role, I think these two groups had the biggest impact on defining race and ethnic relations today.

Ethnic and racial make-up of America

US Census Bureau figures show that the predominant races recorded in 1790 were the White and Black populations, and that other races and ethnicities such as Asians and Hispanics didn't make up significant numbers until the mid-part of the twentieth century. Table 14-1 shows you the changing racial make-up of the United States over the past two centuries.

Table 14-1	Racial composition of the United States		
	Race figures in millions (percentage of total in brackets)		*Total population in millions*
Year	White	Black	Other
1790	3.2 (80.7)	0.8 (19.3)		3.9
1800	4.3 (81.1)	1 (18.9)		5.3
1810	5.9 (81)	1.4 (19)		7.2
1820	7.9 (81.6)	1.8 (18.4)		9.6
1830	10.5 (81.9)	2.3 (18.1)		12.9
1840	14.2 (83.2)	2.9 (16.8)		17.1
1850	19.6 (84.3)	3.6 (15.7)		23.2
1860	26.9 (85.6)	4.4 (14.1)	0.1 (0.3)	31.4
1870	33.6 (87.1)	4.9 (12.7)	0.1 (0.2)	38.6
1880	43.4 (86.5)	6.6 (13.1)	0.2 (0.3)	50.2
1890	55.1 (87.5)	7.5 (11.9)	0.4 (0.6)	62.9
1900	66.8 (87.9)	8.8 (11.6)	0.4 (0.5)	76
1910	81.7 (88.9)	9.8 (10.7)	0.4 (0.4)	92
1920	94.8 (89.7)	10.5 (9.9)	0.4 (0.4)	105.7
1930	110.3 (89.8)	11.9 (9.7)	0.6 (0.5)	122.8
1940	118.2 (89.8)	12.9 (9.8)	0.6 (0.4)	131.7
1950	134.9 (89.5)	15 (10)	0.7 (0.5)	150.7
1960	158.8 (88.6)	18.9 (10.5)	1.6 (0.9)	179.3
1970	177.7 (87.7)	22.6 (11.1)	2.9 (1.4)	203.2

	Race figures in millions (percentage of total in brackets)			Total population in millions
1980	188.4 (83.1)	26.5 (11.7)	11.7 (5.2)	226.5
1990	199.7 (80.3)	30 (12.1)	19 (7.7)	248.7
2000	211.5 (75.1)	34.7 (12.3)	35.3 (12.5)	281.4
2010	223.6 (72.4)	38.9 (12.6)	46.3 (15)	308.7

Native Americans: Manifest destiny and marginalisation

Before the United States of America existed, the North American continent was made up of hundreds of different nations: Cherokee, Sioux, Osage and so on. No single homogenous entity existed, and relations between these groups paralleled those in other continents, with trade, alliances, war, peace and all other state-to-state relations. A window to this rich diverse world is the large number of languages spoken on the North American continent: Before Europeans arrived *en-masse,* 300 languages were in use. (Today, over 150 native North American languages are spoken.)

The estimated population for the whole of the Americas (North, South and Central) in the late fifteenth century was between 50 and 100 million. Disease (some of it brought by Europeans) and conflict led to a horrific depopulation by up to 90 per cent. The first Europeans brought measles and smallpox and other diseases that the local population had no resistance to, with devastating effect.

During the 1600s and 1700s, as the Europeans began to establish themselves, multiply and expand, their relations with Native Americans became more problematic. A series of wars and treaties between the English and the Indians led to a gradual extension of the reach of the colonial settlers.

From the establishment of the United States from the 13 former colonies, attitudes towards the Native Americans did not alter. The Native Americans had fought military campaigns and enacted appeasement policies in order to keep some parts of their ancestral homes but the European advance could not be halted. In order to legitimise the expansion out to the West of the continent, the government introduced a series of treaties with the Indians to displace them from their tribal lands, culminating in the Removal Act of 1860 that gave the president authority to move Indian tribes in the South to federal land west of the Mississippi.

This Act brought them into the orbit of the government and also provided an incentive for those involved in making treaties with the Indians to bribe and cajole them into accepting harsh terms.

Within seven years of the Removal Act coming into force, 70 removal treaties moved about 50,000 Indians to a small area of what is now eastern Oklahoma. Although the states attempted to impose any terms they liked on the Native Americans because they did not see them as sovereign nations, the Supreme Court ultimately ruled, in 1831, that the Cherokee Nation was sovereign and immune to Georgia state laws. However, President Jackson effectively ignored this decision by persuading a Cherokee chief to sign a treaty and move west. Other Cherokees disputed this treaty and fought against being removed; as a result, in 1838 federal and Georgia state troops forced around 15,000 of them on a march west during which 3,000–4,000 of them died. By the 1840s no Native American tribes remained in what's now the Southern United States.

The economic and political advantages gained by expanding the land area of the Unites States were made possible by a cultural narrative that legitimised the forcible and brutal removal of people from their lands. That narrative stereotyped Native Americans as both noble savages and savages: noble when compliant and willing to negotiate land treaties with Whites but wild savages that needed taming when they resisted the designs of the White settlers.

Tied in with this appropriation of both Native American and Mexican land (see 'The African American's role as a slave') was the application of a composite of political, economic, cultural and religious reasons into a single framework, called *Manifest Destiny*, that legitimised this westward expansionism. It gave American settlers a mighty and unstoppable justification to acquire new lands through imagining that Americans and their political system were imbued with special virtues, that expansionism was inevitable and that the Wild West needed to be tamed and civilised. And it was their duty to do so.

The African American's role as a slave

Slavery was a key factor in the development of the American colonies from the early seventeenth century. The first African slaves were transported to Jamestown, Virginia, in 1619 to provide labour on tobacco plantations. For the next 240 years, slavery continued to be an important aspect of agricultural production in America.

By the start of the American Revolution in 1775 nearly 100,000 Africans had been transplanted as slaves to the Charleston area alone. And in this region, nearly 90 per cent of the population was black. In the late 1700s, the invention of the cotton gin to remove seeds from cotton plants enabled an expansion of the labour-intensive cotton planting in the southern states, further consolidating the economic importance of slavery to the American economy. Cotton production stood at about 3,000 bales in 1790, nearly 200,000 in 1812 and 4.5 million in 1860. Cotton accounted for half of all exports. This massive increase in cotton production meant an equally large increase in the number of slaves. In 1790, 700,000 people were enslaved in the United States but by 1860, just before the beginning of the Civil War, that number had risen to about 4 million, and those were predominantly in the Southern states.

During the constitutional debates following independence, Southerners were able to obtain three main concessions allowing for the continuation of slavery in spite of growing opposition to it among Northerners:

✔ The continuation of the slave trade with Africa.

✔ The three-fifths clause in the Constitution, which counted each slave as three-fifths of a person when determining the number of seats a state would have in the House of Representatives, and the number of votes for each state in the Electoral College (see Chapter 10 on the electoral process for further details). Because the Southern states had the greatest number of slaves, they had a disproportionate representation in the House and thus more impact in determining who won the presidency.

✔ The Federal Fugitive Slave Act of 1793, which gave local and state governments the authority to seize and return slaves to their owners, enabling slave catchers to cross state lines in pursuit of runaways and impose penalties on those aiding them.

The colonies north of Virginia had less use of slaves, principally because it was difficult for the Quakers in Pennsylvania and the Puritans in New England to fit the institution of slavery into their idealised views of the New World. And the cooler climates of the North meant that the cash crops of tobacco and sugar were not suitable and so enslaved labour was not ideal for the more diversified economy.

By 1804, all the northern states, whose economy was not contingent on slavery, had abolished the practice. Various anti-slavery societies developed to support African Americans escaping the plantations and travelling north. The Underground Railroad was one such organisation that helped upwards of 100,000 people escape slavery by connecting a series of safe houses through to the North and on to Canada. All of the states that maintained slavery instituted state laws and codes that defined what slaves were able to do. The long-term impact on the position of African Americans in society after slavery had been abolished has been dramatic. They were defined as chattel property of the owners, and their lives were controlled in a number of ways, including brutal punishment for those who transgressed these laws. They were prevented from learning to read and write, sexually exploited and encouraged to have children who were likely to be sold on to other slave owners. As well as everyday forms of resistance to slavery, rebellions also occurred whereby slaves attacked the people controlling them. Such rebellions created cultural justifications for continuing slavery by suggesting that Black people were incapable of being civilised and so needed to be repressed further.

The Westward expansion (legitimised through Manifest Destiny) from the early 1800s and the establishment of new states further divided the North and South. Whether these new lands would become free states or slave states became a subject of dispute. These disputes led to violence, federal military intervention and referenda that typically favoured the pro-slavery side.

In 1860, Abraham Lincoln was elected President of the United States, and by February 1861 (a month before he took his oath), South Carolina, Florida, Mississippi, Alabama, Georgia, Louisiana and Texas had claimed secession from the US. Six of these set up a new country called the Confederate States of America, which was understandably rejected by US President Buchanan and the incoming President Lincoln.

On 12 April, the Confederate Army attacked Fort Sumter in Charleston and the Civil War began. Slavery did not become a rationale for the war until Lincoln issued the Preliminary Emancipation Proclamation in September 1862. It declared that by 1 January 1863, if those rebelling against the Union did not give up the fight, 'all persons held as slaves within any State, or designated part of a State . . . shall be then, thenceforward, and forever free'. On that first day of 1863, around 3.1 million people who had been enslaved were liberated.

By the end of the war in 1865, 620,000 to 850,000 people had lost their lives out of a population of about 35 million. Slavery was abolished, but that didn't mean African Americans were treated as equals in American society in terms of politics, economics or culture. The next big step to gaining equality was the Civil Rights Movement.

Celebrating the Civil Rights Movement

The 1960s were a time of revolutionary change in American society. Among an increasing number of Americans, and the government, the dominant White Anglo Saxon Protestant culture (affectionately known as WASP) was recognised as being in need of an overhaul. It needed to better reflect the racial and ethnic diversity of the country in the political, cultural and economic realms.

Martin Luther King's landmark 'I have a dream' speech

On 28 August 1963 at the steps of the Lincoln Memorial in Washington, DC, Martin Luther King Jnr., gave a 17-minute speech that even today is phenomenally stirring – a speech that uses the language of justice found in the Declaration of Independence and the Constitution to explain what the future America can look like. The following two extracts to the speech illustrate its beauty, although I do recommend you listen to a recording to get the richness and power of King's voice.

In a sense we've come to our nation's capital to cash a check. When the architects of our republic wrote the magnificent words of the Constitution and the Declaration of Independence, they were signing a promissory note to which every American was to fall heir. This note was a promise that all men, yes, black men as well as white men, would be guaranteed the "unalienable Rights" of 'Life, Liberty and the pursuit of Happiness.' It is obvious today that America has defaulted on this promissory note, insofar as her citizens of color are concerned. Instead of honoring this sacred obligation, America has given the Negro people a bad check, a check which has come back marked 'insufficient funds.'

But we refuse to believe that the bank of justice is bankrupt. We refuse to believe that there are insufficient funds in the great vaults of opportunity of this nation. And so, we've come to cash this check, a check that will give us upon demand the riches of freedom and the security of justice.

And so even though we face the difficulties of today and tomorrow, I still have a dream. It is a dream deeply rooted in the American dream.

I have a dream that one day this nation will rise up and live out the true meaning of its creed: 'We hold these truths to be self-evident, that all men are created equal.'

I have a dream that one day on the red hills of Georgia, the sons of former slaves and the sons of former slave owners will be able to sit down together at the table of brotherhood.

I have a dream that one day even the state of Mississippi, a state sweltering with the heat of injustice, sweltering with the heat of oppression, will be transformed into an oasis of freedom and justice.

I have a dream that my four little children will one day live in a nation where they will not be judged by the color of their skin but by the content of their character.

I have a dream today!

I have a dream that one day, down in Alabama, with its vicious racists, with its governor having his lips dripping with the words of "interposition" and "nullification" – one day right there in Alabama little black boys and black girls will be able to join hands with little white boys and white girls as sisters and brothers.

I have a dream today!

The drive for change was particularly focused on the status of African Americans, although ultimately all minority groups benefitted. The racial and ethnic path of America changed course in three important ways: the drive for civil rights, the reform of immigration policies that no longer favoured White Europeans and the introduction of political, economic and cultural government policies designed to change America into a more multicultural society.

Moving America into civility

The distant antecedents to the Civil Rights Movement are the three amendments made to the Constitution in the years after the end of the Civil War (1861–1865), a period referred to as the *Reconstruction Era*:

✔ Thirteenth Amendment related to the banning of slavery and involuntary servitude (1865)

✔ Fourteenth Amendment related to the citizenship rights of all Americans, stating that all citizens had 'equal protection of the laws' (1868)

✔ Fifteenth Amendment stated that all Americans irrespective of 'race, color, or previous condition of servitude' had the right to vote in elections (obviously not women as they weren't seen as equals until early in the next century!) (1870)

However, in the early 1890s a series of Southern states introduced what became known as the *Jim Crow* laws. They enabled states to introduce separate facilities for Whites and African Americans in every facet of an individual's life, including public facilities such as swimming pools, medical centres and schools, the workplace, transportation, restaurants and shops.

While you may think, 'hang on a minute, doesn't this contravene the Fourteenth Amendment?' my answer would be no, not if you were a Supreme Court justice during the 1896 case of *Plessy vs. Ferguson*. Plessy, an African American, refused to move from an all-White to an all-Black railway carriage and was arrested under an 1890 Louisiana law stating that segregation was legal as long as equal facilities were provided. He argued that this statute was illegal under the Constitution because it violated the Thirteenth and Fourteenth Amendments. The Supreme Court decided against Plessy in a 7–1 ruling and declared that *separate but equal* did not violate the rights of citizens, and thus a state could now legally enact legislation that supported segregated facilities. This ruling effectively reversed the achievements gained as a result of the Union victory in the Civil War.

Another great advance in the civil rights movement came with the establishment of the National Association for the Advancement of Colored People (NAACP) in 1909 to fight for an end to race discrimination. From the 1920s, it began supporting legal battles that litigated and investigated a range of issues such as lynching and segregation in public and private facilities. It made big strides when it took a series of cases to the Supreme Court contesting the Constitutional legality of *white primaries* that enabled the Democratic Party to exclude members of other races from participating in choosing candidates for upcoming elections. In 1944, and in an 8–1 ruling, the Court overturned a previous ruling by stating that 'the right to vote in a primary for the nomination of candidates without discrimination by the State, like the right to vote in a general election, is a right secured by the Constitution'. The ruling ushered in a new, second era of reconstruction, more popularly known as the modern Civil Rights Movement, and increased voter registration among African Americans from about 150,000 in 1940 to about 700,000 in 1948, to a million in 1952.

A number of distinct moments from the 1950s onwards define the modern Civil Rights Movement:

- The 1954 Supreme Court ruling on segregation determined that separate educational facilities between African-Americans and Whites did not mean equal.

- The freedom rides on interstate public transport from 1961 by civil rights activists forced the question of the 1960 Supreme Court ruling that determined segregation in interstate travel was unconstitutional.

- The consequences of the 1963 march on Washington, DC, represented a growing opposition to the status quo of White supremacy.

- The Civil Rights Act of 1964 determined that segregation in public facilities and hiring based on race, ethnicity, religion, sex or national origin was illegal.

- The Voting Rights Act of 1965 ensured that unfair restrictions on access to the constitutional right of all people to vote, such as literacy tests,were illegal.

- The Civil Rights Act of 1968 provided equal opportunities for access to housing, making it illegal, for example, for landlords to discriminate based on race.

- Rosa Parks refused to give up her bus seat for a White man. As a consequence of her refusal she was arrested, charged and convicted under the state's segregation laws. That incident incited a boycott and brought the segregationist policies of the country into question. On 13 November 1956 the Supreme Court ruled that segregated transport was unconstitutional as it violated the due process and equal protection clauses of the Fourteenth Amendment.

✔ Various civil rights organisations held a rally in Washington, DC, on 28 August 1963 to call for jobs and freedom for all races and ethnicities. About 250,000 people attended the march, and prominent religious and civil rights leaders spoke. Notably, Dr Martin Luther King gave his famous *I have a dream* speech.

✔ In June 1963, President Kennedy spoke to the nation explaining the right of the Black students to attend the University of Alabama, and strongly encouraged Congress to introduce civil rights legislation designed to enable 'all Americans the right to be served in facilities which are open to the public' and 'authorize the Federal Government to participate more fully in lawsuits designed to end segregation in public education'.

✔ The Civil Rights Act was passed in July 1964. States could no longer segregate between races and ethnicities in businesses or public facilities, such as restaurants, swimming pools and hotels. Neither could businesses nor government discriminate based on colour, religion or gender.

✔ In Mississippi, in the summer of 1964, the NAACP, among others, set up the *Freedom Summer* project aimed at increasing black voter registration. Freedom Schools taught students about black history and the importance of the Civil Rights Movement, as well as provided legal and medical advice. In that summer alone, 17,000 Black Mississippians registered to vote.

✔ In early January 1965, the clergy-driven Southern Christian Leadership Conference (SCLC) and other organisations put together a campaign for African Americans to register to vote in Selma, Alabama. At one protest, in the adjoining county, on 18 February, a church deacon, Jimmie Lee Jackson, was shot by a state trooper while protecting his mother from attack. He died a few days later.

✔ In response to this attack, on 7 March 1965, the SCLC, led by King, organised a protest march from Selma to the state capital in Montgomery. On the bridge outside Selma, police attacked the protesters using sticks and tear gas. The media were recording the attacks and the event became known as *Bloody Sunday*. A second march, two days later, involving even more protesters, was again broken up. On that night, Reverend James Reeb, a White minister, was beaten up; he later died in hospital. A week later, President Johnson spoke to a joint session of Congress about what was happening in Selma, and delivered the message to America, the world and Congress that 'every American citizen must have an equal right to vote. There is no reason which can excuse the denial of that right. There is no duty which weighs more heavily on us than the duty we have to ensure that right.'

✔ On 17 March 1965, the Voting Rights Act was submitted to Congress as a Senate bill (see Chapter 7 for details on how a bill becomes law). Key to the bill was its determination that states or local governments could employ 'no voting qualification or prerequisite to voting, or standard, practice, or procedure . . . to deny or abridge the right of any citizen of the United States to vote on account of race or color'.

On 21 March 1965, with a Supreme Court ruling enforcing their right to march, and protection provided by FBI agents and the Alabama National Guard (which had been taken under federal control), King led thousands of people on a five-day march to Montgomery. On 3 August the bill was passed by the House of Representatives by 328–74 and a day later in the Senate by 79–18. Two days later, in the presence of Martin Luther King, Rosa Parks and other civil rights leaders, President Johnson signed the bill into law. The impact of the Voting Rights Act was impressive in its speed and coverage. By the end of 1965, almost 250,000 more African Americans had registered to vote. At the end of 1966, in 9 of the 13 Southern states 50 per cent of African Americans eligible to vote were registered to do so. Obviously, greater numbers of African Americans voters meant an increase in African Americans elected to office. From 1965 to 1985, in 11 of the Southern states, African American state legislators increased from 3 to 176. And across the United States between 1970 and 1980, the number of African Americans in state-wide elected positions more than tripled, to 4,912.

✔ The Civil Rights Act of 1968, also known as the Fair Housing Act, prohibited anyone from refusing to sell or rent a property based on their race, colour, religion or national origin. Neither could any statement or advertisement be printed or published that preferred or intended to prefer one group over another. It also prohibited a property owner from denying that a property was for rent or sale solely because they didn't want a member of a particular group to live there (gender and family status were added to this legislation in 1974 and 1988, respectively). This Act had a big impact on an individual's right to live in a place of his own choosing.

Immigration reform

As America continued to change the way it addressed its ethnic and racial identity, immigration priorities shifted away from privileging Whites. The 1965 Immigration and Naturalization Act (otherwise known as the Hart–Celler Act) changed US immigration policy, and thus the future racial and ethnic path of America. It replaced a former and overwhelmingly racial policy that encouraged White European immigration at the expense of others.

Rosa Parks' legacy and non-violent protest

The protests initiated by Rosa Parks' refusal to give her bus seat to a White woman led to the founding of the Southern Christian Leadership Conference (SCLC). Martin Luther King was the president of this clergy-driven organisation. Its three-pronged mission statement

✔ Pressed for White Americans to join African Americans in their struggle for equality

✔ Urged African Americans to fight for justice

✔ Promoted non-violent activism

Its first major non-violent campaign, in late 1961, involved protesting against Georgia's segregation laws. Not until the Birmingham, Alabama non-violent protests in 1963 did King garner the national and international media attention the Civil Rights Movement needed. The Birmingham march was protesting against the segregation of businesses and attempting to persuade the owners to end segregation for customers in public facilities, shops and restaurants, and open up employment opportunities for African Americans and others.

King and others disobeyed a court injunction against the protesters and were jailed as a result. On 20 April, following the involvement of President John F. Kennedy's administration,

King was released. The protests continued and on 2 May, the SCLC organised a march involving in excess of 1,000 students marching into downtown Birmingham.

One of the town's commissioners, Eugene 'Bull' Connor, not renowned for his desire to improve racial equality, authorised the local police and fire services to attack the protesters with guard dogs, batons and water hoses. This protest was shown on television all over the world and there's nothing like non-violent protesters being beaten up by government agents for grabbing people's attention. One of these people was President Kennedy.

On 10 May 1963, the *Birmingham Truce Agreement*, discontinuing segregation, was signed by both officials and protesters. Businesses would hire more Black people, and toilets, restaurants and public facilities would be open for everyone to use. Because a number of places frequented by protesters were subsequently bombed, and in response to the state government not dealing with the situation, President Kennedy ordered 3,000 federal military troops to be stationed nearby the town and threatened to remove the Alabama National Guard from state control.

From the 1880s onwards, immigration reforms were implemented to control who was allowed to enter the country. In 1882, the Chinese Exclusion Act was passed by Congress banning Chinese immigration because of fears of increasing unemployment and the lowering of wages. The Act also had friends within the eugenic movement who determined that the Chinese were racially inferior, and it excluded other unwanted groups such as mentally incapable and insane people and those who had committed political crimes. By 1902 this temporary legislation had become permanent.

Over the next 50 years, other immigration laws were passed, reinforcing existing laws against immigration and expanding who should be excluded from entering the country. Some examples include:

- A series of naturalisation safeguards enacted in 1906 to ensure that the dominant Anglo culture was protected. It included making the English language a condition of acceptance.

- The Emergency Quota Act passed into law in 1921, which implemented a quota system that limited immigration to 3 per cent of the number of people from that country based on their numbers as determined in the 1910 US Census. The impact on immigration was two-fold. First, it reduced the number of immigrants from around 800,000 in 1920 to about 300,000 in 1922. Second, and this was the reason for its introduction, it disproportionately favoured immigration of White Northern Europeans because they were the predominant group in the US at the time of the 1910 census.

- The Immigration Act of 1924, which further limited immigration via a more stringent quota system. Immigration from a country was now capped at 2 per cent of the number of people from that country living in the US based on the 1890 US Census. It meant that around 70 per cent of immigrants came from three countries: Germany, Ireland and the UK. The Act also excluded Asian people from emigrating to the US.

By 1943, in part in response to the Second World War, immigration laws were loosened. Agricultural workers were being allowed to enter from the rest of the Americas, and the Chinese Exclusion Act was repealed, allowing for Chinese immigration for the first time in 60 years. By 1952, the Immigration and Nationality Act (otherwise known as the McCarran–Walter Act) had consolidated all these various Acts into one and maintained the nationality-based quota system – and maintained a bias towards Western immigration. By the time of the Civil Rights Movement in the 1960s growing dissatisfaction was evident among hyphenated Americans – for example, Polish-Americans and Italian-Americans – that immigration rules favoured Northern Europeans.

In 1965, when the Voting Rights and the Civil Rights Acts were being introduced into law, the Immigration and Naturalization Act responded to the biased US immigration and naturalisation policies. The Act replaced the national quota system with one focusing mainly on immigration favouring relatives of already existing US citizens and people with US residency and preferring those with skills required by the economy. No restrictions were placed on the number of familial-based immigrants, while those entering the country for other reasons were capped at 290,000 people a year.

While various supporters of the Act, at the time, had argued that it wouldn't have a dramatic impact on the racial and ethnic make-up of the country, the reality has been somewhat different:

✔ Even in the years immediately after the Act was passed, dramatic changes occurred when Asian immigrants, effectively barred under the quota system, entered the country from places such as Vietnam, China and Japan.

✔ Not only has the absolute number of immigrants increased following the 1965 Act – and the later 1990 Immigration Act (which increased the number of immigrants able to come to the country to 700,000 a year) – from about 6 million in the 30 years before the Act to 18 million in the 30 years after the Act, so too has the racial and ethnic profile of those who have migrated:

  • In 1960, 9.7 million people in the US (9.7 per cent of the population) were foreign born. Of those 9.7 million, 75 per cent were from Europe, 10 per cent North America (that is, Canada and Mexico), 5 per cent Latin America and 5 per cent Asia.

  • In 2012, 40 million Americans were foreign born, equating to 12.9 per cent of the population. Of those 40 million, immigrants from Europe declined dramatically, to a mere 12 per cent, 53 per cent came from Latin America and 28 per cent from Asia.

Not only has legal immigration had an impact on the racial and ethnic make-up of America but so too has illegal immigration. According to the Pew Research Center, in 2010 about 11.2 million unauthorised immigrants were resident in the US, and of those, 8 million were working. Looking at country of origin, as a result of the border with the US the majority came from Latin America:

✔ 6.5 million (58 per cent) from Mexico

✔ 2.6 million (23 per cent) from other Latin American countries

✔ 1.3 million (11 per cent) from Asia

✔ Just under 500,000 (4 per cent) from Canada and Europe

✔ Around 400,000 (3 per cent) from Africa and other countries

Throughout this rapid expansion, opposition to immigration reforms and illegal immigration has been expressed. The 1986 Immigration Reform and Control Act, for example, was an attempt to deter illegal immigration by increasing inspection and enforcement at the borders, mainly at the one with Mexico, imposing penalties on businesses that employed unauthorised migrants and, rather paradoxically, giving 2.7 million illegal immigrants already in the country the right to claim citizenship. Its principal objective of deterring illegal immigration clearly didn't work when you consider that 11.2 million such migrants were believed to be in the country in 2010. Illegal immigration has declined only once in the last 20 years and that was the product of a downturn in the economy following the 2008 financial crisis. More recent attempts to deal with illegal immigration have stalled in light of the upcoming mid-term elections in November 2014. No political party or elected official is willing to contravene party lines and risk losing the election for the sake of a rational solution that involves making compromises.

Multiculturalism

Multiculturalism isn't just about race and ethnicity, it also involves sexual preference, gender and lifestyle choice. Whilst multiculturalism can simply refer to multiple cultures existing within one geographic location, this chapter looks at it from a nuanced definition that includes relationships among the multiple cultures living and working in one location, discussions on the relative dominance of cultures over others, and the impact this has in determining economic, political and educational success of members of the different cultures.

In the United States, multiculturalism is also a public policy designed by the government at the local, state and federal levels to address the imbalances that exist within American society. It supports a space that happily allows a plurality of groups to have their own voice and not be dominated by one particular narrative. In other words, someone can be Hispanic-American, and not be restricted in their access to education because their first language is Spanish and not English.

Policies addressing multiculturalism developed out of the 1960s Civil Rights Movement and resulting legislation as an attempt to break down the inequalities within society. The impact of these policies can be divided into three strands – political, cultural and economic – each of which is subject to controversy. Each strand's actions influence the other strands in one way or another. As just one example, this section discusses affirmative action and its economic impact from the 1960s onwards.

Changing the politics of America

Multiculturalist policies have served to increase the representation of ethnic and racial minorities in government, including elected and appointed positions. One example is policies regarding the redistricting of electoral areas (see Chapter 10 for more on redistricting) based on two sections of the Civil Rights Act, which prohibit discrimination against minority voters and require state governments to seek preclearance for redistricting.

In 1986, the Supreme Court, in *Thornburg vs. Gingles*, provided a two-part test to determine whether a state redistricting plan was acceptable. It reinforced the position of the federal government under Section 5 of the Civil Rights Act to actively support redistricting to ensure a majority for the minority groups, thus raising the possibility of minority representation in office. The power of the federal government to approve districts did, however, lead to some questionable districts, such as those with populations connected solely by an interstate road. These types of district were curtailed by the Supreme Court's ruling in the 1993 *Shaw vs. Reno* case.

While this policy (and others) hasn't created a representative balance of officials based on racial and ethnic identity, the situation has changed significantly over the years. Take, for example, the number of Black and Hispanic elected officials at the local, state and federal levels. These positions include municipal and school board officials to state governors and legislators to members of Congress.

- ✔ According to the National Roster of Black Elected Officials, in 1970 1,469 Black elected officials existed; by 2011 that number had grown to over 10,500.

- ✔ According to the National Association of Latino Elected and Appointed Officials, in 1996 there were 3,743 elected officials; by 2011 5,850 were in office.

Changing the dominant American culture

At a cultural level, multiculturalism is about enabling expression from cultures other than the dominant one. It can include an increase in the development of media programmes targeted towards particular groups, which both elevates that group's culture and educates other people to it, and can also include an acceptance of different cultural practices such as the wearing of particular religious dress when working for the government. These all contest and expand the definition of the dominant culture.

Educational policies to address the recognition of other cultural narratives within school curricula, such as the stories of Native Americans and African Americans, were borne out of the 1960s Civil Rights Movement. Over time, schools and colleges have expanded the range of texts used in class and encouraged greater discussion of different groups and their practices within the classroom. Take, for example, the discussion of the founding of the US in high school history classes. No longer is the idea that the Native Americans required civilising, the dominant narrative when the United States was being established, reinforced by the school curriculum. Multicultural education policies also address the issues raised by the changing demographics of the US, including accommodating students for whom English is a second language.

Changing the economy: Affirmative action

The historic favouring of one ethnic or racial group within the political, economic and social realms limits the opportunities of people in disadvantaged groups. These three areas of favouritism lead to a constant denial of opportunities for disadvantaged groups because they reinforce each other. Having minimal political rights, for example, ensures that you do not get a seat at the table, which can further drive your isolation by reducing resources, such as educational funding. This poor resourcing can lead to poor education and limit economic opportunities, as people are not sufficiently educated to attain good and well-paid employment. One way of addressing this inequality is by directly impacting the educational aspect and improving the economic opportunities of disadvantaged groups.

Affirmative action is a tool for addressing these inequalities, and it provides a helping hand to people to ensure they're able to gain access to employment or educational opportunities. President Johnson, rather inspiringly, best described the logic behind affirmative action in a 1965 address to the historically Black Howard University. He said, 'you do not take a person who, for years, has been hobbled by chains and liberate him, bring him up to the starting line of a race and then say, "you are free to compete with all the others," and still justly believe that you have been completely fair'. Unfortunately, the federal government took some time to take this idea on board.

Since the early 1940s the federal government has employed programmes designed to elevate the status of disadvantaged groups. Initial affirmative action-based programmes focused almost exclusively on African Americans but, as the decades went by, included other disadvantaged groups too:

- ✔ In 1941, President Roosevelt issued *Executive Order* (EO) 8802 (an EO is an order from the president without Congressional or judicial input that directs the actions of federal or state agencies). It required defence contractors for the federal government to implement non-discriminatory employment policies. By 1943, this order had been extended to all federally-employed contractors and subcontractors.

- ✔ Building on Roosevelt's policies, President Kennedy's 1961 Executive Order 10925 established the federal Equal Employment Opportunity Committee (EEOC) to oversee equality of opportunity within the executive branch of government. It also ensured that government-appointed contractors and subcontractors had to actively promote equality within their workforce and equality of their treatment 'without regard to their race, creed, color, or national origin'.

- ✔ President Johnson introduced Executive Order 11246 in 1965. This order transferred responsibility for enforcing affirmative action in employment on the part of contractors and subcontractors from the EEOC to the new

Office of Federal Contract Compliance Programs (OFCCP) regulated by the Department of Labor. It also included monitoring affirmative action programmes in university colleges. In 1967 it was amended by Executive Order 11375, which added gender discrimination as being prohibited alongside race, colour, religion and national origin.

✔ By the time Richard Nixon became president, the systemic pressures that maintained inequality in employment were being addressed head-on by the federal government, in particular the construction industry. By 1969 Nixon gradually implemented a programme that required federally-appointed contractors along with the unions to act in good faith to appoint minority groups at a level determined by the government. In the early 1970s, a series of cases questioning the legitimacy of affirmative action reached the Supreme Court; however, the Court favoured a broad understanding of affirmative action.

✔ In the late 1970s, reflecting a sea-change in government and public attitudes to its scope and range, the courts questioned the Constitutional status of affirmative action and refined its reach. This narrowing in scope has continued to the present day.

To demonstrate the impact these changes in attitudes and court opinion have on American society, I examine the case of university enrolment based on race and ethnicity. Huge inequality existed between the numbers of Black and White students attending university. In 1965, for example, only 5 per cent of undergraduates, 2 per cent of medical students and 1 per cent of law students were African American. Affirmative action in education aimed to redress this historical imbalance by increasing the number of students from underrepresented groups by providing financial and academic support programmes to increase their chances of success. It was aimed at elevating their earning potential and economic status in-line with non-discriminated groups. Affirmative action was also intended to increase cultural equality among ethnic and racial groups; by seeing each other as equals, it was hoped that future workplace interaction between Black and White employees would be improved.

In 1978, the Supreme Court ruled on the admissions policy at the University of California's medical school, in *Regents of the University of California vs. Bakke*. The regular admissions policy was based on a series of metric tests and interviews; a special policy existed for people who declared themselves 'economically and/or educationally disadvantaged' or a member of an ethnic minority (Black, Native American, Asian or Hispanic). Those in the second category did not have to achieve the same high school grades. Of the 100 places offered each year, 16 were reserved for students in this special category. While no clear majority opinion was reached (in fact, six different opinions were written), the Supreme Court did declare that the fixing of a quota for special admissions violated the 1964 Civil Rights Act (prohibiting discrimination based on race for federally-funded programmes). However, it also declared that race could be considered a factor in admissions programmes, and that affirmative action could be encouraged in order to establish a racially diverse student body.

By the late 1990s – and the appointment of more conservative Supreme Court justices – affirmative action in university admission policy was increasingly restricted. It was seen by some as *reverse discrimination* – a policy of favouring the minority group at the expense of admission based on academic achievement. Likewise, it was argued that affirmative action was unconstitutional according to the equal protection clause within the Fourteenth Amendment because it favoured one group over others, and contravened the 1964 Civil Rights Act because it discriminated based on race. Opponents also argued that the beneficiaries of affirmative action were predominantly middle- and upper-class students from minority groups and not those from the working class, and that low admission grade requirements were a disincentive to hard work on the part of minority students. The by-product of affirmative action was seen as a reinforcement of racial prejudice – on the part of both the majority group and minority groups – rather than a diminution because race and not ability determined admission.

In 1994, opponents to affirmative action in education were winning a series of court cases and legislative and executive orders across the county. Supporters of affirmative action took their case to the Supreme Court but their request for a hearing (grant of *certiorari*) was denied.

Around the same time, one case did make its way to the federal appeals court and the court's opinion had a profound effect on university admission policies around the country. In *Hopwood vs. Texas* (1996) four White prospective students complained that they had not been accepted for the law school programme at the University of Texas, even though they had better scores than a number of Black and Hispanic students who had been offered places. They argued that they were being discriminated against under the equal protection clause of the Fourteenth Amendment. The judges ruled overwhelmingly in favour of the four prospective students and decreed that the law school could not use race as a factor in determining 'which applicants to admit in order to achieve a diverse student body, to combat the perceived effects of a hostile environment at the law school, to alleviate the law school's poor reputation in the minority community, or to eliminate any present effects of past discrimination by actors other than the law school'. This ruling forced universities to rethink their admission policies.

Two similar cases, involving the University of Michigan and its law school, went through the lower courts and both reached the Supreme Court in 2003. In each case, the plaintiffs argued that they were subject to reverse discrimination. The rulings restricted affirmative action by defining the terms under which it could be employed. Cases following this decision have also maintained a limited application of affirmative action within university acceptance policies.

Affirmative action was once widely applied but over time was curtailed by a series of criteria determining that it could not discriminate against others irrespective of whether they came from advantaged groups. Herein lies the dilemma. I think that providing structural support to historically disadvantaged groups is necessary as a means of increasing their chance of achieving economic success – even at the expense of others. A significant period of transition is needed to address over 200 years of inequality. If one is serious about creating equality, advantaged groups (that is, White people) who've benefitted from this history of inequality need to make sacrifices.

Defining Life in America Today through the Lens of Race and Ethnicity

How far has America come in terms of embracing its immigrants? I'll let the stats tell the story. Earlier sections show the difficulties people have faced during America's history as a result of their race or ethnicity, and although progress is evident, statistics reveal that, in spite of advances in terms of the rights afforded to minority groups and their apparent equality before the law, serious differences in achievement levels still exist. They are a reflection of remaining structural and cultural impediments to equality.

Employment and unemployment

Table 14-2 shows 2012 Bureau of Labor Statistics on employment, unemployment, and weekly earnings for Americans based on their racial and ethnic identity. A couple of key take-homes are that Blacks, American Indians and Alaska Natives had the lowest levels of employment. Blacks and Hispanics had the lowest levels in managerial and professional careers, which was further reflected in the lower earnings of Blacks and Hispanics. And unemployment figures were greatest for Blacks, with all indigenous American groups not that far behind.

Table 14-2	Employment and unemployment statistics based on race and ethnicity (2012)			
Race or ethnic group	*Employment %*	*Employment in management, professional, and related occupations %*	*Median weekly earnings $*	*Unemployment %*
American Indians and Alaska Natives	52.1	*	*	12.3
Asians	60.1	49	920	5.9
Blacks	53	30	621	13.8
Hispanics	59.5	21	568	10.3
Native Hawaiians and Other	63	*	*	11.8
Whites	59.4	39	792	7.2

* Data unavailable

Education

In 2013 there were nearly 207 million people over the age of 25 in the United States. Of those, two thirds were non-Hispanic Whites, three out of twenty were ethnic Hispanic (of any race), just over one out of ten were Black, and one out of twenty were Asian. Table 14-3 shows you the racial breakdown of the population. The percentage breakdown in each race and ethnic category regarding education levels shows a discrepancy in who's earning degrees.

Table 14-3	Population figures of people over the age of 25 by race or ethnic group (2013)
Race or ethnic group	*Population figures of people over the age of 25 (millions)*
Asian	11.2
Black	24.4
Hispanic	29.1
Non-Hispanic White	139.7

For those who had taken three years of college but did not have a degree the biggest figures were for Black people, with less than one out of ten Blacks over the age of 25, whilst the lower figures were for Asians with less than one out of twenty. But whilst the differences in this category are not that big, when the education qualifications rise there is a dramatic change in the percentage of each group. Nearly one quarter of Asians had a bachelor's degree, whilst only one out of ten Blacks and less than one out of ten Hispanics had one. This divergence continued through to master's programmes as well. In other words, the chances of you having employment, a good wage and a good education increase if you are either an Asian or White non-Hispanic. Table 14-4 breaks down education by race or ethnic group.

Table 14-4	Education level of population over the age of 25 by race or ethnic group (2013)			
Race or ethnic group	*Education level of population over the age of 25 as a % of the race or ethnic group*			
	High School Diploma	*Three years of college but no degree*	*Bachelor's degree*	*Master's degree*
Asian	18.8	4.6	23.9	14.7
Black	30.3	8.2	9.8	6.1
Hispanic	27.2	5.3	8.1	3.4
Non-Hispanic White	27	6.4	15.8	9.4

Prison population

According to the Bureau of Justice Statistics, in 2012 there were nearly 1.5 million prisoners in state and federal prisons and .74 million in local jails. In total that is 2.2 million people incarcerated. It works out at about 707 per 100,000. More than one out of every 100 Americans is incarcerated. When compared to other countries this statistic becomes even more mind-blowing. It's nearly seven times more than in most Western nations.

When broken down by race and ethnicity the picture is even starker. Racial and ethnic minorities are more likely to be arrested, convicted and then face tougher sentences than White non-Hispanics. In comparing the prison population to the

US population the discrepancy is as stark. The Black prison population in the US in 2009 was nearly 40 per cent of the total prison population but only 13 per cent of the US population, the Hispanic prison population was over 20 per cent of the prison population and was just under 17 per cent of the country, and the White non-Hispanic prison population was 34 per cent and made-up 63 per cent of the US population. African American men, for example, are about 6 times more likely to go to prison or jail than White non-Hispanic males, and Hispanic males are 2.5 times more likely to be incarcerated than White non-Hispanics men.

Broken down another way, one out of 17 White non-Hispanic men, one out of six Hispanic males, and one out of three African Americans born today will spend time in jail or prison. These figures reflect the racial and ethnic barriers prevalent within American society but also the massive gap between rich and poor. If you are rich, you will have better representation and are more likely to have a lighter sentence if convicted. And if you are poor, you will have poor representation, usually inexperienced court-appointed lawyers, be more likely to be sentenced and have tougher sentences when convicted. The connection of wealth with race and ethnicity is that you are more likely to be poor if you are not a member of the White non-Hispanic or Asian groups.

Law enforcement agencies also show prejudice in dealing with people from ethnic or racial groups. This includes the increased likelihood of police brutality due to reinforcing prejudiced stereotyping. In 2013, for example, a federal judge declared that the New York City Police Department's policy of stop-and-frisk was deemed unconstitutional because it unfairly targeted minorities without any due reason. In making her ruling, the federal judge suggested that this policy contravened the 14th Amendment's equal protection clause (all people must be treated equally under the law) and the 4th Amendment, which protects people against government's unreasonable searches and seizures. The policy had been ongoing for a number of years but under Mayor Michael Bloomberg (2002-2013) its role in policing had been greatly increased. In 2002, for example, New Yorkers were stopped just over 97,000 times and by 2012 they were stopped nearly 533,000 times. When this is broken down by race, the prejudice of racial profiling is apparent. In the 2012 stats, 55 per cent (over 284,000) were Black, 32 per cent (165,000 were Latino) and only 10 per cent were White (50,000).

Chapter 15

Examining Fault Lines in American Society

The United States has a population of about 320 million – a lot of people with plenty of ideas about how lives should be led, not just their own but those of others, too. One of the ways in which these ideas can be classified is by observing whether people support a progressive position whereby they seek to expand current notions of what's acceptable and create a new norm or a traditional position in which they hold on to an often idealised and sometimes imagined past.

This chapter examines the contentious issues of gun control, capital punishment, abortion and reproductive rights, gay rights and healthcare to identify the relevant arguments and work out how they map on to the big divide in American society.

Looking at the Big Five Issues in American Society from Two Different Angles

Modern moral debates often involve competing claims about rights. And these claims navigate around the two extremes of conservatism and progressivism. Typically, the proponents of these extremes are the most vocal, and what tends to happen is that the rights of one group are supported at the expense of those of other groups. This paralysing extremism of 'us and them' creates a locked-horn situation whereby discussion of alternatives is structurally dissuaded and compromise is negligible. Luckily, and more often than not, the proponents of these extremes do not reflect the views of the American public. The majority of the public tend to sit somewhere in the middle.

The terms *conservative* and *progressive* have come to be acceptable short-hand for the two most prevalent sets of beliefs about humanity informing political ideas. They were introduced in James Hunter's influential 1992 book, *Culture Wars: The Struggle to Define America*, which details how key debates in American society collectively reflected a conflict that divided America. These ideas are dependent on differing interpretations of *moral authority*, or basic beliefs that inform a person's worldview.

Hunter suggests that the divide between conservatives and progressives differs from previous fault lines that have haunted American society since its foundation. It cuts across religious divides between Catholics, Protestants, Jews and others, and instead focuses on ideological battles:

✔ In the conservative interpretation of the world, morality is definable, absolute and unchanging. Irrespective of the era in which we live, we need to obey the same moral code. While conservatives can be secular, moral codes are typically defined by religious texts.

✔ From the progressive perspective, morality is defined by our experiences and not some external and absolute defined force. It is a product of the changing society in which we live.

From this ecumenical battle, the fight to dominate the narrative of public culture in contemporary America evolves.

When I talk about extremes in this book, I'm referring to the position furthest from the other perspective, not the value or content of that extreme. I'm using it to give a sense of position rather than to pass judgement on the content of that position.

Can American society be so easily reduced to a number of cultural markers that define its political and social landscape? If we answer *yes,* then we're accepting that everyone sits on either one of the extreme polar narratives that ask Americans to decide whether 'you are with us or against us'. This situation is quite clearly not the case. Although the public discourse may exacerbate these extremes and drown out the voices of nuance and sliding scales, the American population is somewhat different.

In understanding these varying fault lines in contemporary American society, it's essential to describe the two extremes. Doing so gives a picture of the alternating positions that Americans can align themselves with. While they are extremes and don't reflect the average American's position, the organisations, politicians and commentators that represent these ways of life do, however, play an important role in American political life and hence cannot be excluded from the discussion (for further details on the power of interest groups, see Chapter 13). But I don't want to give the impression that these extremes are what every American ascribes to; think of the American population as the antidote to the extremism of the culture wars. Each issue that I discuss in the upcoming sections raises a different fault line that appears to rip American society apart. But while, at times, vitriolic animosity does exist between the extremes, the American population sits somewhere in the middle, dispelling the apocalyptic visions of the future.

Reviewing Gun Control

The Constitution's Second Amendment guarantees every American the right to own a gun. To buy a gun from a dealer, a background check is required; however, most states allow people to buy guns from a private seller without any of these checks. Americans can purchase many different types of guns, ranging from a pistol to a shotgun, rifle or a semi-automatic assault rifle. In other words, it is easy to get a gun in America.

On the one side of the debate about gun rights, you have the *traditionalists* (pro-gun), supported in their views by interest groups such as the National Rifle Association (NRA) that are vehemently against all forms of gun control. On the other side, the *progressives* (pro-gun control) aren't against gun ownership as such but, rather, are against the ease with which guns can be purchased. Whether this situation reflects the success of the pro-gun lobby to dictate the terms of the discussion and ensure that banning guns isn't a political reality is up for debate.

Estimated figures suggest that anything between 270 and 310 million guns are owned in the United States. That's approximately one gun per American, although of course some people have none and others have plenty. In 2013, about a quarter of Americans stated that they owned a gun whilst over a third said they lived in a home where a gun was held. And with a lot of guns in circulation come a lot of deaths. In 2010, over 30,000 people were killed by guns, with just over a third being murders and the rest suicides. This rate of death by guns is three times that of other developed countries such as Sweden or the UK.

The gun control lobby

The progressives observe gun-related statistics, along with the infamous multiple massacres such as Columbine and Sandy Hook (see the sidebar 'Shooting massacres since 1999'), and suggest gun legislation is urgently required. Pro-gun control organisations, such as the national Coalition to Stop Gun Violence, lobby for the following:

- ✔ Running universal background checks on people wanting to buy a gun.

- ✔ Banning semi-automatic guns for home-ownership.

- ✔ Micro-stamping bullet cases so that every bullet can be traced back to the gun that fired it.

- ✔ Opposing the laws in over 38 states that enable people to carry a loaded gun in public with minimal or no checks on their suitability or otherwise for doing so.

- ✔ Opposing Stand Your Ground – legislation in 27 states that enables someone to shoot another they fear could cause them 'great bodily harm' such as in a fistfight.

- ✔ Raising debate between the role of mental health and gun violence (including suicide) to explore how to restrict gun use for some mentally ill people without stigmatising them.

- ✔ Opposing a bill signed into law by President Bush in 2005 that removed the right for a plaintiff to sue the gun industry, both manufacturers and retailers, in US courts in relation to suspected negligent practices.

The high rate of murders is a key factor in the lobby's argument for increasing controls on access to guns. Attached to this is their opposition to the pro-gun narrative that suggests gun murders are a product of the 'other' class, that is, criminal outsiders, and not of law-abiding citizens. The gun control people object to this narrative because it paints a picture that criminals are responsible for most shootings and they can always have access to guns, so why should innocent law-abiding citizens have to suffer restrictions on the constitutionally granted rights because of the actions of the few?

If the pro-gun argument was accurate, then the stats would show that most people who were murdered with a gun were shot by someone they didn't know, i.e., a criminal. However, this argument is somewhat thwarted by crime statistics reported by the Federal Bureau of Intelligence (FBI), which shows that more than three times as many people are murdered by someone they knew than by a stranger. The gun control lobby suggest this debunks the pro-gun argument that it's the fault of criminal outsiders.

The gun-control lobby do not have the same level of influence as the pro-gun lobby, and this is particularly evident in the funding levels that the lobby has to give to politicians running for election or to promote their political agenda amongst the public. In congressional elections, for example, in the ten years leading up to 2010, the gun-control lobby gave 28 times less (only $245,000) the amount to House and Senate contenders than the gun lobby.

Shooting massacres since 1999

Date	Incident and location	Number of deaths and injuries
23 May 2014	Young man in La Isla, California opens fire on people whilst driving his car	6 killed (3 not killed by gun) and 13 injured
16 September 2013	Lone gunman enters the US Navy Yard in Washington, DC and shoots people	12 killed and 3 injured
14 December 2012	Young man kills his mother and then travels to Sandy Hook Elementary School in Newtown, Connecticut and starts shooting	20 children and 6 adults killed
20 July 2012	In Aurora, Colorado a young man enters a cinema showing the new Batman film and opens fire on the audience	12 killed and 58 injured
5 November 2009	A US Army psychiatrist opens fire at Fort Hood in Texas	13 killed and 29 injured
16 April 2007	Student at Virginia Tech in Virginia opens fire at the university campus	32 killed and 17 injured
2 October 2006	Man shoots children in an Amish school in Nickel Mines, Pennsylvania	5 children killed and 5 injured
21 March 2005	In the Red Lake Indian Reservation in Minnesota, a young man killed his grandfather and partner and then went to the Senior High School and shot people	5 children and 4 adults killed and 5 others injured
15 September 1999	White Supremacist in Fort Worth, Texas shoots people at the Wedgwood Baptist Church	4 children and 3 adults killed and 7 others injured
29 July 1999	In Atlanta, Georgia a man opens fire in two financial trading offices	12 killed (3 not killed by gun) and 13 injured
20 April 1999	Two students at Columbine High School, Colorado open fire at the school	12 children and 1 adult killed and 21 injured

The pro-gun lobby

In an argument centred on the rights of the individual to possess a gun, traditionalists suggest that the decent law-abiding majority of gun owners shouldn't be prejudiced against because of the actions of a few. In an effort to contextualise the level of deaths by guns, the gun lobby compare the approximately 30,000 deaths caused by firearms, in 2010 with the 33,000 people killed by motor vehicles.

The gun lobby, represented most notably by the National Rifle Association (NRA), has been very successful in thwarting the ambitions of those who want to restrict gun ownership. The NRA aims to ensure that Americans continue to have access to guns. In that effort, it supports legislation such as Stand Your Ground (which enables someone to shoot another they fear could cause 'great bodily harm') and the right for people to carry a concealed gun in public, and opposes legislative proposals such as restrictions on owning assault weapons, background checks on people buying guns at gun shows, databases that keep records of gun purchases and changes in how guns are registered.

The power of the NRA to effect its agenda is impressive. It focuses on using its 5 million grass roots members to support its campaigns to halt gun restrictions by writing letters to elected politicians, and it provides funding, lobbying and campaign support to elected representatives who support its agenda. In the 2011–2012 election cycle, for example, the NRA spent over $18 million on supporting and opposing particular candidates and lobbied nearly 70 bills passing through Congress. Perhaps one of its most controversial strategies is targeting areas that have recently experienced a gun massacre. In late March 2013, three months after the Sandy Hook elementary school massacre in which 20 children and six adults were killed in Newtown, Connecticut, residents in the area received postcards and automatic phone calls asking them to put pressure on state legislators to 'stop dangerous anti-gun legislation'.

I suggest that the NRA's power within the American political system has resulted not merely from its financial clout but also its message, which speaks to the American experience. Whether or not you agree with the logic of the argument, a successful public narrative intertwines gun ownership with the birth and growth of the United States. Particularly striking is the role of the Second Amendment to the US Constitution. Ratified in 1791 as part of the Bill of Rights, it discusses the right for Americans to bear arms. It states that 'a well regulated Militia, being necessary to the security of a free State, the right of the people to keep and bear Arms, shall not be infringed'. Central to understanding the importance of this amendment, then and today, is the fear of a tyrannous government. This amendment is interpreted by the traditionalists as the right of all individuals to own a gun, which off-sets any attempt by the government to control the citizens.

What the American public thinks

The near complete success of the pro-gun lobby in the political arena doesn't fully reflect the views of the population. The polling agency Gallup has been collecting statistics on firearms for over 50 years. One thing it tells us is that the appetite for gun control is waning. By October 2013, 49 per cent of those polled wanted stricter gun controls compared to 78 per cent in 1990. And when it comes to gun massacres, multiple explanations exist. Three out of five people think it is the ease in a gun can be purchased, whilst nearly two-thirds think violence in the entertainment industry are responsible, and four out of five people think it is the failure of the mental health system.

Gun killings lead Americans to think that some kind of gun control is required: a quarter of them think that only authorised people such as the police should have access to guns and nearly two thirds think gun control legislation should be passed by Congress.

Considering Capital Punishment

Is it right to punish someone convicted of a crime, typically aggravated murder, with death? Opponents of the death penalty gravitate towards one of two positions. First is the moral argument that no one, including a state, should kill people. Second is the suggestion that the death penalty involves too many problems, which renders it inoperable as a fair and just system of punishment. These positions tend to operate in conjunction but aren't dependent on each other. Those in support of the death penalty focus on its strength as a deterrent and the recognition that some crimes require the ultimate act of retribution.

The following statistics evidence the broad scope of the death penalty in America:

- ✔ As of 2014, 32 states, together with the federal government and the US military, have the option of seeking the death penalty.

- ✔ Currently, around 3,105 people have been convicted and are waiting on death row.

- ✔ Sixty-three people await execution in federal and military court systems.

- ✔ As of January 2014, 1,364 people have been executed since 1976.

- ✔ Since 1976, 273 clemencies for people on death row have been granted.

Death penalty abolitionists

To purist abolitionists, killing someone is a simple act of immorality because all life is valuable and should not be devalued even for those who have committed murder. Others oppose the death penalty because it's an unfair and unjust process. I concentrate here on that second group of abolitionists, who offer four main criticisms of the death penalty:

- ✔ **Racial bias:** Nearly two out of five people on death row in April 2013 were Black, and similar figures were White. But if the demographics of the general public and death row inmates aligned, just over one out of ten people would be Black and three out of five would be White.

- ✔ **Unsound convictions and wrongful executions:** Since 1973, 143 people have been freed from death row and either acquitted or had the charges against them dismissed. On average, such people have had to spend 10 years on death row before being exonerated.

- ✔ **Quality of representation:** The effectiveness of someone's legal representation is a key factor in whether they'll receive the death penalty. Most defendants in cases in which the death penalty is sought have a state-appointed attorney because they can't afford to hire an attorney whom they choose. Those attorneys typically are overworked, lack trial experience and may even be incompetent. According to the *Dallas Morning News*, in 2000, 'nearly one in four condemned inmates has been represented at trial or on appeal by court-appointed attorneys who have been disciplined for professional misconduct'.

- ✔ **Low deterrence effect:** Those in favour of the death penalty argue that it acts to deter others from committing serious crimes. A number of academic studies have suggested that anywhere from between three to 32 murders (dependent on the study) have been deterred by each execution. Abolitionists question these findings and have produced evidence of their own. A study carried out in 2012 by the National Research Council, for example, suggested that statistical models employed by these studies made faulty assumptions and included incomplete or implausible views on a murderer's perceptions of capital punishment.

Death penalty supporters

Supporters of the death penalty tend to sit on the conservative side of politics and see the individual as totally responsible for his actions. They're tough on criminals and think some crimes just can't be forgiven. Seekers of the death penalty make two key arguments:

✔ **Deterrence:** Despite the argument to the contrary, those in favour of the death penalty stick to their guns about its role as a deterrent. Accordingly, they take issue with the National Research Council study mentioned above. The study suggested that because only one in six people on death row has been executed since 1976, the death penalty isn't actually much of a deterrent. Supporters of the death penalty state that this figure is flawed and also that the study itself did not address whether the murderers themselves were aware of the low death row to execution conversion statistics.

✔ **Constitutional retribution:** While the Supreme Court (in *Gregg vs. Georgia* (1976) confirmed a 1949 opinion that 'retribution is no longer the dominant objective of the criminal law', it also suggested that 'capital punishment may be the appropriate sanction in extreme cases as an expression of the community's belief that certain crimes are themselves so grievous an affront to humanity that the only adequate response may be the penalty of death'. And it is this concept of retribution that provides a rallying cry for supporters.

What the American public thinks

In concert with government and court opinion gradually turning against the death penalty (since 2006, six more states have abolished it), public opinion is also changing. While support for the death penalty remains high, at 60 per cent according to Gallup in 2013, it is still at its lowest since the mid-1970s. Support has been falling every year since a high of 80 per cent in 1994, which means that roughly six out of every ten Americans support the death penalty.

Clearly, the public is subjecting the issue to greater scrutiny. Since 2010 the number of people concluding that the death penalty is applied unfairly has gradually increased. Viewing support for the death penalty from the perspective of adults adhering to different political positions, a clear divide between conservatives and liberals is evident. Of those polled in late 2012, 75 per cent of conservatives were in favour of the death penalty and 18 per cent were against it, while only 47 per cent of liberals were in favour and 50 per cent were against it.

Addressing Abortion Rights

This battle doesn't just play out in heated discussions in court, the media or elections, it's also spilt out on to the street and people have been threatened and even murdered and buildings bombed because they're connected in some way to an abortion clinic. And because the two sides disagree even in terms of what they're arguing about, dialogue on this one is very difficult.

A landmark event in this debate occurred in 1973 when *Roe vs. Wade* (1973) came before the Supreme Court. The Court declared most existing state abortion laws unconstitutional and limited the right of the state to interfere in a woman's choice to have an abortion. Since this time the pro-life movement has attempted to change the status quo by actively eroding its terms through political and legal means and attempts to change public opinion, while the pro-choice movement has been playing a holding game, using similar methods, to minimise the impact of the pro-life efforts on the right of women to choose.

The defining terms of the fight are that pro-choice supporters (progressives) claim restricting access to abortion violates the right of a woman to control her own body while pro-life advocates (traditionalists) claim that abortion is a violation of the right of the foetus to life. Tapping into the language of the culture wars, a progressive position suggests that the individual should make her own decisions free from moralist interjection, while traditionalists criticise the drive to undermine the traditional family structure and believe the state should step in to protect society, the family and children.

Political polarisation on the issue

Over the years a steady partisan polarisation has occurred whereby Republicans are seen as the pro-life party and Democrats the pro-choice party. Interest groups have a significant impact on public debates concerning abortion. In the 2011–2012 election cycle, for example, nearly $3.4 million was spent on lobbying, advertising and donations to members of Congress by pro-life groups. In the same cycle, nearly $4.6 million was spent on similar activities by the pro-choice groups.

The funding given to the main pro-life and pro-choice organisations shows a much more revealing picture of their power they wield. Planned Parenthood is a not-for-profit family planning and reproductive health organisation with a left-leaning super PAC that supports pro-choice candidates. It has a large war chest, and in the 2012 election cycle spent around $65 million on informing the public on its politics, on pro-choice candidates, on lobbying and on campaigns against Republican pro-life candidates.

Perhaps the largest pro-life organisation is National Right to Life (NRTL). Unlike Planned Parenthood, it is an interest group alone and not also a health service provider and so has much lower revenue. It does not have a public education programme like Planned Parenthood but in its engagement with electoral politics it employs a similar approach by using its two super PACs to advertise in favour of pro-life candidates.

The pro-life argument

The pro-life, or traditionalist, position adheres to a few key assertions:

- ✔ The rights of a foetus are the same as those of a human who lives outside the womb.
- ✔ The *innocent* foetus is morally superior to the pregnant woman and should be protected.
- ✔ The right of the foetus to live is greater than the right of the woman to choose.

When a foetus can survive outside the womb (viability) has played into ideas about when it deserves state protection. But traditionalists argue that viability changes over time as a result of improvements in medical capabilities. They maintain that all attempts to nominate a specific point of viability are problematic and rights should thus be afforded to the foetus at conception.

The pro-choice argument

In moral terms, the pro-choice argument suggests that a woman owns her body and therefore she should choose what happens to it; being able to choose an abortion without state interference is thus an important element of attaining that right.

Having the option to choose an abortion is also an important aspect of supporting gender equality in the political, social and economic spheres. Having a child has a greater detrimental impact on the opportunities of a woman in terms of education and employment than on a man.

Other points made in support of abortion include the fact that, rather than reducing the number carried out, making abortions illegal would make the practice more dangerous for women and also criminalise their behaviour when making a choice about their own bodies. And one of the current issues the pro-choice are fighting against is the gradual erosion of the rights of women to choose when they reproduce. In 2013 alone, 24 states enacted 53 different types of anti-choice legislative measures.

What the American public thinks

The average American's views on abortion sit somewhere in the middle. In mid-2013, Gallup conducted a poll giving Americans one of three options concerning their position of the legality of abortion: that it should be legal under all or certain circumstances or should be made illegal. Of those polled,

52 per cent believed that it should be legal in certain circumstances and 26 per cent in all, while 20 per cent thought it should be made illegal. As expected, more Republicans oppose abortion than Democrats.

Taking a Look at Gay Rights

The modern gay rights movement has sought equality in all spheres of life. To achieve that position it has used a range of measures, including involvement in federal, state and local politics, improving the portrayal of gay people within the media, changing the attitudes of the general public and introducing legislation to protect and expand the rights of gay people. Strategies range from repealing laws that criminalise sexual acts at the state level, to responding to police harassment of gay people at the local level, to fighting for legal equality of gay relationships at the legal level.

Opposition to the gay rights movement, on the other hand, is not a movement as such; it is a series of different groups responding to what they conceive as problems with homosexuality and the impact of the advancing demands of gay rights. At various times since the 1950s this fight has played out on a series of different battlefields. The following sections look at the shifting interplay between the conservative and progressive positions, in the areas of gay marriage and national security.

Striving for marriage equality

Opponents to same-sex couples marrying include mainstream religious faiths such as evangelical, Mormon and Roman Catholic churches, as well as faith-based and conservative political organisations. These groups have a range of reasons why same-sex marriage should be opposed, including:

- Through interpreting various religious texts, homosexuality is seen as immoral and a sin against God.

- Legalising gay marriage makes homosexuality more culturally acceptable which is problematic because it destroys public morality.

- Marriage represents a human design to reproduce, and so is between a man and a woman, not two people of the same sex.

- Marriage is good for society and the state because it creates the conditions for raising well-rounded and stable people, and this order would be disrupted by marriage between gay people.

- In a 'slippery slope' argument, opponents think gay marriage may lead to other forms of marriage such as incest, paedophilia and bestiality.

Supporters of same-sex marriage include interest groups, various religious and political leaders, and businesses and labour organisations. They suggest it is a matter of civil rights and that all people should be treated equally under the law. Their arguments include the following:

✔ Same-sex marriage is a civil not a religious matter.

✔ Denying equality for all Americans fosters discrimination as it suggests gay couples are second-class citizens.

✔ Marriage is a commitment between two people irrespective of sex.

✔ Marriage would enable same-sex couples the legal rights that opposite-sex couples have, such as next-of-kin visitation rights if the partner is in hospital, spousal healthcare as well as taxation and inheritance rights.

✔ The values of same-sex couples are the same as opposite-sex couples; they want to live ordinary lives and create stable environments that enable their children to prosper.

✔ Gay marriage would make it simpler for gay couples to adopt and foster children, and evidence suggesting that children with same-sex parents are not impaired in any social, psychological or physical way is an opportunity to give more children better life chances.

Recent developments in the federal courts, political developments in state legislatures alongside a growing cultural progressivism to support equality of sexual preference in the everyday lives of people have all contributed to same-sex marriage becoming a reality for more and more Americans. In June 2013, two Supreme Court rulings paved the way for same-sex marriage to be accepted at state and federal levels. By mid-2014, same-sex marriage was legal in 19 states and in the remaining states there are various levels of acceptance of gay unions from full bans to unions that provide same-sex couples with the same rights as married couples. And to the chagrin of those in opposition, more referenda and bill proposals in the other states for legalising same-sex marriage are emerging.

Gay rights and national security

In 1953, President Eisenhower had declared that any federal employee found to be gay would be fired. In an era of McCarthy-driven hysteria, the fear was that gay people working for and with the government were a threat to national security. Throughout the Cold War, there was a ban on gay people joining the military because of a fear that it would adversely affect military discipline, and those found to be homosexual were discharged. Between 1980 and 1990 approximately 1,500 members a year were forced out under this directive.

Change came during the Clinton administration's 'don't ask, don't tell' policy, which meant that commanding officers couldn't ask about a person's sexuality but it also meant that a gay enlistee could not talk about his sexuality or engage in sexual activity. And when Democrat President Obama came to power, the cause had another champion.

Support for gay rights was playing out through the courts. In October 2010, a federal judge ruled that the 'don't ask, don't tell' policy violated gay military people's constitutional rights and demanded the government immediately discontinue the policy. Whilst the Department of Justice represented the institutional conservatism by requesting a delay, the writing was on the wall to discontinue the policy. Particularly because the Pentagon had issued a report determining that openly gay people did not harm military discipline. By mid-December 2010, Congress had approved a bill allowing gay people to openly serve, on 22 December Obama signed the bill into law, and on 20 September 2011 the law came into force.

What the American public thinks

The American public clearly has different attitudes to different issues affecting gay people. What it does overwhelmingly agree on, however, is that gay people do face discrimination. In a 2012 Gallup survey, 9 per cent thought discrimination was *not at all serious*, 26 per cent thought that it was *not too serious* and 63 per cent thought that it was *somewhat* to *very serious*. The public also shows a continuing and growing increase in support for gay rights in all areas of public and private life. Some issues clearly attract more support than others:

- ✔ In a long-term *Washington Post*/ABC poll on whether openly gay people should be allowed to join the military, support rose from 44 per cent in 1993, when *don't ask, don't tell* was first introduced, to three-quarters in 2008. And by December 2010, support had increased slightly further.

- ✔ A consistently high level of support has been demonstrated for inheritance rights for same-sex couples if one of them dies. According to Gallup, in late 2012 nearly four out of five Americans were in favour.

- ✔ From 2009 the number of Americans who supported same-sex partners receiving health insurance and other social benefits from their partner's policy increased from nearly seven out of ten to nearly eight out of ten. However, in the same survey, support for same-sex couples having the right to adopt a child was lower, at nearly six out of ten Americans in 2009 to just over six out of ten in 2012.

- ✔ Support for gay marriage in the mid-1990s was low, at just below three out of ten Americans. However, by 2011 over half of Americans supported gay marriage.

> ✔ Asked if they would support a federal pro-gay marriage law, more than
> 60 per cent of progressives supported gay marriage, with the liber-
> als pulling in nearly eight out of ten. More than half of conservatives
> opposed, and regular church attendees hit the highest figures with over
> seven out of ten against.

Scrutinising Healthcare

Some fault lines are created when legislation or a cultural shift in the public's
perception on an issue so upset the *status quo* that a fundamental change
in the direction of the country occurs. The healthcare legislation passed by
Congress and signed by President Obama in 2010 is a great example.

On the progressive side you have those aligned behind the need for health
care provision for all Americans whilst on the conservative side you have
groups that believe the government should not force an unwarranted and
unpopular policy on Americans. In making their respective cases, the two
extremes tapped into key issues that define the line that divides them, such
as the rights of the individual vs. the group, big government, and federal vs.
state rights. Similar to the other fault lines, the evidence suggests that the
American public sit somewhere in the middle between the two extremes.

Healthcare in the past

State-supported healthcare provision didn't just appear out of the blue in
2009. It was always a political and social issue that had been a part of America
since the 1860s, when it was introduced as a way of providing social care to
African-Americans released from slavery after the Civil War. Since that time,
it has been attempted in various configurations and with differing tactics,
almost always by Democratic politicians. And all these attempts to institute
healthcare were directed by the progressive nature of politicians.

It was during President Harry Truman's efforts to continue Roosevelt's New
Deal policies, which included a national healthcare plan, that a federally-
funded programme was first dubbed 'socialist', by the Republican senator
Robert A. Taft. That insult (and keep in mind that whenever mainstream
American politicians call something *socialist*, it's never meant as anything
but an outright criticism) was sustained through the decades as Presidents
Eisenhower, Kennedy, Johnson and Clinton worked toward a federally-funded
healthcare system. Its first iteration came in the Johnson administration,
which saw the establishment of Medicare and Medicaid – health insurance
for citizens over age 65 and for those who couldn't otherwise afford it,
respectively.

Conservative opposition to the progressives' healthcare ambitions in the 1960s included Ronald Reagan who at that time was developing his conservative credentials, the American Medical Association (AMA – an organisation that represents the interests of medical doctors), and the 1964 Republican presidential candidate Barry Goldwater. The rhetoric predictably equated health care with socialism.

Under President Bill Clinton (1993–2001), supporters of healthcare reform received a major boost on the national political stage. Having campaigned for greater access to healthcare for all Americans, Clinton initiated a task force, controversially headed-up by First Lady Hilary Clinton, to develop a package of reforms to be submitted to Congress and voted on. In a strategic move to bring in support from business and conservative elements, and fearful of accusations of a socialised medical system, Clinton's proposal was to involve private insurance companies in its delivery and yet ensure the progressive agenda whereby healthcare coverage was universal and insurance prices were held low. Opposition by Republicans and business interest groups successfully framed the bill as complex, expensive and enlarging the size of government to a dangerous extent. Even a compromise proposal that would have exempted small businesses from having to provide healthcare insurance for their workers, for example, did not stop the bill from dying.

There had been no more significant progressive healthcare reforms since Clinton's failure in 1994 until the proposal instigated by Obama in 2009. Bear in mind that 45 million Americans had no access to healthcare at that point. On 23 March 2010, President Obama signed the Affordable Care Act (ACA) into law. The law made substantial changes to US healthcare provision, including:

- ✔ An individual mandate, which means that anyone who doesn't have insurance through her employer or with Medicare or Medicaid has to take out her own plan.

- ✔ Expansion of Medicaid to include families that are 33 per cent above the poverty level.

- ✔ Guaranteed coverage without increased premiums for those with pre-existing medical conditions who wish to change insurance plan.

- ✔ Establishment of health insurance exchanges, which compare available plans and allow small businesses and individuals to buy insurance cover.

Healthcare reforms under Obama

The strategies utilised by those conservatives who oppose President Obama's reforms – known by detractors as *Obamacare* – can be seen in the public, political and legal arenas. As ever, when healthcare reforms are proposed, you find a combination of business interests fearful of having to provide healthcare for employees, healthcare insurers afraid of being forced to accept people with pre-existing conditions and a Republican Party fearful of an increase in taxation, a negative impact on the economy and the need for small businesses to pay for worker contributions.

Lobbying played an integral role in shaping the opponents' position. According to analysis released by the non-partisan campaign finance watchdog Public Campaign Action Fund (PCAF), for example, the top 13 private health insurers and their industry association, America's Health Insurance Plans (AHIP), spent nearly $23 million lobbying Congress and the administration from January to September 2009 alone. The health industry doesn't operate alone; it provides support to those elected politicians who are equally opposed to the reforms. According to the Center for Responsive Politics, when the House of Representatives passed its version of the bill in early November 2009 with 220 votes for and 215 against, those who opposed the bill had received on average just over $500,000 from health insurance companies, employees and the health industry since 1989. On average, this financial inducement worked out at about 15 per cent more per politician ($65,000) than the payments made to those who supported the bill.

The Republican Party has had a series of political opportunities to fight the Affordable Care Act but each time failed to deliver the decisive blow. In the summer of 2009, when the President and other key supporters of the reforms argued their case and opponents raised their objections in town hall meetings throughout the country. Tea Party heroes, such as former Republican Vice-Presidential nominee Sarah Palin, also stirred up the debate by stating that the federal government would appoint bureaucrats to serve on death panels choosing which old people to kill because resources would be limited. In response, Obama concluded that no one would 'pull the plug on grandma'. The Republican Party also failed on countless occasions to pass repeals of the ACA.

Legal challenges to the Affordable Care Act

On the legal side, opponents issued a number of challenges to the implementation of the ACA. One such challenge involved 26 states opposing the individual mandate aspect of the bill that required all Americans to have a health insurance plan. The Supreme Court duly heard oral arguments for elements of a series of cases that concerned the legality of Congress passing healthcare reform under the Affordable Care Act and its supporting Health Care and Education Reconciliation Act (2010). These cases were heard under *National Federation of* *Independent Business vs. Sebelius*. In an act of judicial restraint, the Supreme Court voted 5–4 (with Chief Justice Roberts voting alongside the liberal justices), accepting the argument that the individual mandate of the Affordable Care Act was an example of the taxation powers of Congress and should not be halted. It wasn't all good news for President Obama, however, as the conservatives did win minor victories, including restricting the powers of the federal government to impose conditions on its funding of states.

What the American public thinks

It is difficult to determine the middle ground when considering universal healthcare, as the debate has been successfully defined by the extremes: you are either for or against it. And the public opinion polls show a divided America. In fact, the polls show that Americans are moving ever towards the conservative position:

✔ In the past 14 years, support for federal government-sponsored healthcare coverage for all Americans has reduced significantly from nearly three out of five Americans in 2000 to about two out of five in 2014. And those American who are against federal involvement demonstrated similar changes, but in reverse.

✔ When asked specifically about the 2010 Affordable Care Act, February 2014 figures showed that 51 per cent disapproved of President Obama's restructuring of the healthcare system while only 41 per cent approved.

The 2013 US government shutdown

In late 2013, right-wing elements of the Republican Party in the House of Representatives, referred to as the *Tea Party* (which opposes large government and supports reducing the national deficit) forced a government shutdown. Each year the federal budget has to be approved by Congress and, if it isn't, most federal departments and agencies are suspended and their employees not paid and told to stay at home (*furloughed*). In this instance, Tea Party members of the House of Representatives included a provision to the federal budget that stripped the ACA of funding. Because the Republicans had a majority in the House, the bill was passed but as soon as it arrived at the Democrat-controlled Senate, it removed these funding restraints and sent it back to the House. An *impasse* ensued and a shutdown was put in place on 1 October, whereby 800,000 federal employees were furloughed. On 16 October, the Senate Democrat and Republican leaders agreed to halt the shutdown until 15 January 2014 and to extend federal funding until 7 February to enable negotiations to continue. An appropriations bill was reached by the 15 January deadline and the federal government was no longer subject to a further shutdown. The Republican drawdown on federal funding for the ACA was thus defeated.

Chapter 16

Understanding the Impact of Financial and Economic Crises

A boom and bust cycle is an inevitability of the liberal economic system. And more and more people find themselves attached to in this rapidly expanding globalised world. But while the world being closer together brings definite benefits, it also means that when one country catches a cold the others are likely to sneeze, too. And this is no truer than of a cold started in the largest and most important economy in the world – the American economy.

In this chapter, I provide details about two major economic crises and the impact they had on the United States and the world. I also describe the responses of two very different administrations as America worked to climb out of its most recent economic woes.

Boom to Bust: Economic Cycles

I know that the sun will set tonight and rise again tomorrow morning, and with the same degree of confidence it's safe to predict that the liberal economic model of the modern world will also experience sunsets and sunrises.

This *boom and bust cycle* basically describes the ebb and flow of economic stability. I express this degree of confidence despite the arrogant claims to the contrary made during the heady days of economic growth in the early twenty-first century. For example, in 2007 the UK Chancellor of the Exchequer (equivalent to the US Secretary of the Treasury), Gordon Brown, claimed that 'we will not return to the old boom and bust'. Unfortunately, this statement was no slip of the tongue; he made this claim over a hundred times in the House of Commons. Oh, how foolish does he feel now?

The boom and bust cycle seems an inevitable part of the governed human condition. A *boom* includes times of

- **Continued growth in the economy over a period of time.** Growth is reflected in continued increases in GDP (Gross Domestic Product, a measurement of the productivity of a nation), higher rates of employment, and growth in the market, as reflected in higher prices on the stock exchange.

- **Ready credit.** Banks broaden the availability of loans with low interest rates for investments such as stock market share purchases, housing and business expansion.

- **Low interest rates.** With a continued low interest rate, the economic cycle continues to spiral upwards as it encourages people to borrow more because their repayments won't be that much greater than what they borrowed.

During a boom, easy credit and low interest rates lead people to think that, if they speculate on continued growth, they'll make more profit in the future. People max out their credit cards because high employment and rising wages lead them to believe they can afford to do so.

The continued low interest rates along with increases in the amount of money in supply are facilitated by the national bank – in the US, the Federal Reserve (known as the Fed). The Fed does this in order to ensure sufficient money and credit is in the economy in order for it to grow, although if it does this too successfully then a knock-on effect is high inflation. High inflation is bad for the economy because it means what you can buy for a dollar today costs more tomorrow. So, the Fed controls these two sides through a balancing act of changing interest rates and manipulating access to money in order to control its supply in the economy.

The bust side of the economic cycle is what the world's been living with since the summer of 2008. This economic downturn is referred to as a recession or, when really bad, a depression. Economic growth declines or even goes into reverse. The problems that appear during a bust are the product of what went on in the boom years (which is why it's a cycle):

> ✔ Overinvestment as a result of low interest rates leads to what econo-mists refer to as *malinvestment*. Thus people invest in industries that look good on paper but which ultimately fail to make a profit, and more homes and offices are built than demand exists for.

> ✔ The stock exchange follows a downward trajectory, which means that the face value of shares decreases, investors are less likely to invest and more likely to get rid of assets which they deem dangerous, and businesses are less likely to expand and more likely to shed workers to manage costs.

> ✔ Employment levels inevitably fall, which means that people have less money to spend, which negatively affects the economy and further exac-erbates the situation.

All in all, a bust is not a happy period of time in which to live. The credit card bills come in and people can no longer afford to pay them off because they've either lost their jobs or their wages have shrunk.

Controlling the economy is an important element of the political agenda of elected officials. The president and Congress can influence the boom and bust cycle. Their *fiscal policy* is tasked with lowering unemployment, influ-encing interest rates and controlling inflation. The logic is that a government can impact economic performance by changing government spending and tax rates. *Monetary policies* are those plans that are proposed by the central bank of the country, in this case the Federal Reserve, and are aimed at con-trolling the supply of money predominantly through raising or lowering inter-bank interest rates; that is, when banks borrow money from each other. The Federal Reserve's decision making is independent of the elected government.

The Great Depression

The Great Depression, a worldwide economic depression that really got roll-ing when the US stock market crashed in 1929, demonstrates the impact that economics can have on the welfare of the American people, politics and soci-ety, and how what happens in one nation can ripple out through the world.

To put it simply, the economic crash was preceded by overinvestment. With the mass movement of people from rural to urban areas, increase in steel pro-duction to support expansion of the construction industry and an increase in consumer spending on homes, household goods and cars, the 1920s were indeed swinging. Businesses were making large profits, which itself fuelled further investment in the stock exchange. As share prices continued to rise, people borrowed more and more money with which to invest. And so the boom continued.

A terrible irony for a president touting a 'triumph over poverty'

The son of Quakers, the 1928 presidential candidate for the Republican Party, Herbert Hoover, was a good guy by all accounts. Although a businessman before he entered politics, he had demonstrated on numerous occasions his commitment to public service. At the outbreak of the World War I he helped thousands of Americans to travel back to the US; under President Wilson he was involved in the Food Administration's efforts; and after the war he was responsible for providing famine relief to Soviet Russia in the early 1920s. In his acceptance speech for the presidential candidacy, he concluded that

We in America today are nearer to the final triumph over poverty than ever before in the history of any land. The poorhouse is vanishing from among us. We have not yet reached the goal, but given a chance to go forward with the policies of the last eight years, and we shall soon with the help of God be in sight of the day when poverty will be banished from this Nation.

In an ironic twist, just a few months after Hoover won a resounding victory in the general election, with over 58 per cent of the popular vote and 444 (out of 531) Electoral College votes, and just over a year after this speech, the Wall Street crash occurred. In October 1929, stock prices on the US stock market fell by over 12 per cent on two consecutive days (29 and 30). This crash had an enormous negative impact on the economy and its effects were felt by nearly all Americans – and people and markets throughout the world – for years.

This type of boom is based on speculation (investing in shares that one predicts/hopes will rise in price), and at some point the bubble will burst and the house of cards will fall down.

The effects of the Wall Street crash rippled around the world and investors lost billions of dollars as a result of the depreciation in share value. But its impact went far beyond the value of the stocks on the exchange. By 1933 US GDP was half the 1929 figure. Because banks in the US had used customer deposits to fund their investments, it meant that many could no longer operate and thus closed. This caused a run on other banks (people panicking and getting their money out), which meant these banks were also forced to close because they couldn't cover people's deposits. And those deposit holders who couldn't get their money out in time lost their savings.

In 1929 unemployment stood at about 3.2 per cent. Within a year this had risen to 8.9 per cent and in 1932 it hit 24.1 per cent, which equated to about 12 million people (one in four). And because unemployment benefit didn't exist, people who lost their jobs were unable to make rent or mortgage payments and thus became homeless. They couldn't afford food so went hungry.

Poverty was extreme. Even for those who still had a job, hourly rates were about half of those of the boom years. In the Midwestern and Southern States a drought in 1931 and 1932 destroyed farmers' crops.

As you can imagine, come the 1932 presidential election incumbent President Hoover stood no chance against the Democratic candidate Franklin Roosevelt. Roosevelt won a stonking victory. His administration's solution to the crisis was the *New Deal* – a set of programmes intended to tackle the problem from several angles:

- **Banking:** Roosevelt reorganised the banking and finance industry. He kept open those banks that had sufficient capital, reorganised others and closed those that were doomed to fail. As soon as confidence in the banks was restored, Americans began re-depositing their money. In 1933 the Glass–Steagall Act was introduced, which prevented high street banks from investment speculation and guaranteed the savings of the average bank account holder.

- **Public assistance:** To off-set the poverty and starvation experienced by the average American, the government implemented a series of welfare programmes through the Federal Emergency Relief Administration (FERA). It gave resources to state governments to pay unemployment benefit, for example, and funded the Civilian Conservation Corps (CCC), which by 1935 had given 500,000 young men employment doing things such as building bridges and planting trees.

  The Social Security Act (1935) provided federally-funded programmes to protect vulnerable people, such as retirees, the unemployed, children and the blind, from poverty. Other programmes included the Tennessee Valley Authority (TVA), which was tasked with providing electricity to the area between Virginia and Mississippi. By constructing hydroelectric dams the federal government created employment for the unemployed, which enabled them to put food on the table for their families, and by giving people in the region electricity they opened up new markets for businesses.

- **Infrastructure:** The Works Progress Administration (WPA), established in 1935, provided jobs and carried out large-scale infrastructural projects such as building roads and bridges. Within eight years, it had provided employment for about 8 million people.

The era of large government had emerged as the solution to the country's problems. The New Deal had shifted attitudes within government and society about the roles and responsibilities of the federal government. It led to around 40 years of the federal government being the acceptable salvation of society's problems.

The Great Recession

The financial and economic crises that hit the world in the first decade of the 21st century don't make for a particularly warm story. Millions, if not billions, of people were, and currently *still are*, negatively affected.

The bursting of the housing bubble

Two key factors help explain the cause of the economic crisis: the housing bubble and creative accounting on the part of the finance industry. By 2007 a huge housing bubble was ready to explode and, although the industry knew about it, it did not, or could not, do anything about it.

Between 1990 and 1998 house prices remained fairly consistent and showed only small growth. However, in the eight years thereafter house prices more than doubled. This rise reflected a massive demand in housing, and was created by two principal factors:

- **Low interest rates:** Sustained low interest rates from the late 1990s onwards meant that more and more people thought they could afford to buy their own home. It also meant that increasing numbers of people thought, and were encouraged to think, they could afford larger mortgages to buy larger properties. The Federal Reserve encouraged the maintenance of low interest rates that facilitated continued borrowing by lending to its own customers, such as commercial banks, on lower rates.

- **Subprime mortgages:** In ordinary English, this term refers to mortgages provided to people who are at risk of defaulting, hence the term *subprime*. In the early 2000s access to these mortgages was greatly expanded. To attract lower earners, mortgages with very low interest rates were advertised with minimal conditions. Lending rose from approximately $180 billion in 2001 to $625 billion in 2005. In part, this was facilitated by Congress and the Clinton and Bush administrations pressuring mortgage companies such as Freddie Mac, Fannie Mae and other government-sponsored enterprises. Another structural reason for this increase in lending was the 1999 Financial Services Modernization Act (during the Clinton administration), which repealed the 1933 Glass–Steagall Act. It deregulated the financial industry and gave banks, brokerages and insurance companies the opportunity to give people mortgages and then sell that risk on for profit to some other company as a mortgage-backed security.

By 2006 the housing bubble had burst and negative effects were slowly trickling down. An increase in house prices wasn't matched by an increase in hourly wages during this period, which meant that people could no longer afford to buy houses. Property prices plummeted.

Negative equity (when the current price of your property is lower than what you paid for it) isn't the end of the world if you can afford to continue to pay the interest rates and carry on living in the property. The serious problems unfold if you can't afford to live in the property: the lender forecloses; you have to sell the house; house prices have collapsed so what you get from the sale won't cover the mortgage; you remain in debt but without a home.

In 2005, 3.3 per cent of homes with subprime mortgages were in the process of foreclosure; by 2008 that had risen to a record 13.7 per cent. Millions of the most disadvantaged people in America were losing their homes.

Subprime mortgages knocked about $1 trillion off the US housing market, and this was only the beginning of their legacy to the world's economic situation. By turning these high-risk loans into securities that were traded worldwide, the effects of the subsequent housing market crash were felt around the world. Here's how it happened:

1. **More loans were being granted, but their interest rates were higher.** Interest rates depend on a borrower's credit rating and history. A higher interest rate is applied to those at greater risk of defaulting, thus subprime interest rates were higher.

2. **Lenders sold off their risk.** If the mortgage lender didn't want to accept the risk of a borrower defaulting on his mortgage, he'd sell it to a mortgage banker such as Freddie Mac or Fannie Mae. After deregulation (reduced governmental oversight of the financial sector), the mortgage banker could sell the mortgage on to an investment bank for profit.

3. **Mortgage risk became tied in to other types of investment.** When the investment bank received the mortgage it would combine it with a number of other similar loans. These were then traded in the financial markets as a security, for example a mortgage-backed security (MBS). Combining subprime mortgages with other less risky mortgages spread the risk of the whole package defaulting.

4. **Too many subprime loans were brought into the markets.** Investment bankers got cocky. Instead of sprinkling a few subprime loans into the mix, they started to chuck in bucket loads. In 2000, subprime loans equalled about $100 billion, with half of those being *securitised* (traded in the financial markets as a security). By 2006, total subprime loans had increased to $600 billion, and about $450 billion of those were securitised. Because securities were sold on to the wider financial world, such

as to pension and hedge fund investors, if something went wrong in the housing market the entire financial system around the world would be affected. And that's exactly what happened.

5. **Faulty credit ratings were assigned.** In order for purchasers to determine the securities' level of risk, credit rating agencies such as Moody's were employed to rate them. The greater the risk, the lower the price. The problem with the subprime mortgages was that, because they were wrapped up with other loans, ratings were higher than they would have been if they were on their own. Approximately 80 per cent of subprime MBSs had the highest credit rating, indicating the least risk and making these securities prize investments. As more and more people in the subprime loan category were defaulting, and with house prices falling, the collateral was worth a lot less than was originally presumed. As a consequence, the credit rating of these security products went down dramatically, which further exacerbated the economic crisis. In 2007–08 Moody's alone downgraded over 36,000 of its security products.

6. **Banks and investors developed a false sense of security.** In order to protect against the riskier elements of the securities, investors were insured against the risk of homeowners defaulting through what's called a credit default swap (CDS). The cost of the insurance was a slice of the profit from the return of the securities. This policy gave banks the false belief that they were immune from risk. By 2007 this market was worth $62 trillion. Unfortunately, CDSs weren't regulated so companies could create one willy nilly and no collateral was needed so long as the insurer had been given the highest possible rating from the rating agency.

7. **And then everyone got spooked.** In the complicated scenario of securities being banded together with different risk levels, banks, pension and hedge funds were uncertain of the value of their securities, so were held back from loaning more money in case they needed to cover large losses. This had a dramatic impact on the world economy: no one wanted to lend money, and economic success is contingent on the money supply flowing freely.

September 2008 and the Collapse of Lehman Brothers

In the run-up to September 2008, the American government was actually responding to the growing economic and financial crisis. The Federal Reserve had dropped interest rates to encourage a continuing flow of money, Congress had provided support for low-income families with mortgages in the form of tax relief and the government had bailed out the investment bank Bear Stearns (a *bailout* is when the government provides financial support to a struggling business to prevent it from failing and causing further problems within the wider economy). However, this approach wasn't sufficient to halt the spread of the crisis.

At the beginning of September, the federal government declared that it would place the mortgage lenders Fannie Mae and Freddie Mac under conservatorship (basically take control of them). Between 2004 and 2006 these lenders had purchased $434 billion in securities that were composed of subprime loans. However, with the fall in house prices, continuing defaults on loan repayments and increases in foreclosures the two companies were in trouble. In 2007 they recorded losses of $14.9 billion. The US Treasury provided up to $100 billion capital for each company in order to keep them operating and stop their failure from damaging the American financial system.

It was different, though, for Lehman Brothers. Established in the mid-19th century, it had become one of the largest investment banks in America by the beginning of the 21st century. Between 2000 and 2008, Chairman Dick Fuld earned $310–500 million. By the end of 2007 Lehman had made $4 billion in profit. It was the largest underwriter of real estate loans in America. And, as a result of the 2007 property crash, it was in financial trouble.

By August 2007, for every $1 Lehman owned it was borrowing up to $44. This arrangement is called *leverage* (it enables a company to increase its investment portfolio without having to increase its equity) and, in comparison to its competitors, Lehman's was high. Morgan Stanley's leverage was in the low 30s and Goldman Sachs' was in the 20s.

On 10 September 2008 Lehman posted a $3.93 billion third-quarter loss after having to devalue its mortgage portfolio by $5.6 billion. Within 48 hours the bank's share price had fallen by about 52 per cent. On 15 September Lehman filed for bankruptcy and became the first big bank to collapse since the crisis began. Its bonds and loans lost about 50 per cent of their value, and the $70 billion it owed was unrecoverable. The collapse of Lehman created a domino effect, and financial markets around the world also lost value. The Dow Jones (an index of 30 large publicly-owned American companies that shows how their shares are trading) recorded a 4.4 per cent drop.

Meanwhile, American International Group (AIG), the largest insurer in the world, was going through an equally dangerous capital problem. It had sold insurance protection (credit default swaps) for $441 billion worth of securities that were originally given the highest rating. Unfortunately, $57.8 billion of these swaps were securities comprising subprime loans. Its credit rating was downgraded, and it had to ask the Federal Reserve for help. On 16 September the Federal Reserve announced that it had given AIG an $85 billion loan to prop up the company. Any chance the AIG bailout may have had at calming the markets was lost when the Dow Jones fell by a further 4 per cent on 17 September.

On 18 September the Treasury Secretary proposed that the federal government should buy $700 billion of bad mortgage assets from financial companies so that they did not go bankrupt and impair the economy. In response to this proposal, the Dow Jones climbed 3.3 per cent but the bill had to pass Congress before it could be enacted.

Following a rating downgrade, the Washington Mutual bank experienced a run when $16.7 billion worth of deposits was withdrawn. As a result, on 25 September the federal government was forced to close it down. At the time, it was the sixth-largest bank in the US. Four days later the Citigroup bank was involved in a government-arranged deal to buy the banking operation of Wachovia. Wachovia had been hit by the subprime mortgage crisis and, in the second quarter of 2008, had reported losses of $8.9 billion.

On 28 September, Congress voted on the proposal to bail out financial institutions embroiled in the financial crisis. It was rejected by the House of Representatives, and by the close of day, the Dow Jones had lost 7 per cent, or $1.2 trillion, of its value – the biggest fall ever recorded in one day.

The impact was felt around the world. The bill was amended and passed in the Senate on 1 October, in the House of Representatives on 3 October and signed into law by President Bush immediately afterwards. On 18 October the Treasury announced that, rather than buying up bad banks, it would inject capital into the markets by buying shares in financial companies. Within days, nine of the largest banks, such as Citigroup and JPMorgan Chase, had asked to be part of the scheme.

However, this scheme didn't halt the downward trajectory of the economy and the day-to-day lives of American citizens were unaffected. According to the Bureau of Labor Statistics, in the final four months of 2008 unemployment shot up from 6.1 to 7.3 per cent. In numbers, it meant 2.385 million jobs were lost from the economy. Retail sales had gone down by 3.6 per cent from September to October, by a further 3.4 per cent in November but then picked up for Christmas and recorded only a 2.5 per cent decrease.

With the stream of financial organisations failing, the Bush administration had to constantly adapt its recovery plan. And the public were dismayed at the economic problems facing the country.

Obama's plan

The presidential and congressional elections were held in November 2008, and Democrat candidate Barack Obama won a convincing victory against the Republican, John McCain. In the House of Representatives the Democrats increased their dominance by 21 seats and in the Senate became the majority party. The American public were dissatisfied with the Republicans' leadership in a number of issues, including the 'War on Terror' and its response to the recession. The public wanted a new way of dealing with the issues that America confronted, including the ongoing financial and economic crises.

The Obama administration pursued a series of monetary and fiscal policies to halt the crisis and get America back on the path to financial stability and continued economic growth. Its plan was fourfold:

- Stabilise the financial markets
- Keep Americans in their homes
- Create jobs
- Ensure federal government fiscal responsibility

During the Obama administration, the Federal Reserve continued to lower interest rates in an attempt to encourage lending between banks and thus increase the money supply and provide more loans and mortgages to people and businesses to stimulate the economy. The Treasury continued to inject capital into financial companies that needed it but also ensured that caps were placed on the size of corporate bonuses following a government bailout. When it was revealed that nine of the financial companies that had received federal financial support had given around 5,000 of their traders and bankers more than $1 million each in bonuses in 2008, public disgust prompted the implementation of such a cap.

On 18 February 2009 President Obama announced the creation of the Homeowner Affordability and Stability Plan (HASP) aimed at stabilising the housing market. The plan had three core components:

- It helped homeowners who were paying high interest rates but couldn't refinance their mortgage because they had insufficient equity in their homes as a result of depreciating house prices. The aim was to reach 9 million homeowners and halt further foreclosures.

- For those in imminent risk of defaulting on their repayments, it provided incentives for lenders to renegotiate loan repayments to off-set foreclosures.

- In order to provide affordable mortgages it provided an additional $200 billion to Fannie Mae and Freddie Mac.

The cornerstone of the Obama administration's efforts at halting the financial and economic crises facing America was to push through Congress a big-government spending and tax-relief programme plan called the American Recovery and Reinvestment Act 2009 (ARRA), otherwise known as the Stimulus or Recovery Act. The initial Senate and House of Representatives versions of the bill were sufficiently different to warrant a conference between the two chambers. A synthesised bill was proposed and submitted to a vote on both floors on 13 February (for details on how a bill becomes a law, see Chapter 8). The House passed it by 246–183 and the Senate by 60–38.

Unlike Paulson's plan to help Wall Street's financial companies by offering them $700 billion, ARRA was intended to support Main Street's small businesses and the average American with what transpired to be $840 billion. And coming in at 407 pages, this Act covered a lot of ground. Its self-declared ambition was to provide jobs and promote economic growth, give support to those impacted by the recession, invest in science- and health-related technology, provide capital for infrastructural projects and support maintenance of state and local government budgets regarding essential services. Among its dictates were the following:

- ✔ To support employment growth by providing $54 billion to incentivise small businesses to hire people. For example, tax credits were provided if they hired the long-term unemployed, veterans or students, and fees on economic development loans were eliminated.

- ✔ To support those impacted by the recession and stimulate growth by providing $260 billion worth of tax cuts, tax credits and unemployment benefits. Examples included a deduction on sales tax when buying a new car in 2009, a tax credit of $8,000 for first-time homebuyers and extension of unemployment benefit for an extra 33 weeks.

- ✔ To invest in scientific research by providing $4 billion and to modernise research facilities and fund research positions by investing a further $10 billion.

- ✔ To improve infrastructure by providing $46 billion for transportation projects, $31 billion for modernising federal government buildings and $4 billion for improving broadband access in both rural and urban areas.

- ✔ To ensure key services are kept running by providing states and school districts with $54 billion for educational programmes and teachers' salaries and $87 billion of federal match-funding to enable states to pay for the increase in Medicaid (health coverage for those unable to afford private health insurance) as a result of the recession.

It is now some years since President Obama signed the stimulus package into law. In hindsight it should be possible to examine its effectiveness in terms of stimulating the economy and pulling the country out of recession. But of course people view it through different lenses: politicians who supported the stimulus claim that it worked; those who didn't say it failed. To help you reach your own conclusion, here are some facts:

- ✔ **The good news:** During 2009 and early 2010 the US economy continued to haemorrhage jobs; over 4.3 million were lost from the economy.

However, from March 2010 onwards, more jobs were created than lost. In May 2009, for example, about 516,000 new jobs were created. According to the Bureau of Labor Statistics, in the 18 months following the passing of the stimulus package by Congress, approximately 2.4 million private sector and 1.7 million public sector jobs were created. According to the same source, the economy contracted (measured in GDP) in 2009 by 2.8 per cent but by the following year had grown by 2.5 per cent. GDP has grown by at least 1.8 per cent each year since then.

✔ **The bad news:** The injection of billions of dollars into the economy has dramatically increased federal debt. By late 2013 the *public debt* (amount of money the government owes the public) stood at nearly $12 trillion. That's over 126 times the National Health Service's budget for 2013/14 and about a 90 per cent increase since President Obama took office. The national public debt has doubled since Obama became president, currently standing at about $600 billion a year

The Occupy Movement

The international Occupy Movement aims to expose and fight social and economic inequality. By 2012 members had protested in 951 cities in 82 countries, mostly in Europe and America. In mid-2011 the people behind the Canadian anti-consumerist magazine *Adbusters* proposed an occupation of Wall Street (New York City's financial district) for later that year to express dissatisfaction with the current financial system. The idea took hold and on 17 September protestors occupied a park in that district. The demonstration publicly criticised Wall Street's role in causing the financial and economic crisis, and opposed the major banks' and large corporations' negative influence on democracy.

Occupy's campaign slogan 'We are the 99%' highlighted the plight of the majority of the world's population in contrast to the 1 per cent of people who dominate the unequal economic system. And they may just have a point when you consider the following statistics – statistics supported by the Congressional Budget Office (CBO), the US Congress' research arm,

so no tree-hugging not-for-profit organisation. Its October 2011 report on income distribution trends between 1979 and 2011 stated that 1 per cent of the population owned *a third* of US net wealth. The income gap was widening; for the top 1 per cent wages grew by 275 per cent while for the bottom 20 per cent they grew by 18 per cent. And the 24 million least-wealthy households in the US saw average income go down 10 per cent from 2006 to $11,034 in 2010. Compounding this figure, according to the US Census Bureau, in 2013 about 15 per cent of Americans lived in poverty, which works out at about 46.5 million people.

On 15 November New York City mayor, Michael Bloomberg (the thirteenth-richest person in the world and founder and owner of a global financial data and media company), tasked the New York Police Department with evicting the protestors from the park. In return, the protestors successfully sued the city, stating that the raid contravened their rights under the constitution. They were awarded $360,000 in damages and legal fees.

Affecting American Interests – and Economies Far and Wide

Over the last six years the global financial crisis has had significant political, social and security implications in terms of America's ability to promote its national interests for reasons like the following:

- ✔ The financial crisis has meant a loss in jobs for people around the world, impacting their ability to sustain themselves.

- ✔ It has put pressure on the political leadership of these countries and in some cases has led to mass opposition to the powers that be.

- ✔ It has also increased poverty levels, causing political instability in numerous countries and thereby impairing American national interests such as having stable nations to trade with.

- ✔ A resurgence in state capitalism has occurred throughout the world whereby governments, including the US and the UK, have had to financially support companies by buying shares or completely taking them over. Coupled with this state-driven capitalism has been a growth in protectionism. In the US, for example, part of the 2009 stimulus package was a commitment that federally-funded construction projects would buy American steel, iron and manufactured goods.

- ✔ America's ability to take a leadership role in world affairs has taken a hit because the crisis is seen by many as the result of American greed.

The ability of America to project its power has been damaged by the crisis. Failure to succeed in promoting democracy in Afghanistan and Iraq (and the subsequent loss of prestige) and the results of the financial crisis have also limited the scale of foreign intervention. According to a Harvard University report, these wars cost the US $6 trillion (that's half of America's national debt!). As a result of the financial crisis, these types of intervention are no longer possible.

All of these issues have had a detrimental impact on America's ability to project its power in the world. Protectionist economic policies on the part of the US can encourage other states to behave in a similar manner, thus restricting the international flow of capital and further hampering economic growth. If a state is in political turmoil its prior allegiance to America in the 'War on

Terror' could also be compromised. If a state can't provide basic services for its people civil unrest may result, as demonstrated by the Arab Spring that began in 2010 (see Chapter 18 for more on the Arab Spring and its impact on American foreign policy).

Connecting the Dots between the Great Depression and the Great Recession

Significant parallels exist between the Great Depression of the 1930s and the Great Recession of the late 2000s:

- ✔ Excesses in the financial industry led to significant malinvestment during the boom years, which then led to crashes.

- ✔ The impact of these crashes went beyond their origins in the financial industry and had significant negative consequences for the American people.

- ✔ The contracting economies led to rising unemployment, increasing numbers of people living in poverty and a surge in homelessness.

- ✔ The federal government's response to both crises was also similar: pumping billions of federal dollars into the economy to stimulate growth.

A capitalist-based market economy will never be able to escape the boom and bust cycle. In fact, global warming, the increasing fight for finite natural resources and growing national debt limiting the ability of national governments to respond means that the impact of economic crises on the world can only intensify.

Part V
Looking Into American Politics on the World Stage

Examining Whether America Is in Decline

The debate over whether America is in decline has been a steady source of discussion since the 1960s, when American economic and military power, relative to other states, was identified as shrinking.

✔ After World War II, American dominance declined relative to other states as their economies began catching up. Japan's emergence throughout the 1980s led it to be the world's second-largest economy in the early 1990s and the biggest creditor of the US. This era of decline was somewhat replaced with President Clinton's administration when the American economy increased by about 40 per cent.

✔ The decline debate resurfaced after the 9/11 attacks. It was spurred on by a number of coalescing factors. The failures of American missions in Iraq and Afghanistan alongside the loss of prestige due to the tactics employed in the 'War on Terror', and the 2008 financial and economic crisis as well as the continuing economic and military rise of China and its growing assertion of its position as a major player in international affairs have all had an impact in re-opening the debate.

✔ China is of particular concern to commentators on American foreign policy when talking about the decline of the US compared to other states. By 2012, China had become the second-largest economy in the world behind the US, and since 2008 it has been the largest holder of US government debt. All of which means that China can assert itself on the international stage in a way it was previously unable to.

Get the details on the times government ground to a halt at www.dummies.com/ extras/americanpoliticsuk.

In This Part . . .

✔ Examine the American mission, and the narratives that enable and legitimise US actions in the world.

✔ Delve into America's relations with a number of friendly and not-so-friendly nations such as the UK, China and Cuba, in order to understand how American foreign policy affects its engagement with other nations.

✔ Discover the many ways the terrorist attacks of 11 September 2001 defined and shaped American foreign policy.

Chapter 17

Revealing the American Mission

*F*oreign policy is about the way in which one state interacts with other states in the world. It's about pursuing a state's national interests. And these interests can be shaped by a number of practical factors, such as its military prowess, and ideological issues, such as its political identity. This chapter explores the historical reasons why the United States acts in the way it does throughout the world. It details how America's unique character was formed and how this narrative influences its foreign policy.

I first clarify what *foreign policy* is before going on to discuss why the United States is an *exceptional* state, and what that exceptionalism looks like. To help you understand the character of American foreign policy, I provide a tour of the ideas it contains, and discuss historical cases to emphasise my points. Finally, I discuss the circumstances in which the American value of promoting a world in its democratic image can be successfully combined with the ambition of promoting its national interests.

Understanding the Role of Foreign Policy

A state's foreign policy has two key ingredients; its actions and its strategies for achieving its goals. The aim of a country's *foreign policy* is to attain its national interests without incurring a diminution of its position in the world relative to other states, or the loss of its prestige, resources and so on.

When I talk about national interests, I refer to the political, economic, military and cultural aims and objectives of a state. An example of a goal in the national interest could be for a state to open up foreign markets for American products. Another aim could be to create an alliance of states and non-state actors to oppose the actions and behaviour of another state, such as President George H. W. Bush's United Nations-backed alliance to remove the invading Iraqi troops from Kuwait in 1990–91.

A country's national interests are determined by a mixture of factors. First are the domestic influences on foreign policy, for example:

✔ The values that define a country's culture (such as the importance of individual rights).

✔ Interest groups aligned to a particular issue or way of seeing the world (such as the pro-Israeli American Israel Public Affairs Committee).

✔ Constituents (such as the Cuban-Americans in Florida influencing American policies on Cuba).

✔ The collective attitudes of the various government departments involved in foreign affairs such as the State and Defense Departments.

✔ The actions and ambitions of previous governments, which to some extent shape what options are available to the current government.

External factors also shape the state's national interests and influence how they can be attained, including:

✔ The foreign policies of other states.

✔ The geopolitics of a region (such as the demands for natural resources).

✔ The influence of international and regional institutions such as the United Nations, African Union, Organization of American States, Arab League and European Union.

The interaction a country has with other countries is considered the *act* of its foreign policy. This act typically takes place via interactions between government personnel through a process called *diplomacy*. Diplomacy involves negotiations between professionals (called diplomats) on a range of subjects, such as peace treaties, military issues, economics, and environmental issues.

Diplomacy is also often considered an art and refers to how people interact with each other. *Protocols* are established ways of behaving and they inform the etiquette of foreign relations. Think of protocols as the norms of an international culture that enable states to interact with without offending each other's sensibilities (of course, such interactions aren't always managed successfully!). How states demonstrate respect to visiting heads of other states will be informed by accepted protocols.

The ease and speed of communication and travel has made the world smaller and closer. A state on one side of the world, for example, can now respond to a crisis in another part of the world almost instantaneously. Alongside states, non-state actors also play a role in international relations. Within this globalised world, non-state actors such as non-governmental organisations (Oxfam, Greenpeace), multilateral organisations (the United Nations) and multinational organisations (British Petroleum and Coca-Cola) all have significant political influence in shaping the world but are aligned to their own interests as opposed to those of a particular state.

Spreading the Ideas of an Exceptional State

The United States of America was borne from an idea, a revolutionary idea of power of the government residing in the people and not a monarch. And it is this fact that marks it as an *exceptional* and special state.

Following a kerfuffle about taxation, the 13 United States of America declared their independence from Britain on 4 July 1776 (celebrated since as Independence Day), claiming that 'all men are created equal, that they are endowed by their Creator with certain unalienable Rights, that among these are Life, Liberty and the pursuit of Happiness'. In arguing their case, the newly-freed colonists claimed that, when a government is unable to offer these rights to the people, the people have the right to replace it and establish a new system of government. And the United States is an exceptional nation because no state previously, and only one state since (the Jewish state of Israel, in 1948), has adopted wholesale at birth these liberal-inspired *inalienable* rights.

It is this exceptionalism that has invoked a sense of duty on the part of the United States to promote its political system of liberal democracy around the world. (The word *liberal* refers to the political and economic philosophy that emphasises the rights of the individual, and *democracy* refers to a system of government whereby people are represented by elected officials.)

Religion and Secularism in Making America Special

America's special status was defined by the religious and politico-philosophical landscape of its first European immigrants. The first settlers, in the seventeenth century, were predominantly Puritans and other people seeking escape from religious persecution. These people emigrated in order to create a utopian society, free from persecution, which would also enable them to progress and obtain material advantages. Emigration offered them a chance to put the failures of the old world behind them and to start afresh in a new world.

The journey undertaken by these early immigrants had both physical and metaphorical meaning – America became both the actual land and the 'promised land'. This view was somewhat similar to the rationale of Enlightenment political thinkers who saw the promised land as an opportunity to create a secular civil society and system of government free from European corrupting influences. In time, the combination of religion and Enlightenment reasoning established a state and institutions to reflect these morals and principles. The influences of these two traditions on the American mission have changed over time but are still evident in shaping how the country defines its role both in domestic affairs and in its relations with the world.

Religious identity of America's mission

The principal religious influences on the American mission stem from the Protestantism of the Puritans, and their experiences. The Puritans believed that Europe could be saved from itself by following their example of a prosperous, free and moral society; they would provide the libertarian 'beacon of light' for the European states to follow.

John Winthrop, a Puritan leader during the seventeenth century, was one of many who believed that all nations had a covenant with God. The Church of England, in accepting Catholic rituals, had broken that promise. By moving to Massachusetts, Winthrop intended to create a new Puritan covenant. Reflecting on Matthew 5:14, in the sermon *A Model of A Christian Charity* (1630), he famously declared the new land be considered 'as a citty upon a hill', a place from whence to demonstrate to the rest of the world how great life can be if committed to God's will. The sermon also covered political and economic life. It explained how the new settlers should work together, live together and pray together.

Integral to the religious dimension of the American mission is the *Great Awakening*, an evangelical revival that swept the nation in the middle of the eighteenth century. The Great Awakening adapted the Puritan belief system by recognising the importance of individual religious experience. It prompted non-Puritan sects' greater acceptance of the Puritans' vision of America as the shining city on the hill to be emulated. It was responsible for creating a specific American identity by fostering an independent and self-determined character in the settlers. In part, it helped the colonies unify around a common identity: being an example for all other people to emulate translated into a foreign policy that suggested America's political system should equally be emulated by others.

This shining city metaphor isn't the only Protestant image that explains the religious aspect of America's mission. Another Christian influence in America's future foreign policy is the acknowledgement that the apocalypse – the final battle between good and evil – informed its understanding of international affairs. Invoking the ideas contained in the apocalypse introduced the importance of standing up to evil when determining America's engagement in the world and, by default, if it fought evil then it meant the country was good. This religious outlook explains America's firm mission to counter evil in the world.

Secular identity of America's mission

Buttressing the religious identity of the American mission is the Enlightenment and its belief in a secular civil society and system of government. Although all of America's *founding forefathers* could be seen as Christians, the majority could not be called devout. These non-devout Christians included:

- George Washington (first US president)
- John Adams (second US president)
- Thomas Jefferson (third US president)
- James Madison (fourth US president)
- Benjamin Franklin (first US ambassador to France)

These founders were products of the Enlightenment ideas of reason and science, and played important roles in establishing enlightened institutions such as societies and places of learning. Franklin, for example, was key in establishing the University of Pennsylvania.

The enlightened political thinkers looked over the pond to Europe and saw a system that had failed to provide for the people and viewed the *New World* (the American colonies) as an opportunity to redress those faults. In *Common Sense* (1776), the famous political activist, Thomas Paine, reflected on the revolutionary Enlightenment belief that America had the opportunity to rectify the faults of the *Old World* (Europe) by preserving 'freedom and other republican virtues, and construct[ing] an order based in the dictates of reason free from the abuses of monarchical egotism'.

Enlightenment philosophy was concerned primarily with domestic politics but this didn't preclude the discussion of international relations. The American followers of the Enlightenment reasoned that the failed European monarchical government system that was responsible for so many conflicts should be replaced with a system of republican states. In a *republic*, power to govern is held by the people and the politicians they elect to represent them and not by a pre-determined leader such as a monarch.

This republican state would support the rights of people and support an increase in economic trade between states. Free and fair economic relations were integral to these early goals of the United States. It did not want political and military alliances to hamper its economic development, so it disengaged from the political shenanigans of international relations. This pragmatic motivation went side-by-side with the American belief in the peace-inducing effects of liberal economic policies. This idea remained prominent throughout the nineteenth century, and the promotion of economic interdependence is still a prevalent force in US decision making today.

Glimpsing the American Mission

The United States has forever proclaimed its unique sense of mission and suggested that it is a beacon of freedom and righteousness for the world to admire and follow. It sees its mission as providential; it has been 'chosen' to share its blessings by engendering political reform on both the international and domestic level and by opposing 'evil' throughout the world.

American governments have long suggested that the liberal project lies at the heart of their foreign policy and national interest. This project's aim is to ensure the security of the United States while leading and building a political and economic liberal world order. This world order will favour American interests while also benefitting those like-minded states that buy in to it. Acknowledging the religious past, American officials have typically used quasi-religious language to define and describe their actions, suggesting that America has a divinely sanctioned mission to spread its own version of liberal democracy to the rest of the world.

Promoting liberal democracy is at the core of the American mission. To a large extent, it legitimises this objective through the rhetoric of opposing evil in the world, and achieves this goal through advancing international norms and institutions that promote them.

Promoting liberalism and democracy

The core ideas and ideals adhered to by mainstream America focus on individual political and economic freedoms. These concerns were as relevant at the founding of the nation as they are today. They include:

- Freedom of religion, enterprise and speech
- Protecting minority voices in a majority-ruled society
- Separation of government between Congress, the judiciary and the executive
- Equality before the law

Some of these central tenets are enshrined in the Declaration of Independence (1776). The Declaration defined the rights of individuals, the inalienability of these rights, the manner in which people should be governed and the course of redress if government should break its *social contract* with the people (when individuals consent to losing certain freedoms in exchange for protection from the state).

Looking back on American relations with the rest of the world during its two centuries of history, it is possible to pull out two main strategies for promoting liberalism and democracy:

- The *isolationist* approach means that America sets itself up as a role model. America is the Winthrop-inspired 'citty on the hill' that shows the other countries in the world how they should conduct domestic and international relations free from corruption and immorality. Other states and their people would see the success resulting from America's liberal approach to economics and politics and wish to emulate it.
- The *internationalist* approach means that America actively engages with the world to advance economic liberalism and democracy.

Policy makers over the course of US history have employed both strategies at different times, dependent on context. After the end of the First World War, for example, America retreated from active international engagement (see the 'Developing a pacific international system' section, later in this chapter, on Congress's failure to ratify the treaty establishing the League of Nations), whereas after the Second World War it has actively engaged with the world to promote its system of governance.

Opposing evil in the world

The rhetoric of evil is an essential element of American foreign policy in the Twentieth Century and is a product of the Christian religious identity of the US. It imbues American actions against other states with a religious-like meaning, and ensures defeating evil is essential to the reform of politics and international relations; one that follows the American political model. Talking about evil provides a framework to legitimise how the US has decided to respond to a particular threat to the nation, its people and its allies.

In other words, there are two ways in which the American fixation on the language of evil has an effect on its foreign policy. It can be used to legitimise its actions by calling the 'bad guys' evil and by default the US becomes the 'good guys', and therefore all the actions of the good guys become legitimate. Following on from this, the very act of applying the language of evil to a particular country, individual or event can itself determine the policy response by America.

During the two world wars America's enemies were depicted as evil, and in the Cold War President Ronald Reagan depicted the Soviets and other communist states as being part of an 'evil empire'. Communism was *the* competing ideology thwarting American efforts to make the world a better place through the promotion of liberal democracy. Whilst not explicitly mentioning evil, an example of the US application of evil-inducing rhetoric can be seen in the 1950 US National Security Council (part of the President's Office, consisting of national security advisors) report, more commonly known as NSC-68. The report concluded that the

> *'Kremlin's policy towards areas not under its control is the elimination of resistance to its will and the extension of its influence and control. It is driven to follow this policy because it cannot [...] . . . tolerate the existence of free societies; to the Kremlin the most mild and inoffensive free society is an affront, a challenge and a subversive influence.'*

Years later, during the *Détente* of the 1970s – a thawing of relations between the US and the Soviets which led to international treaties designed to ease tensions between the two – some American conservatives employed the language of evil when describing the Soviet Union and communism's ideology. And some of these Soviet critics were appointed to foreign policy positions in the Reagan administration (1980–88), confirming the evil identity of the Soviet Union. Critics included people such as Jeane Kirkpatrick, who became the US Ambassador to the United Nations (UN). In 1983, for example, President Reagan gave a speech to the National Association of Evangelicals that clearly demonstrated religious-inspired rhetoric. In a fit of religious zeal, Reagan declared that, 'there was sin and evil in the world, and we're enjoined by Scripture and the Lord Jesus to oppose it with all our might'. It set the scene for one of the most famous lines of his administration. In referencing the upcoming nuclear weapons negotiations with the Soviets, he asked the audience to not 'ignore the facts of history and the aggressive impulses of an *evil empire*', and suggested it was dangerous 'to simply call the arms race a giant misunderstanding and thereby remove yourself from the struggle between right and wrong and good and evil'.

The language of evil continued into the twenty-first century with the Bush administration. Five days after the terrorist attacks in 2001, President George W. Bush commented that America would respond by 'rid[ding] the world of evil-doers'. A few months later, in his 2002 State of the Union Address on the danger facing the free world from rogue states, President Bush spoke about the pursuance of weapons of mass destruction by Iraq, Iran and North Korea. He declared that, 'states like these, and their terrorist allies, constitute an *axis of evil*, arming to threaten the peace of the world'. And because these weapons could be passed to terrorists who 'could attack our allies or attempt to blackmail the United States', he clearly stated that action needed to be taken because to do nothing 'would be catastrophic'. And one way of dealing with this evil was, as you've probably guessed, to promote liberal democracy.

Developing a pacific international system

In the years after the Declaration of Independence (1776) the United States conducted its foreign policy with as little political contact as possible with the European–international political system. Its solution was to base its foreign policy with Europe on commerce issues only. In future years, this policy came to be known as isolationism.

But in the twentieth century, the United States became more interventionist. It took on the role of devising a world order that would no longer follow the great power politics that had dominated the international arena since the *Westphalian peace* established by a 1648 treaty between European powers decreeing that the sovereign rights of a state would not be interfered with by other states. The American mission was to change this system by creating a new world order to bring about a sustainable peace between states and, in so doing, secure the position of America as a dominant force in world politics.

President Woodrow Wilson's famous *fourteen points* speech at the end of the First World War outlined his commitment to, among other things, free trade, democracy for all and disarmament. That notion marked the first time that a US president had proposed the replacement of the old European balance of power system – whereby states create alliances with other states in order to provide a balance in relation to the more powerful state or states to minimise their influence on international affairs – with a new system of collective security.

Wilson's policy marked the development of a pacific international system as a core element of the American mission. This system was to be operated through the League of Nations. It was an attempt to create a new world order by insisting that countries work together to ensure aggression by one state was collectively opposed – that is, a system of *collective security*. Wilson demanded that other states pay a price for a new interventionist United States. He required that the liberal victorious European powers acquiesce in their power politics and support a change according to American specifications.

While other states might have been keen to get the United States involved in their defence, ultimately the US Senate didn't ratify the treaty establishing the League of Nations (see Chapter 5 for Congress's responsibilities). President Wilson was not capable of persuading his own country-people of its value. Hence, the US did not become a member of the League of Nations and by its inaction resoundingly supported a continued political isolationist approach to the international community. Without its political, economic and military might behind it, the League of Nations failed in its ambition to sustain peaceful relations between nations. It can be argued that this retreat from international affairs enabled the Germans and the Japanese to pursue their expansionist foreign policy agendas.

This new world order, as shaped and defined by the United States, got its second chance after the Second World War. America and its allies created a system of international norms and institutions that was consistent with its liberal political and economic values. In 1945 the Senate overwhelmingly voted in favour of the Charter of the United Nations by 89 to 2. This outcome was because most American politicians accepted that a return to isolationism was not a viable option in the context of the rise of the communist threat.

The charter outlined how this new world would operate, including how states should behave towards each other and how international disputes should be settled. It provided a framework for deciding when to collectively act militarily to deal with threats to international peace, and recognising the rights of individuals to political, economic and social opportunities such as access to education, healthcare and the protection of their human rights. The charter was an agreement between international states but it also fulfilled the desire of the US – and other Western states – to shape the world in their own image. For example, the US established an international financial system – *Bretton Woods* – that encouraged financial deregulation to enable private investment, a clear reflection of its belief in a liberal economic system. Its aim was to ensure economic development and co-operation among states and it established the International Monetary Fund and the International Bank for Reconstruction and Development (now known as the World Bank) to that end. This liberal agenda benefitted the US because it ensured that the future world economy was to be conditioned by practices and behaviours that reflected American needs.

The ability of the US to pursue all of its national interests via the medium of the United Nations changed during the Cold War. It stated that the UN was failing in its aim of providing collective security as a result of Soviet infiltration. This lack of trust in the UN system reflected resolutions and declarations made by the *General Assembly*, the talking-shop of the UN; all 193 members have the opportunity to represent their views and shape UN policy on all issues related to its charter. The US believed that recent resolutions and declarations showed either Soviet influence or a growth in confidence among developing nations that deviated from US interests. One such example is the resolution adopted in 1975 determining 'that Zionism is a form of racism and racial discrimination'. By 1975 Israel had become a firm ally of the US. This difference in ideologies has led the United States, since the end of the Cold War in 1991, to increasingly pursue its interests either by acting alone or through using other organisations such as NATO (North Atlantic Treaty Organisation – a political and military alliance between Western states, which promotes democratic values and provides collective defence of its members), or ad hoc alliances should it need to respond to an international crisis such as the 2003 *coalition of the willing* that forced regime change in Iraq. Today, the US still claims that it will create mini-alliances in order to further its interests or act unilaterally if need be; however, since the hostile rejection of multilateral institutions (including the UN) during the Bush administration (2001-2009), the Obama administration has been making a concerted effort to engage much more with international institutions in order to mend relations with allies and other states.

Combining Values and Interests

As you see throughout this chapter, American values and interests are combined in designing and justifying how the US acts in the world. The two are joined at the hip, so much so that they're both required whenever an American official explains why the country is responding to a situation in a particular way.

Promoting liberal democracy has been an active aim of American foreign policy since 1945. It enabled the US to advance its national interests and its values at the same time:

- ✔ Promoting democracy ensured that it attained its **national interests** regarding political, economic and security needs. This was best expressed in the *democratic peace theory* that emerged during the 1980s, which suggested democracies were the best political system because they did not go to war with each other, were better trade partners and behaved better towards their citizens than other systems. The more democracies, the more stable and peaceful the international order, thus benefitting the US by maintaining its position as the leader of the free world.

- ✔ **Values** such as individualism, equality and political, economic and social developmental progress are benefits that the US offers the world and its population by promoting a free market and democratic political system. President Reagan expressed this view best in 1982 when, in explaining the importance of helping the world reach for democracy, he claimed that, 'the objective I propose is quite simple to state: to foster the infrastructure of democracy, the system of a free press, unions, political parties, universities, which allows a people to choose their own way to develop their own culture, to reconcile their own differences through peaceful means'.

To give you a few more examples of how these two aspects of foreign policy – national interests and values – are intimately connected, take a look at the following quotations. Taken from a Republican and a Democrat president, they demonstrate the bipartisan nature of the American mission. In 1999, President Clinton spoke about his vision of how the US should engage with the world. With the rise of civil wars and conflicts around the world in places such as Bosnia and the Horn of Africa, he explained that it was in American interests to intervene by rhetorically questioning 'the consequences to our security of letting [these] conflicts fester and spread'. It was important that the US dealt with problems before they could impair the attainment of its interests. In providing a guide as to how America would carry out this objective, he concluded that, '[while] we cannot, indeed, we should not, do everything or be everywhere . . . where our *values and our interests* are at stake, and where we can make a difference, we must be prepared to do so'. And the method for doing so is promoting democracy.

In the 2002 National Security Strategy report, the Bush administration outlined its future US foreign policy in response to the 2001 terrorist attacks on American soil. It neatly encapsulates this combination of national interests and values. In describing how the US was victorious in the battle with the Soviet Union and communism during the Cold War, it explains how the US, as the remaining superpower, has the opportunity to turn this position of 'influence into decades of peace, prosperity, and liberty'. The solution was to employ an internationalist foreign policy, which, the report states, 'reflects the union of our values and our national interests'. In explaining why this is the case, it declares that 'the aim of this strategy is to help make the world not just safer but better' by promoting 'political and economic freedom, peaceful relations with other states, and respect for human dignity'. And promoting liberal democracy was a way to achieve these goals.

The legacy of the American mission has enabled successive administrations to rhetorically combine the roles of interests and values when explaining and legitimising its foreign policy actions. However, it doesn't provide much detail on the hierarchical relationship between the two. At certain times, promoting democracy has coincided with how the US government achieved its national interests. It includes examples such as providing support to establish stable democracies in Japan and Germany after the Second World War (post-1945).

But you also find times in the nation's history when it has not promoted democracy because doing so would not be in its economic or security interests. Its need for natural resources from Saudi Arabia, for example, is a good example of when an economic-based national interest trumps any discussion on the value of promoting democracy.

If the combination of values and interests was based on an equal footing, examples would also exist of the value of democracy trumping American national interests. I have been unable to find a single significant example, however. This situation isn't surprising; no state would act in accordance with its values at the expense of its interests.

Examples do exist, however, of the US providing token support to democracy in states in which it has no major economic or security interests. Such commitment is superficial, as demonstrated by the limited resources applied, and in reality is a public relations exercise.

If the aim of the state is survival, then being an altruistic value-laden nice-guy isn't going to get you far in the rough and tumble of international relations! Thus the US picks carefully where it deploys its democracy promotion wagon, and will only do so when doing so supports the promotion of its national interests.

Chapter 18

America and the World Today: A Brief Survey

. . . .

In This Chapter

▶ Understanding the special relationship between the US and the UK

▶ Learning to live as neighbours: America and Canada

▶ Exploring the America-Australia bond

▶ Facing the rising superpower: The US and China

▶ Analysing the power balance between the US and Israel

▶ Explaining tensions with Cuba

. . . .

*E*very country that's a friend of the United States likes to think that their relationship is a special one. In fact, even those that have bad relations with the US like to think they're special. Because America is a superpower and involves itself in all four corners of the globe, all states define their identity, in part, in terms of their relationship with America.

The reality is that America is the dominant partner in almost any relationship with another state, irrespective of whether it's a friend or foe. Since the end of the Second World War, the only state that's had any real opportunity of claiming equality with the US has been the Soviet Union and even that proved ultimately futile, collapsing as it did in 1991. International relations are a messy, complicated and often paradoxical state of affairs whereby different government agencies often promote different strategies. I can't show you all those nuances, so in this chapter I highlight a number of countries that provide an illustration of the types of relationships the US has with other states.

Family Bond: The US and the UK

Relations between these countries have always been intimate. After all, the United States evolved out of what were 13 British colonies. Relations between the two peoples got off to a bad start with the colonists' increasing sense of resentment that the British weren't responding to their needs. This resentment kicked off the War of Independence in 1775. The War of 1812 was a continuation of the hostilities initiated in the revolution, and British interests in the Confederate cause during the American Civil War (1861–1865) didn't help matters, either.

In spite of the rocky start to their relationship, cultural and economic ties always existed between the two that, once the dust settled, would reinforce good political relations. This section looks at relations between the US and the UK throughout the twentieth and twenty-first centuries from the perspective of their changing roles on the world stage and the importance of friendships between particular leaders.

Changing roles in international relations

At the start of the twentieth century through to the beginning of the Second World War, the British were a dominant power on the world stage. During this time, the US was focused on expanding its sphere of influence in the Americas while simultaneously ensuring that European powers weren't encroaching further. In the early stages of the First World War (1914–1918), the US was officially neutral, although it conducted zero trade with Germany as a result of the British blockade and the British government borrowed heavily from American banks. When Germany launched unrestricted submarine warfare, the US joined the British and its allies and declared war against Germany in April 1917. At the end of the war in 1918, the US was in a much more financially and politically stable position than its allies because it hadn't endured the full five years of conflict. As a result, the US could assert itself more vigorously on the international stage. And it did so at the postwar conference at Versailles in 1919. President Woodrow Wilson's plans for a system based on collective security (see Chapter 17 for details on the League of Nations) was instituted even though the US ultimately chose not to join. By the end of the First World War, Americans demonstrated a strong domestic and Congressional reluctance to engage in international politics and a move towards isolationism, which was reinforced with the focus on internal issues during the Great Depression of the 1930s.

During the first few years of the Second World War (1939–1945), the US was, once again, officially neutral. Congress instituted a number of Neutrality Acts that prohibited involvement, and Americans didn't want to engage in another European war. However, President Roosevelt was a supporter of Britain and her allies, and provided munitions and established a lend-lease programme to enable Britain to 'borrow' military supplies for the war effort – hardly a neutral programme. At the end of December 1941, the Japanese bombed Pearl Harbor in Hawaii and the Americans joined the allies in the fight against the Japanese and their German allies. This war effectively led to the collapse of the British empire.

In the post-war era, the US instituted a new world order in which it was the lynchpin. It played key roles in establishing the United Nations (UN) and the World Bank and set up the Marshall Plan (1948–1951) to provide funding to help Europe get back on its feet. Meanwhile, Britain lost its superpower status but still played a significant role in international politics. It was a founding member of the UN and a permanent member of its Security Council. It benefitted from the new world economic system and was a liberal democracy like the US. Britain's role as an important ally of the US throughout the Cold War against the Soviet Union and its communist allies consolidated their relationship. Britain was also a member of the North Atlantic Treaty Organisation (NATO), which guaranteed military and political support to other members in case of an attack.

A clear expression of how much power the British had lost on the international stage and how much America had gained is revealed by the Suez Crisis of 1956 – a diplomatic and military confrontation between Britain, France and Israel with Egypt. Rather than remaining localised, the US feared that the invasion of Egypt would involve the Soviets at some point, and so pressured the British and French to withdraw. This exertion of American power over Britain strained their relationship but didn't break it. The British were an important ally in the fight against communism and accordingly shared intelligence material and military secrets. In the early 1960s the US had provided nuclear weapons to the British military, an act indicative of the trust and alliance between the two states.

By the 1990s, although Britain and the US continued to maintain good relations, the end of the Cold War meant that the *special relationship* was no longer as important to the US as previously. It was now a multi-polar world, and the US was developing special economic relationships with other countries. However, that special relationship was reinstated when Britain's government (but not its people) supported the American 'War on Terror' post-9/11.

Great friends defined through leaders

Personal connections can play an important role in our perceptions of particular relationships. Those between President Ronald Reagan and Prime Minister Margaret Thatcher during the 1980s and President George W. Bush and Prime Minister Tony Blair during the 2000s are two such special relationships. Both developed during periods of international political turmoil that enabled the two countries to demonstrate their resolve in working together. During the 1980s it was the Cold War that pitted the West against the East, and in the 2000s it was the fight against rogue states, coined the War on Terror.

Thatcher came to power in 1979 and Reagan in 1980. The two leaders shared a similar conservative political outlook in domestic politics, a belief that free markets were the drivers of economic growth and a zeal for opposing communism on the international stage. Disagreements did occur in relation to foreign policy issues but had little impact on their overall working relationship or strategic priorities. Disputes included the refusal of Reagan to support the British against Argentina in the Falklands in 1982, the American invasion of the British Commonwealth of Grenada in the Caribbean in 1983, and the attempt by Reagan and Gorbachev to initiate the decommissioning of nuclear weapons at the 1986 Reykjavik summit.

The personal relationship between Reagan and Thatcher enabled advice to be offered and acted upon; they trusted each other. Thatcher, for example, famously called Reagan in 1984 after her first meeting with Mikhail Gorbachev (then a young light in the Soviet cabinet) to recommend him to Reagan as someone 'who you can do business with'. Gorbachev ultimately became the Soviet General Secretary and led the Soviet Union to end the Cold War. This support for each other even included Thatcher travelling to the US during Reagan's seeming implication in the torrid Iran-Contra scandal during 1985–1987 (see Chapter 20 for further details), politically standing beside him to demonstrate international support. However, it can't be denied that Thatcher (and Britain) needed Reagan (and America) as a friend more than was the case in reverse. Thatcher thus made many more trips to the US than did Reagan to the UK.

A similar power dynamic arose within the relationship between Blair and Bush. This strong relationship was reinforced after 9/11, when Blair immediately called the attack 'not a battle between the United States of America and terrorism but between the free and democratic world and terrorism'. It hinted at British involvement in any retaliation, and over the coming weeks Blair initiated a diplomatic campaign gathering support for the Bush administration's future response. Blair's approach could be seen as centring on getting in early and thereby helping shape Britain's importance in international politics.

The problem with this approach is that independence of thought and action are compromised for the sake of supporting an ally. And in the case of Blair, the most important issue was supporting Bush in a war with Iraq despite questions being raised about its international legitimacy. As a result, Blair is portrayed by critics as the the Bush administration's poodle. The war in Iraq also disconnected Blair from domestic public opinion and those European leaders who were opposed to it. His argument made in defence of invasion ultimately transpired to be less than reliable – Iraq did not possess weapons of mass destruction.

America will always be the stronger partner in this special relationship. When it wants Britain to support its actions, the US lays claim to this alleged kinship; when its interests don't coincide, however, the US will always do what it wants. This situation won't change. The question remains whether Britain will ever adopt a policy that doesn't involve putting the US at the centre of its foreign policy decision making.

Next-Door Neighbours: The US and Canada

When talking about the history of US–Canadian relations, Britain's role as the colonial boss is inevitably part of the equation. The US and Canada both were once a part of the British colonies in North America but, with the War of Independence, became political adversaries. This situation was reinforced when, at the end of the war, about 50,000–75,000 Loyalists (American colonists who supported the British Crown) left the US for Nova Scotia, New Brunswick and Ontario in what's now modern-day Canada. This influx of people loyal to Britain pretty much guaranteed that the Canadian colonies weren't going to suffer the same fate as those in America. In spite of this political separation on the matter of allegiance to the Crown, the cultural bonds between the two peoples were strong. Both cultures had similar British ancestry and led similar lives in the New World.

The War of 1812 was the only military conflict between the two countries, when the US attacked Canada, and the colony was used as a base for attacks into US territory by the British. After the War of 1812, as the years went by, a series of territorial disputes occurred but they never reached open warfare again. In 1867, Canada became a dominion government, meaning that it had full control over its domestic politics but foreign policy was still controlled by Britain. Around the same time the border disputes between the US and Canada were being resolved. Migration between the US and Canada further cemented cultural ties and, as importantly, economic links. By 1910, the Canadian immigrant population had peaked at 1.2 million.

By the 1920s, Canada was asserting itself in foreign affairs, in particular in its relations with the United States. One such example was the decision by the Canadian dominion government in 1923 to sign the Halibut Treaty with the US regarding North Pacific Ocean fishing rights. In this instance, in contrast to previous agreements, Canadians chose to go it alone in their relationship with the US and did not seek a British signature.

By the 1940s, the US and Canada had fought together in two world wars, were both democracies and were both allies in the Cold War against communists. The two nations' political and economic ties are further illustrated by their membership of a number of multilateral organisations, including being founding members of NATO, the World Trade Organization (WTO) and the Organization of American States. In 1994, the relationship was further cemented by membership of the North American Free Trade Association (NAFTA), an economic trade agreement between the US, Canada and Mexico. Figures on the economic impact of NAFTA are dramatic. Trade between the three countries has tripled since its implementation in 1994. Canada is America's largest trading partner. In 2013, for example, goods exported from the US to Canada totalled $300 billion, while goods exported from Canada to the US totalled $332 billion. In the services industry, American exports to Canada amounted to $61 billion, and exports to the US from Canada amounted to $30 billion. That's a lot of money crossing the border.

This close co-operation has led both countries to fight side by side in military engagements from Korea (1950–1953), the Gulf War (1990–1991), Kosovo (1998–1999) and Afghanistan (2001–the present). However, Canada did not involve itself in the Vietnam War in the 1960s and 1970s. And Canadian prime minister Jean Chrétien caused controversy when, in 2002, he warned that Western countries were seen by the world as 'arrogant and self-satisfied, greedy and with no limits' as a result of their accumulated wealth. He also commented that he was wary of the American response to the 9/11 attacks because 'you cannot exercise your powers to the point of humiliation for the others. . . . There are long-term consequences'. Chrétien's comments created difficulties with the Bush administration, although Canada did support the war in Afghanistan and send troops. The relationship became frostier still when Chrétien refused to publicly support the invasion of Iraq in 2003 without the support of a new UN resolution, although it was later suggested that Canada was involved in supporting that military campaign, including using its navy to protect supply lines.

Canada and America are mutually dependent in terms of trade and economic growth. But while they hold similar positions on a number of international issues, Canada has asserted its independence in foreign affairs. Perhaps Canada listened to President Nixon's comments in a joint session of the Canadian Parliament in 1972, when he described how American foreign policy rested 'on the premise that mature partners must have autonomous, independent policies: each nation must define the nature of its own interests; each nation must decide the requirements of its own security; each nation must determine the path of its own progress'.

The Shared Democratic Ideals of the US and Australia

Good relations between America and Australia are primarily a product of the need for each other in the Pacific as fear of Japanese dominance in the region grew during the 1930s. By 1940, Britain had dropped its claim to manage Australia's military and diplomatic relations. Australia was gaining status as a nation in its own right on the international stage and the US and

Australia had official legations representing their interests in Canberra and Washington, DC, respectively. By 1946, these legations had become embassies with ambassadors. In 1951, Australia, New Zealand and the US signed the ANZUS (Australia, New Zealand, and United States) treaty establishing collective military security between the three nations. Australia invoked this treaty following 9/11. Australia determined that an attack on the US was an attack on itself, and therefore would be involved in any future US responses. Australia is one of the only nations to have supported the US militarily in every one of its major conflicts from Korea to Vietnam to the Gulf War to Afghanistan and ultimately to Iraq.

Once again, the power dynamics in this relationship favour the US. However, the Australian government offers a much more pragmatic explanation of why it supports the US. Part of the strong relationship is based on shared democratic ideals and similar cultural and immigrant heritages. However, it's also true that close ties with the US are essential for Australia's ability to secure its security and economic national interests. Australia's relative isolation and small population of 22 million means that it depends greatly on its alliance with the US in terms of security in the region and maintenance of shipping lanes. The Obama administration's decision in 2011 to refocus its foreign policy strategy on 'pivoting' towards Asia was particularly good news for Australia. This new policy has included expanding the US military presence in Australia, for example basing 2,500 Marines in Darwin.

The positive relationship between the US and Australia is also based on economic benefits. Although trade disputes do occur between the two, the US is one of Australia's biggest economic partners.

A part of this economic relationship between the US and Australia is defined through the 2005 Australia-United States Free Trade Agreement (AUSFTA). In 2013, goods exported from the US to Australia totalled $24.89 billion, while goods exported from Australia to the US totalled $8.91 billion. In the services industry, American exports to Australia amounted to $11.56 billion and exports to the US from Australia amounted to $5.5 billion. Although these figures are high, compared to Australia's economic relationship with China, which stands at $139.55 billion for both imports and exports, they're peanuts.

Considering the importance of China's trade with the country, it's surprising that Australia is not less receptive to American national interests, at least visibly (American and Chinese interests compete). The key strategic and political issue facing Australia in the coming years will be its ability to successfully manage Chinese and American interests now that both see Australia as a place to play out their own strategic games.

Push and Pull between America and Israel

The relationship between the US and Israel has been short but packed with controversy. When the Israeli state was established out of mandate Palestine (an area controlled by the British after the First World War) in May 1948, the Truman administration was in dispute over whether to recognise the new Zionist state. Some believed that it could precipitate bad relations with Arabs in the region whom the US was courting to access their oil. But within two days of the declaration, the US responded in a diplomatic telegram from President Truman recognising 'the provisional government as the de facto authority of the new State of Israel'. While recognising Israel, the US still maintained a policy of supporting Arab states to maintain access to oil and off-set Soviet attempts to dominate the region.

During the 1950s, American support for the fledgling country was limited. When Israel participated in the Suez Canal crisis in 1956, the US supported Egypt and in the process was able to persuade Egypt to come under the US sphere of influence; as part of the sweetener, the US took a neutral stance in Egyptian–Israeli relations. American–Israeli relations improved during the 1960s when Presidents Kennedy and Johnson began aiding the country militarily as well as economically. At the time, the US was fearful of the intensity of Israeli reprisals following attacks by surrounding its Arab and Palestinian neighbours.

The strong relationship between the US and Israel that you see today developed during the Yom Kippur War of 1973, when Israel was attacked by Egypt and Syria. America's superpower rival, the Soviet Union, was supplying arms to the Arabs; in response, the Israeli prime minister ordered planes equipped with atomic weapons. In order to halt Israeli preparations for using such weapons, the US decided to supply it with attack aircraft, tanks and helicopters. US support of Israel ultimately lead to the 1973 oil embargo placed upon it by Arab producers, which precipitated a four-fold increase in the price of a barrel of oil.

During the 1970s American aid to Israel increased dramatically, especially in terms of military support. According to a 2014 US government report, during that period it gave Israel $16.3 billion in loans and grants, 71 per cent of it being spent on military hardware. In the 1980s that rose to $28 billion, 56 per cent of which was spent on military support. Obviously these weren't acts of charity on the part of the US; rather, they were a recognition that US national interests would best be served in the region by a militarily strong Israel counterbalancing expansion of Soviet interests. US aid to Israel continued even after the end of the Cold War; currently it amounts to around $3 billion per annum. Such aid is essential to the economic and political survival of the country.

One would think that this degree of financial support would result in substantial US control over Israel's actions. In fact, the American government has had very little control over what Israel chooses to do. Contrary to its relationships with most other states, the US is by no means the dominant partner in its relations with Israel. Regarding occupied territories and Israeli acceptance of a Palestinian state with full nationhood, for example, various US administrations have been unable to exert any significant influence on the Israeli position. This situation is partly the result of Israeli influence in American politics.

Approximately 300,000 American citizens live in Israel, out of a population of 7.9 million, and about 10 per cent of them vote in US elections. Being pro-Israel is an essential element of their political manifesto if a candidate wants to get elected, irrespective of party. Add to the mix Christian evangelical support for the state of Israel together with the power of the pro-Israel lobby to exert its influence on American politics and you can clearly see why the US is pressured to support Israeli actions.

An example of the inability of US administrations to exert their authority is demonstrated repeatedly in the history of the two countries. For example, no sooner than a US Secretary of State flies over to negotiate resumption of peace talks between the Palestinians and Israelis does the press report the approval of a new and illegal settlement (under international law) by the Israeli government. In recent times, actions like these, together with Israel's aggressive posturing towards Iran, have led to some very hostile relations between President Obama and Prime Minister Benjamin Netanyahu.

In September 2012, while attending the UN's annual conference, the Obama administration publicly made it known that Obama was unable to arrange a meeting with the Israeli PM. Obama's attitude towards Netanyahu was reflected in an accidental recording of him discussing Netanyahu with French President Nicolas Sarkozy at a 2011 G20 summit meeting. Sarkozy declared, 'I cannot stand him. He's a liar' Obama responded, 'You're fed up with him, but I have to deal with him every day!'

At United Nations Security Council meetings the US has vetoed every proposed resolution criticising Israel, and it's voted against every General Assembly proposal to take action against Israel. While this demonstration of support is admirable and consistent with US national interests, unfortunately the sentiment isn't reciprocated. In early 2014, the US proposed a resolution in the General Assembly criticising Russia's annexation of the Crimea (see Chapter 19 for further details). Israel decided that it had friendly relations with both states and didn't want to get involved. As a general with the Israeli Defence Ministry stated, 'the US is involved in its own way, but our security interests should not be defined as identical to those of anyone else, even the US'. Time will tell whether this break in relations between the two allies is permanent or merely a temporary fault line.

The Long Association between the US and China

Relations between China and the US have come a long way since they were first connected as a result of trade and migration. Today, Sino–American relations are a complicated mix of political, economic and military posturing between a superpower and a rising power.

But power relations weren't always this complicated; in the past the US was much more dominant (which made things pretty simple). During the 1800s, US relations with the Chinese were a consistent story of the US exerting its power over them. American missionaries demonstrated their racial superiority as they educated the Chinese masses; Chinese immigrants worked as labourers constructing the US railroads. Later, the US banned further immigration using the 1882 Chinese Exclusion Act, and pushed for trade concessions for American businesses in Chinese ports.

Much the same commercial approach to China was applied in the first part of the 1900s. America recognised that China was run by one government, the Republic of China. The emergence of Japan as a threat to the US in the Pacific was intensified by a series of colonial wars Japan initiated against the Chinese. The Chinese government, led by Kuomintang (KMT) leader Chiang Kai-shek, ultimately fought a war against the Japanese imperialist army from 1937. The US supported the Chinese government by providing economic and military aid in order to counterbalance the power of Japan. The Sino–Japanese war ended in 1945 when the US dropped atomic bombs on the cities of Hiroshima and Nagasaki and Japan surrendered. The US continued to support the KMT government throughout the 1940s in its fight against the communists led by Mao Zedong. In October 1949, Zedong defeated the Kuomintang and established the People's Republic of China (PRC). The remaining KMT forces left for the island of Taiwan and established a Chinese government in exile. The US continued to support the KMT nationalists, thereby creating hostile relations with the communists for a generation. In 1953, President Eisenhower signed a mutual defence pact with the KMT, ensuring that invading the island would be too costly for the PRC.

With China becoming a member of the atomic weapons group in the mid-1960s, and supporting the Vietnamese during the Vietnam War against the US and South Vietnam, relations continued to be strained. However, in a classic case of *my enemy's enemy is my friend*, Chinese disputes with their communist Soviet allies enabled America to begin opening formal relations with them. By the early 1970s, thawing of relations included a secret trip by the US Secretary of State to China, which led to the PRC taking over the KMT's permanent seat on the UN Security Council in October 1971. It was a major step in improving relations between the two countries as it recognised the sole authority of the communist government. Thawing continued when President Nixon visited China in 1972. This event was a big deal; remember that China was a member of what the Americans perceived as an evil communist gang attempting to take over the world. By the end of the decade, China had received full diplomatic recognition by America under President Carter. However, in recognising that the PRC was the legitimate government of the Chinese people, it also recognised that Taiwan was a part of China, thus reducing Taiwan's diplomatic status. The US did, however, enable the *de facto* political independence of Taiwan by providing it with political, economic and military support.

In the 1980s and 1990s a series of disputes between the US and China strained relations and between them. From the American perspective, they focused on China's abuse of political dissidents' human rights, such as the protestors in Tiananmen Square in Beijing in 1989. By mid-1989 the protest had been crushed, hundreds of protestors killed and many thousands imprisoned. The accidental NATO bombing of the Chinese embassy in Belgrade, which killed Chinese diplomats, caused another negative spike in relations.

While these disputes may have given commentators a lot to talk about, the fundamental issue changing the power relations between these two countries is the meteoric rise of the Chinese economy. From 1979 onwards, when China opened up its economy to foreign investment and instituted free market reforms, its gross domestic product (GDP) has increased on average by 10 per cent every year. Admittedly, it started from a low base but compared to US data during the same period – the world's largest economy – these figures are impressive.

The economies of the two nations have become much more entwined since the Clinton administration signed the 2000 US–China Relations Act normalising trade relations. As a result, China was able to join the World Trade Organization, the effects of which on trade between the rest of the world and China has been phenomenal. Take trade between America and China as an example: in the three years after China joined the WTO, US exports to China increased by 81 per cent and exports from China to the US increased by 92 per cent. According to US government statistics, in 2000 trade between the two totalled $116 billion and by 2013 totalled $552 billion.

After Canada, China is the second-largest trading partner of the US. However, while the overall amount of trade between the dyads of US–Canada and US–China isn't that dissimilar, the power relationship strongly favours the Chinese. In 2013, China exported to the US nearly four times as much as it imported from the US, a pattern repeated pretty much throughout the 1990s and 2000s. It became the second-largest economy in the world by 2012, and by late-2008 was the largest holder of US government debt. By 2013, the US owed China $1.2 trillion, about 8 per cent of total US government debt. China can thus now assert itself on the international stage – and other countries have to listen. It's also expanded its foreign investment in Latin America and Africa, demonstrating its emergence as a global power. It's involved in resolving international disputes, including negotiations with North Korea and Iran regarding their nuclear capabilities. And, worryingly to the US and its allies, China is increasingly flexing its muscles in territorial disputes in the South China Sea with Japan, Vietnam, Brunei, Taiwan, Indonesia, Malaysia and Philippines.

China's newfound economic power is backed up by its increasing military expenditure. While US military expenditure dwarfs all others at $640 billion in 2013 (about 37 per cent of world share), China's is $188 billion (11 per cent of world share). The gap between the two is shrinking. In response to the rise of China and increasing economic and military threat it poses to America's allies in the region, in 2011 the US redefined its foreign policy approach to focus on Asia rather than the Middle East. As part of this pivot, President Obama initiated negotiations between the US and several other nations regarding creating a free trade zone (Trans-Pacific Partnership) in the region. China isn't invited to the party. Although rivalry between the two sides will undoubtedly continue to grow, hopefully neither will resort to military solutions to resolving disputes.

Stuck in Time: America and Cuba

Truly a David versus Goliath story, the relationship between the US and Cuba is also a confusing combination of deep-seated suspicion and animosity that's gone well beyond its usefulness date. It's now an anachronism of the legacy of the Cold War and the political influence of the Cuban lobby in Washington, DC, politics.

Under the 1950s dictatorship of Fulgencio Batista, Cuba, and in particular Havana, was a playhouse for America's rich and famous – and the mafia. The dictatorship was increasingly violent and repressive towards the Cuban people, leading to an armed revolution starting in 1953 and ending with Batista's overthrow in 1959 by Fidel Castro. The response of the US government towards the new government was negative from the very outset, and had only gotten worse by 1960, when Castro nationalised all foreign businesses in the country, increased import duties on America goods and established economic ties with the Soviet Union.

Castro's changes hit the US particularly hard because most imports to Cuba were from the US, and most foreign companies were American. Add the Cuban economic slap to an ideological schism and potent enmity is the result. The Eisenhower administration naturally responded in kind, imposing a heavy embargo and cutting diplomatic relations with the country. This inauspicious beginning defines the relationship between the two countries to this day.

In an attempt to mimic the actions of the small band of Cuban revolutionaries who had hidden out in the Sierra Maestra mountains in the south of the country before taking over the country, in April 1961 the CIA organised an invasion comprised of Cuban exiles against the communist government. Intending to overthrow the socialist government run by Castro, the invasion of the Bay of Pigs was a disaster because it was detected by the Cuban military. US antipathy towards Cuba wasn't just because it had been snubbed; it also represented an ideological threat – a Cold War enemy situated a mere 50 miles off the coast of America. Its well-established policy of denying adversaries any foothold in the Americas meant that the US was determined to end this socialist experiment. Undeterred by this military failure, the Kennedy administration continued its assault on the Cubans by introducing a full economic embargo in early 1962. This embargo is still in existence today.

When the Soviet Union attempted to locate nuclear weapons in Cuba, ideological enmity almost resulted in nuclear war. The *Cuban Missile Crisis* in 1962 ultimately lead to the establishment of a direct phone line between the two superpowers to thwart any future misunderstanding. The missiles were removed, the US committed to not invading Cuba and then secretly retrieved from Greece and Turkey nuclear weapons pointing at the Soviet Union. Despite these agreements, relations remain very frosty between Cuba and the US. Their fight continued during the 1960s as the Cubans exported the communist revolution to other parts of Latin America and even to the Congo in Africa.

During the early 1980s, the Cuban economy was suffering as a result of the economic embargo imposed upon it. When President Carter opened America's doors to them, about 125,000 disillusioned Cubans left and headed to the US. Castro sanctioned their exit, presumably thinking it was better to have them out of the country than causing problems inside it. The Cuban lobby in the US now has tremendous impact on national politics.

The collapse of the Soviet Union in 1991 had an enormous negative effect on the Cuban economy: it lost its Soviet subsidies, exports declined by about 85 per cent and GDP fell by a third. Cuba entered a *Special Period* of fundamental changes; agricultural production changed from petro-chemical to organic, it sought foreign investment and marketed itself as a tourist resort. In 1995 Congress passed the Helms–Burton Act formalising the US embargo into law. President Clinton was initially reluctant to sign it but went ahead in March 1996 after the Cuban government shot down two planes in its airspace belonging to a US–Cuban anti-Castro organisation. The Act effectively restricted US presidential engagement in meaningful relations with the Cubans unless very restrictive measures were met, including the need for Cuba to become a democracy. It also caused problems with US allies as it imposed sanctions on them if they traded with previously American companies that had been nationalised. One of the first to be affected was a Canadian mining company involved with the Cuban government in extracting nickel from an allegedly US-owned mine. The executives of the company were barred from entering the US in July 1996.

Other key moments defining the intense US–Cuban relationship include the arrest in 1998 and subsequent imprisonment of five Cubans for attempting to infiltrate Cuban exile organisations in the US, and the 1999 Elián González crisis that erupted when a six-year-old boy was one of only three survivors of a trip across the Gulf of Mexico to Florida. His father was still a resident in Cuba and wanted his son to return while other family members in Florida wanted him to stay. The case was heard in a federal court, which declared that the child would have to be returned. The family objected but the Supreme Court refused to hear the case. Elián and his father returned to Cuba in June 2000.

In early 2008, as a new administration was entering the White House, so too was a new president, albeit unelected, heading up the Cuban government. Barack Obama replaced George W. Bush, and Raúl Castro replaced his brother, Fidel.

Raúl Castro introduced a series of economic reforms: Cubans can now own mobile phones and computers, wage equality is no longer enforced and more land is given to private farmers. Within a year relations between the two countries warmed and the US lifted restrictions on Cuban-Americans sending remittances to Cuban friends and family and allowed Americans to travel to Cuba. In June 2009, Cuba emerged from political isolation in the region when the Organization of American States lifted its ban on Cuban membership. Cuban political and economic reforms continue apace. Dissidents have been released; to boost the economy, no longer is a job guaranteed for every Cuban; people are able to buy and sell property; and Cubans can leave the country without dealing with the complicated bureaucracy that restricted their movements previously.

In March 2014, the European Union opened negotiations to improve economic relations, and in May President Raúl Castro met a US trade delegation from the Chamber of Commerce to discuss establishing trade relations between the US and Cuba. The future appears to be bright in regard to changing the political and economic relationship between the two countries. The remaining difficulty is economic embargo. The US president has to abide by law, and the Helms–Burton Act is very restrictive. Relations can thus only be normalised in one of two ways: Congress must repeal the Act, which is very unlikely, or Cuba must become a democracy. Interestingly, the definition of what constitutes a democracy is open to Congress to determine, but the likelihood of that happening in Cuba anytime soon is minimal. Raúl Castro must also leave office and that, too, is unlikely to happen in the foreseeable future.

Chapter 19

Analysing 9/11 and Contemporary American Foreign Policy

- -

In This Chapter

▶ Describing the end of the Cold War and the new world order

▶ Detailing what happened on 9/11

▶ Looking at the Bush administration's response to 9/11

▶ Checking out Obama's approach to foreign policy

- -

*O*n 9 September 2011, the United States was attacked by terrorists. According to the Bush administration, the US was living in a new world. A world where the threat of rogue states combined with the actions of non-state actors (read *terrorists*) could combine meant a new foreign policy was required.

This chapter explains the backstory to 9/11, what happened on the day and the US response to those attacks. It includes a discussion of President Bush's and President Obama's foreign policies and what they achieved. The post-9/11 US policy is not just about America's immediate response to the attacks but about the actions taken in this entirely new international environment – actions that would not have been implemented had 9/11 not happened.

Setting the Scene: The End of the Cold War and Post-1991

The Cold War lasted for 45 years and pitted the *free world* led by the United States against the *communist world* led by the Soviet Union. Within it, two great powers fought for world dominance – and to win a battle of opposing ideologies.

While some dispute exists regarding whether it was America's foreign policy actions or the internal dysfunction of the Soviet state that led to the end of the Cold War, it ended rather abruptly. In June 1989, free elections were held in Poland and the previously banned trade unionist party, Solidarity, under Lech Walesa won the election. Unlike previous cases of opposition to communist rule in Soviet-dominated Eastern Europe, the Soviets did not militarily intervene. A new precedent had been set and heralded revolutions across Eastern Europe. By November 1989, the Berlin Wall had come down and plans were afoot for German reunification. In 1991, Russia, Ukraine and what became Belarus declared independence and the Soviet Union collapsed.

At the end of the Cold War the US didn't want another superpower rival to emerge as its bi-polar opponent. President George H. W. Bush set out to prevent this scenario by establishing a *new world order* that maintained America's dominance while accepting its capability of and responsibility for improving the living conditions and standards of the world's population. In his 1992 address to the United Nations, he spoke of the end of the Cold War and his belief that there was 'a unique opportunity to [create] a genuine global community of free and sovereign nations – a community built on respect for the principle of peaceful settlement of disputes, fundamental human rights and the twin pillars of freedom, democracy and free markets'.

US promotion of democracy and involvement in multilateral engagement in resolving the world's problems was seen to serve the new interpretation of national interest. This new order began with the US invasion of Panama in 1989. American troops removed the military dictator General Manuel Noriega from power. Previously, the American government had tolerated that of Noriega in exchange for the maintenance of an anti-communist regime and American influence over the Panama Canal. The Panama invasion was followed by the US-led international ejection of Iraq, under President Saddam Hussein, from Kuwait in 1991 and US engagement in the UN humanitarian operation in Somalia in late 1992.

The new world order seemed to be going well; the UN could now operate without the previous Cold War posturing. But no sooner was it set up than it seemed to unravel during President Clinton's first term in office.

Clinton was the first American president in over 50 years who didn't have to contend with an ideological, military and economic superpower rival. But he was also the first US president to have to deal with the new tensions of a post-Cold War world. For example, the independence of former Yugoslav states led to wars between the Serbian-dominated former Yugoslavia and Slovenia in 1991, against Croatia (1992–1995), Bosnia (1992–1995) and Kosovo-Albanians (1998–1999). Over 250,000 people died in these wars and millions more were displaced from their homes. In Africa, hundreds of thousands of lives were being lost in events such as the Somali and Sierra Leone civil wars and the ethnic cleansing in Rwanda.

Under Clinton, the US took action in some of these conflicts (such as Bosnia) but stood back from others (such as Rwanda). And in light of these conflicts, Clinton identified the need to increase the number of nations in the democratic community. The solution was to promote democracy and free markets in the mould of the American liberal democratic system.

The Clinton administration gradually institutionalised and prioritised the promotion of democracy and particularly focused on developing the political infrastructure of countries by supporting

- Free elections
- An independent judiciary
- Free press
- A civil society
- Accountable police service
- Economic reforms that privatised industries and encouraged free enterprise
- Reconstruction of infrastructure such as roads, hospitals and schools

In January 2001, George W. Bush became the forty-third president of the United States. President Clinton presented President Bush with a foreign policy that both engaged the world and promoted US democracy as the state-system to emulate. US promotion of democracy had increased dramatically under Clinton; it had become a principal foreign policy tool for the attainment of US national interests. However, Clinton also bequeathed Bush a legacy of increasing criticism of America.

Seen as the epitome of globalisation, America provoked opposition to its capitalist and hegemonic profile. Political Islamists were becoming increasingly active in their opposition to American influence in the Middle East and the rest of the Muslim world. Osama Bin Laden, for example, spearheaded extremist Islamic opposition to American policy in the region by organising a loose conglomeration of Muslim organisations called al-Qaeda. Attacks by al-Qaeda members had already occurred: on the World Trade Center in New York in 1993 (when a truck bomb exploded, killing six people and injuring about 1,000); on the US embassies in Tanzania and Kenya in 1998 (killing 234 and injuring over 4,650); and on the *USS Cole* in the port of Aden in 2000 (a suicide mission, killing 17 sailors and injuring 39).

Recounting the Day That Changed Everything: 11 September 2001

On 11 September 2001, the course of America's engagement with the world changed radically. Terrorists hijacked four planes over the continental United States and used them as weapons. The timeline is as follows:

- ✓ 8:45 am: American Airlines Flight 11 was purposefully crashed into the North Tower of the World Trade Center in New York City.

- ✓ 9:03 am: United Airlines Flight 175 was crashed into the South Tower of the World Trade Center.

- ✓ 9:30 am: President Bush announced that two planes had crashed into the World Trade Center in 'an apparent terrorist attack on our country'.

- ✓ 9:37 am: American Airlines Flight 77 was crashed into the Pentagon, the US military headquarters, in Washington, DC.

- ✓ 9:59 am: The South Tower of the World Trade Center collapsed.

- ✓ 10:03 am: A fourth plane, United Airlines Flight 93, was crashed into a field in Pennsylvania before it could reach its destination.

- ✓ 10:28 am: The North Tower of the World Trade Center collapsed.

Official figures state that 2,996 people died on 9/11, and because the victims included people of 78 different nationalities an automatic connection was felt between members of the international community. Intense questioning took place in the following days regarding the perpetrators.

The hijackers, their leader and their explanation

Nineteen people hijacked the four planes that comprised the attack – 15 from Saudi Arabia, one from Egypt, one from Lebanon and two from the United Arab Emirates. They were all working for al-Qaeda, an Islamist terrorist organisation, and were organised into four teams: one member in each team was the pilot and the others were to subdue the cabin and flight staff in order to gain access to the cockpit. The pilots arrived in the US in 2000 in order to begin flight-training courses in South Florida and Southern California. The remainder of the hijackers flew to the US in early to mid-2000.

Osama Bin Laden, the head of al-Qaeda, was the son of a Saudi billionaire who owned a construction business and had good relations with the Saudi royal family. He was thus a well-connected and rich individual. He was a devout Wahhabi Muslim (an ultra-conservative form of Sunni Islam practised in Saudi Arabia). By 1979 he'd moved to Pakistan and developed relations with the Pakistani secret Inter-Services Intelligence (ISI) agency in order to train Muslims from all over the world to fight the Soviet forces occupying Afghanistan. By 1988, al-Qaeda had been established to protect the Islamist cause around the world. When Iraq invaded Kuwait in 1990, Bin Laden offered al-Qaeda forces to protect Saudi Arabia from possible Iraqi attack. His offer was declined and, instead, US and other military forces from around the world were invited in. Bin Laden publicly denounced Saudi Arabia for allowing non-Muslims to protect the holy sites of Mecca and Medina. Disillusioned with his birth country, he fled to Sudan in 1992.

Hostility to the US intensified, and al-Qaeda attacked symbols of American power in Africa, the Middle East and in the US itself. The attacks on 9/11 were a continuation of a trend that had started 11 years earlier. And Bin Laden was a politically savvy operator, seeking to explain and legitimise al-Qaeda attacks in interviews with Western and non-Western journalists.

Defending the attacks against the US, Bin Laden commented in numerous interviews that they were in response to 80 years of foreign domination. As evidence of this domination, he cited supposed US-sanctioned Israeli invasion of Lebanon in 1982, US complicity in Israeli attacks on Palestine and the US-driven UN sanctions imposed on Iraq in the early 1990s, which were responsible for killing 1 million Iraqi children. In an October 2001 interview, Bin Laden concluded, 'May God mete them the punishment they deserve.' In a 2004 interview, regarding whether 9/11 was a response to the great wrongs experienced by Muslims, he rhetorically asked if a man [should] be blamed for defending his sanctuary'. He then answered that, '[if] defending oneself and punishing the aggressor in kind' is 'objectionable terrorism . . . then it is unavoidable for us'.

Bin Laden's argument that the attacks were a product of US actions in the Muslim world counter the claims by Bush and his administration that the US was attacked because it espoused the values of freedom and liberty.

How the world responded to 9/11

The days and weeks after 9/11 saw an international outpouring of symbolic support for America:

- ✔ On 12 September, the French newspaper, *Le Monde*, best captured the moment with its headline 'Nous sommes tous Américains' ('We are all Americans').

- ✔ In London, the military band played the Star Spangled Banner instead of the British national anthem during the Changing of the Guard at Buckingham Palace.

- ✔ In Palestine, Kuwait and Israel people donated blood.

- ✔ In Berlin, thousands of people gathered at the Brandenburg Gate.

- ✔ In other places, such as Lebanon, Cuba and India, people demonstrated their support through public displays of sympathy, prayer and mourning.

International leaders also provided their support for America. UK Prime Minister Tony Blair stated that, 'this is not a battle between the United States of America and terrorism but between the free and democratic world and terrorism'. Hinting at British involvement in any retaliation, he continued that 9/11 was 'perpetrated by fanatics who are utterly indifferent to the sanctity of human life and we, the democracies of this world, are going to have to come together to fight it together and eradicate this evil completely from our world'. German Chancellor Gerhard Schröder stated that, 'they were not only attacks on the people in the United States, our friends in America, but also against the entire civilized world, against our own freedom, against our own values, values which we share with the American people'.

These public declarations of support for the US government and the American people were backed-up by diplomatic responses, too:

- ✔ On 12 September, an emergency meeting of the United Nations Security Council passed a resolution calling on all states to bring the perpetrators to justice and expressing 'its readiness to take all necessary steps to respond to the terrorist attacks of 11 September 2001'.

- ✔ On the same day, NATO (North Atlantic Treaty Organization) invoked Article 5 of its Treaty for the first time ever. This Article declares that an attack on one member nation is an attack on all others and military action can be justified as an act of self-defence.

- ✔ Members of the Organization of American States (OAS) passed a resolution on 21 September stating that, 'these terrorist attacks against the United States of America are attacks against all American states'.

✔ Signatories to OAS' Inter-American Treaty of Reciprocal Assistance (1947) invoked its Article 3 for the first time, confirming a policy of collective defence.

✔ Australia invoked Article 4 of the 1951 treaty between Australia, New Zealand and the United States of America (ANZUS), also for the first time, which stated that an attack on one state was an attack on the others.

Understanding Bush's Foreign Policy Response to 9/11

President Bush contended that 9/11 was an attack on the American way of life. In his address to a joint session of Congress on 20 September 2001, he answered the question being posed by many Americans: 'Why do they hate us?' He responded: 'they hate what they see right here in this chamber: a democratically elected government. Their leaders are self-appointed. They hate our freedoms: our freedom of religion, our freedom of speech, our freedom to vote and assemble and disagree with each other.'

A few days earlier Congress had passed a joint resolution authorising the president to use all necessary and appropriate force against those nations, organisations or persons he determined had planned, authorised, committed or aided the terrorist attacks that occurred on 11 September 2001, or harboured such organisations or persons, in order to prevent any future acts of international terrorism against the United States by such nations, organisations or persons. This authorisation provided the Bush administration with Congressional consent to implement a foreign policy that started with Afghanistan but ultimately became a worldwide war against terrorism and states with whom the US was in conflict. In this section, I discuss these events by looking at what's become known as the Bush Doctrine. Abandoning previous foreign policy strategies such as containment and deterrence, it took a much more aggressive and proactive approach.

The Bush Doctrine

As the days wore on after 9/11, communications by and from the administration showed that foreign policy was no longer just about retribution on al-Qaeda in Afghanistan but an opportunity for America to more aggressively assert itself in the international arena. Central to this assertiveness was the continuation of a long-term policy that saw the US as the driving force in establishing a more peaceful and stable world order (see Chapter 17 for more on the American Mission).

Every couple of years, the president publishes a document detailing how the US government intends to interact with the world. The 2002 National Security Strategy (NSS) published in September defined the new foreign and security policy of the Bush administration. It had five key elements:

✔ **A new definition of threat:** The Bush administration identified three dangerous actors in the post-9/11 world – terrorist organisations, weak states that provide support and protection for terrorists, and rogue states. Al-Qaeda was identified as a terrorist organisation, Afghanistan a weak state, and Iraq, Iran and North Korea as rogues. Bush, in his 2002 State of the Union Address, famously spoke of these three rogue states as an 'axis of evil'.

✔ **Rejection of deterrence and containment:** Deterrence was seen as unlikely to work against rogue states because they weren't rational actors and were 'more willing to take risks, gambling with the lives of their people, and the wealth of their nations', or terrorists who, unlike states, don't experience territorial pressure to conform and 'whose avowed tactics are wanton destruction and the targeting of innocents'.

✔ **A willingness to act unilaterally:** The Bush administration doubted whether its national security interests would be met by international and regional institutions such as the United Nations. Bush declared that the US would act, if need be, *unilaterally* – that is, on its own.

✔ **Expanded definition of pre-emption:** With containment and deterrence no longer suitable for dealing with the security concerns facing America, a new strategy was required to deal with rogue states and non-state terrorists who'd obtained or attempted to obtain WMD. The doctrine suggested that the dangers faced were imminent, extremely dangerous and implemented by actors who couldn't be deterred. The US had never had to deal with such a situation before and, as such, required an immediate and unprecedented response. A danger, if considered clear and present, enables a state to pre-emptively strike in order to protect itself. Controversially, the Bush administration widened the definition of pre-emptive to also include preventative attacks, which have no legal sanction in international law.

✔ **Domestic identity of a state important in international relations:** Attached to the strategy of pre-emption, the administration committed itself to thwarting terrorism by promoting democracy in these weak and rogue states. This strategy promoted US national security and economic interests by enforcing democracy, human rights and free markets over state sovereignty. Promoting democracy became an overarching narrative that defined all American foreign policy actions. And it justified this disregard for national sovereignty by claiming that it would minimise terrorism focused on the US and its allies. According to this logic, democratic states

are more stable, less likely to go to war with each other, better trade partners and better to their citizens. Such a policy would therefore not only
benefit America but make the world a safer and better place.

Afghanistan and the ascendancy of the Bush Doctrine

When President Bush addressed Congress and the nation on 20 September,
he spoke of the coming war against terrorists and suggested that the fight
would be a 'lengthy campaign unlike any other we have ever seen'. He issued
a stark warning that those 'nations that provide aid or safe haven to terrorism' had to make a decision: 'either you are with us or you are with the terrorists'. Any regime that was seen to 'harbor or support' terrorists would be
regarded as 'hostile'. And this good-versus-evil dichotomy became a defining
feature of American foreign policy in the post-9/11 world.

In spite of their denials, the evidence suggested that al-Qaeda was responsible for 9/11, and in late September the US requested that the Taliban government in Afghanistan surrender Osama Bin Laden and other members of the
organisation and close al-Qaeda training bases or risk attack. Although negotiations did take place with the Taliban and the Taliban did ask Bin Laden to
leave Afghanistan, for the Americans this response wasn't good enough. On
7 October 2001, US military operations began.

The American mission was to create a stable liberal democracy in
Afghanistan. By as early as December 2001, it was clear that President
Bush was determined that Afghanistan would have a political system that
responded to the needs of the Afghan people, unlike the previous Taliban
government. And as the Bush Doctrine suggested, establishing a secure and
stable democratic Afghanistan that would no longer be a haven for terrorists
was essential to securing US national interests.

The American promotion of democracy was given international legitimacy
by the *Bonn Accords*, the international conference designed to map out
Afghanistan's future. The Accords committed the new interim Afghan government, under the leadership of Hamid Karzai, to establishing an *Emergency
Loya Jirga*, a traditional vehicle for selecting political leadership, to be held
within six months to decide on a transitional administration. It also committed the interim government to writing a new democratic constitution to be
established within 18 months of the transitional administration's inaugura-
tion. In order to support this change the international community provided
diplomatic and financial support, and established the International Security
Assistance Force (ISAF) under NATO command to help stabilise the country.

Unfortunately, Afghanistan's chance of becoming a stable and secure democracy was considerably reduced by the actions of the US and UK governments (among others):

✔ About 20,000 civilians have been killed in Afghanistan. According to the UN Assistance Mission in Afghanistan (UNAMA), between 2006 and 2012 alone 10,737 civilian deaths occurred. While anti-government forces were responsible for 66 per cent of these fatalities, 34 per cent were caused by pro-government forces – the very agents supposed to be protecting them. The Afghan people were disillusioned with the transitional government, the democratisation process and international military support as a result.

✔ The state-building project installed a new government to replace the defeated Taliban. The democratisation process in Afghanistan impeded the country's transition to consolidated liberal democracy. By introducing a Western liberal democratic model in Afghanistan, the US government developed conditions that led to future violent conflict. The Taliban and al-Qaeda opposed democracy as modern and Western, and have resisted the new state's attitude to the rights of women.

✔ Short-term compromises were made that ultimately impeded the long-term goal of liberal democracy. While it was deemed necessary to gain the support of Afghan warlords, drug lords and military commanders to secure victory against the Taliban and al-Qaeda, their co-option into the democratic process was problematic. These figures held significant sway in the country and did not want to see the rule of law usurp their powers or stop their opium production. Some of these figures even ran for local and national elections, further consolidating their power. The US and its allies thus incorporated opponents to democracy within the system.

✔ High levels of corruption within central and local government have affected the democratising process. Official US government reports of misappropriation of funds and resources are legendary. One report, for example, stated that security for road construction projects was being outsourced to members of the Taliban – the very people such security was meant to offer protection from!

Moving on to Iraq

The Bush Doctrine elevated the fear that rogue states possessed WMD and were passing them on to Islamic terrorists opposed to America. Any country that was seen to fit this bill was in trouble.

Former Bush administration officials have suggested that Iraq was on its radar in the immediate aftermath of 9/11. In the 18 months before the March 2003 US-led invasion, officials made the legal and public relations case for intervention in Iraq. The focus on Iraq is evident in President Bush's September 2002 speech at the UN. He suggested that the Iraqi government was 'gaining and deploying the most terrible weapons' and a possibility existed that it could 'supply these weapons to terrorist allies'.

Using the framework of the Bush Doctrine, an invasion seemed inevitable, although its authorisation under international law was questionable. In spite of years of sanctions, the Bush administration suggested that Saddam Hussein's government still had WMD and that the Iraqis had a working relationship with al-Qaeda. Although the CIA had informed Bush that no connection existed between Iraq and 9/11, key officials, such as Vice President Dick Cheney, had commented in late 2001 that one of the 9/11 hijackers had previously met the Iraqi intelligence services.

The Bush administration, with support from allies such as the UK, sought to deal with this new Iraqi threat. In the 2002 September speech to the UN, Bush called on Iraq to destroy all its WMD and end its support for terrorism. He called on the UN Security Council to pass resolutions to support these goals, including the threat of military intervention if Iraq did not comply. Together with a lightly veiled threat of unilateral action, he warned that 'the purposes of the United States should not be doubted'. In providing a moral argument concerning the need to engage with Saddam Hussein, and supporting the argument of the Bush Doctrine that a state's domestic identify was important in relation to international affairs, he suggested that that free societies were better because they did not intimidate or occupy other states (clearly the irony was lost on him!).

As a consequence of the Bush administration's commitment to dealing with Iraq, the UN Security Council passed a resolution demanding that Iraq allow weapons inspectors to enter the country and disarm its WMDs and related materials. The head of the inspectors, Hans Blix, issued a report on 7 March 2003 declaring that Iraq was not providing them with full documentation of chemical agents that had gone missing but had increased its co-operation; the inspectors required more time to investigate. The Bush administration determined that Iraq was in breach of UN resolutions and thus the Security Council should meet immediately to issue a new resolution on the matter, condemning the Iraqis and authorising military force. Other members of the Council, such as France, refused to authorise such a resolution and it wasn't passed. However, an international 'coalition of the willing' – around 40 states – did support an invasion.

On 19 March, the US, UK, Australia and Poland launched a military campaign against Iraq, aiming to make the world a safer place by ridding Iraq of WMD, ending its support for terrorists and freeing its people from tyranny. In May 2003, Bush declared that 'major combat operations in Iraq have ended'. However, while military operations against the Iraqi military had indeed ended, things weren't working out as anticipated.

The argument for the invasion began to unravel. No credible evidence suggested a working relationship existed between Iraq and al-Qaeda, and the Iraq Survey Group tasked to find WMD declared that Iraq had never had any. Further, the expectation that the Iraqi people would see the international forces as liberators and welcome them with open arms proved wildly optimistic and in reality completely unrealistic. American support for post-Saddam Iraq helped escalate violence by reinforcing sectarian divisions.

Similar to its Afghan mission, the US aimed to restore infrastructure such as roads, schools and hospitals, support private sector development, establish a representative government, and hold free and fair elections. However, such a programme had little chance of success. And its impact on Iraqi society was appalling. According to the British-based Iraq Body Count, between 2003 and the end of the Bush administration in January 2010, over 110,000 civilians died; other reports actually suggest that this figure is too conservative. According to a US, Iraqi and Canadian report, between 2003 and mid-2011 500,000 Iraqis had been killed either directly in the fighting or indirectly as a result of ill-health or poor sanitation.

While responsibility for post-2003 Iraq, becoming a sectarian battlefield between Sunnis, Shiites and Kurds was primarily driven by the insurgent Sunni groups such as al-Qaeda, the US-led mission did play a role in fostering the conditions that led to the civil war (2005–2007). America established the Coalition Provisional Authority in 2003 to run the country in the interim while a transitional government made-up of Iraqis could be established. However, its first two orders were a disaster, engendering distrust among Sunnis and former military personnel, and exacerbating sectarian relationships among Sunnis, Shiites and Kurds.

The first order purged the government of former personnel, effectively removing any institutional memory and thus opportunity for efficiency. The second disbanded the military and security services. In excess of 350,000 people suddenly became unemployed and unable to provide for themselves or their families. Sunnis and Shiites protested the move, and evidence suggests that some former soldiers became embroiled in the insurgency, as well as engaging in criminal activities.

Treatment of prisoners

One of the greatest criticisms levelled at the Bush administration is its treatment of people suspected of terrorism and prisoners of war. That treatment exposed America to worldwide criticism, and severely undermined its professed mission to promote a democratic and peaceful world order. Its engagement in Afghanistan and Iraq and treatment of prisoners obviously confirmed to many Bin Laden's claim that the US was aggressive towards Muslims and were very good recruitment tools for al-Qaeda and related organisations.

By January 2002, America was transferring captured al-Qaeda and Taliban fighters from Afghanistan to a prisoner of war camp in the US naval base in Guantánamo Bay, Cuba. In the following years, people from Iraq, Pakistan, Yemen and other countries were picked up and detained in the camp, but without prisoner of war status, which would have granted certain rights under the Geneva Convention, including the right to be treated humanely and not suffer humiliating or degrading treatment. The Bush administration argued that because they were considered *unlawful enemy combatants* and not prisoners of war, the Geneva Convention didn't apply. Further, placing these people in territory outside the US meant not having to grant them constitutional protection such as not being held indefinitely without charge and release if insufficient evidence exists.

By 2004, treatment of prisoners was becoming a humiliating public relations disaster. In a former Iraqi torture centre, Abu Ghraib, US military prison guards and CIA officials were committing gross human rights violations, including killing, raping and torturing prisoners. Various human rights organisations such as Amnesty International were reporting this situation by as early as mid-2003. Not until April 2004, however, when an American news programme showed images of abuse, did worldwide condemnation force the US to respond to the situation.

If these apparently isolated incidents weren't bad enough, by mid-2004, evidence showed that the US was employing interrogation techniques that were considered by multiple organisations, including the International Committee of the Red Cross and Human Rights Watch, as torture. In a 2002 legal opinion by the US Department of Justice's Office of Legal Counsel, the case was made that specific interrogation techniques could be employed and were not torture. These *enhanced* techniques included the simulation of drowning called *waterboarding*, which involved pouring water down the throat of someone being held down so that they gag continuously.

A number of people from around the world suspected of Islamic extremism were detained by US-friendly governments, flown by Central Intelligence Agency (CIA) chartered planes and deposited in secret interrogation facilities in other friendly nations. This process was referred to as *extraordinary rendition*. Initiated by the Clinton administration, it was expanded under President George W. Bush. According to a 2013 Open Society Justice Initiative report, around 136 people were transferred to these secret facilities, interrogated and tortured and 54 countries were apparently involved. One such country was Macedonia, which was found by the European Court of Human Rights to have been complicit in torturing a German citizen, Khaled El-Masri, in a case of mistaken identity.

One element of the US federal government did not bow to pressure from the president, however. In 2006, the Supreme Court heard *Hamdan vs. Rumsfeld*, in which a Guantánamo detainee concluded that the military tribunals established to try prisoners for war crimes contravened both the Geneva Convention and the US military's Uniform Code of Military Justice. The Bush administration responded by getting Congress to pass the 2006 Military Commissions Act, which authorised military tribunals to try suspected enemy combatants and prevented them from challenging their detention in the federal courts. However, in *Boumediene vs. Bush* (2008), the Supreme Court declared that preventing those who were accused from petitioning the federal courts for an explanation of why they were being detained was unconstitutional.

Taking a Look at Obama's Version of a Post-9/11 Foreign Policy

Some presidents, such as Reagan and Bush, are visionary; they see the world as something malleable that they, representing the superpower, have the power and duty to change. The other type of president, and Obama's in this camp, tends to respond to the world as it is rather than advance an activist agenda for change. This isn't to say that these presidents don't want to influence the world in America's favour; rather their approach is less openly aggressive and unilateral. This type of president is more pragmatic about foreign policy.

When Obama was elected in 2008, engaging in large-scale military interventions was no longer viable as a result of the failure of the missions in Afghanistan and Iraq. Too much hostility existed toward the Bush administration's foreign policy approach. The 2008 economic crisis also meant that America couldn't afford further military action. (See Chapter 16 for details of the economic crisis.) But it would be unfair to say that Obama's foreign policy is all about responding to the world in a pragmatic way; he is also committed to promoting American values as laid out in the American mission (see Chapter 17).

The Obama administration's foreign policy doctrine became known as *strategic engagement*. It defined how Obama would renew America's role in leading the world while ensuring that its national security was protected. Obama saw that the two wars in Afghanistan and Iraq, as well as the fight against extremism, were important aspects of American foreign policy but they shouldn't be the only defining features. His administration's approach, as stated in its National Security Strategy in 2010, was built on three themes:

- ✔ **Building our foundation:** A successful economy can finance American engagement with the world, funding the military, development programmes and diplomatic efforts. Interestingly, in suggesting that US 'national security begins at home', the strategy document stated that long-term global success was being hampered by not fully supporting a range of domestic issues such as 'education, energy, science and technology, and health care'. In driving its leadership role in the world, in a swipe at the Bush administration's aggressive imposition of democracy through armed intervention, it suggested that the US would set an example for the world to follow by supporting human rights and other democratic values at home. And while it declared that 'America must demonstrate through words and deeds the resilience of our values and Constitution', as the Arab Spring and National Security Agency debacle demonstrate, this particular tenet was hot air.

- ✔ **Pursuing comprehensive engagement:** The US must play a role in shaping the international system and so will engage 'nations, institutions, and peoples around the world on the basis of mutual interests and mutual respect', not only its allies but also the newly emerging twenty-first-century powers such as China, India and Russia. The document also issued a warning to states such as Iran and North Korea that, if they wanted the political and economic benefits resulting from integrating into the international community, they needed to abide by international norms or face increasing isolation, including sanctions.

- ✔ **Promoting a just and sustainable international order:** America would use international institutions to isolate states hostile to the current international order (a swipe at the Bush administration's willingness to subvert them). Strengthening these institutions and international norms of acceptable state behaviour was seen as an important means of legitimising and imposing economic sanctions. Ultimately, the US saw supporting a stable international order as essential for promoting its national economic and security interests.

Obama's successes

Obama's administration has achieved some notable successes. One of his first Executive Orders, signed in January 2009, would close Guantánamo Bay detention camp by January 2010, halt the use of military tribunals and provide detainees with the power to question their detention in court and not be permanently detained without a fair trial. That order kick-started a positive change in attitude toward America. Obama also declared that the US government would not be involved in torture or apply the Bush-sanctioned enhanced interrogation techniques. Acts like these saw him awarded the Nobel Peace Prize in October 2009 (although some people were a little surprised that he was thought worthy of it).

From the beginning, Obama had disapproved of the Iraq war, and when in office upheld his election promise to withdraw US troops. On 18 December 2011, the last remaining US troops left the country.

Despite the proclamation in the 2010 National Security Strategy that the US would re-balance its priorities, the fight against Islamic terrorists was still a key priority. Perhaps the greatest victory in the fight against al-Qaeda was the May 2011 killing of Osama Bin Laden by US Special Forces in Abbottabad, Pakistan. According to Obama, it was the 'most significant achievement to date in our nation's effort to defeat al-Qaeda'.

Another, more domestic, political success was Obama's ability to reorient the Democrats as the middle-ground in national security discussions, in part by ensuring the US was not involved in another costly war based on skewed idealism. Perhaps the most important success of the Obama administration's strategic engagement has been its policy towards Iran and its nuclear weapons development programme. After Obama took office, he sponsored a range of sanctions on Iran by the US, UN and the European Union. They have negatively impacted Iran's economy and even caused Iraqi citizens to express dissatisfaction with their own government. In November 2013, Iran, the US, the UK, China, France, Germany and Russia agreed to a six-month interim deal that would enable both sides to negotiate a final settlement on Iran's nuclear programme. In order to receive up to £4.3 billion ($7 billion) worth of sanctions relief (including unfreezing oil assets) during the interim period while negotiations for a final agreement continue, Iran is committed to

- ✔ Limit uranium enrichment to 5 per cent in order to power reactors but not create nuclear weapons

- ✔ Neutralise its current 20 per cent uranium stockpile (it is only a short step from 20 per cent to nuclear weapon-grade uranium)

- ✔ Halt development of a plutonium site (also used in developing nuclear weapons) and increase access to nuclear sites by international inspectors

Negotiations are still underway and, despite Iranian, American and Israeli detractors, a final agreement may soon be reached that will reintroduce Iran into the international community.

Obama's failures

Key aspects of Obama's policy of strategic engagement haven't been too successful:

✔ He has been unable to succeed in Afghanistan. Obama had used the War in Iraq as a political tool for bashing the Republicans in the 2008 presidential election because it directed attention away from the fight in Afghanistan, leading to resurgence in Taliban attacks. After taking office, and in response to the growing destabilisation of the country, through 2009 to September 2010, Obama employed a new strategy that included 98,000 extra troops.

The new strategy focused on dealing with the Taliban and other insurgents but also training Afghan military and police to secure the country when the US and its NATO allies pulled out in late 2014. Unfortunately, this surge in troops has not had that much of an impact in stabilising Afghanistan, making its government more accountable or making the country a safer place for civilians to live.

✔ As the years went by, the Obama administration's ethical stance on dealing with the legacy of US human rights abuses conducted under the banner of the 'War on Terror' became less defined. In true pragmatic style, this commitment to American values was jettisoned when faced with other competing interests. As an example, the deadline for closing Guantánamo Bay passed, and it is currently still open. Part of the problem was that none of the 50 states were willing to take the detainees and hold them while awaiting trial. This failure was compounded by Obama reneging on his commitment to halt trying detainees in military tribunals rather than civilian courts.

✔ In April 2009, Obama made public a series of CIA memos discussing the use of enhanced interrogation techniques during the Bush administration, including waterboarding and placing people in stress positions. Obama aimed to distance himself from Bush. While claiming that it was a 'dark and painful chapter in our history', Obama refused to consider prosecuting the CIA personnel responsible for torture because the US government had sanctioned it. This decision smacks of double standards because these arguments were rejected in the trials of Bosnian-Serbs responsible for murdering people in Bosnia during the 1992–1995 break-up of Yugoslavia, and during the Nuremberg trials of Germans responsible for war crimes during the Second World War.

✔ Part of Obama's foreign policy aim was to improve relations with Russia, which had been problematic during the Bush administration. In March 2009, Secretary of State Hillary Clinton suggested a "resetting" of relations between the two nations. After initial success with agreement on reducing stockpiles of nuclear weapons, relations hit problems regarding the March 2011 US-led NATO mission in Libya. Russian support for the mission in the UN Security Council did not include regime change, but that was what happened when opposition rebels were supported by NATO air strikes in destroying Colonel Muammar Gadhafi's military. Russians rejected US requests for UN military authorisation including resolutions condemning the Syrian President Bashar al-Assad's attacks on his people.

✔ In late 2013, Ukrainian President Yanukovych rejected closer ties with the EU in favour of Russia. Opposition responded by protesting in the capital, Kiev, reaching upwards of 800,000 people. Protests continued, and by February 2014, parliament passed and then repealed an anti-protest law. Over 100 protestors were killed by the government. By the end of February, Yanukovych left Ukraine, and pro-Russian forces invaded the ethnically Russian Crimean peninsula. By the end of March, the peninsula held a referendum and was annexed by the Russians. Americans objected; Russians ignored them; and relations between the two countries were at their worst since the end of the Cold War. Obama's initial response to declare limited sanctions on associates of Putin was criticised by US right-wingers as not sufficiently robust to deal with Russia. They suggested that Obama's 'reset' policy emboldened Russia to dismiss US opposition.

More of Obama's foreign policy actions

Some cases can be defined either as a success or failure depending on where you're sitting. In this section I consider a couple of such cases: the US response to the war in Syria and the use of military drones.

Syria

In March 2011, the Syrian civil war began between President Bashar al-Assad's Syrian government and a series of disunited secular and religious opposition groups.

In August 2012, Obama first discussed the use of chemical weapons in Syria as a *red line* that couldn't be crossed or the US would militarily intervene. By June 2013, the US claims, Assad had used chemical weapons but military intervention did not occur. By late August, it was reported that Assad had used chemical weapons and killed 1,400 people. Over a week later, Secretary of State John Kerry called for military attacks on the Syrian government, blaming them for the chemical-related deaths. Obama requested Congress to approve military intervention, but they're opposed and don't vote on the bill. By September 2009, Syria agreed with Russia to hand over its chemical weapons.

Deciding whether this was a success or failure depends on your perspective as to what is most important, the continuing humanitarian disaster, or keeping the US out of another conflict.

Drones

Obama expanded the use of *drones* (unmanned air vehicle that can be used to spy and fire missiles on people) to kill those it sees as a threat to national security.

On one side, the argument is the drone use has restricted the abilities of al-Qaeda affiliated groups' abilities to conduct attacks. As of January 2014, over 390 drone attacks had happened and 2,400 people had been killed since Obama became president. There were only 51 attacks during the entire eight years of the Bush administration. Drones have enabled Obama to conduct counterterrorist operations in remote areas such as Northwest Pakistan, Yemen, and Somalia where it is unlikely he would be able to send people in to detain them. The counterargument is that drones are morally and politically questionable. People are being killed without recourse to a fair trial, and the President gets to choose who lives and dies. It also causes a lot of public opposition in the countries that are attacked because national sovereignty is being subverted by the US, and a large number of civilians are still being killed by them (250 out of the 2,400 killed by drones under Obama).

Reducing the role of democracy promotion

Part of the Obama Doctrine was for democracy promotion writ-large to be replaced with a policy of promoting democracy only in certain circumstances. The international political realities made any attempt to impose a political system on a country foolhardy, whilst there has been greater recognition and insight that national interests can be attained without engaging in large-scale missions (i.e., Afghanistan or Iraq). It means that the opportunities for promoting democracy are limited, and large-scale missions non-existent. However, whilst no longer an overarching narrative, democracy promotion remains a part a part of the Obama foreign policy toolkit. It has been particularly useful in responding to the Arab Spring pro-democratic movements since 2009.

In December 2010, a young Tunisian street vendor, Mohamed Bouazizi, set himself to fire because officials had stopped him from selling vegetables and confiscated his products. Protests at his death forced the Tunisian president, who had been in power for 23 years, to resign. Protests spread across the Middle East and North Africa collectively became known as the *Arab Spring*. In Tunisia, Egypt, Libya, and Yemen, the protestors were able to replace the previous dictators with new leaders or new governments. However, in the other instances, the regimes were able to suppress the demonstrators and the desire for change.

With promoting democracy no longer central to American foreign policy, the question was how Obama was going to respond to these domestic uprisings that fought against authoritarianism. Whilst not all the protestors were requesting democracy *per se*, they were demanding greater representation and less corruption, ideals that sit alongside democracy. Obama responded by suggesting that the domestic identity of a state (i.e. whether or not it was a democracy) was not important if that country's support was required in gaining its national interests. With these interests being to maintain reliable access to oil so the global economy is not negatively impacted, to cooperate with states in order to counter terrorism, deal with the Arab-Israeli conflict, and counter WMD development or use.

Effectively, Obama's approach has produced very few cases that include democracy promotion missions because the criteria are so constraining. If the society is sufficiently agitating for political change and if maintaining support for the current regime is too destabilising to the pursuit of American interests, the US would support a transition. Likewise, if supporting the current regime is not destabilising to securing its national interests, the US would maintain its current policy (for example, Bahrain). And because the Arab Spring countries are in a state of heightened instability, political realities are constantly changing. As a result, US conceptions of how its interests can be attained also differ. Thus the US has been able to change its support for the removal of President Mubarak in late 2011, to supporting the deposal of the Muslim Brotherhood's Mohamed Morsi as president in 2013.

Part VI
The Part of Tens

Certain elections bring more impact than others. Find out about ten particularly important elections at www.dummies.com/extras/americanpoliticsuk.

In This Part . . .

✔ Check out political scandals that made an impact on American culture, including bad moves by presidents and missteps by wannabes.

✔ Get the details on candidates who gave it their level best but couldn't quite make it to the presidency.

Chapter 20

Ten Political Scandals That Shook the Nation

*G*reed. Lust. Hubris. The stuff of soap operas also is regularly (and delightfully for those watching along at home) the stuff of politics. The quick-moving world of ego and intrigue is readymade for scandal – and scandals most certainly abound.

All but one of the scandals here are from the 1970s onwards. That's not because scandals didn't exist before the invention of the colour TV (I could write a book on the scandals of Ben Franklin alone) but because more recent scandals help show you the shape of American politics today. And in varying ways, these cases demonstrate Lord Acton's famous maxim that power tends to corrupt and absolute power corrupts absolutely.

Bill Clinton and Monica Lewinsky (1998)

Monica Lewinsky was employed as an intern in 1995 in President Clinton's Office of the Chief of Staff and began an intimate relationship with him. This was not his first indiscretion; in 1994 Paula Jones had filed a civil case against Clinton accusing him of sexual harassment. Following rumours of her affair with Clinton, Lewinsky was asked to file an affidavit (a statement under oath) explaining the situation. She denied ever having had an affair with the president. However, Lewinsky had confided details about the affair with a former colleague, Linda Tripp, who secretly taped the conversations. A few years later, Tripp contacted an independent counsel, Kenneth Starr, and suggested that Clinton had asked Lewinsky to lie about the affair under oath. Tripp met Lewinsky again, and the FBI working for Starr recorded Lewinsky talking about the affair and the Paula Jones case. The Attorney General granted Starr the ability to expand his investigation to include possible perjury, and from then on in, Clinton was doomed, particularly because he gave a deposition denying he had had a sexual relationship with Lewinsky.

At a press conference, standing next to his wife, Clinton claimed rather forcefully, 'I did not have sexual relations with that woman, Miss Lewinsky. I never told anybody to lie, not a single time; never. These allegations are false.' Under oath, however, he offered a pretty flimsy defence of his previous comments by claiming that he didn't believe receiving oral sex constituted sexual relations. (This wasn't the first time he'd tried to wriggle out of something on a technicality – he also famously claimed that, while he had smoked marijuana, it didn't really count as he 'did not inhale'.)

On 19 December 1998, the House of Representatives suggested that grounds for impeachment existed in relation to obstruction of justice and perjury). A trial was set for an impeachment of a sitting president, only the second time in US history.

Ultimately, the Senate concluded that the president was guilty of neither obstruction of justice nor perjury. Partisanship pretty much defined this vote. The Republicans had the majority with 55 Senators to the Democrats' 45. All 45 Democrat senators voted 'not guilty' for both counts whilst most Republican Senators voted against Clinton on both charges. Only ten Republicans voted 'not guilty' for the perjury charge and five for the obstruction of justice. Unlikely as it may seem, the impeachment trial did not do lasting damage to Clinton's reputation. In fact, according to a Pew Research Center poll conducted in December 1998, he gained a 10-point increase in approval ratings – to 71 per cent – including among Republican voters.

The Florida Election Debacle (2000)

In the early morning of 8 November 2000, Vice President Al Gore had 260 electoral college votes (and would go on to gain 266), and Republican Nominee George W. Bush had 246. That left 25 EC votes in Florida, and whoever won that state would become president.

Later that day, the evidence suggested that Bush had won by less than 2,000 votes in the state, automatically incurring a recount by Florida state electoral law. And then things really got hairy:

- ✔ On 9 November, Gore requests a hand recount in four predominantly Democratic-leaning counties as allowed under Florida electoral law, and it proceeds. The deadline for both recounts is 14 November.

- ✔ Within a few days, the Bush team request a federal injunction to stop the recount in some states claiming that it violated, among many issues, the equal protection clause of the Fourteenth Amendment by suggesting that all people in a state must be treated equally under the law. The federal judge rejects Bush's plea for a federal banning of the recount in some counties in Florida.

- ✔ Three of the counties recounting continue after the 14 November deadline. Republican-appointed Secretary of State, Katherine Harris, petitions the Florida Supreme Court to halt the recount but is rebuffed.

- ✔ By 18 November, overseas absentee ballots show that Bush is leading Gore, across the state, by only 930 votes.

- ✔ The Gore team asks the state court to consider whether the type of ballot used in Palm County was so confusing to voters that a number of people may have inadvertently voted for conservative Reform Party candidate Pat Buchannan. He received 3,407 votes when the Reform Party itself suggested he should only have gained about 500. The state judge declares he has no constitutional right to question the results in this way.

- ✔ On 21 November, a new recount deadline is set. The Bush team submits a case to the Supreme Court requesting it to review the Florida Supreme Court ruling allowing the recount to continue. In Palm Beach the electorate had chosen their preferred candidate by punching a hole next to their name. Unfortunately, some votes have not pierced the card correctly. A state judge declares that these cards cannot be automatically excluded from the recount if they indicate an intentional choice.

- ✔ On 24 November, the US Supreme Court enters the fray and decides that it will hear Governor Jeb Bush's (yes, the younger brother of George W. Bush) and Secretary Harris' case that the Florida Supreme Court decision to hold selective recounts was constitutional (*Bush* vs. *Palm Beach County Canvassing Board 2000*).

- ✔ On 26 November, Secretary Harris declares that Bush is the winner of the 25 EC votes in Florida by a margin of 537 votes. And Florida Governor Jeb Bush signs the certificate awarding the EC votes to his elder brother.

- ✔ Another round of requests to state and federal courts to have votes countered or discounted ensues.

✔ On December 1, the US Supreme Court hears oral arguments for *Bush vs. Palm Beach County Canvassing Board 2000* on constitutional grounds regarding whether the Florida Supreme Court had the right to support selective recounts in some counties and not others. The election results stay up in the air while an incredibly intricate back and forth among the parties, the State of Florida and the Supreme Court ensues. In the end, the Court decides that the decision by Governor Bush and Secretary Harris to award the 25 votes to George W. Bush stands.

On 13 December, Gore conceded defeat to Bush. Interestingly, in a 2001 report on what would have happened in Florida if the Supreme Court had allowed the partial recount in the four Democratic-leaning counties concluded that Bush would probably still have won. A recount of all disputed votes state-wide would probably have meant that Gore gained anywhere between 42 and 171 votes out of the 6 million cast – it's thus way too close to call.

Illinois Governor Rod Blagojevich Selling Obama's seat (2009)

The state of Illinois is renowned for its tainted political scene; accusations of corruption are rife. Democratic Governor Rod Blagojevich has only enforced that reputation.

Although Governor Blagojevich actually ran on an anti-corruption ticket, about a year after he'd been in office he was accused of involvement in corrupt appointments, kickbacks and illegal campaign fundraising.

During his 2006 re-election campaign, Blagojevich's fundraiser, Antoin Rezko, was indicted on corruption charges (and ultimately convicted and sentenced to 10 and a half years) and his wife was also investigated for corruption. FBI investigations into Blagojevich himself also revealed hard evidence of the extent of his corruption.

Because Obama had vacated his Illinois Senate seat upon becoming president, Blagojevich was responsible for filling it. He saw it as a wonderful financial opportunity. Wiretapped by the FBI, he said: 'I've got this thing, and it's *** golden. I'm just not giving it up for *** nothing.' He was arrested and charged with selling multiple positions, including the recently vacated Senate seat.

Before the case could come to trial, the Illinois House of Representatives overwhelmingly voted to impeach the governor. Blagojevich was ultimately convicted and sentenced to 14 years in prison. A rich man, a successful politician and still he wanted more.

Keating Five Savings and Loan Scandal (1988)

During the 1980s and 1990s deregulation was the prevailing principle regarding the financial industry. *Savings and Loan Associations* (S&Ls – known in the UK as building societies) are specialist financial institutions for savings deposits and mortgages. They especially benefitted from this relaxation of controls, enabling them to use their depositors' money and invest in riskier real estate and junk bonds deals because the return was so much greater.

From the mid-1980s to the mid-1990s, over 1,000 S&Ls failed. A government report published in 1996 stated that bailing out this industry had cost the taxpayer approximately $132 billion. Any number of corrupt and illegal acts were going in this industry during this period, but a particularly juicy one involves five US senators.

Federal Home Loan Bank Board (FHLBB), which regulated the industry, concluded in 1996 that one company, Lincoln Savings and Loan, had exceeded its capital in these risky investments by in excess of $615 million and had unreported losses of $135 million. Charles Keating, the head of Lincoln, was fearful that the company might be forced into insolvency and so initiated a series of strategies to halt further FHLBB action. He requested the help of five senators: Alan Cranston (D – California), Dennis DeConcini (D – Arizona), John Glenn (D – Ohio), John McCain (R – Arizona) and Donald Riegle (D – Michigan). Previously, Keating had given about $1.4 million in campaign contributions to these five members of Congress (does anyone smell corruption?).

In 1987, Keating asked them to meet with the regulators and intervene in their deliberations on Lincoln to enable the company more time to deal with the situation. In May 1988, the FHLBB agreed that it would give Lincoln the opportunity to correct itself. Lincoln's assets grew during this period but Keating transferred money into its estates and property parent company, the American Continental Corporation. Continental was losing money because the property market had bombed. And in order to cover these losses, Lincoln persuaded its customers to invest more of their money away from federally-secured deposits to unsecured high risk bonds.

In 1988 Keating tried to get the FHLBB to give him more time by getting Cranston and DeConcini to talk to them, however, this time the delaying tactic failed. In April 1989, Continental went bankrupt and Lincoln failed, costing the taxpayer $3 billion, and over 20,000 depositors lost their savings. In 1993 Keating was convicted of 73 counts of fraud and imprisoned.

Following an Ethics Committee investigation, the political careers of four of the senators were ruined. McCain is still a senator today, representing Arizona, and was the 2008 Republican Party presidential candidate, made famous as a result of having the former Governor of Alaska, Sarah Palin, as his running mate.

Iran–Contra Affair (1985–1987)

Republican president Ronald Reagan was a committed anti-communist and believed that the US should do everything within its power to halt the spread of this political ideology. Because of its close proximity to the US and its Latin American allies, Central America was seen as being of particular significance.

During Reagan's first term in office (1981–1985), his fear of communism led him to support a number of operations that sought to counter their influence. In Nicaragua, for example, the dictatorship of General Somoza was replaced by a left-leaning revolutionary group called the Sandinistas. While it never claimed to be communist, it did redistribute wealth and practise agrarian land reform, practices seen by Reagan as very dangerous. Opposition to the Sandinistas was provided by the Contras (meaning 'against'), and they fought a civil war against the government.

Reagan decided to provide the Contras with assistance but a Democratic-led Congress got in the way: the 1982 Boland Act restricted the Central Intelligence Agency (CIA) and the Department of Defense (DoD) from providing military support for the Contras. In late 1984, the Act was expanded to restrict not just military but also financial support for the Nicaraguan opposition. The Reagan administration wilfully ignored the law. And in the same year, the Islamic Republic of Iran, which had made an enemy of the US after capturing its embassy officials in 1979, requested US military support for its war against Iraq. The Reagan administration was divided over whether to provide military support because an arms embargo rendered doing so illegal. However, the Iranians claimed that they would help release the American hostages captured by Hezbollah in Lebanon. Reagan approved the arms deal to Iran, claiming that he was selling them to moderates within the government. American hostages were duly released.

In late 1986, a Lebanese newspaper broke the story on the Iran part of the deal, and Reagan was panned by the American media and public for going back on his word regarding never negotiating with terrorists.

An investigation set up by the attorney general uncovered evidence suggesting that $12 million of the $30 million received from Iran was diverted to the Contras in Nicaragua to pay for their campaign. Reagan then realised that he could be impeached by Congress for ignoring the Boland Act.

Reagan established the Tower Commission in December 1986 to investigate what had happened. Published a year later, the report effectively cleared Reagan of knowledge of the ultimate destination of the funds raised by the arms deal but implicated National Security Council member Lieutenant Colonel Oliver North, National Security Advisor John Poindexter and Secretary of Defense Caspar Weinberger. A Congressional committee report criticised the National Security Council, run by the Executive, for breaking the law while another report (written by Republicans) suggested that conflict between the Executive and Congress enabled funds to be channelled to the Contras.

North was found guilty of, amongst other things, ordering the destruction of documents relating to the arms deal. Unfortunately, his guilty verdict was quashed because his testimony was protected by immunity from prosecution. Poindexter was involved in organising the transfer of missiles to Iran and was convicted of obstructing the Congressional committee. His conviction was also overturned, because several witnesses at the trial had listened to his testimony for the Congressional committee at which he was granted immunity. Weinberger escaped the clutches of the law slightly differently. He was indicted for perjury and obstruction of justice in mid-1992 but, before trial, was pardoned by President George H. W. Bush along with a number of CIA and other national security officials. Interestingly, note that Bush was both a former CIA director and the vice president during the Reagan administration; he was also implicated in the Iran–Contra affair. Thus members of the executive broke the law, a likely cover-up insulated Reagan from being impeached and no one was ever held to account. Sounds like a typical day in politics.

National Surveillance Scandal (2013 and Onwards)

In early 2013 Edward Snowden, a former US secret intelligence contractor, released thousands of US national intelligence documents detailing the country's complicit involvement in illegal mass-surveillance activities. He leaked the documents to a number of international newspapers, including the *Washington Post* and the *Guardian*. *Guardian* journalist Glenn Greenwald detailed how the National Security Agency (NSA) was involved in collecting millions of telephone records from a US telephone provider as the result of a secret court order. It then transpired that a much wider data-mining programme was in place. It included mining the data of American citizens, which is against the Fourth Amendment of the US Constitution. The *Guardian* and *Washington Post* also reported that the NSA was capturing digital data such as online chat via Facebook and search histories on Google. By mid-June, these revelations had become a matter of international diplomacy. The European Union (EU) requested assurances that these surveillance programs were not infringing the rights of European citizens The US government strove to limit the political fall-out.

On 22 June, US prosecutors charged Snowden with espionage and theft and he fled to Russia. On the international front, the German news magazine, *Der Spiegel*, published documents claiming that the US had bugged EU offices in New York and Washington. The EU sought clarification. By August, Snowden had been offered asylum in Russia. France, Spain, Portugal and Italy refused to allow a plane carrying Bolivian president Evo Morales to travel through their airspace. Morales was returning from Moscow and Snowden was suspected of being on his plane. The plane was forced to land in Austria and searched by the authorities, without success. President Obama cancelled a meeting with Russian President Putin in protest at Snowden being given asylum.

And on the domestic front, further revelations from a leaked internal audit showed that the NSA, contrary to official statements, knew that it was breaking privacy laws and going beyond its legal authority. American companies were also implicated when it was revealed that the NSA was paying them for access to their communication networks. In September, Brazilian president Dilma Rousseff cancelled an official state visit to Washington, DC, after a Brazilian newspaper reported that the NSA had spied on her and her colleagues. The NSA was also found to have intercepted mobile phone conversations held by the German chancellor, Angela Merkel.

Today, numerous investigations are examining the actions of the NSA and Snowden is still in exile. He'll probably spend the rest of his life on the run because he challenged what he saw as un-American and illegal behaviour. Obama and the executive have begun to change, rhetorically at least, their approach to surveillance and the legislature and judiciary are doing their constitutionally appointed job of checking the abuse of power on the part of the other branches – perhaps indicating that the American political infrastructure does still work.

ABSCAM Scandal (1978–1981)

Recently made into a Hollywood film, *American Hustle*, this is a classic story of greed, stupidity and sex – three ingredients required for a worthy scandal. The FBI initially began an investigation to recover two stolen paintings but it morphed into an investigation into corrupt US government officials.

Melvin Weinberg, a New York con artist, was convicted of fraud in 1977, and then persuaded by the FBI to set up a fake company, Abdul Enterprises Ltd (supposedly funded by Arab sheiks), to capture dodgy politicians. The FBI recorded a series of meeting with a number of public officials, asking them to arrange a series of tasks from shipping money out of the US to organising political asylum for certain individuals. In order to create a legitimate cover, the fake sheikhs had to live a decadent and opulent lifestyle to convince politicians that they had serious capital and wanted to invest in the US.

New Jersey senator Angelo Errichetti was the first fish to take the bait. Errichetti was willing to arrange for other politicians to help the sheikhs obtain casino licences and political asylum. The sheikhs would pay each person $50,000 immediately and the same amount following assistance. As the weeks and months went by, the fake sheikhs had to persuade the politicians to agree to the deals and to physically take money in order to establish a case against them. In this first sting, Errichetti was accompanied by New Jersey Democratic senator, Harrison Williams, who said he'd help the sheikh invest in a Virginia mining operation. Williams was recorded saying, 'You tell the sheikh I'll do all I can. You tell him I'll deliver my end' (cue comic moment number one as the interpreter speaks gibberish to the sheikh and passes it off as Arabic).

Williams committed to a deal whereby he convinced officials that the government should do business with the mine, as a result of which he would personally receive a share of the mine's profits. The next stage of the sting involved Errichetti introducing a Philadelphia lawyer to the second sheikh, who required help gaining immigration approval. A number of Congressmen were recorded claiming they would help (cue comic moment number two as the sheikh claims he needs bright light to remind him of the desert sun when actually it's necessary for the video recordings). Republican South Dakota Representative Larry Pressler was also asked if he wanted some money but stated that it was illegal and left the meeting. He then went on to tell the FBI what had happened, and rather insightfully commented on current attitudes to politics: 'I find it somewhat repulsive that I'm on tape, but now I'm called a hero. It's a sad state of affairs when it's heroic to turn down a potential bribery situation'.

By the end of the investigation 31 officials had been targeted, and 19 were prosecuted for bribery and conspiracy. This number included six Congressmen, a senator, a mayor a Philadelphia city councillor and a lawyer. They received prison sentences of between one and six years for their crimes.

Pentagon Papers (1971)

In 1967, Secretary of Defense Robert McNamara commissioned a team of analysts to write a top secret history of US involvement in Southeast Asia from the time of the Second World War. The study, completed in 1968, was huge, comprising 47 volumes. Later it became collectively known as the Pentagon Papers. Because the papers documented some very sensitive areas of American foreign policy in relation to the Vietnam War, they were highly classified and only those with top level clearance had access to the full set.

Daniel Ellsberg, one of the original contributors to the papers, was doing some follow up research and had been given clearance to access all of the papers. A Vietnam veteran, he'd originally been supportive of US foreign policy. However, he became increasingly disaffected and began attending anti-war rallies in 1969. He was unhappy that so many soldiers were being sent to die in a war that he now viewed as unwinnable. And his research had shown decades of corrupt practice in relation to it.

Ellsberg battled with his conscience. In 1969 he was working as a consultant on the Vietnam War for President Nixon and Secretary of Defense Henry Kissinger. As far as he was concerned, however, the Pentagon Papers showed US involvement in Vietnam to be 'a quarter century of aggression, broken treaties, deceptions, stolen elections, lies and murder'. At the end of the year, he and a colleague, Anthony Russo, secretly made copies of the papers.

Gradually, Ellsberg told more and more people about what the papers revealed. He spoke to sympathetic senators, analysts and academics. In 1971 he shared the documents with *New York Times* correspondent Neil Sheehan, who promised that he wouldn't write about them. But Sheehan also had information about the papers from other sources and ultimately the temptation posed by such a sensational scoop was too much. He broke his promise to Ellsberg and in June 1971 the *New York Times* published excerpts from the papers. The Nixon administration requested a court order to prevent the publication of further material but Ellsberg seized the moment and released the documents to 18 newspapers. The media fought the injunction and the Supreme Court accepted that the papers should be published. The hornets' nest had been well and truly stirred.

The information now in the public domain was to create serious ruptures in the relationship of trust between US citizens and their government. It was revealed that a succession of administrations had lied to the people about the extent of US involvement in Vietnam. Air strikes over Laos, raids along the coast of North Vietnam and offensive actions by the Marines had taken place long before the American public was informed. This was a particularly dirty scandal because the lives of nearly 60,000 Americans (and nearly 1.5 million on both sides) were lost in a war about which top level politicians had been so dishonest.

While the papers were allowed to legally print the papers, Ellsberg's actions were not viewed as legal. He accepted that he might go to prison for what he'd done and he very nearly did. He and Russo faced charges of espionage, theft and conspiracy. However, in an ironic twist, the government corruption that they had exposed actually then saved them. During the trial it was revealed that the prosecution had used a plethora of illegal means to find evidence against Ellsberg and Russo, including unsanctioned wiretapping and breaking into Ellsberg's psychiatrist's office to look for notes about him. The trial was dismissed and Ellsberg and Russo walked free.

Ellsberg remains a campaigner for government transparency today and has spoken up for one of his whistleblowing successors, Edward Snowden (see above for details).

Teapot Dome Scandal (1920–1923)

In 1912, the US government claimed ownership of three oil reserves in California (Elk Hills and Buena Vista Hills) and Wyoming (Teapot Dome). The reserves were for emergency use on the part of the Navy if its supplies ran low. In 1920, as part of the Naval Appropriations Act, the Secretary of the Navy was given the power, so long as it benefitted the US, 'to conserve, develop, use, and operate the same in his discretion, directly or by contract, lease, or otherwise, and to use, store, exchange, or sell the oil and gas products thereof, and those from all royalty oil from lands in the naval reserves'.

In 1921, Republican Warren Harding moved into the White House, and appointed former Congressman Edwin Denby as the Secretary of the Navy and Senator Albert B. Fall as the Secretary of the Interior. Fall was against the public ownership of the oil reserves and persuaded Denby to relinquish control of the reserves to his department. President Harding signed the Executive Order in 1921 approving the transfer of powers. Big mistake.

Fall decided that private enterprise was more important than long-term national interests and he secretly leased out the oil reserves to the oil industry. Fall received about $400,000 in sweeteners. In April 1922, the *Wall Street Journal* published an exposé of the Sinclair deal with Fall. President Harding defended both Secretaries but this didn't stop the Senate, a week later, from initiating a committee investigation to get to the bottom of the matter.

Following resolution of the Senate investigation, a joint resolution by both chambers of Congress stating that the deals were fraudulent and corrupt and that the oil fields should be returned to the Navy was signed by the president. Although this affair appears small fry now, not until Nixon and Watergate did it move down the political scandal pecking order.

Nixon and Watergate (1971–1974)

On 17 June 1971, five men were arrested trying to break into the Democrat Party headquarters based in the Watergate Hotel in Washington, DC. One of the arrested men was a former CIA operative and another was a Republican Party security official. In August, it was reported by the *Washington Post* that a cheque for $25,000 made out to one of Nixon's re-election finance organisers was deposited into the bank account of one of the arrested burglars. And so began one of the greatest cover-ups of all time.

As the year went by, more and more was revealed about the FBI investigation suggesting that the Republican Party had a secret group of people hired to spy and disrupt opponents' election campaigns. In spite of this scandal, Nixon was able to win a landslide victory in the November 1972 general election and enter the White House for a second term. He got a whopping 520 EC votes and over 60 per cent of the popular vote. In January 1973, the five men caught in the Watergate Hotel pleaded guilty to burglary, and a further two men, who were officials in Nixon's re-election campaign team, were convicted of conspiracy, burglary and bugging the Democratic Party's headquarters. A few months later, Nixon addressed the nation claiming, 'there can be no whitewash at the White House'. In this light, he accepted the resignation of two key White House advisors and the Attorney General and sacked John W. Dean III as a result of their involvement in the break-ins and their subsequent cover-up. Nixon took full responsibility for what happened but, playing innocent, distanced himself from their actions by suggesting that 'we must reform our political process'.

A Senate committee was established in May to investigate what happened. In June, former counsel Dean claimed in his testimony that the president discussed the cover-up of the Watergate break-in at least 35 times with him. A former presidential appointments secretary then revealed that, since 1971, Nixon had been recording all calls and conversations in his office. Nixon refused to hand over the tapes to the committee and in April the special prosecutor issued a subpoena for them. Nixon instead released edited transcripts. In July 1974, the Supreme Court ruled that the president must hand over the original 64 tapes to the Senate committee. Around the same time, the House of Representatives judiciary committee voted that grounds for impeaching the president existed in relation to obstruction of justice, abuse of power and contempt of Congress. The final nail in Nixon's coffin was the release of a previously uncatalogued tape of his Chief of Staff discussing the break-in with him a few days after it happened and suggesting that the CIA should pretend to the FBI it was a national security issue and thus shouldn't be investigated.

Three days later and after realising that he would lose an impeachment trial in the Senate, President Nixon addressed the nation and stated: 'I shall resign the presidency effective at noon tomorrow. Vice President Ford will be sworn in as president at that hour in this office.' And so ended Nixon's political career – in disgrace. While everyone around him had either fallen on their sword or been pushed onto it in order to protect him, Nixon didn't face impeachment, and was given a full and unconditional pardon by President Ford so he could never be charged for his actions. He lived out his life in political ignominy.

Chapter 21

(Almost) Ten Candidates Who Came Up Short

● ●

In This Chapter

▶ Running down the campaigns of notable also-rans

▶ Glimpsing big political splashes who dried up

▶ Remembering the names that nearly made a mark

● ●

*I*magine: You make the big decision to run for office. You sacrifice time, energy, cash and, in some cases, pride. You make the exhausting effort to get your name and ideas out into the world in an appealing package that voters respond to. And you . . . almost get it.

The structure of the system necessitates more candidates than office-holders, which means those who didn't quite make it at least have a lot of company. Some of them make more of a name – good or bad – for themselves before exiting the political stage.

Here, I run through some of the hopefuls who just missed out.

Hillary Clinton (2008)

Hillary Clinton was once known only as the wife of the 42nd president of the USA. In fact, she was always a formidable achiever with a multitude of feathers to her cap. A graduate of Yale Law School, she was twice listed by the *National Law Journal* as one of the 100 most influential lawyers in America. During her years as first lady (1993–2001) she took an active role in politics, including working on healthcare, and she entered electoral politics in 2000, successfully standing as a senator for New York.

Perhaps throughout her two terms as a senator, Clinton was preparing for her possible candidacy for president. She was a well-known and popular figure, and was seen by many as the natural candidate for the next Democratic president. Her ambition to stand was near enough an open secret, but she didn't declare publicly until January 2007, when she posted a message on her website: 'I'm in, and I'm in to win.' And perhaps she would have, if Barack Obama hadn't thrown his hat into the ring.

Early polls indicated that Clinton was marginally ahead of the other candidates, Obama and Edwards. Clinton and Obama eventually left Edwards for dust, and the end of the campaign was a two-horse race. Clinton contrasted herself to Obama by emphasising her experience and presenting herself as a safe pair of hands for a country in economic trouble. Obama, on the other hand, stood for change and a fresh start. As the primaries progressed, the votes remained incredibly close.

In late March things became more difficult for Clinton when she was forced to admit that her previous claims to have been under fire from snipers on a state visit to Bosnia in 1996 weren't true. The media pounced on this admission, which seriously threatened her credibility. On 6 May, a narrower-than-expected win in the Indiana primary coupled with a large loss in the North Carolina primary ended any realistic chance she had of winning the nomination. Not one to bow out, she continued her campaign for another month, albeit making fewer attacks on Obama. By 3 June Obama had won enough votes to become the presumptive nominee and Clinton accepted defeat and pledged her support to Obama, campaigning energetically for him in the general election.

Clinton's career was far from over, though. She was Obama's Secretary of State during his first term, presiding over a change in direction for American foreign policy, as well as increasing troops in Afghanistan. And it may not be the end of ambition to return to the White House as president. When she worked under Obama she denied any ambitions in that direction but she remains an overwhelming favourite among Democrats for the 2016 presidential election nomination. In September 2013, Clinton hinted that she may be considering running. Watch this space.

Barry Goldwater (1964)

Barry Goldwater had a successful political career as a senator for Arizona before he ran as the Republican candidate in the 1964 presidential election – and a successful senatorial career afterwards.

Goldwater did battle for the Republican nomination against more moderate conservatives, including governor of New York Nelson Rockefeller. His staunch conservatism was based on supporting individual responsibility rather than regulation as a driver for change in America. He advocated limited government and reducing the power of the federal government. During the Republican primaries he argued that he was the only real alternative to Johnson and the liberalism of the era and he controversially voted against the 1964 Civil Rights Act in the Senate. On the foreign policy front, he was an ardent nationalist and anti-communist, criticising President Johnson for not taking a tougher line with Cuba and failing strategy in Vietnam and advocating increasing US military power to off-set that of the Soviet Union.

Goldwater was advancing a controversial political platform, which met intense opposition from within the Republican Party. Rockefeller, for example, accused him of extremism that could possibly harm race relations at home and cause agitation abroad. Goldwater won the Republican nomination at the July 1964 national convention and, in his acceptance speech, reiterated his small government, anti-communist stance. In response to those who accused him of extremism, he concluded that it was no bad thing because 'in the defense of liberty [it] is no vice. And let me remind you also that moderation in the pursuit of justice is no virtue.'

In the general election, Goldwater was up against the Democrat incumbent, President Johnson. Unlike most candidates, Goldwater refused to turn down the volume on his conservative views and he stuck by his ideological platform. In a late September 1964 rally speech, Johnson was referring to Goldwater when he stated that, 'it takes a man who loves his country to build a house instead of a raving, ranting demagogue who wants to tear down one. Beware of those who fear and doubt and those who rave and rant about the dangers of progress.' On the domestic front, Johnson portrayed Goldwater as a racist based on his rejection of the 1964 Civil Rights Act, even though he had supported the 1957 and 1960 Acts. Goldwater's defence was that desegregation should be a state not a federal issue.

Goldwater lost the electoral college vote by 52 to 486 and the popular vote by 39 to 61 per cent. He carried only six states, and five of those were in the South.

In 1969, Goldwater re-entered the Senate, and he didn't retire until 1986. His later career suggests that the ultra-conservative caricature of Goldwater wasn't a true reflection of his political identity. He actually had an underappreciated libertarian streak; in the 1990s, for example, he was pro-choice and spoke out against discriminating against homosexuals. Advocating for their right to serve in the armed forces, he once said, 'you don't have to be straight to be in the military; you just have to be able to shoot straight'.

Patsy Mink (1972)

In the political world, white men dominate – even now, and especially in earlier decades. Still, some people who are neither male nor white were able to navigate the political system and become senior elected officials. Hawaiian Patsy Mink was one of these cases. Unable to pursue her goal of becoming a doctor – purely because schools wouldn't accept females – she changed course and pursued postgraduate training as a lawyer at the University of Chicago. Returning to Hawaii after her studies, she was unsuccessful in her applications to established law firms so set up her own. During this time, her interest in politics grew and she became an active member of the Democratic Party.

In 1956 Mink was elected as the first Asian American in the Hawaii House of Representatives, and in 1958 was elected to the Hawaii Senate. She ran for Congress in the 1964 elections and won a seat in the House of Representatives, becoming the first Asian woman to take a seat on Capitol Hill. During her time in Washington, DC, she was committed to speaking out against racial and sexual discrimination and achieved a number of victories, including her 1970 opposition to President Nixon's nomination of G. Harrold Carswell as a Supreme Court justice because of his previous rulings regarding Black Americans and women. Her testimony to his Senate hearings helped ensure that he was not confirmed. She was also critical of American involvement in the war in Vietnam.

In early 1972, Mink ran in the primaries for the Democratic Party on an education, civil rights, social welfare, anti-Vietnam platform. It was a brief foray into presidential politics but important nonetheless. Ultimately, she withdrew her candidacy after receiving only about 0.5 per cent of the overall vote. But her bid was never really about winning the Democratic candidacy – she had neither the support nor the resources of the other candidates – rather it was more about maintaining a public profile for the issues she thought were important and that needed to be kept in the public domain.

Mink continued fighting for these causes as a Congresswoman, winning elections in 1972 and 1974. Returning to Hawaii after two years in Washington, DC, she re-entered local politics as a Honolulu city councillor. By 1990 she was back on Capitol Hill as a Congresswoman, maintaining her commitments to education, civil rights and so on. When she died from pneumonia in 1992, she was actually seeking re-election. In a fitting tribute, her death came too late for the ballot papers to be changed and Mink became one of few politicians re-elected after their death. Over 100,000 people voted for her, and she received 52 per cent of the vote.

Wesley Clark (2004)

A quintessential all-American hero who ticks all the boxes, Wesley Clark studied at Oxford University, joined the military and fought for his country, was successful in his career and retired from the military as a four-star general. And he was good looking, to boot.

Before he ran for office, Clark held some very lofty posts in the army. For example, he was a commander during NATO's 1999 military confrontation with President Milosevic's forces in Yugoslavia, which halted the killing of ethnic Albanians in Kosovo. He retired from the military in 2000 and decided to enter politics. Clark declared that he'd run as a presidential candidate in the Democratic primaries. His campaign quickly gained traction and in the first few weeks raised $3.5 million. He stood on a traditional Democrat platform. Unfortunately, because he'd lived most of his life outside of politics, his ability to be a manicured producer of sound bites was rather limited. Clark often made remarks that were either misinterpreted or made pithy headlines that didn't show him in a great light. For example, after he told journalists that he believed in travel that was faster than the speed of light, the *New York Times* used the ironic headline, 'Clark is Light-Years Ahead of the Competition'.

Despite his gaffes, in early February 2004 Clark was doing rather well, gaining 27 per cent of the vote in Arizona and 24 per cent in North Dakota. By 10 February, however, his race was effectively over when he didn't win sufficient votes in Tennessee or Virginia. His strategy was to win the South and these defeats meant that he wasn't going to, so the next day he withdrew from the primaries and supported John Kerry for the nomination.

Since his exit from the race, Clark has continued to play a role in Democrat politics by campaigning for party candidates in national elections. In 2008, he endorsed Hillary Clinton early in the primary cycle for the Democrat presidential candidate and then Obama in the general election against Republican John McCain. In mid-2013 he endorsed Clinton again as the 2016 presidential candidate. This is pure speculation but it's hard not to think of cold calculations in a national security expert supporting a candidate so early in order, perhaps, to garner a position in the cabinet.

Sarah Palin (2008)

Sarah Palin emerged on the national political scene in a blaze of glory in 2008 when she was nominated by Republican presidential candidate John McCain to run as his vice president. She became a darling of the right and a source of criticism from the left as a result of her unconventional way of talking about hot political issues.

Palin was a local councillor in the Alaskan town of Wasilla from 1992 and in 1996 became the mayor. In 2002 she unsuccessfully ran as the Republican candidate for the Alaskan lieutenant governor, although she got to within 2,000 votes of winning. In 2006, she ran for governor, beating the incumbent Republican governor, Frank Murkowski, in the primaries. At the age of 42 she beat the Democrat candidate 48.3 per cent to 40.9 per cent to become governor of Alaska. Her governorship was based on, among other issues, cleaning up Alaskan politics from its cloud of dodgy dealings and reducing the state budget.

Palin was a political activist, with an ability to connect with constituents. Moreover she was a die-hard conservative, member of the National Rifle Association and supporter of family values. She was fiscally responsible and against abortion. These traits brought her to the attention of Senator McCain's presidential campaign team. The steam had gone out of that campaign and it needed a boost, something different. In late August 2008, McCain nominated Palin as his vice presidential candidate for the upcoming general election against Democrats Obama and Biden. It was only the second time that a woman had been nominated for this position. Despite a three-week presidential boot camp in September 2008, Palin made a spectacular series of gaffes, including not being able to name a single newspaper or magazine that she might have read, telling US military personnel that Afghanistan was a 'neighboring country' and claiming that New Hampshire (in the Northeast of the country) is in the Northwest. After a series of such errors, people were questioning her credentials as a vice presidential candidate. Interestingly, whilst she was criticised by some, she was also lauded for her ability to appeal to the conservative base. Unfortunately, her wildcard entry as the Republican vice presidential candidate did not appeal to the voters it was aimed at, and McCain and Palin lost the election in no uncertain terms (EC votes: 173 to Obama's 365; popular vote: 45.7 per cent to Obama's 52.9 per cent).

Since losing the election, Palin has taken up political commentary. She's set up her own PAC (see Chapter 10) to support political candidates who support her views and maintains a prominent role in the Tea Party movement (see Chapter 10 for details) by commentating on American politics via outlets such as Fox News. Unsurprisingly, she's become a vocal critic of the Obama administration, particularly its 2010 healthcare reforms. She's also fostered a media personality by publishing her memoir (which sold over 300,000 copies on its first day!) and starring in a reality TV show featuring the life of her family in Alaska.

Herman Cain (2012)

Cain ran in the 2000 Republican primary for the presidency but exited before the primaries began. In 2004 he ran in the 2004 Republican primary for a Senate seat in Georgia but was beaten into second place. He had a better chance for candidacy in the 2012 Republican primary for the presidency, but ended up in this chapter nonetheless.

Cain had a successful career outside of politics before deciding to enter that world. He was a CEO of a famous pizza chain, and then the CEO of the National Restaurant Association (the other NRA). His previous forays into national electoral politics had given him the opportunity to develop a profile as a public commentator through radio and print. Maintaining his interest in Republican politics, he spoke at a number of Tea Party events, aligning himself with its position on small government, low taxes and a balanced budget.

In May 2011, he decided to enter the ring for the Republican primaries. Initial polls of Republican voters were favourable; his outsider status served him well with the Tea Party and other Republican activists. According to him, the country should be run as a business; as a successful businessman, he'd also make a successful CEO of the United States.

During Cain's campaign, events took a damning turn: four women who worked with him at the NRA accused him of sexual misconduct. He confirmed paying them off but denied acting improperly with them. Another woman then claimed to have had a 13-year affair with Cain, a suggestion he denied. The scandal hit him hard and polls showed that support for him had dipped dramatically. He effectively withdrew from the campaign.

Even though he was out of the contest, it was too late to remove his name from the ballot sheets. In the late January primary he gained 6,326 votes. Not bad for a non-runner – although the winner did poll over 240,000.

In May 2011, when Cain had just announced that he was running for the Republican presidential candidacy, he claimed in a *Washing Post* interview, 'I don't have this long-term ambition of I want my own show on Fox . . . I want to be president.' In February 2013, Fox News issued a press release stating that Cain was going to be a political and business commentator on the channel.

William Jennings Bryan (1896)

A great public speaker, William Jennings Bryan was a committed Baptist and liberal who ran as the Democratic Party's candidate for presidency three times. A lawyer from Nebraska, he joined the Democratic Party and was elected as a Congressman in 1890. He was re-elected again in 1892, and then lost to the Republican candidate in the 1894 Senate race.

Bryan's nomination as a presidential candidate in 1896 was based on one speech (the *Cross of Gold*) at the Chicago Democratic convention. It was a populist call to increase the amount of money in circulation by coining silver as well as gold. He suggested that this move would help the average person pay off their debts. Big business and the Democrat and Republican party bosses weren't thrilled; they supported the gold standard. Bryan's speech had Marxist overtones when he asked the Democratic convention delegates whether they wanted to be on the side of the 'struggling masses' or the 'idle holders of idle capital'. He suggested that prosperity should rise up through the classes rather than filtering down. His speech was also heavily imbued with religious overtones when it concluded by talking about people who supported the gold standard, 'you shall not press down upon the brow of labor this crown of thorns. You shall not crucify mankind upon a cross of gold.' The speech was an instant success, and even though he wasn't openly up for nomination, the 36 year old won and became the Democratic Party's presidential candidate. Bryan's running mate was chosen by the convention – a wealthy shipbuilder from Maine, Arthur Sewall. He supported the silver cause and could help fund the general election in November.

Bryan fought on a populist platform and travelled the country meeting the people while his Republican opponent, William McKinley, ran a more conventional – and static – campaign, receiving delegations at his Ohio residence. McKinley's pro-gold standard campaign out-spent Bryan and, in a further twist of fate, those Democrats who'd supported the gold standard held their own convention and nominated a 79-year-old John Palmer and a sprightly 73-year-old Simon Bolivar Buckner to run against Bryan in an effort to ensure that McKinley would win by splitting the Democrat vote. It worked: Bryan lost to McKinley by 176 EC votes to 271, by 47 to 51 per cent in the popular vote and about 600,000 fewer votes than McKinley's 7.1 million. Although he lost the election, his politics maintained a key role in Democratic Party thinking and Bryan ran again in 1900 and 1908. He was appointed Secretary of State in Woodrow Wilson's administration in 1912 and was responsible for introducing arbitration as a means of settling international disputes rather than declaring war.

Bryan's 1896 campaign has two interesting legacies. First, his decision to travel around the country speaking directly to the people was a new campaign strategy. Second, it effectively destroyed the populists' chance to end the dominance of the two-party system.

Michael Dukakis (1988)

Michael Dukakis was a career politician who served in the Massachusetts House of Representatives as a Democrat from the age of 29. In 1974, he won the Democrat candidacy for the Massachusetts *gubernatorial* (governor) election. He beat the incumbent Republican by 53.5 to 42.3 per cent of the popular vote. His reformist platform was popular with the voters but Democrat party bosses in the state were disillusioned and deselected him for the 1978 gubernatorial election. He was selected for the Democrats again in 1982, and won the general election with an even bigger share of the votes than the last time.

His success as governor was a product of improving the state economy, decreasing the state government's budget and improving the transport infrastructure. This track record was enough to drive success in the 1986 election. He once again improved his popular vote, to 65.15 per cent, the Republican share dipping below 30 per cent. All that political success led him to run in the Democrat primaries for the 1988 presidential election. His success continued: up against Jesse Jackson, he won the nomination when 70 per cent of the delegates at the national convention voted for him.

His political platform was based on combining his success as the instigator of the Massachusetts Miracle with rhetoric of the American Dream. The *Massachusetts Miracle* referred to the sustained period of economic growth in that state, a balancing of the state government budget, a reduction in taxes and a fall in unemployment from 12 to 3 per cent. The *American Dream* rhetoric tapped into what voters could expect from a President Dukakis and what the Republican nominee George H. W. Bush could not deliver because he was part of the failed Reagan administration.

Dukakis was topping most of the polls against Bush at the beginning of the campaign. However, a serious dirty tricks campaign by the Bush team and a failed response strategy meant Dukakis was caricatured and ridiculed. First, the Republicans leaked a false report that Dukakis had sought psychiatric help after his brother was killed. Republican President Reagan, when asked to comment on this story, commented, 'I'm not going to pick on an invalid'. The Dukakis team responded too slowly to effectively counter it.

Then a Republican senator falsely alleged that Dukakis' wife had burnt the American flag at a political protest in the 1970s, and then criticised Dukakis for opposing a bill that supported schoolchildren pledging allegiance to the flag. Once again, Dukakis responded slowly and ineffectively to these claims. Dukakis was also slated regarding a prison programme enacted during his time as governor, which released prisoners for short periods of time. A convicted murderer, William Horton, was released under this programme and committed a rape and a stabbing. Dukakis was portrayed as being soft on criminals and opposed to the death penalty – an unfair criticism when 40 other states were running similar programmes at the time. This attack was compounded in the second presidential debate when the interviewer asked Dukakis whether he'd support the death penalty if his wife had been raped and murdered. He responded: 'No, I [wouldn't], and I think you know that I've opposed the death penalty during all of my life'. This comment was spun by the opposition as an example of Dukakis' dispassionate side.

Overall, his decision not to respond to these attacks immediately and consistently was a strategic error that ruined his chance of winning the election. Ultimately, he did devise a proactive strategy but by then he'd not only lost his majority in the polls but was too far behind to catch up. Bush emerged comfortably on top, winning 53.4 per cent of the popular vote compared to Dukakis' 45.7 per cent. Dukakis remained as governor until 1992, but the Massachusetts Miracle was short-lived, and he decided not to run for another term. He now teaches political science at UCLA.

Eugene Debs (1920)

Every now and then a candidate outside the Republican and Democratic parties finds some success in a national election. Eugene Debs' story is one of the relative successes experienced by a socialist in the early part of the twentieth century.

Originally, Eugene Debs was a Democrat, and an elected one at that. In 1884, he was elected to the House of Representatives (representing Indiana) but served one term only. He then worked for the trade union movement and, by 1893, had established the American Railway Union (ARU). His status as an effective union leader was cemented after he successfully campaigned for better wages and working conditions for staff on the Great Northern Railway. Dissatisfied with the capitalist system, Debs then declared himself a socialist and joined the Socialist Party.

In 1900 Debs began his first of five presidential election campaigns. While acknowledging that he wasn't going to win, his key aim was placing social-ist values in the public arena so that Americans could encounter alternative ways of looking at the world. He supported equality on the basis of race and gender, decent working conditions and rights for workers and the restriction of child labour.

Each election campaign was more successful than the last. In the 1908 elec-tion, for example, on a train called the *Red Special*, Debs travelled around the country spreading the socialist message. He gained 420,852 votes as a result. The 1920 presidential election, however, is the discussion point of this sec-tion. America entered the First World War in 1917 on the side of the allies; Debs was opposed to this action. In 1918, he delivered an anti-war speech knowing that it probably violated the Espionage and Sedition Acts (1917 and 1918, respectively). In that speech he stated that Wall Street would make money out of the war, that he supported the Russian Bolsheviks' surrender to the Germans, that the working class would pay the ultimate price in terms of their lives and that the ruling class would 'declare war and . . . alone make peace'. He was convicted and sentenced to 10 years' imprisonment under the terms of these Acts.

In 1920, from his prison cell in Atlanta, Debs decided to run for the presi-dency again. Seen as a political prisoner, his campaign was a classic case of David versus Goliath. His campaign poster was titled *From Atlanta to the 'White House', 1920*. Debs polled 914,191 votes – not bad for a candidate in prison. President Wilson refused to commute his sentence but the new presi-dent, Warren Harding, did so on Christmas Day, 1921.

Index

• G •

• Q •

• R •

e Author

Dr Matthew Hill is a Senior Lecturer in American Politics in the School Humanities and Social Science at Liverpool John Moores University. Previous to this he has held lectureships at Anglia Ruskin University, and the School of Advanced Study at the University of London. He has contributed to teaching American politics at several other universities including Cardiff, De Montfort and Birkbeck. Matthew's research on US Foreign Policy and democracy promotion is published in international journals and as a book. As well as trawling the shelves in dusty libraries and archives, Matthew has interviewed a number of prominent figures for his research, including former US Secretary of State Madeleine Albright and former ambassadors.

Matthew has lived and worked in the US in the past including a stint as an intern at *The Carter Center,* where he worked for former President Jimmy Carter. He now gets his fix of favourite American foods on annual research trips. At home, he likes to appease the American part of his soul by calling films 'movies' and pronouncing tomato to rhyme with potato. He can be heard walking the streets of London recounting famous skits from *Saturday Night Live*.

Author's Acknowledgements

So many people have been instrumental in bringing this book into being. The team at Wiley have been wonderful to work with. I'm grateful to Mike Baker, my Commissioning Editor, for his creative thinking and efficiency in getting the ball rolling, and his helpful input at the later stages too. Most importantly, I have felt so lucky to have my editor Traci Cumbay on my side (and on my case!) throughout this project. Traci's sharp and thorough editing skills are second only to her ability to write funny, morale boosting emails. Numerous times she has reeled me back from the end of my tether and helped me to get this book finished. I would also like to thank Terri Jett for her technical review and Kate O'Leary for turning my scribbles into a Dummies book.

I am grateful to both Liverpool John Moores University and Anglia Ruskin University for their support in allowing me the time to write this book. Alex Miles, my History Head John Moores, took me on in the middle of writing this book.

Finally, I want to thank my partner, Charlotte. For the last six months she's barely seen me because the laptop has got between us. But when I've looked up, I'm delighted to find that she hasn't gone away, and she sometimes even tolerates a 'fascinating' story about the US constitution, or electoral anomalies. I don't know how I got so lucky.

Publisher's Acknowledgments

Acquisitions Editor: Mike Baker

Project Editor: Traci Cumbay

Copy Editor: Kate O'Leary

Technical Editor: Terri Jett

Art Coordinator: Alicia B. South

Project Coordinator: Melissa Cossell

Project Manager: Steve Edwards

Cover Image: ©Marilyn Nieves/Getty Images